MW00772146

Joyce's Ghosts

Joyce's Ghosts

IRELAND, MODERNISM, AND MEMORY

Luke Gibbons

The University of Chicago Press   Chicago and London

The University of Chicago Press, Chicago 60637
The University of Chicago Press, Ltd., London
© 2015 by The University of Chicago
All rights reserved. No part of this book may be used or reproduced in any
manner whatsoever without written permission, except in the case of brief
quotations in critical articles and reviews. For more information, contact
the University of Chicago Press, 1427 E. 6oth St., Chicago, IL 60637.
Published 2015.
Paperback edition 2017
Printed in the United States of America

23 22 21 20 19 18 17   2 3 4 5 6 7 8 9

ISBN-13: 978-0-226-23617-9 (cloth)
ISBN-13: 978-0-226-52695-9 (paper)
ISBN-13: 978-0-226-23620-9 (e-book)
DOI: https://doi.org/10.7208/chicago/9780226236209.001.0001

Page ii: Louis le Brocquy, Study Towards an image of James Joyce (1978).
Oil on canvas. 70 x 70 cm. © Estate of Louis le Brocquy.
Reproduced from color. Photograph: Adams Showrooms, Dublin.

Library of Congress Cataloging-in-Publication Data

Gibbons, Luke, author.
Joyce's ghosts : Ireland, modernism, and memory / Luke Gibbons.
pages ; cm
Includes bibliographical references and index.
ISBN 978-0-226-23617-9 (cloth : alk. paper)
ISBN 978-0-226-23620-9 (ebook)
1. Joyce, James, 1882-1941—Criticism and interpretation.
2. Dublin (Ireland)—In literature. 3. Modernism
(Literature)—Ireland. I. Title
PR6019.09Z533474 2015
823.912—dc23
2015010762

♾ This paper meets the requirements of ANSI/NISO Z39.48-1992
(Permanence of Paper).

In memory of
Tom Duddy (1950–2012)
and
Siobhán Kilfeather (1957–2007)

Nothing of that time or place remains.
Death and history have passed through them,
I-now a distant relation of me-then.
There are only these images, too familiar
for imaginings, too orderly for dreams.

TOM DUDDY,
"The Problem of Memory"

For much of the nineteenth century, Irish Gothic cannot be defined
so much in terms of a subgenre . . . as in terms of an extra dimen-
sion apparent in many works of Irish fiction . . . and "gothic" traces
continue to surface in the twentieth-century novel.

SIOBHÁN KILFEATHER,
"The Gothic Novel"

CONTENTS

List of Figures xi

Preface xiii

Acknowledgments xvii

INTRODUCTION: "A GHOST BY ABSENCE" *1*

1: TEXT AND THE CITY *21*
Dublin, Cultural Intimacy, and Modernity

2: "SHOUTS IN THE STREET" *53*
Inner Speech, Self, and the City

3: "HE SAYS NO, YOUR WORSHIP" *79*
Joyce, Free Indirect Discourse, and Vernacular Modernism

4: "GHOSTLY LIGHT" *103*
Visualizing the Voice in James Joyce's and John Huston's "The Dead"

5: "PALE PHANTOMS OF DESIRE" *138*
Subjectivity, Spectral Memory, and Irish Modernity

6: "SPACES OF TIME THROUGH TIMES OF SPACE" *165*
Haunting the "Wandering Rocks"

7: "FAMISHED GHOSTS" *188*
Bloom, Bible Wars, and "U. p: up" in Joyce's Dublin

8: "HAUNTING FACE" *207*
Spectral Premonitions and the Memory of the Dead

Notes 227   Index 269

FIGURES

1.1   Carola Giedion-Welcker, "James Joyce at the Platzspitz" (1938) 22

2.1   Frances Hegarty and Andrew Stones, *For Dublin* (City Hall, 1997) 54

2.2   Frances Hegarty and Andrew Stones, *For Dublin* (City Hall, 1997) (detail) 55

2.3   Frances Hegarty and Andrew Stones, *For Dublin* (River Liffey, Ormond Quay, 1997) 56

2.4   Frances Hegarty and Andrew Stones, *For Dublin* (Clarence Hotel, Wellington Quay, 1997) 57

2.5   Frances Hegarty and Andrew Stones, *For Dublin* (College Green American Express Building above Thomas Cook Sign, 1997) 58

2.6   Amanda Coogan, *Molly Blooms* (2004) 69

2.7   "Justice," Dublin Castle, Dublin 69

4.1   John Huston, *The Dead* (Gabriel, Lily, and Gretta, 1987) 104

4.2   John Huston, *The Dead* (opening shot, 1987) 118

4.3   John Huston, *The Dead* (recitation scene: Gabriel, 1987) 121

4.4   John Huston, *The Dead* (recitation scene: Gretta, 1987) 121

4.5   John Huston, *The Dead* (recitation scene: Mr. Grace and Lily, 1987) 122

4.6   John Huston, *The Dead* (Gretta and Lily, 1987) 123

4.7   John Huston, *The Dead* (ruins of Round Tower, 1987) 134

6.1   "Injustice to Ireland" 166

6.2   Rev. J. Conmee, SJ (1895) 169

6.3   "On Board of the *Bugaboo*" (1891) 172

6.4   Mary Rochfort, Lady Belvedere (date unknown) 175

6.5   Timeball, Ballast Office, Dublin (c. 1900) 179

6.6   Sidney Ollcott, *The Lad from Old Ireland* (Terry and Aileen on deck, 1910) 185

7.1   Rev. Thomas Connellan (1908) 192

7.2 Lough Ree, County Westmeath (scene of Rev. Thomas Connellan's disappearance, 1887) *195*

7.3 Rev. Thomas Connellan and converts (1908) *195*

7.4 "U. P. UP," *Celtic Times* (1887) *200*

7.5 Front page, *Celtic Times* (15 October 1887) *202*

8.1 John Howard Parnell (late nineteenth century) *208*

8.2 Pro-Boer demonstration outside Trinity College, *Le Petit Journal* (31 December 1899) *209*

8.3 Title page, Patrick J. P. Tynan, *The Irish National Invincibles and Their Times* (1896) *217*

8.4 Charles Stewart Parnell (1886) *223*

8.5 General Christiaan De Wet (1902) *223*

PREFACE

In the hauntings of Seamus Heaney's "Station Island" (1986), the unrequited ghosts of modernity are left until last. Returning from the penitential site of pilgrimage to the shore, the poet is greeted by an unnamed shade, tall and seemingly blind, but walking "straight as a rush / upon his ashplant." As they move through the car-park, the spectral figure hits "a litter basket / with his stick," a fitting symbol of contemporary purgatory: "A waste of time for somebody your age." Poetry may offer no redress for the injuries of history, but there is a glimmer of hope, if by that is meant approaching the future from a new angle, free from a compulsion to return to the scene of the crime: "Keep at a tangent / when they make the circle wide," and "fill the element / with signatures on your own frequency, / echo soundings, searches, probes, allurements."

It is this capacity to change the station, to turn echo soundings of the past into new frequencies, that catches the spirit of Joyce's ghosts. The undead in Joyce do not belong to the Gothic, for that genre only makes sense historically in cultures that have given up the ghost and no longer succumb to haunting. *Hamlet* and *Macbeth* are not Gothic tales, strictly speaking, for the specter had not yet passed from life into literature and was an everyday affair, despite the efforts of the Reformation to dispel superstition. The cultural milieu of Joyce's upbringing had similarly to undergo the full rigors of disenchantment but was no less integrated into modernity for all that. It is not so much that the ghost was general all over Ireland but that belief itself was kept at bay, including the belief that colonial modernity offered the only path to the future. In Joyce's work, the ghost appears in moments of crisis where the past slips through the private nets of memory but has not yet become public history, hovering in a liminal zone between inner and outer life. It is common to see the revenant as a sign of mental breakdown, as a failure of the mind to police

xiv   PREFACE

its own boundaries, but that presupposes inner life and individualism are already securely in place, which was far from the case in early twentieth-century Ireland.

This has important implications for rational attempts to explain away the ghost by relegating it to psychology, for Joyce's skepticism about the "Viennese school" is as concerned to raise questions about specters of the self as about specters from the otherworld. In this study, I show how key features of modernity—subjectivity, the city, commodity culture, technology, democracy, empire—harbor their own phantoms, particularly as they impinge on the dislocations of the colonial periphery. The shadows thrown by the Great Famine and the fall of Parnell in Ireland become part of the involuntary memory of the colonial subject, in which personal traumas are inseparable from wider social catastrophes. It is in this sense that the "nightmare of history" presided over Joyce's modernist innovations, much as "mad Ireland," according to W. H. Auden, hurt Yeats into poetry. Joyce's Irishness, on this reading, is intrinsic to his modernism, thus countering a tendency in the first generations of Joyce criticism to attribute his formal breakthroughs to exile on the European mainland, and to his association with the metropolitan avant-garde of Pound, Eliot, and others. In *Joyce's Ghosts*, I question this once conventional view, arguing that the pressures of late colonial Ireland, a country at once inside and outside the world system, acted as a cultural laboratory for many of his most distinctive stylistic experiments.

Ireland thus achieves articulation not only as subject matter or content but also as *form*, allowing Joyce to pioneer a mode of vernacular modernism. Vernacular in this sense does not mean native or indigenous but the demotic: language as practiced in its most unstable, everyday settings. Central to this is the idiomatic cast given to the narrative technique of free indirect discourse, according to which language simultaneously carries voices from both inside and outside a culture—the "dialect of the tribe" as well as third-person Standard English (and other registers). This dual voice also raises questions about the well-known stream of consciousness technique, for free indirect discourse challenges the sovereignty of the self, opening inner life to other voices and external forces. Interior monologue is closer to silent dialogue, having as much to do with the frequencies of cultural intimacy as with the innermost recesses of the self.

Contrary to Sigmund Freud's view that the ghost is a projection of inner life, the specter emanates from an incomplete project of self-formation, as in the failure to internalize memory itself in a colonial culture. It is not that the ghost is of one's own making but that it does not make it to the mind in the first place. Rather than being a given, the self is an essentially contested subject under imperial modernity, conforming to but not fully internalizing the individualist ethic of capitalism in early twentieth-century Ireland. Holding on to relational ties from the past, the ghost also holds out for alternative futures: Joyce's work is set in a city on the verge of revolt, emerging from generations of cultural paralysis. *Ulysses* is a portrait of a city like no other in that, through an array of narrative strategies, language is not at one remove from reality but is stitched into the very fabric of the world it evokes. (It is on account of these narrative devices that the discussion does not extend to *Finnegans Wake*, which raises very different questions about language, self, and reality.) The juxtaposition of the real, on the one hand, and the fictive, on the other, places the real world itself in suspension, as if *Thom's Directory* of Dublin has to rely on the imagination to bring it to life. But, as the work of imagination implies, this kind of vivacity depends not only on what is shown but also on what is screened from view: effects derived from what is off the page, or between the lines. It is no coincidence that the revenants of Heaney's "Station Island" are unnamed: a cloudburst breaks on the last ghost, and as "he moved off quickly / the downpour loosed its screens around his straight walk."

Instead of banishing the ghost, Ireland's uneven entry into modernity cast its own shadows, as street lighting, photography, and cinema added to an awareness of unseen presences in Joyce's work. As critics noted from the outset, Joyce's fiction had a highly cinematic quality, culminating in the montage effects of the cascading images in *Ulysses*. Joyce's "The Dead" had to await John Huston's memorable *The Dead* (1987) to find its expression on the screen, for the film not only addressed the substance of the story but also captured "the old Irish tonality," visualizing the voice itself. Though Huston initially filmed the apparition of Michael Furey, this was wisely deleted from the final cut, as the film hints, in the spirit of Joyce's own formal techniques, that the camera itself is the ghost, carrying vestiges of cultural as well as personal memory.

In the final chapter of the book, I chart the manner in which memory under modernism breaks free of romantic regression. While colonial melancholia acknowledges loss, it also holds on, as Judith Butler maintains, to an open-ended *relation* with the lost object that offers a presentiment of hope. In this, history repeats itself with a difference, and it is only when experience fixes on one object, and precludes a generality directed toward others, that pathologies of despair set in. Joyce's "the seim aniew" can thus be seen as preempting foregone conclusions, bearing out Joseph Brodsky's claim that there is always something left over from the past, and that is the future.

ACKNOWLEDGMENTS

This book is the product of "echo soundings" from friends and colleagues over many years. At a time when Patrick Kavanagh's attitude — "Who killed James Joyce?" — still held sway in some academic circles in Ireland, leading Joyce scholars such as Maud Ellmann, Karen Lawrence, and Jennifer Wicke convinced me that Irish voices could play more than a walk-on part on the global stage of Joyce criticism. Seamus Deane, Enda Duffy, Declan Kiberd, David Lloyd, and Emer Nolan brought a new intellectual verve and erudition in pioneering Irish approaches to Joyce, and conversations with them over many years have found their way into this book. Luca Crispi, Ronan Crowley, Anne Fogarty, Terry Eagleton, Vivien Igoe, Terence Killeen, Barry McCrea, Christine O'Neill, Stephanie Rains, and Sam Slote have continued the conversation, as have critics, students, and Joyceans who have shared their knowledge and insights at Joyce conferences, film events, or Irish Studies seminars: Dudley Andrew, Derek Attridge, Murray Beja, Valérie Bénéjam, John Bishop, Katie Brown, Joseph Buttigieg, Gregory Castle, Vincent Cheng, Jeffrey Chown, Jim Collins, Ciara Conneely, Elizabeth Butler Cullingford, Chris Fox, Renée Fox, Andrew Gibson, Susan Cannon Harris, Laura Izarra, Ellen Carol Jones, Peter Kuch, Greg Kucich, Sean Mannion, Amy Martin, Julie McCormack-Weng, John McCourt, Rebecca McGlynn, Tekla Macsnober, Vicki Mahaffey, Katherine Mullin, John Nash, Peggy O'Brien, Vike Plock, Michael Rubenstein, Jessica Scarlata, Fritz Senn, Clare Wallace, John P. Waters, Julie Ann Ulin, Siân White, Catherine Wynne, and Robert Young.

The "Semi-Colonial Joyce" panel convened by Derek Attridge and Marjorie Howes at the Zurich colloquium (1996), subsequently expanded to a full conference at the University of Miami (1998) and a timely publication, *Semi-Colonial Joyce* (Cambridge University Press, 2000), was a key event in concentrating my energies on recasting Joyce from an Irish perspective, but within wider cross-cultural frames.

My colleagues and students in the School of Communications at Dublin City University provided valuable support for my work on Joyce at an early stage, and I would like to thank them for keeping a firm grip on the Humanities homestead when the Celtic Tiger started prowling at the door. When I moved to the University of Notre Dame (Indiana), the English Department and the Keough-Naughton Institute for Irish Studies, under the stewardship of Seamus Deane and Chris Fox, provided the kind of research environment that brought new advances in Irish Studies into dialogue with critical theory and Modernist Studies. I would like to thank all those colleagues who helped me re-create home away from home in Indiana, and also those graduate students in the "Joyce and Irish Modernism" seminars who put me repeatedly through my paces. I was lucky on my return to Ireland to take up a position at Maynooth University, where the intellectual vitality of the English Department and the commitment of colleagues to new directions in Irish Studies and World Literature have helped me to think things through, in keeping with a university ethos that, in a grim period of austerity, provided the time and resources to undertake innovative research in the humanities.

Much of this book is dedicated to showing that, contrary to popular accounts of Jacques Derrida, there are things outside the text, and the company of friends is primary among these. I wish to thank friends whose warm support and encouragement have helped to bring this book to completion, as well as bringing me to book when it was necessary: Desmond Bell, Mary Burgess, Jean Butler, Anne Bernard Kearney, Lisa Caulfield, Denis Condon, Claire Connolly, Maeve Connolly, Lucy Cotter, Michael Cronin, Michael G. Cronin, Dermot Dix, Bairbre Dowling, Sheila Duddy, Michael Foley, Oona Frawley, Debbie Ging, Colin Graham, John Horgan, Aideen Howard, Mary Jones, Richard Kearney, Gerry Kearns, Roisín Kennedy, Sinead Kennedy, Aphra Kerr, Linda King, Kathryn Kozarits, Trish Lambe, Joep Leerssen, Chandana Mathur, Stephanie McBride, Conor McCarthy, Sinead McCoole, Fiach MacConghail, Seona MacReamoinn, Brendán MacSuibhne, Paschal Mahoney, Chris Morash, Catherine Morris, Willa Murphy, Barbara Novak, Éamonn Ó Ciardha, Mary O'Connell, Barbara O'Connor, Maureen O'Connor, Elizabeth O'Connor Chandler, Brian O'Doherty, Sunniva O'Flynn, Diarmuid O'Giolláin, Jean O'Halloran, Cormac O'Malley, Stephen Rea, Ann Rigney, Kevin Rockett, Elaine Sisson, Jamie Saris, and Eamonn Slater.

If, as I also argue in this book, one's voice is only as good as the other sustaining voices in one's life, then some friends, far and near, will hardly be surprised to hear echoes of thinking out loud coming back to them: Jim Chandler, Joe Cleary, James Coleman, Pia Conti, Farrel Corcoran, Rachael Dowling, Tadhg Foley, Marjorie Howes, Tanya Kiang, Christina Kennedy, Niamh O'Sullivan, and Clair Wills. The diverse interests of the extended Gibbons family in Ireland, Wales, and the United States have broadened my horizons over many decades. Since the passing of our parents, my regret is that they are not around to benefit from the example they set us. Bringing it all back home, Joyce's dedication to the everyday shows that, in the end, daily love is more constant than eternal love, and for this I cannot thank Dolores, Laura, and Barry enough.

This book is dedicated to the memory of Siobhán Kilfeather and Tom Duddy. The only consolation for those who knew them is that death does not have the last word, and, as Joyce himself put it, "no life, no moment of exaltation is ever lost."

* * *

I would like to express my deepest thanks to Alan Thomas at the University of Chicago Press for taking this publication on board: it was his editorial vision that led, among other achievements, to the translation of key writings of Nicolas Abraham and Maria Torok into English, and I would like to see this book as a further act of "translation," albeit into a wayward Irish idiom. The editorial guidance of Randy Petilos and Joel Score was invaluable, and India Cooper's fastidious copyediting made working with her a particular pleasure. I wish also to extend my thanks to the anonymous readers whose meticulous, perceptive reports greatly enhanced the final work.

I wish to thank Pierre le Brocquy and Anne Madden for permission to use Louis le Brocquy's *Study Towards an Image of James Joyce* (1978), and also to thank Christina Kennedy and David Britton at Adams Showrooms for their help in providing the photography. Frances Hegarty and Andrew Stones went to considerable lengths to provide me with photographs of their *For Dublin* project (1997), and Amanda Coogan did likewise with her photograph of *Molly Blooms* (2004). Both of these works proved inspirational for the arguments in chapter 2. Fritz Senn was kind enough to forward Carola Giedion-Welcker's photograph of Joyce at the Platzspitz (Zurich) in chapter 1. Rachael Dowling, Bairbre Dowling, and Maria Hayden enriched my understanding of life on the set of John Huston's production of *The Dead* (1987), and helped me greatly to appreciate Huston's eye for the uncanny. I wish to thank the generosity of the owner and Ian Whyte at Whyte's of Dublin for the photograph of John Howard Parnell in chapter 8, and also Professor Donal McCracken for the photo of the cover of *Le Petit Journal*. Ciarán Deane and Anne Fogarty furnished me with digital versions of images used in previous publications of chapters 6 and 7, respectively, and Niamh O'Sullivan and Barry Gibbons did much behind-the-scenes work to bring these images to the page.

I wish also to thank the editors and publishers of books and journals that printed earlier versions of some of the chapters in this book: chapter 1, "Text and the City: Joyce, Dublin, and Colonial Modernity," in *Making Space in the Works of James Joyce*, ed. Valérie Bénéjam and John Bishop (New York: Routledge, 2011), 69–90; and chapter 3, "'He Says No, Your Worship': James Joyce, Free Indirect Discourse, and Vernacular Modernism," in *James Joyce in the Nineteenth Century*, ed. John Nash (Cambridge: Cambridge University Press, 2013), 31–46. Parts of chapter 4 were published in "'The Cracked Looking Glass of Cinema': James Joyce, John Huston, and the Memory of *The Dead*," in "The Theatre of Irish Cinema," ed. Dudley Andrew and Luke Gibbons, special issue of the *Yale Journal of Criticism* 15, no. 1 (Spring 2002): 127–48; "Visualizing the Voice: James Joyce and the Politics of Vision," in *A Companion to Literature and Film*, ed. Robert Stam and Alessandro Raengo (Oxford: Blackwell, 2004), 171–88; and "'Ghostly Light': Specters of Modernity in James Joyce's and John Huston's 'The Dead,'" in *A Companion to James Joyce*, ed. Richard Brown (Oxford: Blackwell, 2007), 359–73. Chapter 6 first appeared as "'Spaces of Time through Times of Space': Joyce, Ireland, and Colonial Modernity" in *Field Day Review* 1 (2005): 70–85; and chapter 7 was first published as "'Famished Ghosts': Bloom, Bible Wars, and 'U.P. UP' in Joyce's Dublin," in *Dublin James Joyce Journal* 2 (2010): 1–23.

INTRODUCTION

"A Ghost by Absence"

As I think of Joyce a haunting figure rises up in my memory.

JOHN EGLINTON, *Irish Literary Portraits*

W. B. Yeats is often viewed as being away with the fairies in the Celtic Twilight, but James Joyce, by contrast, is considered very much a man of this world, grounded in the prose of everyday life.[1] George Sigerson's claim in *Ulysses* that "[o]ur national epic has yet to be written" (*U* 9.309) could be taken as an ironic comment on Joyce's own future contribution to the Revival, but few see *Ulysses* as a response to the request made to Stephen Dedalus in the classroom at Dalkey: "Tell us a story, sir. — O, do, sir. A ghoststory" (*U* 2.54–55). That the ghost is on Stephen's mind, however, is clear from the spectral memory of his dead mother that haunts *Ulysses*, and Joyce himself was no stranger to ghosts, or to the grief that takes leave of the senses.[2] On the night of his mother's funeral in 1903, Joyce kept a vigil with his sister Margaret ("Poppie") for their mother's ghostly return, and though only his sister purported to see the ghost, wearing the brown habit in which May Joyce had been buried (*JJ* I, 136), it closely resembles the revenant of Stephen's mother in *Ulysses*: "In a dream, silently, she had come to him, her wasted body within its loose graveclothes giving off an odour of wax and rosewood" (*U* 1.269–70). Notwithstanding his well-known skepticism, Joyce was susceptible to superstition and had an almost primeval fear of thunder: the seismic roar of the heavens one hundred letters long precipitates the Fall at the beginning of *Finnegans Wake* and rumbles throughout the work. As Bloom ruminates in *Ulysses*: "Something in all those superstitions because when you go out never know what dangers" (*U* 13.1159–60).

Although deeply critical of religious belief, and particularly doctrinal orthodoxy, Joyce also directed his suspicions of received wisdom at the

presumptions of science and psychology—"the new Viennese school Mr
Magee spoke of" (*U* 9.780) in the National Library—to explain the mysteries of life. To a friend who asked him what he thought of the next life,
Joyce replied: "I don't think much of this one" (*JJ* 661). Stuart Gilbert
observes that Joyce did not share his own esoteric beliefs in theosophy
and magic but adds that Joyce was also equally unimpressed by their
secular replacements:

> I doubt if Joyce, though he owned to several deeply rooted super-
> stitions (as they are called), believed in any such doctrines. But he
> accepted their existence as a fact, on a footing of validity no higher
> and no lower than that of many of the fashionable and fluctuating
> "truths" of science and psychology. He had none of the glib assur-
> ance of the late nineteenth-century rationalist.[3]

For all Joyce's aversion to Catholic guilt, he commented, perhaps provocatively, that he preferred Catholic confession to the talking cure of
the couch and saw psychoanalysis as a form of blackmail (*JJ* 538).[4] Opponents of the Catholic confessional in Ireland charged that inner life was
nonexistent since priests were regarded by the faithful "as the reposito-
ries of their private thoughts,"[5] but as Maurice Halbwachs points out,
this scrutiny is no different, penitential judgments aside, from the exposure of inner self to the gaze of the psychologist: "From the moment
the psychologist claims to explain to others what they should see within
themselves, he exposes states of consciousness and exteriorizes them."[6]
A person who, like Mr. Daedalus in *Stephen Hero*, is put off by the title
of Ibsen's *Ghosts* because it suggests little more than "some uninterest-
ing story about a haunted house" (*SH* 93) would be equally mistaken in
reducing a haunted house to the contents of Ibsen's mind. "Why all this
fuss and bother about the mystery of the unconscious?" Joyce remarked
to Frank Budgen. "What about the mystery of the conscious? What do
they know about that?"[7]

One of the underlying impulses behind Joyce's recourse to the ghost
and the uncanny is to raise as many questions about the mind itself as
about its putative spectral manifestations. "Mourning," writes Maud Ellmann, summarizing Freud, "is the struggle to release the ego from the
very ghosts it is attempting to revive."[8] From the inception of the Gothic
genre, the rational response to haunting was to consign it to the subjective realm, as in the anticlimactic psychological resolutions that explained away the supernatural in Ann Radcliffe's tales of terror.[9] Joyce's
ghosts, by contrast, are closer to Tzvetan Todorov's concept of the "fan-

tastic," which oscillates "between a natural and a supernatural explanation of the events described." In this, Joyce's style constantly exploits an
uncertainty principle that exposes the limits of the literal at precisely
those moments of crisis when inner and outer worlds lose their bearings:
"The fantastic occupies the duration of this uncertainty. Once we choose
one answer or the other, we leave the fantastic. . . . The fantastic is that
hesitation experienced by a person who knows only the laws of nature,
confronting an apparently supernatural event."[10]

It is in this light that the questioning of interiority and egoism in
Joyce's fiction is best understood, notwithstanding perceptions of the
centrality of the individual subject in his work.[11] *Ulysses*, according to
Fredric Jameson, is that "quite different thing" in modernism, "the construction of a form of discourse from which the subject — sender or receiver — is radically excluded."[12] In chapters 1 and 2, the dissolution of
the self in its individualistic form is related to what the Soviet psychologist Lev Vygotsky termed "inner speech," a mode of interior dialogue
that comes across as monologue since the same person is both sender
and receiver. Vygotsky relates inner speech not only to introspection but
also to outer forms of interpersonal communication and codes of intimacy, in which much is left unsaid because of context and shared experience: the closer the relationship, the more abbreviated and concentrated
the modes of communication.[13] Inner speech is not only a psychological phenomenon but also a cultural process, embodying the background
knowledge, physical contexts, and somatic responses through which we
negotiate the external environment as well as inner life. Joyce's Dublin
might thus be seen as conveying the inner speech of a city, releasing it
from nativist assumptions of privileged knowledge and providing the
reader with new modes of access to the everyday life of its inhabitants.
As David Pierce describes it, "At times a knowledge of Dublin is assumed
by Joyce. We can think what we like about this, whether or not it's delib-
erate, a form of resentment perhaps by the colonized against the colo-
nizer, or part of Joyce's unconscious peripheral vision. But the upshot is
that there is an onus on readers and commentators alike to make explicit
some of these assumptions or contexts."[14] The cultural intimacy afforded
by *Ulysses* is, of course, far from effortless (as readers initially deterred
by its demands on concentration often attest) and is conditional on a
grasp of literary form — the peculiar syntax, linguistic compression, and
cultural codes of the novel — and, as such, has to be earned; but it is still
in principle open to all. More to the point, Joyce's style derives much of
its disruptive power from the manner in which it picks up on the transformations of a culture in which the majority of the population has lost

one language and is not too sure about its grasp of another. In an influential account, Harry Levin noted that it is through *form* that the novel
forges sympathetic ties to the reader but also opens up the inner life of
the city to the uninitiated: "The act of communication, the bond of sympathy which identifies the reader with the book, comes almost too close
for comfort. The point of view, the principle of form which has served to
integrate many amorphous novels, is intimate and pervasive."[15] On this
reading, the "stranger to Dublin what place was it and so on" (*U* 18.92)
who tired Molly out "about the monuments and . . . statues" might be
better off carrying *Ulysses* than a copy of Baedeker's guide on his or her
tours of the city.[16]

Inner speech, then, applies to public as well as mental life, and there is
an important sense in which Joyce uses it to prise open the sealed boundaries of the psyche. Writing of the maintenance of a clear division between inner and outer in fixing the coherent subject, Judith Butler asks:
"From what strategic position in public discourse and for what reasons
has the trope of interiority and the disjunctive binary of inner/outer
taken hold? In what language is 'inner space' figured?"[17] Joyce's writing
can be seen precisely as the figuring of such language, and one of the
recurrent concerns in his narrative strategies is the irreducible external
component in inner life, whether at a personal or cultural level. It is for
this reason, as I show in chapter 3, that the use of stream of consciousness in *Ulysses* is recast in idiomatic terms to bring it closer to a more
socially oriented use of *free indirect discourse*, the merging of two or more
voices (or viewpoints) in one utterance. Free indirect discourse, according to Dorrit Cohn, is a technique "for rendering a character's thought in
his own idiom while maintaining a third-person reference and the basic
tense of narration," thus challenging the assumption that inner speech
of any kind is the sole preserve of the native or insider.[18] Just as the outsider or third party can gain access to inner experience, so also inside
knowledge is dependent on an external vantage point, and is not compromised by integration into a wider, cosmopolitan world. The material
environment itself bears the traces of interior histories, and as Joyce's
characters move through the city, it is as if the streets and buildings speak
back to them, much as the Kingsbridge train in "A Painful Case" in *Dubliners* whispers the syllables of Mrs. Sinico's name to the haunted Mr.
Duffy. Tom McCarthy's judicious plea to forgo the association of interior
monologue with "unassigned first person narrative" in *Ulysses* might thus
be extended to the "exterior consciousness" of the city itself in the novel:

> People should desist, once and for all, from using the term "interior
> monologue" to describe the novel's outbreaks of unassigned first-

person narrative. This is not interior monologue: it's exterior consciousness, embodied (or encorpsed) consciousness that has ruptured the membrane of conventional syntax.[19]

Psychological explanations of the supernatural seek to convince the deluded that though they imagine they are conversing with other forms, they are really talking to themselves. As Jacques Derrida describes Freud's undue haste in debunking the encounter with the ghost in Wilhelm Jensen's story *Gradiva* (1903): "[The character Hanold] thinks that he speaks for a whole hour with Gradiva, with his 'mid-day ghost' (*Mittagsgespenst*), though she has been buried since the catastrophe of 79. He *monologues with* Gradiva's ghost for an hour, then the latter regains her tomb, and Hanold, the archaeologist, remains alone. But he also remains duped by the hallucination."[20] It may be pure monologue that is the delusion here, for the persistence of dialogue, even in the privacy of inner speech, suggests that there is never an absolute lone voice, except in psychosis.[21] Apparitions, while appearing to the person experiencing them as real, are reduced by Freud to projections of the mind, and the cure proceeds in reassuring the patient that it is all of his or her own making.[22] As Bruno Latour wryly explains:

> Someone who (naively) believed he was hearing voices would then turn into a ventriloquist. Having become aware of his own double-dealing, he would be reconciled with himself. Someone who believed he was dependent on divinities would actually notice he was alone with his own inner voice, and that divinities own nothing he has not given them. Once the scales had fallen from his eyes, he would see there was nothing to see. . . . [H]umans would finally realize they are sole masters in a world forever emptied of idols.[23]

But these reductionist explanations fall short, for no sooner has the otherworld been relegated to the mind than the mind itself is uncovered, on a strict materialist reading, as a phantom in its own right. On purely scientific terms, there is no subjectivity in the first place to produce the flights of the imagination that turn into ghosts: the Self Illusion, as a recent book puts it, is as potent as the God Illusion.[24] According to Latour, "the free and autonomous human boasts, a little too soon, that he is the primal cause of all his own projections and manipulations," for a materialist critique "reveals how determination works, beneath the illusion of freedom. The subject believes he is free, while 'in reality' he is wholly controlled": "The laws of biology, genetics, economics, society, and language are going to put the speaking subject, who believed himself to be master of his own deeds and acts, in his place."[25] In substituting the self for the specter, "the human actor has merely exchanged one form of transcendence for another."[26] Or as Shane McCorristine expresses it: "[T]he spectral self [is] the true ghost in the modern age."[27]

It is striking that the most notable success in the therapeutic treatment of "hearing voices" consists not in medication but in establishing agency through turning hearing into speaking, thus enabling a variation of the two-way logic of free indirect discourse.[28] This infusion of subjective life can take on a dynamic of its own, for just as ventriloquism can lead to the hearing of voices, so the polyphony of free indirect discourse may result in delusions or hallucinations—precisely the hysteria that affects, as Stephen Ullmann points out, the overheated imaginations of Flaubert's characters.[29] If the dual voice of free indirect discourse makes it difficult to tell which of two voices is speaking, then it is not always possible to construe one as a projection of the other—"my multiple Mes" (FW 410.12), as it is relayed in Finnegans Wake.[30] For this reason, according to Ullmann, the technique "is well suited to the evocation of hallucinatory states of mind where the borderline between imagination and reality is temporarily obliterated."[31] This is seen to telling effect in Gabriel Conroy's desolation in the final paragraphs of "The Dead," as inner and outer worlds shade into one another:

> The tears gathered more thickly in his eyes and in the partial darkness he imagined he saw the form of a young man standing under a dripping tree. Other forms were near. His soul had approached that region where dwell the vast hosts of the dead. He was conscious of, but could not apprehend, their wayward and flickering existence. (D 224)

In the first sentence the ghost is not only imagined but perceived: "he imagined *he saw* . . ." (my emphasis). In the second sentence, written ostensibly in the third person, there is an impression of objective narration—"Other forms were near"—but this is voiced through semisubjective descriptions of the regions of the dead in the last two sentences. The borders between inner and outer experiences are indeed temporarily obliterated, before their ultimate "dissolving and dwindling" (D 225). To ask if the ghost literally exists is to miss the point, for it is precisely the equation of literalism with truth that is being called into question, as the opening line of the story suggests: "Lily, the caretaker's daughter, was literally run off her feet" (D 175). As grief and loss weigh heavily on the minds of Joyce's characters, language and emotion give way to other

voices: "It is clear," writes Cóilín Owens, "that some of the most affect-
ing moments in his [Joyce's] fiction are those in which the living are
accosted by those whose deaths they mourn. . . . [Hence the] familiar
Joycean scenario—persisting from 'The Sisters' to *Finnegans Wake*—of
an encounter between a living character and a revenant."[32]

It may even be the case, as Steven Connor suggests, that free indirect
discourse—or the failure to detect its operation—was responsible for
the reemergence of the ghost in the early modern period, prompted by
scriptural controversies over apparitions in the Bible. This concerns the
scene in the Old Testament in which the Witch of Endor summons up
the ghost of Samuel before Saul: "And when the woman saw Samuel,
she cried with a loud voice" and described the ghost to Saul: "And Saul
perceived that it was Samuel, and he bowed with his face to the ground
and did obeisance" (1 Samuel 28). It is not clear that Saul actually sees
the apparition (another translation states "he *knew* it was Samuel"), so
that scripture is *reporting* what others saw, rather than narrating the objective facts:

> Scripture might have been employing a little of what rhetoricians
> nearly 2000 years later would have got into the habit of calling "free
> indirect discourse." One way of reading the phrase . . . is to separate
> out the two voices compacted in it, [whereas a literal-minded com-
> mentator] finds it impossible to conceive or tolerate the idea of two
> voices speaking at once, or the muddying of the narrative voice of
> scripture with the implied voice or perspective of others.[33]

Seizing on an interpretation that Saul was merely responding to the
witch's description, opponents of witchcraft were not slow to exploit the
charge that the witch was ventriloquizing the ghost and impersonating
the voice of Samuel.

In "Hades," in *Ulysses*, the possibility of voices beyond the grave introduced by the new media technologies of the telephone and the phonograph allows Joyce to play with the persistence of the ghost under modernity.[34] Watching lumps of clay fall on Paddy Dignam's coffin in Glasnevin
Cemetery, Bloom experiences last-minute anxieties that the corpse may
still be alive, and that pronouncements of death are not rigorous enough:
"They ought to have some law to pierce the heart and make sure or an
electric clock or a telephone in the coffin and some kind of a canvas air-
hole. Flag of distress" (*U* 6.867–69). The capacity of the new communications media to redress this situation then presents itself, as Bloom
imagines an open line to the next world:

> Besides how could you remember everybody? Eyes, walk, voice.
> Well, the voice, yes: gramophone. Have a gramophone in every grave
> or keep it in the house. After dinner on a Sunday. Put on poor old
> greatgrandfather. Kraahraark! Hellohellohello amawfullyglad kraark
> awfullygladaseeagain hellohello amawf krpthsth. (*U* 6.964–67)

As Connor notes, this passage exploits a subtle confusion between sound
technologies, for while the gramophone could indeed play back grandfather's voice without any ghostly trappings, it is not *live*: Bloom's imagining of a conversation from the grave is closer to a telephone than a
gramophone.[35] Chapter 5 will examine the possibility that media technologies also intervene at the end of "Circe," since the apparition of Rudy
that transfixes Bloom may be a mechanical image, thrown by a projec-
tor. In "The Dead," as will be shown in chapter 4, the spectral modernity of the city extends to street lighting, as the "ghostly light" (*D* 217)
from gas lamps that enters the bedroom of the Gresham Hotel where
Gabriel and Gretta Conroy are staying prefigures the gasworks in which
Michael Furey worked at Galway. The "gathering forces" (*D* 222) that
assail Gabriel Conroy also disturb his speech, for at times it seems that
another voice is speaking through him, derailing his train of thought. In
"The Sisters," the opening story of *Dubliners*, the young boy's anxious
dreams about the dead Father Flynn come alive and acquire a voice of
their own:

> I imagined that I saw again the heavy grey face of the paralytic. . . . It
> murmured; and I understood that it desired to confess something.
> I felt my soul receding into some pleasant and vicious region; and
> there again I found it waiting for me. It began to confess to me in a
> murmuring voice and I wondered why it smiled continually and why
> the lips were so moist with spittle. (*D* 3)

The dialogical imagination is explored repeatedly in *Ulysses* to allow
for transsubjective experiences not fully contained within the self—what
Joyce referred to as the "curious telepathic experiences" that enabled his
fiction.[36] As John Rickard notes, this emerges as "metapersonal memory,"
a process akin to telepathy in which recollections, perceptions, and impressions slip through the nets of individual minds, "gradually loosening
the boundaries of personality and memory."[37] John Gordon has written
of the hallucinations in the "Circe" chapter that they "were essentially
psychological, not textual, in origin," but then he concedes that "this
thesis leaves some loose ends"—"that is, its ever-problematical open-

ness to the possibilities of the psychic transmigrations through some not-only-physical ether."[38] If the phantasmagoria of "Circe" represents for the most part Bloom's unconscious, it still has to be explained how thoughts crop up in Bloom's mind that have featured earlier in Stephen's consciousness, or in exchanges where Bloom was not present. There is even a problem explaining how some thoughts got into Stephen's head in the first place. In the opening "Telemachus" chapter, the "gloomy domed livingroom" where Buck Mulligan is shaving is described, apparently in third-person narration: "Two shafts of soft daylight fell across the flagged floor from the high barbacans: and at the meeting of their rays a cloud of coalsmoke and fumes of fried grease floated, turning" (*U* 1.315–17). Later, echoes of this description mysteriously surface in Stephen's head as he walks on Sandymount strand: "Turning, he scanned the shore south, his feet sinking again slowly in new sockets. The cold domed room of the tower waits. Through the barbacans the shafts of light are moving ever, slowly ever as my feet are sinking, creeping duskward over the dial floor" (*U* 3.270–73). The most plausible explanation is that the earlier mise-en-scène was in fact perceived through Stephen's mind (though he was not present), but it reappears again later in the novel, this time in the stage directions of "Circe" as Stephen and Bloom jostle with Private Carr: "*Black candles rise from its gospel and epistle horns. From the high barbacans of the tower two shafts of light fall on the smokepalled altarstone. On the altarstone Mrs Mina Purefoy, goddess of unreason, lies, naked, fettered, a chalice resting on her swollen belly*" (*U* 15. 4689–93).[39] Thoughts seem to drift free of their mental worlds, as if the objective, third-party aspect of free indirect discourse were sufficient to endow inner life with some kind of indeterminate outer form.

The transfer of thoughts from one mind to another is evident in the much discussed example of the "matutinal cloud" (*U* 17.40–41) in the early chapters of *Ulysses*, which is viewed from different locations during the morning and which gives rise to various maternal associations in the minds of those who notice it. The passing of the cloud over the Martello Tower in Sandycove in "Telemachus" prompts Stephen's first traumatic memory of his last visit to his dying mother: "A cloud began to cover the sun slowly, wholly, shadowing the bay in deeper green. It lay beneath him, a bowl of bitter waters" (*U* 1.248–49). As Stephen recalls his dying mother's bedside, it is as if the memories lodged in the bric-a-brac in her room migrate to his troubled mind: "Her secrets: old featherfans, tasseled dancecards, powdered with musk, a gaud of amber beads in her locked drawer. . . . Folded away in the memory of nature with her toys. Memories beset his brooding brain" (*U* 1.255–56, 265–66). The past be-

comes a spectral nightmare when Stephen is visited by a dream, close to
the real-life incident mentioned at the outset, of his mother in her graveclothes:

> Her glazing eyes, staring out of death, to shake and bend my soul.
> On me alone. The ghostcandle to light her agony. Ghostly light on
> the tortured face. Her hoarse loud breath rattling in horror, while all
> prayed on their knees. Her eyes on me to strike me down. *Liliata
> rutilantium te confessorum turma circumdet: iubilantium te virginum
> chorus excipiat.* (*U* 1.273–77)[40]

In the case of Bloom, his glimpse of the same cloud, as he returns from
the butchers in "Calypso," blocks out a political version of another maternal dream — the Zionist return to a desiccated imaginary motherland:

> A cloud began to cover the sun wholly slowly wholly. Grey. Far.
>   No, not like that. A barren land, bare waste. Vulcanic lake, the dead
> sea: no fish, weedless, sunk deep in the earth. . . . A dead sea in a dead
> land, grey and old. Old now. It bore the oldest, the first race. A bent
> hag crossed from Cassidy's, clutching a naggin bottle by the neck.
> The oldest people. Wandered far away over all the earth, captivity
> to captivity, multiplying, dying, being born everywhere. It lay there
> now. Now it could bear no more. Dead: an old woman's: the grey
> sunken cunt of the world.
>   Desolation. (*U* 4.218–29)

It is no coincidence that the osmosis of thoughts from one mind to
another is associated with death, as in "Hades" when Bloom's turn of
phrase, in his musings on hearts no longer beating, "Old rusty pumps:
damn the thing else" (*U* 6.676), is picked up in Martin Cunningham's
explanation a few minutes later of the gravedigger's black humor: "That's
all done with a purpose. . . . .It's pure goodheartedness: damn the thing
else" (*U* 6.736, 737–38).[41] As we shall see in chapter 5, the intermeshing of
thoughts in the minds of Bloom and Stephen that brings them together
at the end of "Circe" turns on the traumatic loss of Bloom's son, Rudy,
who died soon after birth. It is as if Bloom's desire for a son converges
with Stephen's desire for an all but absent father he has missed in his life.
As Stephen walks on Sandymount beach in "Proteus," he notices a midwife carrying a bag in which he imagines "[a] misbirth with a trailing
navel cord, hushed in ruddy wool" (*U* 3.36–37). This foreshadows two
later sequences: Molly's memory of Rudy's ("ruddy") burial in a "little
wooly jacket" (*U* 18.1448), and the apparition of Rudy carrying a "lamb-

kin" that appears to Bloom at the end of "Circe." Later the midwife is described as carrying "an umbrella and a bag in which eleven cockles rolled" (U 10.1275–76), which evokes the eleven days of Rudy's life, but also Ophelia's "My cockle hat and staff and hismy sandal shoon" in *Hamlet*, which Stephen uses to describe himself (U 3.487–88). In the National Library, Stephen is keen to establish that Shakespeare's dead son, Hamnet, is also associated with the same number, having lived for just eleven years. This loss prompts the appearance of the ghost in Shakespeare's play, according to Stephen, but it also provides the basis for strange flickers of collective memory or thought transference between Stephen and Bloom. Stephen's reverie on Shakespeare's contemporary the musician John Dowland—"In a rosery of Fetter lane of Gerard, herbalist, he walks, greyedauburn" (U 9.651–52)—reappears in Bloom's mind in the Ormond Hotel when he reflects on the purple prose of his letter to Martha Clifford: "Too poetical that about the sad. Music did that. Music hath charms. Shakespeare said. Quotations every day in the year. To be or not to be. Wisdom while you wait. In Gerard's rosery of Fetter lane he walks, greyedauburn" (U 11.904–7).[42] Free indirect discourse, one character picking up the words of another, takes on an eerie quality when the original words have not been publicly uttered in the first place.[43] Subjectivity is indeed in crisis when characters, like the narrator of "Cyclops," are in "two minds" (U 12.9), and it is this that gives Bloom pause for thought when he ends up in the early hours with Stephen in the cabman's shelter: "Literally astounded at this piece of intelligence Bloom reflected. Though they didn't see eye to eye in everything a certain analogy there somehow was as if both their minds were travelling, so to speak, in the one train of thought" (U 16.1579–81).

Faced with the difficulties of explaining away apparitions or hallucinations, it is not surprising that psychological accounts conclude that they are symptoms of mental disorder—"the happy hauntingground of all minds that have lost their balance" (U 10.1061–62), to adapt Joyce's own formulation. Joyce may have created the phantom text of Dublin for the same reason that an amputee imagines a phantom limb: to compensate for the pain of loss. Yet, as Oliver Sacks shows, the experience of a phantom limb is far from being an aberration: it is often the absence rather than the occurrence of the phantom limb that requires explanation.[44] The vividness of a phantom limb may extend to external objects associated with the body, such as a wristwatch; by the same token, if a prosthesis is fitted, the "limb" can respond to minute irregularities in the ground sensed by the original leg. When Sacks notes in passing that "a phantom is more like a memory than an invention," it is difficult not to think of Joyce's almost somatic retention of the irregularities of his home ground, the city of Dublin, as in his remark to Jacques Mercanton: "Chance furnishes me with what I need. I'm like a man who stumbles: my foot strikes something. I look down, and there exactly is what I'm in need of."[45] Taking issue with the tendency to reduce phantom effects purely to neurophysiological disorders, especially if they assume palpable forms outside the body, Sacks points out that there is no need to impute mental disorder to children, for example, who have imaginary friends: "Children may also be more accepting of their hallucinations, having not yet learned that hallucinations are considered (in our culture) 'abnormal.'"[46] The crucial phrase here is in parentheses, "in our culture," for it reveals that such experiences need not arise not from neurological disorders but may be due to historically based *cultural* differences: what passes for normal in one society or era may be pathologized in another. Sacks writes that "many recent studies confirm that it is not uncommon to hear voices," and this was more prevalent up to the modern period: "No doubt there was sometimes an overlap between such voices and those of psychosis and hysteria, but for the most part they were not regarded as pathological; if they stayed inconspicuous and private, they were simply regarded as part of human nature, part of the way it was with some people."[47] It is perhaps with this in mind that we might view Joyce's verdict on the exposure of such private worlds in *Ulysses*: only "a transparent leaf separates it from madness."[48]

In the spirit of Roland Barthes's reminder that the critical task in the modern era is "no longer simply to upend (or right) the mythical message . . . but rather to change the object itself," Joyce's undoing of the familiar binaries of objective/subjective, present/past, and material world/ otherworld may be seen as upending the undue certainty that prides itself on freeing the "object" from myth, all the more so if couched in the scientific language of psychological explanation. Freud, in his forthright engagement with "the psychical roots of superstition" in *The Psychopathology of Everyday Life*, argued that superstition results from attributing to events in the external world purposive effects that belong to the accidents of the mind: "The differences between myself and the superstitious person are two: first, he projects outwards a motivation which I look for within: secondly, he interprets chance as due to an event, while I trace it back to a thought."[49] The certitude with which the inner is demarcated from the outer world, and taken as given, is carried over into Freud's account of "projection":

> *Because* the superstitious person knows nothing of the motivation
> of his own chance actions, and *because* the fact of this motivation

presses for a place in his field of recognition, he is forced to allocate it, by displacement, to the external world. . . . In point of fact I believe that a large part of the mythological view of the world, which extends a long way into the most modern religions, *is nothing but psychology projected into the external world.*[50]

This emphasis on projection as a primary psychological mechanism rests on an idealist assumption that the boundaries of the psyche are already in place, before its contents are displaced onto the external world. The conscious/unconscious subject in Freud is, of course, not dependent on the first-person "I" in the narrow sense, as is clear from the manner in which, as Jean Laplanche and Serge Leclaire note, the utterances of the unconscious are voiced not "in the first person, but in the alienated form of the second or third person."[51] This structures the conscious/unconscious subject along the lines of free indirect discourse, but if so, it is clear that the other voices are not derived solely from within but, as the linguistic turn in psychoanalysis under Lacan showed, from the "Other"—the constitutive voices of our social and cultural milieu (family, nation, class, gender relations) to which we will return in chapters 2 and 3.[52] Hence the opening lines of Joyce's *A Portrait of the Artist as a Young Man* in which the "Once upon a time . . ." story that registers baby tuckoo's earliest self-consciousness is framed in terms of the voices, gazes, and proximity of his parents and extended family: "His father told him that story: his father looked at him through a glass: he had a hairy face. . . . His mother had a nicer smell than his father" (*P* 3).[53] As Jeri Johnson notes, the presence of another perspective throughout precludes a first-person narrative—entailing a voice operating, as it were, outside the "I" or the subject.[54]

For Freud, however, what is outside the conscious "I" comes not from others but ultimately from a deeper interiority, the psyche, in Mikkel Borch-Jacobsen's words, being "driven back down to its own primordiality":[55]

To speak of unconscious "representations" was obviously to signal the existence of something beyond the subject, since I—I the ego—was thus supposed to have thoughts (*Gedanken*) that could think without me. But, through an inevitable countercoup, this was also to reinstate another ego (still the same one, of course) in that beyond.[56]

That projections, however, carry genuine traces of external (often oppressive) events, as against being solely of the subject's own making, is the point of Morton's Schatzman's *Soul Murder: Persecution in the Family*, a substantive challenge to Freud's interpretation of the case of Judge Daniel Schreber, in which the judge's delusions were attributed to his own narcissism rather than his social past: the buried memories of the horrific calisthenic experiments and contraptions to which Schreber was subjected as a child by the disciplinary zeal of his father, the educationalist Moritz Schreber.[57] Thus, for all the emphasis on the material basis of the mind in Freud, little attention is given to the social formation of the psyche, or to the historical emergence of individualism and subjectivity. These can be seen as depending on the reverse process of projection, that of *internalization*, according to which objects and practices are redirected from the outer world to fashion the inner world of the self.[58] Subject-formation in Freud is situated outside history, and though his subsequent work, under the influence of Sándor Ferenczi, takes fuller account of *introjection* and *incorporation*, these were largely seen as secondary processes.[59] It was left to later psychoanalysts such as Nicolas Abraham and Maria Torok to investigate what happens when internalization is not possible, as in the failure to introject the phantom, or the lost object, to the psyche in a state of acute melancholia.[60] Loss or guilt does not get past the body, as it were, and is suspended in a state of incorporation involving the senses and physical sustenance (eating and drinking). Hence the almost physical incisions of conscience for Stephen in *Ulysses*, "Agenbite of inwit" (*U* 1.481), and his experience of the ghost as feeding on flesh: "Ghoul! Chewer of corpses! No mother. Let me be and let me live" (*U* 1.278–9). Abraham and Torok mention in passing that in premodern societies, the public ritual of the wake indicated a shared culture that refused to let go of the dead, a world that answers in many respects to the barely incorporated vestiges of the Irish past that prevailed in the Ireland of Joyce's upbringing.

Though it is often claimed that the ghost was banished by the invention of electric light — "the disenchantment of night" — it was the coming of "inner light" and new understandings of subjectivity that helped to transfer marvels from external reality to the inner world of the imagination in the modern period.[61] To reduce the ghost to a projection of the mind presupposes that inner life is already securely in its place, but such conditions did not exist in late nineteenth- or early twentieth-century Ireland, even though there was no shortage of pressure to bring Irish society, and particularly the Catholic middle class, into line with liberal individualism. The fraught nature of the attempt to forge a coherent subject is well captured in the description of Mrs. Kernan's belief in "Grace," in *Dubliners*, socialized to a suburban existence on the Glasnevin road but yet not quite at one with her beliefs:

Her beliefs were not extravagant. She believed steadily in the Sacred Heart as the most generally useful of all Catholic devotions and approved of the sacraments. Her faith was bounded by her kitchen, but, if she was put to it, she could believe also in the banshee and in the Holy Ghost. (*D* 157)

In the absence of an indigenous Reformation or Industrial Revolution in Ireland, it is not surprising that inner consistency and self-regulation did not take hold, and it was left to the Catholic church to compensate for this through its own authoritarian disciplinary codes. As the historian S. J. Connolly points out, moral practices proceeded by "external deterrents," bearing witness to a culture in which "internal constraints and imperatives of guilt, fear or emotion, were not sufficient to shape the behavior of the great majority of Irish Catholics. Instead these had to be supplemented by external pressures."[62] But these external pressures were not all of a worldly or tangible variety. At a moment when the grip of folklore and the otherworld might have been broken, the calamity of the Great Famine threw the population back onto a shattered past, if only by way of attempting to make sense of the overwhelming forces stacked against them. As Connolly explains:

> Popular supernaturalism in all its forms—not calendar custom alone, but also beliefs in fairies, in witchcraft and magical healing, in charms, omens and protective rituals—provided an explanation for what would otherwise have appeared as a meaningless pattern of good and bad fortune, while at the same time enabling people to feel that they exercised some control over the pattern.[63]

The Famine may have dealt a fatal blow to the folk culture that supported the ghost, but, as Sir William Wilde observed, the cataclysm produced its own modern ghosts, "the remnant of the hardiest and most stalwart of the people crawl about, listless spectres, unable or willing to rise out of their despair."[64] The cultural collapse was such that burial rites themselves fell victim to the plague, leaving corpses, in effect, "undead," ready to walk the land. Undoubtedly the impact of the Devotional Revolution after the Famine made considerable inroads on spectral beliefs and practices but for the most part, as Connolly notes, "the suppression of such observances, and of the beliefs out of which they grew, never became a major element in their program of social control":

> Mary Fogarty's memories of the 1860s and 1870s, not to mention the case of Bridget Cleary in 1895, make clear that in the second half

of the nineteenth century there was still a substantial section of the population for whom the third world of the non-Christian supernatural remained an important reality.[65]

While the ghost might have been expected to disappear into subjective life under modernity, the convulsions of nineteenth-century Ireland ensured that subjective life itself had not come out from under the shadow of death: "We obey them in the grave," thinks Bloom (*U* 6.126). Or as Joyce himself put it sardonically, in one of the barbed English-language exercises he set his Berlitz students in Trieste: "Ireland is a great country. They call it the Emerald Isle. The Metropolitan Government, after so many centuries of having it by the throat, has reduced it to a specter."[66]

Ulysses is subject to unheard and unseen presences, much as a literary work is haunted by the spirit of its author: "Hence the otherwise incongruous presence of ghosts," writes Maria DiBattista, "in a novel that purports to be, among other things, an epic of the body."[67] It is a discussion of Shakespeare and literary immortality in the National Library that prompts Stephen to ask: "What is a ghost?" (*U* 9.147). The question is partly answered by his own suggestion that a ghost's relation to reality is akin to an author's shadowy existence in his work: Shakespeare is therefore the true ghost of *Hamlet*, the "player Shakespeare, a ghost by absence" (*U* 9.174).[68] Absence as well as death gives rise to the ghost, but there are also social hauntings: "One who has faded into impalpability through death, through absence, through change of manners" (*U* 9.147–49). "Change in manners" may allude to the possibility of the ghost appearing in modern dress, as a symptom of exile and loss: "Elizabethan London lay as far from Stratford as corrupt Paris lies from virgin Dublin. Who is the ghost from *limbo patrum*, returning to the world that has forgotten him? Who is King Hamlet?" (*U* 9.149–51). The "ghost by absence'" hovers between the lines of *Ulysses* and sets the tone not only for the persistence of the past but also for intimations of the future, the ghost of things to come.

As the funeral cortege in "Hades" passes the Antient Concert Rooms on Great Brunswick Street and turns into D'Olier Street, the eyes of the passengers in Bloom's carriage alight on Blazes Boylan at the door of the Red Bank restaurant, prompting thoughts of Boylan's organization of Molly's forthcoming concert in Belfast. Martin Cunningham, somewhat disingenuously, asks Bloom if good artists are booked for the tour, to which Bloom replies uneasily:

O yes, we'll have all topnobbers. J. C. Doyle and John McCormack I hope and. The best, in fact. (*U* 6.221–22)

Bloom interrupts his answer at the end of the second sentence, and the reason is close to hand: he was thinking of Boylan, Molly's co-singer on the tour, but it proved too painful.[69] A few minutes earlier, anxieties about Boylan's more immediate rendezvous with Molly had sprung up in his mind as the carriage passed playbills advertising musical performances outside the Queen's Theatre, and no sooner had the thought of Boylan occurred to him than his nemesis appeared on the street outside the Red Bank: "Just that moment I was thinking" (*U* 6.197). The uncanny effect whereby a thought materializes in front of a person's eyes becomes, as will be shown in relation to Charles Stewart Parnell in chapter 8, one of the conditions of the spectral: a mental image escapes the mind and takes on external form. But this textual ghost also operates at a linguistic level, giving rise to an "apophatic" process whereby events off the page, or outside the text, complete sentences.[70] There is a possibility that the unnamed performer on the tip of Bloom's tongue was not Boylan but a spectral premonition of Joyce himself—"The best, in fact" (*U* 6.222–23). Joyce shared a platform with J. C. Doyle and John McCormack at the Antient Concert Rooms in August 1904, and it may be an omen of this event that cuts short Bloom's sentence, having just passed the building: "Antient Concert Rooms. Nothing on there" (*U* 6.180).[71] If, as Ellmann claims, Joyce's performance was "the high point of his musical career" (*JJ* 173), it was also special for another reason, as Joyce sang an encore, "My Love She Was Born in the North Countree," for his new girlfriend, Nora, in the audience. "Coming events cast their shadows before" (*U* 8.526).[72] It was, indeed, with music in mind that Joyce remarked of Mozart that his chief "merit is in what he left out."[73]

In "The Dead," absent tenors awaken unrequited pasts, bearing witness, as R. M. Adams notes, to the manner in which "the Dublin dead constantly control the Dublin living, if not directly, at least through complex patterns of memory and association."[74] It is as if language is haunted by its own silences, the ghost by absence again having the last word. Stephen Dedalus's famous depiction of a pier as "a disappointed bridge" (*U* 2.39) might be applied to the sentences of *Ulysses*, at once complete and incomplete, awaiting definition by the material texture of the city. As Enda Duffy notes:

> Although the mass of detail may appear to provide even an excess of data on Dublin, it can divert us from how much of the city is omitted from the text. And the politics of this vast unsaid can be as eloquent as what gets included in the novel.[75]

As in early modernist collages, in which scraps of newspapers, theatre programs, or tickets were pasted onto a work,[76] the meticulous surface detail in *Ulysses*—the recourse to real people, events, journalism, and street directories—is designed to bridge the gap (or pier) between fact and fiction, except that in this case, the tangential details often have a life of their own, and continually lead us outside the text.[77] For all the appearance of a self-contained fictional world, integrated through form, style, and internal cross-references, the narrative is perforated continually by intrusions from outside the text, often oblique and imperceptible. As Nicholas Royle describes these "textual phantoms":

> It is a question, then, of phantom texts—textual phantoms which do not necessarily have the solidity or objectivity of a quotation, an intertext or explicit, acknowledged presence and which do not in fact come to rest anywhere. Phantom texts are fleeting, continually moving on, leading us away, like Hamlet's Ghost, to some other scene, or scenes which we, as readers, cannot anticipate.[78]

The introduction of the word "gnomon" on the opening page of the first story in *Dubliners*, "The Sisters," and the ellipses, enigmas, and blank windows that follow, are an indication of the gaps and "unfinished sentences" (*D* 3) in the stories to some: the causes of Father Flynn's breakdown or of Mrs. Sinico's accident in "A Painful Case"; the josser's actions in "An Encounter"; the meaning of "Derevaun Seraun" in "Eveline"; Bob Doran's showdown with Mrs. Mooney in "A Boarding House"; Maria's forgotten verse in "Clay" or the missing lines of "The Lass of Aughrim" in "The Dead," among others. Worked into *Ulysses* as a structuring principle of language, words are not at one remove from reality but are *implicated*, in Margot Norris's terms, in the world they evoke: implicature "suggests that implied information requires familiarity with an unstated context and additional information in order to be understood."[79] As Bloom and Stephen stumbled from the cabman's shelter in the early hours, the "visible luminous sign" of a lamp in a second-story window "attracted Bloom's, who attracted Stephen's gaze," and the catechism-type language of "Ithaca" elaborates on what is implied by the sign:

> How did he elucidate the mystery of an invisible attractive person, his wife Marion (Molly) Bloom, denoted by a visible splendid sign, a lamp.
>
> With indirect and direct verbal allusions or affirmations: with subdued affection and admiration: with description: with impediment; with suggestion. (*U* 17.1177–81)

Jacques Derrida's notion that the ghost "begins by coming back" underlies the spectral *form* of *Ulysses* as well as its content. "Without this *non-contemporaneity with itself of the living present*, without that which secretly unhinges it," writes Derrida, there would be no ghost: "Turned towards the future, going toward it, it also comes from it, it proceeds *from* the future. It must therefore exceed any presence as presence to itself."[80] This captures much of the spirit of *Ulysses* in that it is never clear whether the mention of a person, place, or event speaks for itself, or is intimating something else. The reference to real-life events is particularly problematic, for while they merit inclusion on the grounds that they occurred on 16 June 1904, or in historical time, they may also release other hauntings latent in the text. In "Lestrygonians," the "famished ghosts" (*U* 8.730) of the Great Famine shadow Bloom as he walks through the center of Dublin, and that hunger is more than a memory is evident from the soup kitchens that sustain the emaciated Dedalus sisters who catch his eye. A hint of the proselytizing of "souperism" during the Famine (and the powers of prophecy) is provided by an evangelical notice announcing "Elijah is coming" (*U* 8.14), and a short time later, Bloom passes the Rev. Thomas Connellan's bookstore on Dawson Street, prompting a more direct memory of evangelism and the Famine. The real-life Rev. Thomas Connellan, as I discuss in chapter 7, left the Catholic priesthood and staged his drowning in Lough Ree on the Shannon in the late 1880s — one of the many spectral returns from a "watery floor" to feature in *Ulysses* — to be born again as the founder of the Connellan Mission and publisher of the reformed *The Catholic* newspaper, based in Dublin. With Mrs. Smyley, the head of the Bird's Nest Protestant orphanage, the preacher returned to Athlone, his former parish and scene of his "death," to proselytize on behalf of his new church. Though Connellan is a marginal figure and receives barely a cursory mention in annotated guides to *Ulysses*, the Bible wars in Joyce's Dublin inspire one of the recurring subplots in the novel, motivating Father Conmee's expedition in "Wandering Rocks" to keep the late Paddy Dignam's son from falling into Protestant hands. The announcement "Elijah is coming" turns Bloom's thoughts not toward salvation but toward the mass-produced special effects of Revivalist meetings, and Pepper's famous technologically produced ghosts: "Paying game. . . . Where was that ad some Birmingham firm the luminous crucifix. Our Saviour. Wake up in the dead of night and see him on the wall, hanging. Pepper's ghost idea" (*U* 8.17–20). Specters emanate from the market and technology as well as spiritual revivals, and capitalist modernity is no less subject to illusory manifestations than its superstitious counterparts. As Seamus Deane writes, the appeal of com-

modity culture in a colonial city is that "it can be swallowed up in the
illusory world, surrendered to it, by those who are, like the Dubliners,
hungry for illusion, grateful to be oppressed by something 'magical' that
somehow dissolves or seems to dissolve the squalor of the capital."[81] The
disenchantment wrought by the spell of modernity falls short of exposing the banality of its own illusions, the exotic allure of the "paying game"
that unravels for the young boy at the end of "Araby."

That the ghost presages alternative futures is central to Stephen's interpretation of *Hamlet*: "[T]hrough the ghost of the unquiet father the
image of the unliving son looks forth" (*U* 9.380–81). As Bloom walks
through the center of Dublin, he passes the railings of Trinity College and
recalls being swept up in an anti–Boer War demonstration broken up by a
police charge a few years earlier, when Trinity granted Joseph Chamberlain, one of the architects of British imperial policy, an honorary degree:
"Up the Boers! — Three cheers for De Wet! — We'll hang Joe Chamberlain on a sourapple tree" (8.434–36). If, as Maud Ellmann notes of the
end of "Circe," the arrival of policemen on a scene is always useful in dis-
persing ghosts, the breakup of the anti–Boer War demonstration can also
be seen as an attempt to dispel the shade of Parnell.[82] No sooner has the
"chief" surfaced in Bloom's memory, however, than he sees his "haunting
face" across the street, in the visage of his less than distinguished brother,
John Howard Parnell. The possibility that Parnell may be revisiting old
haunts is raised earlier in "Hades" when the mourners suggest that, like
the ghost of Paddy Dignam seen later near Barney Kiernan's (or indeed
the resurrected Rev. Thomas Connellan), Parnell "may not be in the grave
at all. That the coffin was filled with stones. That one day he will come
again" (*U* 6.923–24). In "Eumaeus" this wishful thinking goes global in the
rumor that Parnell slipped out of Ireland and reappeared in South Africa,
changing his name (but not his beard) to Christiaan De Wet (*U* 16.1305).
Spectral memory has picked up where Parnell left off, the migration of the
ghost opening a new anti-imperial front: "history repeating itself with a
difference" (*U* 16.1525–26). In chapter 8, the prospect of return without
regression is related to Judith Butler's reworking of Freud's distinction
between mourning and melancholia, contending that the return of the
ghost, a certain kind of holding on to the past, is often best served by a realignment toward the future. In transferring attachment from a lost object
to a new "relational tie," Butler writes that "a certain interchangeability of
objects" is achieved "as a sign of hopefulness."[83] The object may be irre-
trievably lost, but the *relational tie*, the openness to a future response, has
not entirely disappeared. One part, the grieving subject, is still there, but
like Joyce's pier opening into the sea, it is gesturing toward "the now, the
here, through which all future plunges to the past" (*U* 9.89).

CHAPTER 1

Text and the City

DUBLIN, CULTURAL INTIMACY,
AND MODERNITY

Our language can be seen as an ancient city; a maze of little streets and squares, of old and new houses, and of houses with additions from various periods; and this surrounded by a multitude of new boroughs with straight regular streets and uniform houses.

LUDWIG WITTGENSTEIN, *Philosophical Investigations*

Cityful passing away, other cityful coming, passing away too: other coming on, passing on. Houses, lines of houses, streets, miles of pavements, piledup bricks, stones. . . . Big stones left. Round towers. Rest rubble, sprawlingsuburbs, jerrybuilt.

JAMES JOYCE (*U* 8.484–86, 491–92)

Writing of the renewal of her friendship with James Joyce — then "the most famous writer in the world" — in Paris in the 1930s, Mary Colum noted that "when he appeared in a café or restaurant people took tables near to have a look at him." Not being in the business of instant familiarity, Joyce "always had a table facing the wall so that all anybody could see of him was the back of his head: his guests sat facing him."[1] In this cameo, it is possible to catch a glimpse of Joyce's attitude to his work as well as to his personal life.[2] For all its universality and cosmopolitanism — the appeals to myth, everyman, and the human condition — Joyce's writing was also addressed to those who knew him, and his culture, well. Of those who gazed in wonder at the writer, Colum speculates that there may have been a few French people "in whom the life of Paris soaked in to their veins and pores as that of Dublin had done in Joyce's case, but I doubt it":

1.1 Carola Giedion-Welcker, "James Joyce at the Platzspitz" (1938). Photograph courtesy of the James Joyce Foundation, Zurich.

> Nobody has ever written of the life of a city, so identified himself with that city and its history, as Joyce has with Dublin. The fact that he left it early and became a Berlitz teacher in Trieste, far from diminishing his impressions, clarified them, far from clouding his memory, made it more exact. *Ulysses* and *Finnegans Wake* are the epics of a city, the histories of a city, and of all the languages somebody there might have understood or spoken. (*LD* 381)

Accounting for the manner in which Joyce's Dublin opened onto the world, Colum notes that "cities grew up by rivers," and the deposed capital of Dublin was already a tributary of both Europe and empire.[3] Though Joyce quipped on one occasion that his work "would keep the professors busy for centuries" (*JJ* 535), the expertise required for reading his work derived not only from the academy and the literary world but also from familiarity with the streets of Dublin and the by-ways of Irish culture: "For myself, I always write about Dublin, because if I can get to the heart of Dublin I can get to the heart of all the cities of the world. In the particular is contained the universal" (*JJ* 520). It was indeed the intimate address of *Ulysses* to native readers that constituted part of the scandal for his first Irish commentators, leading Shane Leslie, in one of the first reviews, to suggest that

> it would be better for Ireland to sink under the seas and join Atlantis, rather than allow her life of letters to affect the least reconciliation with a book which, owing to accidents of circumstance, probably only Dubliners can really understand in detail. Certainly, it takes a Dubliner to pick out the familiar names and allusions of twenty years ago, though the references to men who have become as important as Arthur Griffith assume a more universal bearing.[4]

Arthur Griffith, who saw himself as Irish and Irish alone, would hardly have welcomed a "universal bearing," and it is precisely Griffith's assumption that a deep immersion in Irish culture precludes a wider embrace of the world at large that is contested in *Ulysses*.[5] It was the constancy of Joyce's engagement with "the familiar names and allusions of twenty years ago" that not only gave his fiction a belated dissonant role in the national revival (though revivalists were slow to recognize Joyce's contribution) but also placed Irish literature at the forefront of international literary modernism. In the universal scheme of things, Ireland—its inhabitants, its culture, the material texture of Dublin itself—was still the interlocutor without which Joyce's work made no sense: it is, after all, Anna Livia Plurabelle herself who directly addresses the city—and the reader—in the "Letter" section of *Finnegans Wake*: "Soft morning, city! Lsp! I am leafy speafing" (*FW* 619.20).

Asked on one occasion by Hannah Sheehy-Skeffington why he did not return to Dublin, Joyce replied: "Have I ever left it?" (*JJ* 717). It was perhaps Dublin that never left Joyce: as late as the 1930s he recounted to Constantine Curran that "every day in every way I am walking along the streets of Dublin and along the strand. And 'hearing voices'" (*JJ* 717). The almost physical awareness of something not present evinced by Joyce is akin to the experience of loss presented by a "phantom limb," as described by Maurice Merleau-Ponty in the *Phenomenology of Perception* (1945).[6] In his account of the phantom limb, Merleau-Ponty asks: "Why can the memories recalled to the one-armed man cause the phantom arm to appear? The phantom arm is not a recollection, it is a quasi-present and the patient feels it now, folded over his chest, with no hint of its belonging to the past" (*PP* 85).[7] In emphasizing that the past is not only a memory but also a "quasi-present," Merleau-Ponty evokes some of the most telling aspects of Joyce's Dublin and the *relational* aesthetic at work in his fiction. The phantom limb arises from the fact that the body is experienced not as an assemblage of discrete parts but *as a whole*: just "as the beating of the heart is felt as far away as the body's periphery" (*PP* 85), so also the periphery extends to the rest of the body, which is disposed to act as it did before the limb was severed.[8] The phantom limb in this sense is close to the operation of "involuntary memory" in Proust or Joyce, in that a shock or acute event summons a specter into existence, even if the ghost is at odds with the world. Instead of being a pathology, moreover, the imaginary limb is on a continuum with the power of phantom histories to shape our lives, for as Robert Romanyshyn notes:

> Just as one's body can project and sustain habitual situations, it can also project and keep alive previous intentions, [and phases] of one's history, which are no longer supported by the world. There can be, in other words, "a phantom history" just like there is a phantom limb, because this body through which one perceives, this sensitive flesh[,] is a history and this history is embodied.[9]

This is close to the version of Dublin that Joyce re-created in exile: the "fixation does not merge into memory: it even excludes memory in so far as the latter spreads out in front of us like a picture, a former experience, whereas this past which remains our true present does not leave us" (*PP* 83). A phantom history may be "no longer supported by the world," but, as many critics have pointed out, part of the attraction of Pola, Trieste, and Zurich for Joyce lay in the resemblance of these cities to Dublin, a divided city on the edge of a ramshackle empire. As Austin Clarke recalled Joyce's words following a visit to Paris: "Dublin is the nearest city to the Continent. Places here in Paris on a Saturday night are like Capel Street and Thomas Street. There are the same joy and excitement, as though bargaining for Sunday's dinner was a holiday." Dublin was "old enough to be viewed as a European capital; small enough to be viewed as a whole."[10] In this can be seen a version of the "working through" that Freud required of painful memories, in which it is not so much an original event or object (Dublin) that is carried over but, as Jean Laplanche and Serge Leclaire point out, the *relations* woven around it: "The Freudian experience of 'memory' has less to do with the recollection of an 'event' than with the repetition of a structure."[11]

The extent to which Joyce's past took on a relational intensity is clear from the circumstances in which he first encountered Martha Fleischmann in Zurich while he was writing *Ulysses*. Fleischmann, the mistress of a wealthy engineer, Rudolf Hiltpold, lived in an apartment in Zurich behind Joyce's:

> One evening at dusk when she was about to enter her house Joyce happened to pass by the door. He stopped abruptly and looked at her with an expression of such wonder in his face that she hesitated for just a moment before entering the house. Joyce then apologized in German and said that she very strongly reminded him of a girl he had once seen standing on the beach in his home country.[12]

Joyce's attachment to the young woman, and her fascination with the writer, came to grief six months later when Hiltpold intervened to protect her from his rival. Joyce's initial heartfelt remark to Fleischmann, that she captivated him because she was a reminder of someone else, may not have been a wise opening gambit, but it draws attention to the manner in which, on Merleau-Ponty's terms, certain affective ties were drawn from Dublin, even if the content had changed: "Some subjects can come near to blindness without changing their 'world': they can be seen colliding with objects everywhere" (*PP* 80). Crucially, however, Merleau-Ponty contends that despite holding on to similarity, the phantom limb hinges on difference, albeit through disavowal, and in this it is not unlike the denial that often follows the death of a friend: "We do not understand the absence or death of a friend until the time comes when we expect a reply from him and when we realize we shall never again receive one; so at first we avoid asking in order not to notice this silence" (*PP* 81). It is as if Joyce's fiction were a sustained attempt to break this silence, an imaginary world that broke into his private life at moments of seemingly irreparable loss.

It is striking that Martha Fleishmann evoked the "real-life" source for the apparition of the bird-girl — half real, half mirage — on Dollymount Strand in *Portrait*, an epiphany that follows Stephen's first decisive break with Dublin, a place imbued with attachments of home and maternal love: "He was made aware dimly and without regret of a first noiseless sundering of their lives" (*P* 178). Yet though an apparition brings with it the obvious risk of disillusionment, Merleau-Ponty sees in the phantom limb vestiges of hope: "To have a phantom arm is to remain open to all the actions of which the arm alone is capable" (*PP* 81). It is only when the experience fixes pathologically on one irreplaceable object, and precludes a generality that extends beyond present loss, that the future is closed down. In an observation that throws light on the stylistic shift from first-person narration to the dual voice of free indirect discourse in Joyce's work, Merleau-Ponty goes on to note that it is only the "transition from first person existence to a sort of abstraction of that existence, which lives on in that experience" (*PP* 83). Just as the body is experienced as a whole, even when incomplete, so also memory is comprised of moments that await completion in the future: "Every present grasps by stages, through its horizon of immediate past and near future, the totality of possible time; . . . time never completely closes over it" (*PP* 84–5). As Joyce was writing *Ulysses*, much of the material texture of central Dublin was being swept away in the rubble of the Easter Rising of 1916, and it is not surprising that many who looked back to the promise of that era should see in *Ulysses* "a former present which cannot decide to recede into the past. . . . [M]emory reopens time lost to us and invites us to recapture the situation evoked" (*PP* 85).

Conventional accounts of Joyce's rise to literary eminence chart a well-worn trajectory from the local to the international, from the constricting provinciality of Dublin and Ireland to the heady freedom and expansive modernism of mainland Europe, whether in metropolitan Paris or the cosmopolitan circles of Trieste and Zurich.[13] The imputation of parochialism to Irish letters overlooks the fact that London as well as Dublin publishing houses were in Joyce's sights from the beginning, in keeping with a colonial condition in which national conversations were rerouted through foreign (and diasporic) locations: "[S]uch concessions to the English market," writes Joseph Kelly, "were inevitable for Irish writers, if they wanted their books to be available in Ireland."[14] Though Joyce's work was addressed to Irish readers—the "nicely polished glass" in which he imagined Irish people "having one good look at themselves"[15]—he was adamant that this did not preclude international audiences: "The second book I have ready is called *Dubliners* . . . . I do not think any writer has yet presented Dublin *to the world*."[16] By incorporating wider vistas into the act of addressing his own culture, Joyce was dispelling the myth of the insular Celt, the view that a society's conversation with itself was at the expense of its entry into the world republic of letters. As Seamus Deane suggests, Joyce's task was preeminently that of the colonial writer, "to take the cosmopolitan form that he has inherited from the colonizing country, the form of the novel, and to repossess that form, to if you like reconquer the territory of the conqueror, but via style: there is no other means by which it can be done."[17] The "shortest way to Tara was" indeed "*via* Holyhead" (*P* 273).

It is for this reason that free indirect discourse was central to Joyce's techniques, a stylistic innovation that had a distinctive Irish as well as an international provenance and was crucial to the project of addressing multiple audiences.[18] Free indirect discourse allows an articulation of a character's voice—an inner point of view—from an external vantage point and vice versa, a series of narrative positions combining both inside and outside perspectives at once. This gave a specific Irish inflection to Joyce's negotiation of a cosmopolitan style, incorporating a national (internal) and international (external) "parallax" in his work.[19] In allowing a porousness between what lies inside and outside an utterance, it also linked the text to extratextual factors, facilitating some of the charged, localized "reality effects" of *Ulysses*. As Martin Jay points out, free indirect discourse is primarily a literary device, for if it was implemented in everyday life—voices emanating outside the self from no immediate source (Joyce's "hearing voices" mentioned above)—it "would sound more like a hallucination than a communicative speech act."[20] But perhaps this latter, spectral force is closer to the imaginative power of Joyce's work. In its constant gesturing to a "real" world outside the text, *Ulysses* constitutes what Umberto Eco termed an open as against a closed artistic work, that is, a work that requires an explicit engagement with an outside—"nontextual" or contextual factors—without which it would be meaningless. For Eco, it is as if Joyce's later fiction seeks to emulate the openness of experience itself in its "indefinite reserve of meanings":

> Clearly, the work of James Joyce is a major example of an "open" mode, since it deliberately seeks to offer an image of the ontological and existential situation of the contemporary world. . . . If Joyce does introduce some keys into the text, this is because he wants the work to be read in a certain sense, but this particular sense has all the richness of the cosmos itself.[21]

It is through Dublin that Joyce's texts open onto "the cosmos," and it is in this sense that the unresolved national elements in his work, the pressures placed on his style by the contradictions of Irish experience, lie at the heart of his modernism. In his essay on *Ulysses* and capitalist modernity, Franco Moretti attributes the "stasis" of Joyce's novel to "his subjection to English society: for Joyce, it is certainly the only society imaginable." Moretti then goes on to elaborate: "[I]f the city of *Ulysses* were the real Dublin of the turn of the century, it would not be the literary image *par excellence* of the modern metropolis."[22] There was no shortage of "subjection to English society" in Joyce's Dublin, but it is precisely because *Ulysses* was not circumscribed by London, and drew on energies coalescing in Ireland to challenge the rule of empire, that Joyce was in a position to imagine new possibilities of form beyond the dominant versions of British modernism.[23] Dublin and Irish culture did not just provide local color or background to innovations in form that Joyce acquired elsewhere (from European modernism, or the international avant-garde): they were constitutive of his most advanced stylistic achievements.

Text/Context/Texture

[Joyce's] two big books must be the most local in any literature, and I doubt if he really cared much for anybody who was not familiar with Dublin's streets and ways.

MARY COLUM (LD 382)

Ulysses is not *about* Dublin, as in conventional mimetic realism: the city continually breaks through the surface of the text, "the cracked looking-glass" (*U* 1.146) of a prose style, in Leo Steinberg's phrase, that "let[s] the world in again."[24] As is widely recognized, Joyce's writing poses particular problems for the reader, for while it displays linguistic virtuosity at every turn, there is still a kind of withholding. Often what is on the page is not as important as what is left out: there is a constant awareness that some "extratextual" matter is required to fill in the silences, ellipses, and "multi-storied symbolic forms" that perforate the text.[25] Meanings are not always decidable (or undecidable) *within* the work, as in nineteenth-century realist fiction, but are unusually dependent on external references, not all of them from other texts but some from local knowledge, popular memory, or street culture, the material texture of everyday life itself in Joyce's Ireland.[26] For some scholars, this store of local knowledge is asking too much, as it requires abandoning the critical altitudes of high modernism to forage in the byways of a cultural backwater, the Ireland of Joyce's day. Hence, according to Clive Hart and Leo Knuth, Bernard Benstock's impatient declaration that

"*Ulysses* is no more about Dublin than *Moby Dick* is about a whale— although no less." In an attempt to counter the parochial assertions of a number of Irish men who have claimed that a knowledge of their capital is the only key to the mysteries of the novel, Benstock challengingly suggests that "Too much familiarity with Joyce's Dublin might indeed be dangerous in attempting a balanced reading of *Ulysses*."[27]

But while it would be inadvisable to look to *Hamlet* for insights into the state of Denmark, *Ulysses* is indelibly stamped with the Dublin of its time — and, of course, more besides. Its *deictic* character — the relation of language to the situation of its utterance — does not mean that the range of reference applies only to its original context, but it does imply that this context is far from negligible, and is not just background.[28] Words may fly up, Dedalus fashion, but Dublin remains firmly below.

It is not so much that "too much familiarity" gets in the way of understanding *Ulysses*: rather, the familiar is presupposed only to defamiliarize it in the act of representation. "Everyday insignificance," wrote Henri Lefebvre, "can only become meaningful when transformed into something other than everyday life," and it is through the disjunctions of form that the everyday is no longer taken for granted but is exposed to new possibilities in thought and action.[29] The difficulty here is not just the modernist task of representing contingency and spontaneity — how to catch people off guard if they know they are being observed — but the related problem of gaining (aesthetic) access to what are essentially intimate situations. How can a trivial everyday incident, whose value derives solely from the fact that people participate in it, be represented to third parties, that is, be represented at all? In his notes collected as *Culture and Value*, Ludwig Wittgenstein wrote:

> I am always reminded of one of those insipid photographs of a piece of scenery which is interesting to the person who took it because he was there himself, experiencing something, but which a third party looks at with justifiable coldness; insofar as it is even justifiable to look at something with coldness.[30]

This — in a single snapshot, one might say — sums up the literary challenge met by *Ulysses*. The task confronting Joyce was how to portray the intimacy of everyday life — events of no great importance, and only accessible to those who experienced them — in a way that made them legible to others. This is the literary equivalent of Wittgenstein's "third party" seeking access to a snapshot that meant so much to the holidaygoers who had firsthand experience of events. In this case, it is not the "objective" worth of what is represented that matters — the historical significance or information value — but the grounds of representation itself, the *texture* of the most desultory everyday exchanges. As Georges Perec complained, only half in jest, one of the ironies of the daily newspaper is that it actually ignores daily life, if by that is meant the humdrum realities that are not newsworthy enough to make it into print:

The daily newspapers talk of everything except the daily. The papers annoy me, they teach me nothing. What they recount doesn't concern me, doesn't ask me questions and doesn't answer the questions I ask or would like to ask. What's really going on, what we're experiencing, the rest, all the rest, where is it? How should we take account of, question, describe what happens every day and recurs everyday: the banal, the quotidian, the obvious, the common, the ordinary, the infra-ordinary, the background noise, the habitual?[31]

It is true that by including the ephemera of the press in a modern epic, *Ulysses* was already gravitating toward the lower end of what makes history happen, incidents or places that would have no significance were it not for their mention in the novel.[32] Yet, by Perec's standards, even the events noted by newspapers are momentous compared to the desultory nature of everyday life. It is these elusive aspects of experience that are caught in the private snapshot cherished by Wittgenstein's holiday-goer, but unfortunately only make sense to him, her, or their friends. The achievement of *Ulysses* is to translate this personal intimacy into "objective" form, to render subjective (or intersubjective) experience accessible, in principle, to third parties. "Joyce's works are letters of desire," according to Karen Lawrence, "that circulate through the texts of culture, letters published for all the world to see."[33]

"Perhaps what is inexpressible (what I find mysterious and am not able to express)," writes Wittgenstein, "is the background against which whatever I could express has its meaning" (*CV* 16e). *Ulysses* puts words on much of this background, thereby ensuring, paradoxically, that it is no longer mere setting, or what is left unsaid. This is in keeping with Wittgenstein's own contention that it is by virtue of aesthetic form that what is normally passed over in silence finds expression. When we see the ordinary in its everyday setting, it does not make "the slightest impression on us," but when it is *represented*, "so that suddenly we are observing a human being from outside in a way that ordinarily we can never observe ourselves; . . . surely this would be uncanny and wonderful at the same time" (*CV* 4e).[34] This capacity to render the familiar unfamiliar is one of the striking achievements of art:

Only an artist can so represent a thing as to make it appear to us like a work of art. . . . A work of art forces us—as one might say—to see it in the right perspective but, in the absence of art, the object is just a fragment of nature like any other; we may exalt it through our enthusiasm but that does not give anyone else the right to confront us with it. (*CV* 4e)

Joyce, however, adds another element to the intricate interweaving of art and experience. In Wittgenstein's formulation, more suitable to the conception of a *closed* work, artistic form tends to act as a substitute for the real world, obviating any need to experience at first hand what is presented. This is in marked contrast to *Ulysses*: its evocation of Dublin is dependent on, or at least greatly enhanced by, the actual experience of walking the streets and cultivating an in-depth acquaintance with the history and culture of the city. In holding the mirror up to the real world, Wittgenstein is concerned to leave things as they are; in Joyce, the real world is *acted on* and defamiliarized in the process of representation. Reading *Ulysses* requires more than a nodding acquaintance with Dublin, but the experience of the city in turn is transformed by its "rendering strange" through the novel's striking innovations in form.

It is in this context, Wittgenstein writes, "that the very things which are the most obvious may become the hardest to understand" (*CV* 17e). Joyce's mimetic skill did not consist in transcribing what lay fully formed In Irish culture, simply awaiting discovery, for much of the inner lives of his characters lay below the threshold of a self-conscious interiority. Raymond Williams was one among many commentators who drew attention to the problems of articulation that pervade *Ulysses*, the richness of a character's experience standing in stark contrast, at times, with its outer expression (an incongruity comically reversed in the "Cyclops" chapter).[35] At stake here is the conviction that everything communicable by nonverbal means is, in principle, capable of linguistic and, indeed, public expression, even if it does not always find its way into words. As the German phenomenologist Max Scheler wrote in *The Nature of Sympathy*, ten years before the publication of *Ulysses*: "The fact is that the articulation of the stream of consciousness and the ascription to it of those specific qualities of vividness which bring certain parts of it into the focus of internal perception, are *themselves governed* by the potential unities of *action and expression* (and the physical significance of these), which they are able to induce."[36] Inner experience, no matter how private, is in principle accessible to others if we are to make sense of it, and it is the opening of subjectivity onto intersubjectivity, the ability to communicate and establish relationships in a culture stunted by loss and paralysis, that affords such glimpses of hope as are to be found in the pages of *Ulysses*. It is true that for the most part, people may not have the command of language commensurate with the complexity of their experience, but this, for Scheler, is where the aesthetic intervenes, providing the structures that "estrange" and renovate calcified forms of life. Crucially, artistic representation does not involve giving people back what they know already (Alexander Pope's "What oft was thought / But ne'er so well expressed")[37] but seeks to expand horizons beyond conventional frames or categories of experience, "soaring," in Dedalian fashion, above the familiar and the given:

> For this reason poets, and all makers of language "having the god-given power to tell of what they suffer," fulfill a far higher function than that of giving noble and beautiful expression to their experiences and thereby making them recognizable to the reader, by reference to his own past experience in this kind. For by creating new forms of expression the poets soar above the prevailing network of ideas in which our experience is confined, as it were, by ordinary language; they enable the rest of us to *see*, for the first time, in our own experience, something that may answer to these new and richer forms of expression, and by so doing they actually *extend* the scope of our *possible* self-awareness. They effect a real enlargement of the kingdom of the mind and make new discoveries as it were, within that kingdom. It is they who open up new branches and channels in our apprehension of the stream and thereby show us for the first time *what* we are experiencing. (*NS* 252–53)[38]

Joyce's characters are having the experiences, but it is by virtue of aesthetic form that they are rendered intelligible in a publicly accessible manner, not only giving characters back their inner lives but acquainting countless readers with hitherto ineffable or unattainable aspects of life. "That is indeed the mission of true art: not to reproduce what is already given . . . but to press forward into the whole of the external world *and* the soul, to see and communicate those objective realities within it which rule and convention have hitherto concealed" (*NS* 252). When the *Freeman's Journal* wrote of Joyce in its review of *Portrait* that "[w]hat he sees he can reproduce in words with a precision as rare as it is subtle," it failed to grasp that Joyce is not reproducing but *re-creating* his city: the "real" is not already there but awaits *realization* through the language of form.[39] Joyce indeed attends to the kind of everyday experience that is taken for granted, what may be viewed in phenomenological terms as "the Heideggerian idea that individuals are enworlded before they make sense of things in rational terms," but he does not give back the world to his readers as he—or they—found it.[40] Cheryl Herr has rightly observed that stream of consciousness in Joyce is "often too easily accepted as a depiction of 'mind,'" as if characters are fully cognizant of their experience, whereas what is at stake is more a "turn from a Cartesian theory" to "the *production* of 'mind,'" the historical process of coming to consciousness.[41] Rather than being at home in the world, the colonial subject is alienated from his or her everyday life, and even "frets in the shadow" (*P* 205) of common speech. For this reason, Joyce's modernist aesthetic can be seen recasting and defamiliarizing the ordinary, releasing it from mindless conformity in the more acquiescent sense. "I go to forge in the smithy of my soul," wrote Stephen Dedalus, "the *uncreated* conscience of my race" (*P* 275–76, my italics). By transforming the paralysis of colonialism into new circuits of knowledge and radically different conditions of reading, Joyce was giving Dubliners a self-image in which they could see themselves in a startling, reflexive light. As Joyce remarked to Jacques Mercanton of the admittedly more challenging work in progress that turned into *Finnegans Wake*: "How can you expect my compatriots to understand me?"—but "all the same," Mercanton adds, "it was to them, his compatriots, that his mind turned most often."[42]

Writing of the impersonality of artistic method under modernism, Joyce famously pronounced, through the persona of Stephen Dedalus, that the identity of the artist "refines itself out of existence, impersonalizes itself, so to speak": "The artist, like the God of the creation, remains within or behind or beyond or above his handiwork, invisible, refined out of existence, indifferent, paring his fingernails" (*P* 233). Remaining aloof, it is as if the role of artist is to simply to *record* reality, a policy of nonintervention that also extends to readers who sees the (fictional) world laid out before them like a self-contained cosmos, answering to its own laws of coherence. As Joyce wrote of *Ulysses* in the early stages of composition: "It is a sort of encyclopaedia. My intention is to transpose the myth *sub specie temporis nostri*. Each adventure (that is every hour, every organ, every art being interconnected and interrelated in the structural scheme of the whole) should not only condition but even create its own technique" (*JJL* I, 146–47). In commending the depiction of life *as it is being lived* as the supreme feat of mimesis, Wittgenstein also envisages art in similar terms: "But it seems to me too that there is a way of capturing the world sub specie aeterni other than through the work of the artist. Thought has such a way—so I believe—it is as though it flies above the world and leaves it as it is—observing it from above, in flight" (*CV* 5e). Wittgenstein's imaginative flight is consistent with his conception of philosophy as a second-order or "meta" discourse that leaves the world as it is, accounting for things without taking account of the presence of the observer, or reducing them to other more fundamental realities.[43] Hence his imagining of a mode of representation that gave the kind of access to the real world afforded by experience, except at one remove:

> Nothing could be more remarkable than seeing a man who thinks he is unobserved performing some quite simple everyday activity.

> Let us imagine a theatre: the curtain goes up and we see a man in a
> room, walking up and down, lighting a cigarette, sitting down, etc....
> We should be observing something more wonderful than anything
> a playwright could arrange to be acted or spoken on the stage: life
> itself. (*CV* 4)

In many ways, this accords with what was perceived as the world of
unprocessed experience in *Ulysses*: life without any mediation, or even
representation (were it not for the difficulty of the book): "The effect of
this great accomplishment," wrote one critic, "is to make the reader feel
he is in direct contact with the life presented in the book . . . to present
life as it actually is, without prejudice or direct evaluations."[44] It does not
follow, however, that the invisibility of the author allows the reader also
to stand back, "paring his fingernails," absorbing life in all its complexity
without any effort or involvement: "see[ing] life as it is when we have no
part in it, " as Virginia Woolf famously described cinema.[45] Ironically, it
is Wittgenstein's work that is of importance here, for one of his central
contributions to the understanding of everyday life was to underline the
importance of *participating* in social practices, or what he termed "forms
of life."[46] Negotiating everyday experience is a matter of "language embedded in action," an exercise not of standing back but of sharing in the
"idiographic and local context[s]" without which language would be unintelligible.[47] In anthropology and the social sciences, this rules out "the
impartial spectator," the myth that through abstraction and detachment
the investigator can uncover the inner life of a society. Access to the ordinary, observing people going about their daily tasks without posing, as it
were, for the camera, only yields understanding for Wittgenstein if there
is already a grasp of *the social context* of these practices—itself the product of a substantial prior engagement with the culture, whether on the
observer's part or through acquaintance with other sources.[48] It is in this
sense that a grasp of forms of life—the idiographic and local contexts
of Joyce's Dublin—are indispensable to *Ulysses*, the constant intrusions
of the real, moreover, bringing this material background into the very
texture of the novel itself.[49] The irony of Joyce's detachment was that it
brought him closer to his material: writing of the often squalid subject
matter treated by Joyce, his brother Stanislaus noted that it had not occurred to him that "by making a story of it in a spirit of detachment and
in a style of 'scrupulous meanness,' one could liberate one's soul from the
contagion of that experience and contemplate from above with tolerance, even with compassion."[50]

Incursions of the Real

To what extent does *Ulysses* break new ground in crossing the often heavily patrolled borders between art and actuality, life and literature? In the heyday of structuralist aesthetics, the autonomy of art was such that an artwork was considered impervious to history, even in the case of overt references to the real world, such as historical personages or real people, place names, topographical descriptions, and so on. In a provocative reading of one of Wordsworth's most famous loco-descriptive poems, "Yew Trees" (1815), Michael Riffaterre contended that though the actual yew tree — "the pride of Lorton Vale" — can still be identified (and is virtually a sacred shrine for local people), its existence and that of the surrounding landscape has no bearing on Wordsworth's poem. Place names recur in the text — "Lorton," "Borrowdale," "Glaramara," not to mention names of historical battles such as "Azincour," "Crecy" and "Poictiers" — but they enact purely formal roles: "In fact, any name will do as a place name, so long as grammar introduces it as such and it is italicized. Put dots or an X after a preposition like 'at' or before a noun like 'Valley,' and you have conventionally but irrefutably localized your story within a setting. Spelling out names only adds to the verisimilitude."[51] In his early response to *Dubliners*, Ezra Pound held a similar position in relation to Joyce's use of place names:

> He gives us things as they are, not only for Dublin, but for every city. Erase the local names and a few specifically local allusions, and a few historic events of the past, and substitute a few different local names, allusions and events, and these stories could be retold of any town.[52]

The use of names and places here is to enhance what Roland Barthes terms a "reality effect" — an effect that is not dependent on knowledge of the actual places but which lends an air of authenticity to what is being said.[53] As Riffaterre explains:

> Why should the commentary have to explain the actual historical circumstances the names refer back to? . . . Adding philological information to the text does not enrich it, or demonstrate how rich the associations are, but only obscures what makes for its literariness: namely, that a poem is self-sufficient. . . . Associations here do not work from outside history to text, but the other way around. (*IDP* 109)

There are indeed grounds for questioning whether Wordsworth ever attends to the specificity of the places and people mentioned in his work, or whether they are absorbed merely as imaginative figures in the service of an all-embracing metaphysics of Nature. In a critical response to Riffaterre, Christopher Butler concedes that though Lorton Vale is named in the poem, "the reference to a specific vale is also strictly speaking unnecessary—a general concept of a vale is all we require."[54] Nothing could be further removed from the sense of person and place in Joyce—"the lie of her landuage" (*FW* 19–20) that infuses his city of words. People, streets, and place names are introduced in all their specificity: local knowledge, popular lore and gossip, personal relationships and networks, awareness of directions, proximity and contiguity. As Frank Budgen noted, whereas in certain generalized descriptions of place "[o]ne blasted heath, one beetling crag will do as well as another . . . it is essential to Joyce that we shall not substitute our own home town for his, and yet in *Ulysses* he neither paints nor photographs it for our guidance."[55]

Of course, this is not to say the reader is presented with an avant-garde tourist's guide or an elaborate fictive treatment of *Thom's Directory*: actual people and places, once designated, are rerouted through often vertiginous circuits of meaning, each draft and proof providing the pretext (or subtext) for additional layers as the book was prepared for publication. In the case of Wordsworth, as Butler suggests, taking a word out of its original (literal) context and reworking it on a symbolic plane operates largely at a metaphoric level, an unpacking of resemblances and internal connections that also extends to the work's generalized relationship to reality: we do not need to know the actual vale or yew tree but only *roughly* what such an English landscape looks like in order to register its meaning.[56] It is not always the case, however, that the original referential level is hollowed out and divested of its specific gravity in the real world. Riffaterre concedes as much when he notes in passing that "names anchor the description solidly in time because of *their metonymic function*, their ability to stand for a whole complex of associations" (*IDP* 110).[57] For Riffaterre, however, these associations derive from *within* the text, the semantic field generated by the relations of words within the poem. For Joyce, by contrast, such semantic fields emanate as much from *outside* the text, the "whole complex of associations" evoked not only by internal resonances but by real-life personages, sites, and streets that disturb the formal composure of the work.[58] For all the organizational unity and totalizing designs of Joyce's system-building, the constant intrusions of actuality disrupt not only formal unity but, ultimately, the deliberations of composition itself, in a manner that prefigures Robert Rauschenberg's collages as described by John Cage: "This is not a composition, it is a place where things are, as on a table."[59]

In *Ulysses*, successive hauntings—of Leopold Bloom by his dead son, Rudy, or by the suicide of his father, Rudolf Virag, and of Stephen by his dead mother—disrupt the material composure of everyday life, but the sense of loss is not confined to personal trauma: Freud also allows that mourning "is commonly the reaction to the loss of a beloved person or an abstraction taking the place of the person, such as fatherland, freedom, an ideal and so on."[60] The historical shadows thrown by the Great Famine, the Phoenix Park murders in 1882, the death of Parnell, and the centenaries of the 1798 and Emmet's 1803 rebellions, are no less pervasive, not to mention the transitory real-life actions and events whose inclusion in the text seems warranted by no other reason than that they happened on or around 16 June 1904.[61] These spectral presences impinge on the lives of the characters in *Ulysses*, much as the presence of Dublin "off the page" unsettles the text of the novel. In rendering fiction permeable to the real world to an unprecedented degree, Joyce's writing presented readers with difficulties that drew not only on the wellsprings of literary modernism but also on the muddy waters of the Liffey, a rather polluted source for a clear stream of consciousness. Though stream of consciousness is often taken as the signature of Joyce's style in *Ulysses*, pure interiority seldom features in the psychic life of Joyce's characters: the world is too much with them as they set out on their rounds of the city, even those who, like Stephen Dedalus, are given to introspection and flights of the imagination. This is not to say that everyone can be read at face value, and that there is no hiding place for intimacies or confidences, but inscrutability belongs to public as well as private space and has as much to do with secrecy, obliquity in language, and gesture, as with a retreat into the recesses of the mind. The sly civility of speech in colonial Dublin, the recourse to ambivalence and innuendo in the simplest of exchanges, is in keeping with the everyday opacity of a culture that not only sought to block surveillance and police intelligence but was divided against itself. The irony in the present day, as observed above, is that it is no longer state officials who are frustrated by local opacity but critics impatient with the recalcitrance of the "national" or the "local" to theory. For Colin McCabe, Joyce's fictions "are not stories 'about' Dublin in the sense that Dublin is an entity understood and referred to outside the text," but it is precisely the proliferation of matter outside as well as inside the text that produces the phenomenon that is Joyce's Dublin.[62] As John Kidd argued in his controversial "The Scandal of *Ulysses*," reality checks are central to the symbolic economy of *Ulysses*, "itself an encyclopedia, street directory, dialect dictionary, census, pub guide, ordnance survey, and vade mecum bound up in blue and white wrappers."[63] There is, again, an important proviso: much of this information is sifted through the sensibilities of characters who do not need such guides, and who often slip through the nets of the classificatory systems and organized schemes that bring such compendiums together.

The associations, memories, and emotions that arise in the minds of Joyce's characters are generated by their immersion in their environment, an awareness not always raised to overt expression or self-consciousness. Topography itself may operate at a textual level, as in John Kidd's example of the passage in "Lotus Eaters" in which Bloom's passing by the Belfast and Oriental Tea Company prompts a chain of associations relating to life in the tropics: "Too hot to quarrel. Influence of the climate. Lethargy. Flowers of idleness" (U 5.34–35). "Flowers of idleness" draws on the submerged memory of Byron's first poetry collection, Hours of Idleness (1807), but this is not the only Byronic subtext. As Bloom passes by the railings of Trinity College a short time later, his attention is drawn to modern-day lotus eaters playing cricket lazily in the sun: "Cricket weather. Sit around under sunshades. Over after over. Out. They can't play it here. Duck for six wickets. Still Captain Buller broke a window in the Kildare street club with a slog to square leg" (U 5.558–61). In the original revised Gabler edition published in 1986 (the target of Kidd's systematic critique), "Buller" is changed to "Culler," a seemingly minor alteration until we turn to Thom's Directory (1904) and discover that a Captain Buller did exist, and lived at Byron Lodge, Sutton.[64] This picks up on one of the most powerful motifs in Ulysses, the romantic striving exemplified by Byron and implicit in Bloom's gift of a copy of Byron's poems to Molly in their early courting days. It is not just tea and cricket that are preying on Bloom's mind: it is mourning for the loss of the desire that first brought the two lovers together.[65] The associations are prompted initially by the casual phrase "Flowers of idleness," but the subsequent link to Byron is established not textually but extratextually by an entirely contingent factor: Captain Buller's (unvoiced) address at Byron Lodge, Sutton.

Commentators have frequently noted that, notwithstanding scrupulous topographical accuracy, there is little descriptive writing in Joyce of the kind to be found in travelogues or realist fiction: "Despite the wealth of reference to streets, squares, houses, and public buildings," write Hart and Knuth, "there is in Ulysses little descriptive writing of the kind commonly associated with novels of the previous century."[66] It is not that the features of buildings are irrelevant: the ambience of the city is filled in by textual absences, that which frequently goes without saying. Though there is a profusion of details, little is obvious, and communication both between characters and with the reader is marked by ellipses, abbreviation, and incompletion. It is for this reason, as Enda Duffy has noted, that *Ulysses* refuses a sense of "unearned recognition" to its readers, any more than a genuine relationship allows unearned access to intimacy:

> The ideal reader of the novel would have been a Dubliner well versed in the physical aspects of the city in 1904. What this achieves is to alienate other readers from the setting: to continually insist that the reader (who is not a 1904 Dubliner) is an outsider, and that the work of collating these clues into a sense of familiarity with the cityscape is a matter of lifelong interpellation that cannot be provided at second hand to provide a false sense of recognition in the text. . . . This is a knowledge that is superficially accessible to all comers, but from which the outsider is in fact always already excluded, in an ignorance about which she is increasingly taunted—if only in a parade of street names—as the novel progresses.[67]

The kind of knowledge at stake in *Ulysses* is not the "genius of the place" beloved of Romanticism, the local color of characters at one with their surroundings, but has more to do with what Foucault described as "subjugated knowledge": "naive knowledges, located low down on the hierarchy, beneath the required level of cognition and scientificity." So "far from being a general commonsense knowledge," this is "on the contrary a particular, local, regional knowledge, a differential knowledge incapable of unanimity which owes its force only to the harshness with which it is opposed by everything surrounding it."[68] It is not always clear, moreover, that this submerged knowledge lies readily to hand in handbooks or directories, or can be reduced to information, for this is precisely the kind of data that the indeterminacy of the novel—the irreducible elements of chance and contingency—throws into question. As the parodic exactitude of the "Ithaca" section demonstrates, the facts do not speak for themselves: endless information can be amassed *about* a subject, but the often recondite connections that link the facts to history, place, and agency may prove more difficult to unravel.

What, then, is the relation of *Ulysses* to history, the aesthetic implications of the actuality that repeatedly forces its way into the text? Does the recourse to the real establish a despotism of fact that stabilizes the endless play of the imagination afforded by fiction? It would seem, on the contrary, that the introduction of factual reportage brings the reader no closer to certainty than fiction. Though Joyce's story "The Dead" affirms

"Yes, the newspapers were right," the press in *Ulysses* is more notable for
its howlers than for getting it right: "The pink edition extra sporting of
the *Telegraph* tell a graphic lie"(*U* 16.1232). The mention of "L. Boom,"
"M'intosh," and "Stephen Dedalus B.A." in the report of Paddy Dignam's
funeral in the *Evening Telegraph*, not to mention the scrambled words
produced by the momentary distraction of the typesetter when Bloom
visited the newspaper office, does not inspire confidence in newspapers
of record (any more than it does in the scientific precision of the entire
"Ithaca" section of *Ulysses*). As Aristotle pointed out in *The Poetics*, real
life or "history" is the domain of the particular, the contingency of the
event, and its introduction at will into a narrative can only disturb the
structural unity of art.[69] *Fictional* characters and events have to be consistent, or at least plausible, in the interests of verisimilitude, and this is
the realm of poetics, as Aristotle conceived it, or what is now understood
as realism.[70] No such logic is required of characters or events in the *real
world*: the fact that they did something, or an event happened, is sufficient
by itself to lay claim to actuality (if not to world-historical importance).[71]
With the introduction of actual people and real events in *Ulysses*, the narrative takes on the haphazard form (and perhaps unreliability) of a newspaper: a collocation of people and events held together by no other logic
than that they all happened on the same day. John Cage's description of
the "combines" (collages) of Robert Rauschenberg applies as much to
Ulysses as to the newspaper: "There is no more subject in a combine than
there is in a page of a newspaper. Each thing that is there is a subject. . . .
[E]ach minute part is at the center."[72]

These are the grounds on which Robert Adams, one of the first to emphasize the value of archival or extratextual research in Joyce criticism,
called for a separation of "surfaces from symbols" in *Ulysses* to counter
the distraction posed by real-life allusions to the overall thematic coherence of the work. Hence the need to separate

> things which were put into the novel because they are social history,
> local colour, or literal municipal detail, from the things which rep-
> resent abstract concepts of special import to the patterning of the
> novel. This is not a clear-cut separation; we may assume that Joyce's
> frequent purpose, like Ibsen's, was to present both a solid surface
> and a luminous symbol at the same time. But in a book as large and
> as complicated as *Ulysses*, it would be inevitable, even if it were not
> desirable, that one of these purposes should sometimes prevail over
> the other. When we know what part of the book is mainly literal Dub-
> lin detail, we can give more, or at least different, weight to what is pal-
> pably symbolic. . . . [W]e need fewer symbolic uses for the name [of a

real person] because it is better accounted for as fact . . . [sometimes] as a very simple fact indeed.[73]

But as Adams himself concedes, the surface tension of fact is never entirely dissociated from symbol, and the inclusion of a literal detail may generate a tangential narrative of its own, often not fully motivated by, or contained within, the text ("each minute part is at the center," in John Cage's terms above). The difficulty here not only lies in detecting that such narratives exist but also concerns the limits of detective work itself, the possibility that the networks of public knowledge *Ulysses* draws on may often be as inscrutable as the secrecy of the home, personal intimacy, or the recesses of "inner speech." It is for this reason, as Terence Killeen argues, that the semiotics of the city may escape not only the consciousness of individual characters but also that of the author:

> It is often unhelpful to think of James Joyce as the direct author of this material at all. . . . It might be better to think of some larger social entity—the collective voice of Dublin, even—as the repository of these various techniques, which the novel draws on. This is not unlike the situation of Homer, who may well be a social construct himself.[74]

In his account of modernist literary language, Derek Attridge contrasts Joyce's linguistic experiments with more prominent currents in modernism that "stake a claim against time and chance," looking to the artwork to wrest "necessity from arbitrariness, permanence from the historical flux, universality from the culturally specific detail." In the latter case, the modernist ideal aspires to a self-sufficient work impervious to context: "[The work] does not willingly interact with the concrete situation in which text and interpreter find themselves. Though meaning may be suspended, everything in the text is presented as self-justified. . . . Think of the superb certainty of a Mondrian painting, the self-authenticating power of a Mies building, the assured self-validation of every note of a Schoenberg twelve-tone composition."[75] Joyce's logic works in the opposite direction, frequently placing the entire architecture of a system at the mercy of context and circumstance. Though much of the historical scholarship brought to bear on Joyce's texts is a kind of detective work, undertaken "in the name of greater fixity, permanence and truth," this is vitiated by the role of chance, digression, and coincidence in establishing patterns and cross-connections within the narrative. The opposition between intended and accidental readings breaks down since Joyce's system-building is designed precisely to allow for "unforeseen connec-

tions" and interpretations "that defy all predictability and programming."
The potential for new, unexpected readings is attributed by Attridge to
the different *cultural contexts* that shape the reader's experience, but the
grounds for such active responses are laid formally by a narrative structure of gaps and lacunae that punctuate the work: "[T]he distinction between what is inside and what is outside the text is precisely what collapses at this moment."[76] In this, Joyce's practice parts company not only
with the self-sufficient modernist work but also with the classic realism
of historical fiction. Real-life individuals such as Napoleon feature in historical novels, as they do in *Ulysses*, but no sooner are they transferred to
a narrative than they become, in Ann Rigney's words, "parts of a unified,
autonomous fictitious system that stands en bloc at a distance from the
world as we know it":

> Although particular story elements ("Napoleon" or "Dublin") may
> originally have referred to things in the real world, then, their occur-
> rence within the context of a story means that this reference is sus-
> pended: they become part of a fictional world that, as a whole, has no
> counterpart in the actual one.[77]

Rigney is discussing the internal coherence of classic realist fiction, but
in Joyce's work, Dublin and real-life individuals are introduced to sus-
pend the distinction between fact and fiction, bringing text and context
into new kaleidoscopic relationships with each other. According to Ruth
Ronen: "Within the fictive universe of discourse, truth is not determined
relative to an extratextual universe, but relative to a fictional world in
which only some of the textual assertions can establish facts"; in *Ulysses*,
however, it is precisely the possibility that "extratextual facts" can derail
the narrative, or introduce new subtexts, that ensures the radical indeterminacy of its fictive worlds.[78]

Discussing the appearance of the panorama as a form of spectacle
uniquely appropriate to mass society, Heyward Ehrlich noted a key feature that attracted the modernist sensibilities of writers such as Walter
Benjamin and James Joyce: "One recurrent subject of the panoramas was
the city itself, capturing all the aleatory diversity of modern life. In divert-
ing the focus from the foreground to background the panoramas were, so
to speak, *texts made entirely of context*."[79] The capacity to convert context
into text, background into foreground, and vice versa, is central to the
narrative structure of *Ulysses*. It is as if "forms of life," in Wittgenstein's
sense, are gathered into language itself, bringing with them in turn the
avid engagement with both literature and the city required by the text.
The integration of context into text was taken by Roman Jakobson to be

characteristic of the poetic function, as if the aesthetic emulated, or compensated for, the lived texture of experience at the level of signification.[80] As Robert Scholes summarizes it:

> The point of this is that poetry may be definable precisely in terms of our having to supply the missing elements in an act of communication. The "fictional" element in literature, including poetry, is definable as an absent context, or perhaps as a distant context. Insofar as a literary work is mimetic it refers to the "real" world by interposing an "imaginary" world between the audience and reality.[81]

Joyce adds a further layer to this, corresponding to what Scholes describes as "double context'" (or "frequently, as in allegory, a multiple context").[82] If unspoken or material contextual cues—for example, tone, bodily gestures, facial expressions, physical setting—find (paradoxically) expression in verbal form in literature, this in turn requires a *new contextual grounding*, pointing once more to features outside the text.[83] In taking over the materiality of context, language itself assumes a dense materiality, drawing attention to its own physical and tactile properties in the process of enunciation. So far from removing the means of expression from its historical circumstances, this has the effect of *accentuating* its cultural orientations, not only those absorbed into the work but the material practices of literature itself.[84] As Attridge has concluded, discerning in Joyce's prose many of the stylistic qualities attributed to poetry:

> Historically, it has been poetry which has found a variety of means to release the bodily dimension of speech . . . to allow the language's open proclivities—which is to say, those of the inherited culture, mediated by an individual and partly unconscious psyche and by the urgings of the body—to determine to some degree the words of the poem. . . . It is here that the historical dimension becomes particularly important.[85]

The Politics of Obliquity

Secrets, silent, stony sit in the dark palaces of both our hearts.
JAMES JOYCE (*U* 2.170–71)

It is these intercalated forms of life, relating style to the archive and material practices, that converts Joyce's colloquy with his native Dublin into a conversation with readers across different cultures and historical peri-

ods, a differential world at large. Capturing the inner speech of a city
is not an act of transcription so much as translation: developing stylistic techniques that relay to multiple audiences effects experienced in a
local setting but amplified and transmuted through literary form. It is
not only a lack of poetic diction and literary skill that prevents the articulation of everyday experiences, for intimacy and familiarity generate their own shorthand ("the bodily dimension of speech," in Attridge's
terms above), and are none the worse for this. Under conditions of emotional and cultural paralysis, however, when both inner and outer lives
are systematically policed by church and state, secrecy, indirection, and
evasion are built into the most routine everyday exchanges. The aspects
of the ordinary that Joyce renders on the page belong to the *unspoken*
as much as to the spoken, "horizons" or "structures" of experience in
Merleau-Ponty's terms (*PP* 83–84) that often lie unresolved or unfor-
mulated beneath the surface civilities of daily life. That such covert codes
may speak to strangers as well is brought out in a telling example in the
western film *Shane* (1952), as noted by Peter Winch. At the beginning of
the film, Shane (Alan Ladd), a lone horseman, arrives at the ranch of the
beleaguered Starrett family, who are being forced off their land by big
ranchers, and encounters Joe Starrett (Van Heflin), the doughty home-
steader:

> Although they hardly exchange a word, a bond of sympathy springs
> up between the stranger and homesteader. The stranger silently joins
> the other in uprooting, with great effort, the stump of a tree in the
> yard; in pausing for breath, they happen to catch each other's eye
> and smile shyly at each other. Now any explicit account of the under-
> standing that had sprung up between these two, and which was ex-
> pressed in that glance, would no doubt be very complicated and in-
> adequate. We understand it, however, as we may understand the
> meaning of pregnant pause (consider what it is that makes a pause
> *pregnant*), or as we may understand the meaning of a gesture.[86]

Much of Joyce's work may be seen as full-scale attempts—"no doubt
. . . very complicated and inadequate"—to convey in language the elu-
siveness of such moments, and it is striking that the epiphany of the
"bird-girl" on Dollymount strand in *Portrait* also turns on the intimacy
of the returned gaze:

> She was alone and still, gazing out to sea; and when she felt his pres-
> ence and the worship of his eyes her eyes turned to him in quiet suf-

ference of his gaze, without shame or wantonness. Long, long she
suffered his gaze and then quietly withdrew her eyes from his and
bent them towards the stream, gently stirring the water with her foot
hither and thither. (*P* 186)

"Sufferance" is to be expected from the experience of being on the re-
ceiving end of the gaze of a stranger, but voyeurism is contested through
the acknowledgment of the presence of another, the addressivity of the
eye incorporating the properties of calling and answerability in speech:
"Her eyes had called him and his soul had leaped at the call" (*P* 186).[87]
The sense of release is forged not from mastery but from the possibility
of failure: "To live, to err, to fall, to triumph, to recreate life out of life!"
(*P* 186). This incident, a transfiguration of a real event in Joyce's life as
noted above, was also integrated into the fraught intimacy of Bloom's encounter with Gerty McDowell in the "Nausicaa" chapter of *Ulysses*. Eyes
are for reading as much as gazing: gaze and voice fuse in "Sirens" ("Miss
gaze of Kennedy, heard, not seen, read on" [*U* 11.240]), and Bloom fan-
cies his own eyes are worth reading: "In my eyes read that slumber which
women love" (*U* 15.2771–72). On Sandymount beach in the "Nausicaa"
chapter, the gaze crosses an emotional abyss as Gerty McDowell's eyes
alight on Bloom:

> Till then they had only exchanged glances of the most casual but now
> under the brim of her new hat she ventured a look at him and the
> face that met her gaze there in the twilight, wan and strangely drawn,
> seemed to her the saddest she had ever seen. (*U* 13.367–70)

If voyeurism is akin to visual monologue, "mutual disclosure of this kind
tends to build trust":[88] the returned gaze constitutes a dialogical vision
that is no less communicative and even caring for the absence of language. The eyes speak back, but of what it is not clear: "[H]aunting sorrow was written on his face. She would have given worlds to know what
it was. . . . [I]f she saw that magic lure in his eyes there would be no holding back for her. . . . [H]er every effort would be to share his thoughts"
(*U* 13.422–23, 652–53, 654).[89] In the story "Eveline" in *Dubliners*, it is the
inability of eyes to even make contact that signals the point of no return — or rather, of no departure: "Her eyes gave him no sign of love or
farewell or recognition" (*D* 34).

The opening of inner life to strangers does not take place in a void
but draws on codes of cultural intimacy that question the impersonality and detachment of certain conceptions of the public sphere, not

least in a divided, colonial society. One of the pivotal moments in *Ulysses* turns on an exchange of glances between two (relative) strangers, Leopold Bloom and Stephen Dedalus. In the "Eumaeus" chapter, Bloom and Stephen end up in the cabman's shelter under the Loopline Bridge in the early hours of the morning after their fractious revelries in Bella Cohen's brothel in "Circe." There they fall in with other late-night ramblers seeking company, including the keeper of the shelter, "Skin-the-Goat" (James Fitzharris), the jarvey who drove the decoy getaway cab after the assassinations of the state secretary, Lord Frederick Cavendish, and his assistant secretary, Thomas Burke, by the Invincibles in the Phoenix Park in May 1882. When the conversation drifts after many wayward turns to the attractions of cold steel for foreign assassins, a speaker, oblivious to the presence of Skin-the-Goat, mentions the Invincibles, at which point "Mr B. and Stephen, each in his own particular way, both instinctively exchanged meaning glances, in a religious silence of the strictly *entre nous* variety however, towards where Skin-the-Goat, *alias* the keeper, not turning a hair, was drawing spurts of liquid from his boiler affair" (*U* 16.593–97). This sets in train a sequence of exchanged glances that pick up where words leave off: Bloom "turn[s] a long you are wrong gaze on Stephen," who returns a "glance also of entreaty for he seemed to glean in a kind of a way that it wasn't all exactly" (*U* 16.1088–90), followed later by Stephen's response to Bloom's defense of the patriotism of Jews:

> Then he looked up and saw the eyes that said or didn't say the words the voice he heard said, if you work.
> —Count me out, he managed to remark, meaning work.
> The eyes were surprised at this observation because as he, the person who owned them pro tem. observed or rather his voice speaking did, all must work, have to, together. (*U* 16.1146–51)

In "Ithaca," as Bloom and Stephen amble toward Eccles Street under the starry sky, their gazes eventually give rise to an underlying but still unspoken sympathy, "[s]ilent, each contemplating the other in both mirrors of the reciprocal flesh of theirhisnothis fellowfaces" (*U* 17.1183–84).

If the dialogical glances between Bloom and Stephen speak volumes, one of the volumes is *Ulysses* itself. The ingénue who pronounced "*where ignorance is bliss*" on the Phoenix Park murders in the shelter resembles a reader coming to the novel "quite in the dark" without any knowledge of Dublin or its inhabitants, not to mention key moments in Irish history. The analogy between the reader and the denizens of the cabman's shelter breaks down, however, at one level: whereas the exchange of glances between Bloom and Stephen is of the "*entre nous* variety," the street knowledge of *Ulysses*, mediated through literary form, is open to all comers, on the condition that readers, like the "voice speaking . . . must work, have to, together." No sooner have Bloom and Stephen established rapport with knowing glances than Stephen, speaking to Bloom, begins to address the world at large, integrating a third party into the "triangle" of intimate dialogue/glances: "Then, Stephen said staring and rambling on to himself or *some unknown listener somewhere*, we have the impetuosity of Dante and the isosceles triangle miss Portinari he fell in love with and Leonardo and san Tommaso Mastino" (*U* 16.885–88, italics added).

In opening up the inner life of the city "to some unknown listener elsewhere," Joyce risked not only voyeurism, the violation of intimacy, but also, at the public level, a breaking of secrecy that aligns the novel with one of its main rivals in charting the underworld, the police. As Enda Duffy has noted, the entire ethos of "Eumaeus" is pervaded by a police presence: approaching the shelter, Bloom and Stephen "turned into Store street, famous for its C Division police station" (*U* 16.50–51), and, as if prompted by their surroundings, Bloom's thoughts turn to other police dealings "recalling a case or two in the A division in Clanbrassil St." (*U* 16.78–79).[90] Duffy further points out that though the interrogative format of the following chapter, "Ithaca," is often compared to both the Catholic catechism and popular scientific compendiums, its manner is closer to that of police interrogation, as if trying to sort out the obfuscation and circumlocutions of "Eumaeus." The implication of "Ithaca," Duffy writes, is

> that for the subaltern, strict realism (here pared down to the question-and-answer of the police interrogator and suspect) will never escape the panoptic intent of those in power who invented it. . . . Hence it is in "Ithaca" that the massive regime of surveillance of the colonial state is made explicit in the form: we are confronted with a series of questions and answers that is at once a catechism (implying a compendium of the important knowledge of the culture) and a police interrogation (implying the grip of a panoptical regime upon the dispersal and even the very existence of the culture's pool of knowledge).[91]

It is mainly out of a determination to obstruct the panoptical gaze or its fictional equivalent, the omniscient narrator, that Joyce sought to *implicate* readers in the text, calling for the kind of active, heterogeneous interpretations that rule out any controlling vision. According to D. A. Miller, the underlying order and narrative logic of the Victorian novel picked up in a crucial sense where the police left off in the regulation of society, bringing norms of respectability and social integration to private areas out of bounds, or to illicit social spaces, such as those of the underworld, that threatened social decorum:

> Characteristically locating its story in an everyday middle-class world, the novel takes frequent and explicit notice that this is an area that for the most part the law does not cover or supervise, yet when the law falls short in the novel, the world is never reduced to anarchy as a result. In the same move whereby the police are contained in a marginal pocket of representation, the work of the police is superseded by the operations of another, informal, and extralegal principle of organization and control.[92]

Hence, on Miller's terms, Dickens's novel *Oliver Twist* makes a passionate case for a proper understanding of the forces that give rise to delinquency rather than a moralistic condemnation of delinquents per se, but in so doing it attempts to bring the underworld within the expanding nets of Victorian social regulation and notions of fate and punishment: "Though the novel is plainly written as a humane attack on the institutions that help produce the delinquent milieu, the very terms of the attack strengthen the perception of delinquency that upholds the phenomenon."[93]

It was perhaps in this spirit that Ezra Pound commented wryly on Joyce's diagnosis of the malaise of his native city: 'If more people had read *The* [sic] *Portrait* and certain stories of Mr Joyce's *Dubliners* there might have been less recent trouble in Ireland. A clear diagnosis is never without its value."[94] Pound's assumption here is that Joyce's dispatches from the front might have helped the forces of law and order, but the thrust of Joyce's challenge to authority, as Shane Leslie rightly noted, aligns him more with the revolutionary upheaval that led to the eventual resistance to colonial rule:

> Irish writers, whose own language was legislatively and slowly destroyed by England, will cynically contemplate [in *Ulysses*] an attempted Clerkenwell explosion in the well-guarded, well-built, classical prison of English literature. The bomb has exploded, and creeping around Grub Street we have picked up a few fragments by way of curiosity. (*JJCH* I, 211)

"This is the first of my explosives," Stephen says to Madden in *Stephen Hero*, handing him the manuscript of his manifesto "Art and Life"—a statement related by Andrew Gibson to the "Proteus" chapter in *Ulysses*, in which "Stephen is absorbing the spirit of the dynamitard in order to translate it into an explosive art."[95] When Stephen Dedalus meets the old Fenian Kevin Egan in Paris, the memory of his participation in the original Clerkenwell explosion (based on the experience of the real-life figure Joseph Casey, a friend of the Joyce family whom James met in Paris) is still vivid:

> Noon slumbers. Kevin Egan rolls gunpowder cigarettes through fingers smeared with printer's ink. . . . Of Ireland, the Dalcassians, of hopes, conspiracies, of Arthur Griffith now, AE, pimander, good shepherd of men. To yoke me as his yokefellow, our crimes our common cause. . . . The blue fuse burns deadly between his hands and burns clear. Loose tobaccoshreds catch fire: a flame and acrid smoke light our corner. Raw facebones under his peep of day boy's hat. . . . In gay Paree he hides, Egan of Paris, unsought by any save by me. (*U* 3.216–17, 226–29, 239–41, 249–50)

In the charged political atmosphere of the early 1880s that led to both the Phoenix Park murders and the Dynamite War in Britain, Jeremiah O'Donovan Rossa, the exiled Fenian leader in New York, proposed that the $30,000 that had recently gone to the Land League would have been better spent if it "had gone to an 'active' policy [which] would have equipped sixty men with sixty boxes of matches, or something better, who would have burnt down the neighbourhood of St Paul's Cathedral."[96] According to a report of one of the first bombs that detonated the Dynamite War, placed at the Town Hall in Liverpool, a constable arrived on the scene as the fuse was being lit: "'Go back to the Town Hall,' he urged his colleague, 'it is being set on fire. I saw them strike the match and heard the fuse.'"[97] It is difficult not to pick up traces of this incendiary politics in the seemingly trivial action described in "Aeolus" that follows the animated discussions of the Invincibles' escape from the Phoenix Park, and Lady Dudley's unwitting purchase of a postcard commemorating the murders from a hawker outside the park almost twenty years later ("CLEVER, VERY" [*U* 7.674]):

> Pause. J. J. O'Molloy took out his cigarettecase.
> False lull. Something quite ordinary.
> Messenger took out his matchbox thoughtfully and lit his cigar.

I have often thought since on looking back over that strange time
that it was that small act, trivial in itself, that striking of that match,
that determined the whole aftercourse of both our lives. (*U* 7.760–
65)

This enigmatic sequence has lent itself to several interpretations, including the suggestion that the "match" in question concerns the coming
together of Bloom and Stephen later in the novel, but the readings are
not necessarily exclusive.[98] The effect of coincidence and chance in
Joyce's text works to bring both private and public spheres together: it
is, after all, in the discussion of the Invincibles that Bloom and Stephen
exchange knowing glances, leading once more to a play on the sardonic
tribute: "Funny, very" (*U* 16:600).

In *Ulysses*, the surveillance of the colonial state is continually called
into question, the kind of invasive knowledge yielded by those "in the
dark" who are not only disengaged from but hostile to the world they are
seeking to decode. The unvarnished truth is at a premium in "Eumaeus,"
and no more so than where the police are concerned — at least in Bloom's
eyes:

> [A] lot of those policemen, whom he cordially disliked, were admit-
> tedly unscrupulous in the service of the Crown and, as Mr Bloom
> put it, recalling a case or two in the A division in Clanbrassil street,
> prepared to swear a hole through a ten gallon pot. Never on the spot
> when wanted but in quiet parts of the city, Pembroke road for ex-
> ample, the guardians of the law were well in evidence, the obvious
> reason being they were paid to protect the upper classes. (*U* 16.76–
> 82)

Later Bloom himself takes to "Sherlockholmesing" (*U* 16.831) the old
seadog Murphy to establish the truth of his tall tales, but in fact the half-
baked truths that circulate as knowledge throughout militate against detective work — including, one might add, the kind of forensic research
on the part of critics that might be expected to clear up the irresolvable
ambiguities of the chapter. "My dear fellow," says Holmes to Watson in
one of Conan Doyle's stories, "if we could fly out that great window hand
in hand, hover over this great city, gently remove the roofs, and peep in at
the queer things which are going on" — then the truth would lie exposed
in all its candor.[99] This accords with Wittgenstein's God-like view that
leaves the world as it is, but instead of letting people get on with their
lives, oblivious to the spectator, it exposes them to the ultimate fantasy of
power — in Franco Moretti's words, "the totalitarian aspiration towards

a *transparent* society."[100] The reduction of reading to searching for clues, solving riddles, or filling gaps in information militates against the questioning of the authority of facts and positivist approaches to knowledge that runs throughout *Ulysses*. The meticulous concern with accuracy, and the interpolation of real people, places, and events in the action, are offset by the paradox that the introduction of actuality into the work disrupts internal coherence, ruling out any possibility of his fictive world functioning as a closed aesthetic system.[101] We cannot be sure what aspects of the real world matter in the text: those that are explicitly mentioned or that come to light elsewhere, whether in the archive or through other chance discoveries. Hence the Borgesian concept of "a labyrinth without a centre," an endless array of codes, schema, and interconnections but without a master key to make sense of it all. "If you take away the transcendent God from the symbolic world of the Middle Ages," wrote Umberto Eco, "you have the world of Joyce."[102] The otherworld, instead of acting as a source of fixity and authority, is brought down to earth as a principle of openness and uncertainty in the novel.

The same lack of authority applies to the circulation of local knowledge in *Ulysses*, notwithstanding its deep grounding in the inner life of the city. There is no romantic sense of place or, still less, an appeal to the native informant, the mythic Dubliner inhaling knowledge along with the smell of the Liffey and Guinness's brewery. The kind of knowledge at stake in *Ulysses* has more to do with characters at odds with their environment, not always in a position to come to terms with colonial modernity or, for all their ways with words, raise it to the level of consciousness. When the conversation turns (as it does several times) to the traumatic memory of Parnell's downfall in the cabman's shelter, Bloom, we are told, was "incensed" by "the blatant jokes of the cabman and so on who passed it all off in jest, laughing immoderately, pretending to understand everything, the why and the wherefore, and in reality not knowing their own minds" (*U* 16.1531–32). This may have been Skin-the-Goat's hard-line response to Parnell, but it was also a symptom of "the gratefully oppressed" (*D* 35), a divided city whose population turned out in its thousands for the 1798 centenary commemorations in 1898 and, in a volte-face, took to the streets again for the visit of Queen Victoria in 1900. In these circumstances, it is not surprising, as Joyce wrote in "The Shade of Parnell," that the ghost of the leader already roamed the Irish countryside and the streets of Dublin even before his death: "He went from county to county, from city to city, 'like a hunted hind,' a spectral figure with the signs of death on his brow."[103] "Recent criticism has attempted to minimize the greatness of this strange spirit by pointing to the different sources of his parliamentary tactics," but none can take away from "the forlorn serenity of his character" when faced with the opportunism of British liberalism: it was indeed the attempt to import fiction back into fact, forging Parnell's links with the Invincibles, that proved his greatest triumph (*OCPW* 193–94). Yet he was no stranger to "the hillside men": "Parnell, convinced that such a liberalism could only yield to force, united every element of national life behind him, and set out on a march along the borders of insurrection" (*OCPW* 195). That those borders also failed to prevent the "real" crossing over into the zone of the imagination was part of Joyce's contribution to an insurrection in print.

CHAPTER 2

"Shouts in the Street"

INNER SPEECH, SELF, AND THE CITY

Nothing is less a monologue than Molly's "monologue."

JACQUES DERRIDA, "Ulysses Gramophone"

Dubliners going to work or on their daily rounds one July morning in 1997 were perhaps surprised to see apparently random fragments of sentences embossed in pink neon on various prominent sites in the center of the city (figs. 2.1 and 2.2). Though it did not advertise itself, passersby were, in fact, encountering the secret life of Molly Bloom, lifted from the privacy of her thoughts and her bedroom and cast up in lights all over public space. Not for the first time, Dublin had become a city of open secrets, some in the know, others not, though the words in question were posted in broad daylight. It may even have been part of the thinking behind the displays that they were less noticeable during the day, and that the "illuminated cadences" (*D* 211) only glowed at night when their incongruity was fully visible. More than any other artistic project, this striking visualization of thinking out loud caught not only Molly Bloom's words but also the spirit of many of Joyce's experiments with language, and their relation to the inner speech of his native city.

The work in question, *For Dublin*, was an outdoor art installation by Frances Hegarty and Andrew Stones and was the first winner of the Nissan Art Project in 1997.[1] It took the form of nine neon texts, placed strategically on prominent sites in Dublin to add "counterpoint and add resonance to the location":

The artwork proceeds from the idea that in Molly Bloom's seemingly intuitive stream of words—no less than in the activities of the male characters in *Ulysses*—we can find a "map" of the city, presented in terms of a humorous and ironic appraisal of its daily life. The work

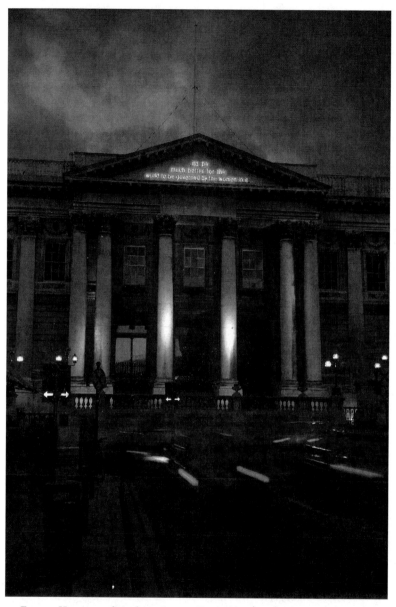

2.1 Frances Hegarty and Andrew Stones, *For Dublin* (1997). From eight manifestations of James Joyce's Molly Bloom in Dublin city center. Photograph: Andrew Stones. © Hegarty & Stones, courtesy Hegarty & Stones (www.brighter.org). View of City Hall from Parliament Street: ". . . itd be much better for the world to be governed by the women in it . . ."

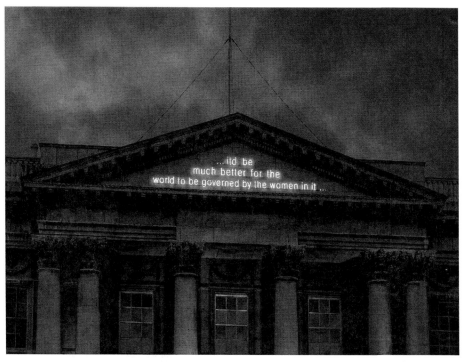

2.2 Frances Hegarty and Andrew Stones, *For Dublin* (1997). From eight manifestations of James Joyce's Molly Bloom in Dublin city center. Photograph: Andrew Stones. © Hegarty & Stones, courtesy Hegarty & Stones (www.brighter.org). City Hall (detail).

renders the fictitious Molly's words in the bold, seductive medium of neon, a form more often associated with the upfront declarations of modern advertising.[2]

As in the case of the whitewashed letters of "Finn's Hotel" still barely visible on the gable end of the redbrick building where Nora Barnacle worked on Nassau Street, *For Dublin* constituted a kind of ghost writing, or afterimage, in which the inner histories of the streets were brought into the open. This might be seen, in the terminology of Lev Vygotsky's *Thought and Language*, as the "inner speech" of a city circulating in public, and it is for this reason that some of the most recondite fragments in Molly's soliloquy seemed to take on a life of their own in their new municipal settings. "O that awful deepdown torrent O and . . ." (*U* 18.1587–88) may refer to Molly's cascading stream of consciousness, but by giving it literal expression on Ormond Quay's lower wall above the Liffey, the metaphor is brought home to base and strangely transfigured (fig. 2.3).

2.3 Frances Hegarty and Andrew Stones, *For Dublin* (1997). From eight manifestations of James Joyce's Molly Bloom in Dublin city center. Photograph: Andrew Stones.
© Hegarty & Stones, courtesy Hegarty & Stones (www.brighter.org). View of River
Liffey, Ormond Quay Lower Wall, and Bachelors Walk Wall: ". . . O that awful deepdown
torrent O and . . . the sea the sea crimson sometimes like fire . . ."

The location is also that of the Ormond Hotel, scene of the "Sirens" episode in *Ulysses*, and across the river on Wellington Quay, another fragment illuminated the Clarence Hotel (now owned by the band U2):
"suppose our rooms at the hotel were beside each other and any fooling went on . . ." (*U* 18.350–51) (fig. 2.4). That the disconnectedness of
Molly's speech only enhances its proliferation of meanings is echoed in
the elliptical associations of the various fragments with the buildings or
sites they illuminate. The departure from the tourist trail and the fixtures
of official history is highlighted in the sequence

> . . . a stranger to Dublin
> what place was it and so on
> about the monuments and he
> tired me out with statues . . . (*U* 18.92–93)

above the parapet of Thomas Cook's travel agency—perhaps the means
by which the stranger came to Dublin (fig. 2.5). This site overlooks one

2.4 Frances Hegarty and Andrew Stones, *For Dublin* (1997). From eight manifestations of James Joyce's Molly Bloom in Dublin city center. Photograph: Andrew Stones. © Hegarty & Stones, courtesy Hegarty & Stones (www.brighter.org). View of Clarence Hotel, Wellington Quay: ". . . suppose our rooms at the hotel were beside each other and any fooling went on . . ."

of the most famous clusters of monuments in Dublin, the three statues of Burke, Goldsmith, and Grattan by John Henry Foley in front of Trinity College and on College Green.[3] It is common to represent public memorials as vehicles of popular memory, the material expression of the imagined community of the nation, as in this description of the fashioning of national myths in Ireland by the Australian cultural critic Donald Horne:

> Between the two grandest porticoes in Dublin, those of the Bank of Ireland and Trinity College, are reminders of the time when Dublin was second city of the British Isles. On a traffic island there is a statue of an eighteenth-century orator in classic pose, hand uplifted. The statue maintains a style of its own—just as Henry Grattan, the great Irish orator whom the statue represents, maintained a stylish eloquence in the successful agitation (backed by hints of force) for the right for an Irish parliament to legislate for Ireland. What became

2.5 Frances Hegarty and Andrew Stones, *For Dublin* (1997). From eight manifestations of James Joyce's Molly Bloom in Dublin city center. Photograph: Andrew Stones.
© Hegarty & Stones, courtesy Hegarty & Stones (www.brighter.org). American Express
Building above Thomas Cook Sign: ". . . a stranger to Dublin what place was it and so on
about the monuments and he tired me out with statues . . ."

known as "Grattan's Parliament" met, as every Dubliner will tell you,
in what is now the Bank of Ireland, for eighteen years, until it was destroyed in British reaction to an Irish uprising.[4]

Grattan's statue is preaching to the converted if Dubliners already know
the story of the Patriot Parliament. The redundancy of statues in the inner
life of the nation, however, is suggested a short time later when Horne
notes that no monuments remain in Dublin to commemorate the Act
of Union that destroyed legislative independence, for the simple reason
that "the Irish have blown them up." Yet, he adds once more, "everyone
in Dublin can tell you where they were." Monuments were indeed more
effective by their absence during the rise of Irish nationalism, ordinary
streets and places themselves furnishing sites of memory of the dead.[5]
    As Molly's seeming indifference to city landmarks indicates, and as
the *For Dublin* installation underlines, Joyce's Dublin is a site of negative topography: glimpses of the unseen, fragments of the unspoken, and

memories of what did not happen compete with actuality in the minds of the living.[6] Joyce's stylistic innovations drew much of their impetus from the modernism of the metropolitan center, but it is also clear that his modernist idiom — its complex allusiveness, its intimacies and exclusions — was inextricably bound up with the Dublin of his upbringing. This was after all a deeply divided city, a center of paralysis, in which alienation, abasement, and ressentiment were integral to the rule of both empire and a compliant Catholic church. The problem with Dublin was not its exclusion from empire but what looked on the surface to be its servile inclusion, as in the case of the thousands who turned out for the pomp and ceremony of Queen Victoria's visit to Dublin, or the less imposing spectacle of the viceregal cavalcade in the "Wandering Rocks" chapter in *Ulysses*.[7] The political authorities in Dublin Castle, with their pervasive network of spies, touts, and whisperers, had few illusions, however, about the sullen unity of hearts and minds under British rule. Habitual conformity — the casual crowds watching the Lord Lieutenant's procession in the "Wandering Rocks" — belied the pressure of conflicting thoughts, as is clear from the reveries of the Unionist Tom Kernan in the episode, whose involuntary memories of the 1798 rebellion as he walks through Thomas Street, awakened perhaps by more recent memories of the centenary commemorations in 1898, foreshadow his missing Lord and Lady Dudley's stately procession through the streets of a deposed capital.[8] The very retreat into subjectivity, as Theodor Adorno notes, is freighted with the world it is trying to forget: "The harder subjectivity rebounds back into itself from the heteronomous, indeterminate, or simply mean world, the more clearly the external world expresses itself, mediatedly, in subjectivity."[9]

The Inner Speech of the City

Terms like "[interior] monologue" then, traditionally defined as "single-voiced" utterances with no expectation of a response, or addressed to no one, can be reassessed as dialogic, addressed to Self as Other. . . . [I]nternal debate is strikingly interwoven with external.

KATIE WALES, *The Language of James Joyce*

Writing of the development of mental life, Lev Vygotsky proposed that even the deepest recesses of the psyche maintain a vital connection to the external world, and the colloquy of voices that give birth to the modern subject. This is already clear, for example, from the colloquial nature of Molly Bloom's inner speech, which bears the imprint of its surroundings as much as the patois of Barney Kiernan's bar, but Vygotsky had in mind a more radical contestation of the boundaries between inner and outer life. Contrary to the Cartesian model that human awareness derives from self-consciousness and works outward, Vygotsky argued by contrast that subjectivity emerges through the process of *internalization,* an inward journey framed throughout by the social horizons of the external world.[10] This is evident in the simple exercise of learning to count: the child counts first on his or her fingers out loud, performing a public action with audible speech, and then gradually moves inward from external forms to counting without physical contact, to eventual "adding in the head" (*TL* 135). Language, likewise, is acquired from social interactions and material surroundings, a process that extends also to "egocentric" speech, the capacity to talk to oneself. As against the Cartesian-type individualism of Jean Piaget, for whom egocentric speech precedes socialization, Vygotsky demonstrated that egocentric speech first takes place in public for the child and is enhanced by the presence of other children.[11] Successful internalization converts (initially public) egocentric speech into (private) *inner speech,* the foundations of thought and mental activity.[12] Inner speech requires an advanced reflexive turn from socially directed language, completing the inner trajectory whereby the child becomes at once both subject and object of communication:

> Every function of the child's cultural development appears twice: first, on the social level, and later, on the individual level; first, between people (*interpsychological*), and then inside the child (*intrapsychological*). . . . All higher mental functions originate as actual relations between human individuals.[13]

Vygotsky added an important rider to this: successful internalization does not part company with the external world but engages with it at different levels throughout the life cycle. Contrary to the view that thought becomes less context-dependent as it grows more abstract and retreats into the psyche, Vygotsky maintained that intellectual complexity is not sacrificed through the grounding of signifying practices in a public, external world.[14] Material and social contexts are not mere scaffolding that can be dispensed with once the (conceptual) building is in place: rather, they *constitute* the structures, the very basis of inner life. The scope (both depth and range) of what is internalized depends ultimately on acknowledgment by, and intelligibility to, a wider interpretative community, and is thus profoundly mediated by the material conditions of its own expression: "Development, as often happens, proceeds here not in a circle but in a spiral, passing through the same point at each new revolution while advancing to a higher level."[15]

Vygotsky moved further away from dominant Western conceptions of child psychology in his argument that interiority is not formed as a matter of course by virtue of genetic development (as proposed by Piaget) but is itself subject to social contexts and historical circumstances. These complex social factors had to do with the onset of modernity in its various manifestations, not all of which were conducive to the construction of inner life. Under conditions of domination or autocratic rule, for instance, the very dynamics of internalization as a psychological process are damaged or compromised—a condition analyzed with acuity by James Wertsch, one of the foremost Vygotsky scholars, in relation to Stalinism and its legacy in the Soviet Union.[16] Outward conformity to a political regime does not entail inner acceptance: indeed, there may be a determined, albeit covert, resistance to internalizing officialdom in any of its manifestations.[17] People go through the motions to appear as "worthy, loyal, and competent members of the total society"[18] but refuse to let its values enter their psychic lives, or to identify with them. On an individualistic or egocentric reading, akin to that of Piaget, this would entail holding on to profound dissatisfactions within the self that never see the light of day and, on Nietzschean terms, may give rise to the psychic futility of ressentiment.[19] In *Stephen Hero*, Cranly objects to Stephen making an "outward show" of his dissent: "But could you not be more diplomatic? Could you not rebel in your heart and yet conform out of contempt? You could be a rebel in spirit" (*SH* 144). On a Vygotskian reading, recalcitrance is not only a mental exercise but is itself out in the open, albeit in endangered spaces and covert forms not open to the casual observer—to the scrutiny of the outsider, the detached third party, the "stranger to Dublin what place was it and so on"—and still less to official surveillance. In the case of Stalinism, much of this furtive "whispering" took place in the apartment kitchen, so much so that the expression *na kukhne* ("in the kitchen") was coined for clandestine, unofficial discourse.[20] In colonial Ireland, dissident speech extended further into public spaces such as the pub, the sports meeting, cultural events, and even the street, all of which provided settings for disaffected solidarities.[21] During the procession through Dublin in 1898 to commemorate the centenary of the 1798 rebellion, in which over a hundred thousand people participated, castle spies and informers paid special attention to pubs along the route, such as Barney Kiernan's, to pick up any loose talk hinting at disloyalty, dissent, or rebellion.[22]

Considered in this light, the bricks and mortar of Joyce's Dublin, the experiences of people coming and going on their daily routines, not only comprise the background to the life of the individual but are the connective tissue of thought itself. As Mary Colum wrote:

> Never was a city so involved in the workings of a writer's mind as Dublin is in Joyce's. In his views of newspaper offices, public-houses, the National Library, the streets, the cemetery, he has got the psychology of that battered, beautiful, eighteenth-century city in its last years of servitude.[23]

It is as if the city itself has a psychology, subject to the same problems of interiority and expression experienced by the individuals who walk through it. Under the twin forces of empire and Catholic rule, the psychological process of internalization was an incomplete project in Irish modernity. Liberal commentators frequently lamented the lack of individualism and inner life among Irish people: "The sense of individualism, the faculty of private judgment, is not fostered," wrote the anti-Catholic writer Michael J. F. McCarthy (whose work was in Joyce's library). Though there was little self-reliance, there was an inflated self-esteem owing to cultural memories of belonging to a higher civilization, to which the Irish person is "yearning to reascend": "Which is why the Catholic Irishman is so secretive about his affairs that, although convivially inclined, he is the least social of men in practice. . . . The chronic state of an Irishman's mind is discontent, a feeling that he ought to be better off than he is. His nerves are sensitive and raw." According to McCarthy, this was suitable material for a Jesuit education, producing a superficial brilliance but devoid of inner depth. As if with Stephen Dedalus in mind, he noted:

> The "embellished memory" imparted by the Jesuits and other Orders enables some of their pupils, especially Irishmen, to pass competitive examinations brilliantly; but such young men, however successful, however crafty, are mostly men of unstable character, devoid of "reflective reason" and power of initiative.[24]

In keeping with Jesuit "craft," the condensation and linguistic density associated by Vygotsky with the mental world of inner speech remain in the open, while possessing all the compression and encryptment of their psychic forms. It is for this reason, Umberto Eco notes, that in *Ulysses* "personal identity itself is questioned": "In the flow of overlapping perceptions during Bloom's walk through Dublin, the boundaries between inside and outside, between how Bloom endures Dublin and how Dublin acts on him, become very indistinct."²⁵ The "secret signs" of "sound and stone" (to appropriate Patrick Kavanagh) resonate in public but, because of the fractured or elliptical nature of such transposed inner speech, are not always immediately intelligible — even to those who imagine, like the stranger who chats up Molly Bloom, that they are participating in the conversation. In his study of the importance of "cultural intimacy" in gaining access to back-stage as well as front-stage existence in everyday life, Michael Herzfeld quotes the historian Eric Hobsbawm to the effect that history and the social sciences are faced with limits in "objective" or dispassionate research: "We know too little about what went on, or for that matter what still goes on, in the minds of most *relatively inarticulate* men and women, to speak with any confidence about their thoughts and feelings towards the nationalities and nation-states which claim their feelings."²⁶ Herzfeld adds that "innermost thoughts are never accessible, despite the rhetoric of hearts and minds," but it may be precisely for this reason that fiction picks up where "third-person" approaches leave off, using the sympathetic imagination to go behind the scenes. The insights and understanding that it yields may not lend themselves to strict verification, any more than knowledge of another person's mind can be established through detached, empirical methods outside of a personal relationship, but this is not to say that people cannot *recognize* themselves in the picture, and react accordingly.

It is in this sense that *Ulysses* is full of loose ends and obliquities, unfinished sentences, half-understood conversations (such as those relating to the horse "Throwaway"), non sequiturs (the man in the brown mackintosh), in-jokes (such as Boylan's prowess as a "great organizer"), colloquial badinage, or seemingly unintelligible remarks (the recurrent motif relating to "U. p: up").²⁷ As Mary Colum wrote in her early review of the novel:

> It hardly seems possible that it can be really understood by anybody not brought up in the half-secret tradition of the heroism, tragedy, folly and anger of Irish nationalism, or unfamiliar with the philosophy, history and rubrics of the Roman Catholic Church; or by one who does not know Dublin and certain conspicuous Dubliners. The author himself takes no pains at all to make it easy of comprehension.²⁸

It is not that there is no subjectivity in colonial Dublin: rather, public spaces are on a continuum with the coded intimacies of private life, and form a semantic barrier, as it were, against the unwelcome intrusions of both faith and fatherland. Sometimes, as in Stephen Dedalus's cogitations in the National Library, it is difficult to tell whether something is said inside or outside the head of a character. In its most liminal forms, it is not clear where interiority ends and the external world begins, as in certain key interpolations of the "Wandering Rocks" chapter, which could pass either for the contents of Father Conmee's head, or ghostly apparitions; likewise, in "Circe" it is the systematic blurring of the boundaries between phantasmagoria and real life that brings the chapter to an end.[29] As Melvin J. Friedman notes of the eventual outward orientation or anchoring of Bloom's interior monologue in *Ulysses*: "Dialogue and authorial or narrative presence . . . work to suggest an intrusion from without on Bloom's thoughts. Joyce, when most heatedly caught up in the flow of Bloom's inner monologue, will always insist on what is outside."[30]

According to Vygotsky, as outer speech contracts and moves inward, it dispenses with explicit formulations, allowing familiarity with context, codes, gestures, and so on to pick up where overt communication leaves off. The more that is conveyed through inner speech, the less needs to be said. In the case of talking to ourselves, where context itself is intrinsic, language can be condensed to the point that single words or verbal fragments can be charged with the semantic density of sentences, paragraphs, or even entire narratives.[31] Vygotsky gives the examples of book titles where a name is sufficient to distill a whole world of experience: "Titles like *Don Quixote, Hamlet,* and *Anna Karenina* illustrate this very clearly: the whole sense of a work is contained within one name" (*TL* 147). This compacted language, for the most part, takes place inside the psyche, or between intimates; but as Wertsch suggests, in a political regime where inner life is at a premium, and the policing of thought is undertaken by both church and state, such hermetic forms of contact are devised not just as a mode of protection against eavesdroppers but to maintain the cultural intimacy of a community. In these circumstances, verbal shorthand, a recourse to the inside track, becomes a feature of outer, everyday exchanges, but with all the ellipses and "cutting of corners" of inner speech. Streams of consciousness flow not only through the mind but through the streets, buildings, and, indeed, bars of the city, competing with other modes of liquid refreshment.

This opens up a further possibility, not fully developed by Vygotsky but implicit in his last writings. Though the capacity to internalize is associated by Vygotsky with abstraction and "the higher mental processes," in certain cultural contexts there may be no less complexity in eluding "reflective reason" and the abstract protocols of scientific method. The capacity to locate the complexity of inner speech amid "shout[s] in the street" (*U* 2.386) to keep it in public circulation may be one of the crucial modes of countering Nietzschean ressentiment, the limited mental revolt against one's own oppression.[32] Resentment undermines the self-esteem of characters in *Dubliners* such as Jimmy in "After the Race," Little Chandler in "A Little Cloud," or Farrington in "Counterparts," and in these cases, inner retreat is a symptom of the stunted civic life of the colonial city. When Mrs. Kearney, in "A Mother," is shortchanged by the organizers of the performances in the Antient Concert Rooms at which her daughter is due to sing, she can barely refrain from giving Mr. Fitzpatrick, whom she eventually ends up with, a piece of her mind—but it ends up staying in her mind:

> Mr. Fitzpatrick, who did not catch the point at issue very quickly, seemed unable to resolve the difficulty and said that he would bring the matter before the Committee. Mrs. Kearney's anger began to flutter in her cheek and she had all she could do to keep from asking:
> —And who is the *Cometty* pray?
> But she knew that it would not be ladylike to do that: so she was silent. (*D* 139)

As against this stifled speech, the philosopher and educationalist Sophie Bryant noted in her contemporary study of "Celtic psychology and its manifestations" that one of the more vital strands of Irish culture lies in the refusal to internalize resistance, redirecting opposition and dissent into alternative public forms:

> This is because he [the Irishman] has a less-developed instinct for pure negative self-control than other people. Some can be cured of their mischievous tendencies, if not of their inmost faults, by a system of pure repressive education.... It is well known that Irish human nature, on the average, does not respond happily to this treatment.... Check its expression in fifty ways, and, after the immediate occasion of repression is past, it reappears in all its multiform humanity as vigorous as ever.[33]

Self-correction takes the form not so much of repressing one's activity but of developing another outlet, even at the risk of contradiction, or without any mediation or resolution into a coherent narrative of the self. Irish practice, writes Bryant, "needs a sphere of social life in which to express [it]self" (*GG* 51) and undertakes "the development of the complementary quality. Thus character is not repressed but developed. Virtue drives a pair of steeds" (*GG* 49). Unlike the patient, step-by-step approach of the Teuton, Bryant continues, the Irish mind "sees many points at once" and, through a process of intense abbreviation, "condense[s] all the main points of an elaborate argument, or a complex conception, into a circle that can be embraced by one sweep of the attention" (*GG* 55). Peripheral details are held in place, promoting a tendency in which a "train of thought explodes in some for the reinstatement of matters remote from present attention, the sudden flash with which the subconscious becomes the conscious in others" (*GG* 54–55). In a passage that would not be out of place as a summary of *Ulysses*, Bryant continues:

> The wide-awakeness of the man in the Dublin street—or, better still, in the streets of Cork—is a direct sign of the lightness with which consciousness slumbers in him. Whatever is in him, or can be in him, awakens on slight provocation, and sits up at once. . . . He is more easily distracted from the particular work which he has in hand by the myriad life of feeling and thought, ever ready to surge up within him. . . . [O]ne quality in excess is a stimulus tending to awake its opposite. (*GG* 59, 61)

The lack of brooding interiority in the Irish person is due to the fact that no one mood takes hold long enough to dominate the personality: "He must be hard pressed indeed before he commits suicide or becomes mad" (*GG* 68). Acknowledging other moods as part of self-consciousness from the outset, Irish inner life is continually divided against itself: "The Irishman, whatever his mood, is conscious or semi-conscious of other moods hanging about him; hence arises a suggestion of incongruity which, without destroying the balance of his central mood, clothes his ideas generally in a subtle veil of humour" (*GG* 67–68). It was perhaps with considerations such as these in mind that Christopher Morley penned his ditty on Judge Woolsey's landmark decision on the publication of *Ulysses* in 1933, which allowed its trade circulation in the United States. Attributing the judge's wise decision to his perception of the undue susceptibility of the "Celtic" psyche to intrusions from the external world, Morley wrote of Joyce and/or his characters:

> He heard the clock its knell tick
> He heard the blackbird sing:
> Reaction peristaltic
> And psychic too, they bring.
> For his locale was Celtic
> And his season, Spring.[34]

Colloquies of the Self

"But the minds, the thoughts of the characters," I began.
"If they had no body they would have no mind," said Joyce. "It's all one."

JAMES JOYCE to FRANK BUDGEN

This appraisal of consciousness and its manifestations places Molly Bloom's soliloquy in a distinctively Irish context, its very (un)intelligibility deriving from the dislocations of the culture that gives rise to it. At one level, various strands in her "monologue," notwithstanding the rich profusion of language, may be at one with her surroundings, in keeping with her British military background: "I love to see a regiment pass in review" (*U* 18.397–8), especially the Lancers or "the Dublins," she muses; or again: "I hate the mention of their politics . . . wasnt I the born fool to believe all his blather about home rule and the land league" (*U* 18.387–88, 1187–88).[35] While patriarchal control of the public sphere is responsible for the confinement of her voice to the bedroom, it does not prevent another Molly, the nationalist Molly Ivors in "The Dead," from speaking forcefully in public. Molly Bloom's soliloquy testifies to an untrammeled interior life, but the confinement to *monologue* may be part of her predicament. Such agency as she acquires derives from the ability to convert monologue into dialogue, drawing on the linguistic energies of a cultural ferment in which gender and sexuality are bound up with wider struggles involving church, class, and state: "itd be much better for the world to be governed by the woman in it you wouldn't see women going and killing each other" (*U* 18.1434–86)—another of the fragments projected by Hegarty and Stones, this time on the façade of Dublin City Hall (fig. 2.1).

Even within the privacy of Molly's bedroom, the separation of mind and body, inner life and physical action, is unresolved, so that the stream of consciousness is not just a mental process, adrift from its public expressions. As a recent commentary notes of the somatic element in Vygotsky's views: "Development takes place both inside and outside the skin, and above all, *on* the skin, *at the border*, that is, at the interface connecting the two systems [public and private]. . . . [T]o a greater or lesser extent, many functions in all subjects remain partially externally distributed throughout the life cycle."[36] Molly Bloom's soliloquy is often taken as the exemplar of inner life in modern fiction, "an instance of pure 'interiority'" in Catherine Whitley's description, and it is not too difficult to see why.[37] Whereas readers of "The Dead," for example, are given no privileged access to Gretta Conroy's inner life, other than through her idiomatic speech and outward appearance, the inverse appears to be true in "Penelope": here "the reader is denied any external point of view at all; the [third-person] narrative seems to disappear, and we are left with Molly's monologue."[38] Yet it is also possible to look at this from a different angle, according to which Molly's reveries represent the reclaiming of the most reclusive areas of the self for a publicly inflected inner speech. In this sense, Joyce's modernism, Hegarty and Stones's *For Dublin*, and Amanda Coogan's artistic project *Molly Blooms* (2004) can be viewed as restoring the suppressed performative dimension to disempowered or consolatory private reveries. In Coogan's performance piece, the austere allegorical figure of "Justice" over Dublin Castle, emptied of its sensual form, is refigured through Molly Bloom's body in terms of an alternative poetic justice that reworks private and public space, love and the formal impersonality of the law, into the landscape of the city (figs. 2.6 and 2.7). Comparing the interiority of Kierkegaard with the *Art Nouveau* of Mallarmé, Adorno noted that while both plunged into the recesses of the self, they were moving in opposite directions: "In place of interiority *Art Nouveau* put sex. It had recourse to sex precisely because only in sex could a private person encounter himself not as inward but as corporeal." By the same token, Molly Bloom's interiority, mixed with bodily needs such as using the chamber pot, attests to the ultimate social affirmation of private space: "The interior should be made transparent as a social function and its self-containedness should be revealed as an illusion—not *vis-à-vis* a hypostasized collective consciousness, but *vis-à-vis* the real social process itself."[39]

In *Thought and Language*, Vygotsky allows for a situation in which inner speech may assume official correctness and formality, as when "it serves as preparation for external speech—for instance, in thinking over a lecture to be given" (*TL* 47). Gabriel Conroy's anxious rehearsals of his after-dinner speech convey this in "The Dead," but Molly Bloom's words travel in a different direction. As Whitley notes, such are the inherent ambiguities and lacunae of her language on the page that her soliloquy cannot be construed as direct access to her mind.[40] Much recent criticism has sought to align Molly's torrent of words with concepts of masquerade, thereby—in some cases, at any rate—imputing a lack of authenticity in the staging, the linguistic effects barely concealing the voice of the off-stage male author.[41] On Judith Butler's terms, however, performance is constitutive of identity formation in the first place, including its openness to other voices and attachments.[42] As Jacques Derrida notes, while falling short of dialogue, Molly's "perfumative" and affirmative "yes"—"all perfume yes" (*U* 18.1608)—"breaches all possible monologue": as an answer to a question, or a recall of another affirmation, "*Yes*

2.6 (*Above*) Amanda
Coogan, *Molly Blooms*
(2004). Performance.
Used with permission
of the artist.

2.7 (*Left*) "Justice,"
Dublin Castle, Dublin.
Photograph courtesy of
Barry Gibbons, Dublin.

indicates that there is an address to the other. . . . *Yes,* the condition of . . . any performative, addresses itself to some other which it does not constitute, and it can only begin by *asking* the other, in response to a request that has always already been made, to *ask* it to say *yes.*"[43]

By the same token, for Vygotsky *all* inner speech is relayed through social mediations, and the task of agency is to recirculate such discourse back into public space by means of one's own distinctive voice. Central to Vygotsky's argument is the contention that successful internalization always remains in contact with the external world, thereby ensuring an ability to act back on it. Contrary to the Hegelian view that mind achieves its apotheosis through an eschewal of material reality, the idiomatic nature of Molly's "well-formed" speech is such that it "comes close to the traditional concept of 'soliloquy,' the dramatic device for speaking thoughts aloud, thoughts in their final stages of processing."[44] The infiltration of inner life under modernity is most evident in the relationship to the commodity and the machine age, what Miriam Hansen refers to as "the mass production of the senses" by new media forms, but also by transport, lighting, and related technologies.[45] In her account of the female body, technology, and memory in "Penelope," Ewa Ziarek notes how Molly's fantasy of extramarital sex in a train simulates the motions of the train in the syncopated rhythms of its language:

> O I love jaunting in a train or a car with lovely soft cushions I wonder will he take a 1st class for me he might want to do it in the train by tipping the guard well . . . 1 or 2 tunnels perhaps then you have to look out of the window all the nicer then coming back suppose I never came back what would they say eloped with him. (*U* 18.366–75)

So far from taking place entirely in her head, moreover, Molly's memories of her tryst with Boylan the previous afternoon are interrupted—or intensified—by the far-off whistle of a train, the mechanical rhythms of the engine recapitulating Boylan's own sexual performance:

> he does it and doesnt talk I gave my eyes that look with my hair a bit loose from the tumbling and my tongue between my lips up to him the savage brute Thursday Friday one Saturday two Sunday three O Lord I cant wait till Monday
> frseeeeeeeefronnnng train somewhere whistling the strength those engines have in them like big giants and the water rolling all over and out of them all sides like the end of Loves old sweeeetsonnnng the poor men that have to be out all the night from their wives and

families in those roasting engines stifling it was today (*U* 18.592–600)[46]

Ziarek highlights the artificial motions of the train to draw a contrast with the natural imagery that pervades Molly's reverie.[47] While technology attests to the intrusion of the outer world on her sensorium, organic imagery relating to flowers, water, and so on seems to draw on a preexistent interiority, invaded, as it were, by mechanical production: "Assimilated to the organic torrents of the sea and the blossoming of flowers . . . female desire retreats to the private and natural space," the promise of an "organic female body that might be a site of resistance to the mechanization of public life."[48] But nature in "Penelope"— "the sea crimson sometimes like fire" (*U* 18.1598–99) emblazoned on Ormond Quay in the *For Dublin* project—is no less an external force, and its materiality as pressing as the obdurate, physical plant of technology. While Ziarek is correct to point out, following Derrida, that "a certain telephonic *techne* not only destroys the intimacy of voice, but also mediates between the self and other," this is also true of an engagement with the natural world.[49] In a gloss on the intimate relation between outer and inner worlds, Cheryl Herr suggests that the fundamental structure of "Penelope" may have to do with the impact of lunar cycles on the female body, Molly's "period piece":

> The breaking of "Penelope" into two handfuls of massive sentences creates a comprehensive rhythm generally taken to allude to the beat of the menstrual cycle, the monthly change of the moon, the flow of the tide, and other natural patterns. So the full-stop is both a grammatical and a natural-biological category that Joyce exploits in staging Molly's star turn.[50]

For Vygotsky, however, such interactions between outer and inner life need not be one way, as is clear from the fact that the fact that "the Russian language has two words for the moon, arrived at by different thought processes that are clearly reflected in their etymologies": one having to do with "caprice, inconstancy, fancy" on account of the ever-changing shapes of the moon, the other relating to measurement or a standard, "the fact that time could be measured by lunar phases" (*TL* 131).

Molly's retrieval of agency through dialogue rather than monologue is achieved most notably, as Kimberly Devlin has shown, in her ventriloquism, the adroitness with which she impersonates the verbal tics and idioms of those who feature in her life.[51] Primary among those is, of course, Bloom himself, and his voice constantly impinges on her own, not always to his advantage:

> the hotel story he made up a pack of lies to hide it planning it Hynes kept me who did I meet ah yes I met do you remember Menton and who else who let me see ... encouraging him making him worse than he is who is in your mind now tell me who are you thinking of who is it tell me his name who tell me who the german Emperor is it yes imagine Im him think of him can you feel him trying to make a whore of me. (*U* 18.37–39, 95–97)

In this hall of echoes, Bloom's voice mingles with his double-tracking of Molly's inquisitorial external speech ("who did I meet ah yes I met do you remember Menton"), both of which are echoed in turn by her surrounding framing voice. Other examples include Milly's friends asking her out to play, "those romps of Murray girls calling for her *Milly come out please*" (*U* 18. 1024–25, italics added), and even the voices of animals: "rousing that dog in the hotel rrrssssstt awokwokawok" (*U* 18.813). As Susan Bazargan notes, "[A]lthough critics have usually referred to the 'Penelope' episode as Molly's monologue or stream-of-consciousness, in fact her discourse is anything but univocal. It is dialogic not only because it seems directed towards an interlocutor, but also because it is formed by a variety of rhetorical stances."[52] Such empowerment as Molly experiences comes from an extension of such performances into the public arena, as in her recall of the feigned voices she used in confession to counter intrusions of the moral police into intimacy:

> theres nothing like a kiss long and hot down to your soul almost paralyses you then I hate that confession when I used to go to Father Corrigan he touched me father and what harm if he did where and I said on the canal bank like a fool but whereabouts on your person my child on the leg behind high up was it yes rather high up was it where you sit down yes O Lord couldnt he say bottom right out and have done with it what has that got to do with it and did you whatever way he put it I forget no father. (*U* 18.106–12)

According to Devlin, her responses may have come across to the priest as contrite, but "for those in the know," the ventriloquism of voices acts as a distancing device, affording a protective space under the very sign of surveillance and control.[53] This conveys a vivid sense of how inner speech may masquerade in public: communicating in one voice, it carries resonances in another that escapes the duff—or "Harvey Duff," as Joyce describes it (U 8.441–42)—ear of a controlling or intrusive third party.[54]

It is not only by means of her actions—the affirmation of her body and sexuality in a milieu of unrequited desire—that Molly emerges from the internalized world of fantasy and resentment: it is also through her capacity to speak her mind in public, albeit through the layered performances of an inner colloquy. Though it is possible to argue that Molly's obsession with her body "saps energies that could otherwise be used to question the extra-sexual order of things—Ireland's colonial situation, for example,"[55] Joyce's contestation of the boundaries between private and public spheres, sexuality and politics, ties one inexorably to the other. It is striking that intimations of rebellion in *Ulysses* ("great times coming") are often voiced in a cryptic inner speech that risks being overheard by "Harvey Duff" informers within the domestic confines of Molly Bloom's world of home, sexuality, and underwear:

> Why those plainclothes men are always courting slaveys. Easily twig a man used to uniform. Squarepushing up against a backdoor. Maul her a bit. Then the next thing on the menu. And who is the gentleman does be visiting there? Was the young master saying anything? Peeping Tom through the keyhole. Decoy duck. Hotblooded young student fooling round her fat arms ironing.
> —Are those yours, Mary?
> —I don't wear such things. . . . . Stop or I'll tell the missus on you. Out half the night.
> —There are great times coming, Mary. Wait till you see.
> —Ah, gelong with your great times coming.
> Barmaids too. Tobaccoshopgirls.
> James Stephens' idea was the best. He knew them. Circles of ten so that a fellow couldn't round on more than his own ring. Sinn Fein.
> (U 8.445–48)

For Joyce, political freedom that stopped at the door of the home, or patrolled the cultural intimacies of inner speech, stopped short of true emancipation. As Frances Hegarty and Andrew Stones write in their brochure accompanying the *For Dublin* project, male figures dominate the public space of the city in Joyce's Dublin, but Molly's voice speaks across the decades, prefiguring the issues that were to become sites of contestation for the women's movement and gender politics in Ireland:

> Within a late 20th century culture shaped by feminist and postfeminist thinking, the singular interest of this character is a measure

of her perceived status as the embodiment of many contemporary issues, for example: the authority of the female voice; female sexuality, femininity and power; the relation of the female persona to language and cultural authority; the nature and status of women in the male imagination; and the "proper place" of the feminine. . . . Although remaining in bed, at the heart of the domestic domain, she becomes mentally hyperactive at a time when the life of the city and its male characters has been played out.[56]

Retrieving subjectivity from its own interiority complex, Molly's voice catches those elusive aspects of inner speech displaced from discourses of power that were now in position to venture through the streets of the *For Dublin* project.

Involuntary Memory

A single voice can make itself heard only by blending into the complex choir of voices already in place. This is true not only of literature but of all discourse.

TZVETAN TODOROV, *Mikhail Bakhtin: The Dialogical Principle*

"What is significant about *Ulysses*," writes Katie Wales, "is that the Bakhtinian idea of 'dialogue,' of inner polemic, pervades the unconscious" as much as the conscious: the very anxieties that Bloom seeks to repress, such as reminders of Molly's rendezvous with Blazes Boylan, are "easily evoked by external stimuli," the side effects of the everyday.[57] Many conventional understandings of the "talking cure" in psychoanalysis envisage it as tying up loose ends, integrating contingencies — often of a traumatic kind — into coherent narratives of the self. For Adam Phillips, by contrast, it is not coherence but free association, the ability to break out of dominant narratives, that promises some release from private torments. "Because of repression," he writes, "the past can only return in disarray as de-narrativized fragments," and part of the function of free association is to produce these fragments, along with other debris from our lives:

Our unspoken lives press for recognition in fragments, in our pauses, our errors and our puns. It is the continuity of our life-stories that we use to conceal the past; through free-association the patient's story loses its composition and becomes more like a collage in which our favorite words find alternative contexts.[58]

In this, it is possible to discern the operation of the stream of consciousness technique in Joyce or, more specifically, its overt dialogical counterpart, which will be explored in the next chapter, free indirect discourse. In his essay "Contingency for Beginners," Phillips makes an instructive distinction between the role of involuntary memory in Freud and Proust that helps to illuminate the specific cast given to inner and outer life in Joyce's works. According to Freud, in *The Psychopathology of Everyday Life* (1901), the involuntary and the accidental are waiting to happen, for their meaning is already *inside us*, placed there by the hidden hand of the unconscious.[59] "Accidents" turn out to be not so much chance encounters as ways of releasing suppressed histories and involuntary pasts: "What looked like accident or chance was in fact voices from the past pressing for recognition: there are lives inside us waiting to be lived."[60] Hence Freud's image of a past "busily and furtively arranging for its own disclosure," stage-managing, as it were, its own unexpected guest appearances in Freudian slips, dreams, and other parapraxes. By contrast, according to Phillips, memory in Marcel Proust is "not seeking attention," or even "waiting to be found," but is truly *involuntary*, in that it belongs to an external world over which we have no dominion. In Proust's own words:

> The past is hidden somewhere outside the realm, beyond the reach of intellect; in some material object (in the sensation which that material object will give us) of which we have no inkling. And it depends on chance whether we come upon this object before we ourselves die.[61]

As Phillips glosses this passage: "'Depending on chance' is, of course, an interesting phrase. For Proust there is no organizing, no technique, for securing access to the past."[62]

Joyce maintains the openness to external promptings found in Proust's involuntary memory, but there is also a sense in which they come from *within*: not from within the self, as in Freud, but from the unrequited pasts *of a culture*. Hidden pasts may lie outside the realm of the self, but this is only to say they lie in other selves, in the intersubjectivity of shared pasts and cultural memory. In the case of Proust, according to Phillips, "we cannot organize a quest for the past, nor is the past pursuing us with its essential messages and unfinished projects." But in Joyce's Dublin, "the moderns of the past" (to use George Sigerson's phrase)[63] are pursuing individuals as they walk through the streets, waiting, as it were, to accost them as they turn a corner, catch a glimpse of a building, or drop their emotional guard. The accidents that prompt involuntary memory in Joyce are precipitated by pressures of unlived pasts akin to those diagnosed by Freud, except they emanate from the histories of a contested public sphere, as well as the inner repressions of the individual. Joyce's narrative methods of direct and indirect speech, of inner as well as outer dialogue, may be seen precisely as "organizing techniques" (adapting Phillips's words above) for "securing access to *alternative* pasts"—and thus to more open-ended futures. If the stream of consciousness device introduces a degree of randomness and indeterminacy into a work, the more socially overt technique of free indirect discourse admits different voices, bringing interiority into contact with other subjectivities and histories within a culture.

And it is a method of sorts, albeit dependent on chance or—quite literally—"throwaways," as in the case of the newspaper handed by Bloom to Bantam Lyons at Westland Row. The difficulty in Joycean narratives is in establishing where exactly narrative coherence ends and accidents begin, and it is this indeterminacy that lies at the heart not only of *Ulysses* but also of earlier stories such as "A Painful Case" in *Dubliners*. Mr. Duffy, the self-absorbed protagonist of the story, is a creature of habit who "abhorred anything which betokened physical or mental disorder" (*D* 104). When he first befriends Mrs. Sinico at a concert, their next meeting is left to chance, but by the third occasion, it is clear that Mr. Duffy is no longer prepared to take risks: "Meeting her a third time by accident he found courage to make an appointment. She came. This was the first of many meetings" (*D* 106). As their relationship deepens, it seems Mrs. Sinico's barely suppressed vivacity is on the point of rescuing Mr. Duffy from himself until, in a moment of spontaneity, she "caught up his hand passionately and pressed it to her cheek" (*D* 107). The involuntary gesture is too much for Mr. Duffy, and he recoils from the shock of physical intimacy, gradually disentangling himself from her company.[64] His life congeals once more into habit and routine until he is assailed some years later by another chance occurrence, a newspaper report of Mrs. Sinico's death crossing a railway line: the verdict of the inquest is that the incident was an unfortunate accident, and that "no blame attached to anyone" (*D* 111), but Mr. Duffy is allowed no such consolation, his inner torments accentuating the suspicion that he had "sentenced her to death" (*D* 113). A throwaway remark by her husband at the inquest alluded to the fact that their marriage was happy until she "began to be intemperate in her habits" (*D* 111) two years ago, and indeed was out late the night of the accident to buy spirits. The story leaves it open whether her death was due to chance, intoxication, or suicide, but one item in the report indicates a chronicle of a death foretold: "The deceased had been in *the habit* of crossing the lines late at night from platform to platform" (*D* 110). Habit, the very means of stabilizing contingency in Mr. Duffy's life, is the source of Mrs. Sinico's—and indeed his own—downfall. For Freud the pressure of the past comes from inside, but in Joyce the boundaries between inner and outer worlds are blurred to the point of breakdown.

It is not that inner life, therefore, is absent in Joyce: as the stream of consciousness technique shows, it is all-pervasive, but its function is more in keeping with the notion of "parallax" propounded in "Lestrygonians": the possibility that at any given moment, different perspectives may open up on a narrative that thought it had the whole world to itself. Interior monologue thus shades into interior dialogue, the merging of inner and outer voices that constitutes free indirect discourse.[65] In this technique, a narrator, whether in the first or third person, is intercepted by another voice in a manner akin to free association, but introducing subtle shifts in tone, register, and point of view. As Deborah Parsons describes its third-person variant: "Because the use of the third-person retains an element of objective narration, free indirect discourse has been described as having a 'dual-voice,' able to convey at once the immediate thoughts of a character and the detached perspective of an impersonal narrator."[66] In "A Painful Case" Mr. Duffy almost stumbles on this device, but instead of drawing close to others, it allows him to distance himself from his own body:

> He lived at a little distance from his body, regarding his own acts with doubtful side-glances. He had an odd autobiographical habit which led him to compose in his mind from time to time a short sentence about himself containing a subject in the third person and a predicate in the past tense. (*D* 104)

As against this studied impersonality, it is precisely free indirect discourse, according to Charles Lock, that enables "the liberation of the modern subject" from "the obligatory and constitutive enunciation of the first person pronoun," the inner isolation that desensitizes Mr. Duffy. As "one word holds two voices, perpetually, without hope or fear of resolution," openness to the other is inescapable, thus affirming, in Bakhtin's terms, the "triumphant carnivalesque of writing from the tight bourgeois individualism of speech."[67] Hence the manner in which the increased polyphony of Joyce's work, according to Joseph Valente, challenges the "systems limiting Irish subjectivity and comes to enjoy a comparatively unencumbered language and perspective. Moving in and out of discrete accents, mind-sets, and evaluative positions, clarifying each by way of others, the narrative voice embodies polyphony as political freedom."[68]

It is this receptivity to other voices that prevents the self from being its own best company in the end. In Molly Bloom's soliloquy, as we have seen, it is the sound of passing trains that disrupts her fantasies, only to launch other erotic trains of thought. Likewise in "A Painful Case," it takes the departure of a goods train from Kingsbridge Station, echoing the syllables of Mrs. Sinico's name, to release Mr. Duffy from the grip that his own self-serving memories exercised over the past:

> Beyond the river he saw a goods train winding out of Kingsbridge Station, like a worm with a fiery head winding through the darkness, obstinately and laboriously. It passed slowly out of sight; but still he heard in his ears the laborious drone of the engine reiterating the syllables of her name. He turned back the way he had come, the rhythm of the engine pounding in his ears. He began to doubt the reality of what memory told him. He halted under a tree and allowed the rhythm to die away. (*D* 13–14)

It is perhaps with this sort of revelation in mind that Sophie Bryant wrote of "the sudden flash with which the subconscious become the conscious in others" (*GG* 54), the echoes of inner speech that release the self from its "incurable loneliness."

CHAPTER 3

"He Says No, Your Worship"

JOYCE, FREE INDIRECT DISCOURSE, AND
VERNACULAR MODERNISM

Though James Joyce is often presented as an adversary of the Cultural Revival and the Irish language, his article "Ireland at the Bar" gives a sympathetic account of the fate of a native tongue struck mute by colonial power. Joyce's article, written for an Italian periodical in 1907, dealt with the trial of "four or five peasants from . . . the ancient tribe of the Joyces" who were charged with the notorious Maamtrasna murders in Connemara in 1882. As the defendants "did not know English . . . [t]he court had to resort to the services of an interpreter," and the "interrogation that took place was at times comic and at times tragic," particularly the inquisition of Myles Joyce, the oldest of the accused:

> On the one hand there was the officious interpreter, on the other, the patriarch of the miserable tribe who, unused to civic customs, seemed quite bewildered by all the legal ceremonies.
> The magistrate said:
> "Ask the accused if he saw the woman on the morning in question."
> The question was repeated to him in Irish, and the old man broke out into intricate explanations, gesticulating, appealing to the other accused, to heaven. Then exhausted by the effort, he fell silent; the interpreter, turning to the magistrate, said:
> "He says no, your worship."
> "Ask him if he was in the vicinity at the time."
> The old man began speaking once again, protesting, shouting, almost beside himself with the distress of not understanding or making himself understood, weeping with rage and terror. And the interpreter, once again replied drily:
> "He says no, your worship."[1]

The coercion masked by the legal proprieties of reported speech lasted
to the end: "Legend has it that even the hangman could not make himself understood by the victim and angrily kicked the unhappy man in the
head to force him into the noose."[2]

It is characteristic of Joyce's finely tuned ear that he should pick up
the barely silenced put-down of the colloquialism "your worship" in the
doomed speech from the dock. The magistrate might well have thought
that the fawning deference emanated from the translator himself had not
the presence of reported speech been indicated through a shift in intonation, signaled in print by Joyce's reproduction of the original gauche
Hiberno-English in the Italian version ("afferma di no, 'your worship'").[3]
It may be that the "officious interpreter" is mocking the hapless defen-
dant, but it is clear that Joyce does not share in this condescension.[4]
Hardly in awe of the majesty of the law, he went out of his way to ridicule its solemn English variant, particularly if backed by "the evidence
of a policeman": writing, tongue in check, to his brother Stanislaus in
1905, he expressed a wish that his fiction should only be judged "by some
jury composed partly of those of my own class and my own age presided
over by a judge who had solemnly forsworn all English legal methods."[5]
It is no coincidence, then, that in *Finnegans Wake*, the police interpreter
at the trial is described as a member of the "royal Irish vocabulary" (*FW*
86.1). The obsequious "your worship" in Joyce's account of the Maamtrasna trial, the only vestige of Myles Joyce's voice retained in the act of
translation, is ambiguous on more than one count, for though given as
reported speech, it is also unclear whether the original was meant to be
in Irish or Hiberno-English. "Your worship" was a comic staple of peasant speech in Irish fiction throughout the nineteenth century, though, as
its ingratiating excess suggested, it was not to be taken at face value and
more often than not hinted at thinly disguised contempt. In Dion Boucicault's *Arrah-na-Pogue* (1864), the vagabond Shaun's use of "your worship" occurs in a context that makes fun of the law:

> MAJOR (*impatiently*): Are you guilty or not guilty? . . .
> SHAUN: I did plade guilty last night, and so I was thin, your worship;
>   but I want to say, that I am as innocent as a fish this morning.
> MAJOR: You wish to withdraw your plea?
> SHAUN: I don't know, sir, but I want to do whatever will get me off.[6]

It is notable that even at an early stage, a single line or phrase in Joyce's
journalism should carry the complex and often undecidable layers of
meaning found in his later work. This awareness of the politics of language, particularly as it affected the nuances of reported speech, is dis-

played at its most telling in Joyce's use of free indirect discourse, a narrative device, as we have seen, that brings language into contact with the clashing communicative idioms, or "idiolects," of a culture.[7]

Vernacular Form

Free indirect discourse, or the "Uncle Charles Principle" as it was famously tagged by Hugh Kenner in Joyce criticism,[8] is a mode of narration in which a character is described from the outside in the third person, but in a manner that catches the tonality of his or her voice from the inside: his or her thoughts, cultural idioms, or points of view. As Ida Klitgaard describes this signature or "initial" style of Joyce:

> In Joyce's works the characters almost always speak in individualised
> or even idiosyncratic ways, and the typically Joycean technique of
> the "initial style" is to have a third-person narrator borrow such a
> character's marked idiom. The traditional objectivity of the narrative
> voice of a prose novel is here suddenly blended with the subjectivity
> of fictional characters to such a degree that the reader is confused as
> to which viewpoint and which attitude belong to the narrator, the
> character and the author.[9]

In Irish literary history, it is not so much psychology — "subjectivity" — as the *cultural* codes of idiomatic speech and oral culture that break into the objective tone of third-person narration. Though free indirect discourse was characteristically used in modernism to register the psychological, inner world of a character, the regular recourse to colloquial idioms and elements of performance to signal its presence in Irish literature opens onto wider social vistas, as if a voice can only make its presence felt by means of the culture that speaks through it. Joyce's use of free indirect discourse was no doubt indebted to distinguished precursors such as Flaubert, but in its most distinctive form it is closer to the "shout in the street" that constitutes the vernacular modernism of *Ulysses*.

In "Eveline," the first story in *Dubliners* narrated in the third person, the description of the avenue where Eveline lives is "invaded" from the outset by her wistful voice, but at this early stage Joyce places the obvious colloquial word in italics:

> The children of the avenue used to play together in that field—the
> Devines, the Waters, the Dunns, little Keogh the cripple, she and
> her brothers and sisters. Ernest, however, never played: he was too
> grown up. Her father used often to hunt them in out of the field with

his blackthorn stick; but usually little Keogh used to keep *nix* and call
out when he saw her father coming. Still they seemed to have been
rather happy then. Her father was not so bad then; and besides, her
mother was alive. (*D* 29)

But as the narration proceeds, voices of other characters are filtered
through Evelyn's "reporting," as in the description of her troubled relationship with her father: "She always gave her entire wages—seven shillings—and Harry always sent up what he could but the trouble was to get
any money from her father. He said she used to squander the money, that
she had no head, that he wasn't going to give her his hard-earned money
to throw about the streets, and much more, for he was usually fairly bad
of a Saturday night" (*D* 31). The sensitivity to local idioms debasing
purity of diction is highlighted in "A Mother," when Mrs. Kearney's dis-
agreement with the organizers of the concert at which her daughter is to
sing in the Antient Concert Rooms betrays her barely disguised patronizing attitude toward Mr. Fitzpatrick's mispronunciation of "Cometty"
(*D* 139), rendered, as we have seen above, through Mrs. Kearney's re-
sentful inner speech. The fate of the bass tenor, Mr. Duggan, in the story
is also sealed when he betrays his lowly station through dialect and
breaches of etiquette:

> He sang his music with great feeling and volume and was warmly
> welcomed by the gallery; but, unfortunately, he marred the good im-
> pression by wiping his nose in his gloved hand once or twice out of
> thoughtlessness. He was unassuming and spoke little. He said *yous* so
> softly that it passed unnoticed and he never drank anything stronger
> than milk for his voice's sake. (*D* 140)

It may be that "yous" would have slipped by unnoticed, like Mr. Fitzpatrick's "Cometty," had not Mrs. Kearney's vigilant ear been in the business of policing the narration itself—and, of course, being exposed in
turn through the withering irony of the story. Viewed in this light, language in much nineteenth-century Irish fiction can be seen as a struggle
for legitimacy between vernacular idioms and dominant discourses intent on keeping colloquialisms in their place—whether quarantined in
dialogue, in italics, or through the isolating device of quotation marks.
As V. N. Volosinov notes of similar containment exercises in Russian fiction, in terms that could apply to Joyce's account of the interpreter in
the Maamtrasna trial, the use of quotation marks for "catchy" idioms
distanced the narrator from the more demotic voices that infiltrated the
narrative:

If these "catchy" terms are to be retained in indirect discourse, [it was important] at least to enclose them within quotation marks. If we were to read the resulting case of indirect discourse aloud, we would speak the expressions within quotation marks somewhat differently, as if to give notice through our intonation that they are taken from another person's speech and that we want to keep our distance.[10]

One of the most noticeable trends in Joycean criticism in recent decades has been a shift in focus from stream of consciousness as the central technique of Joyce's modernism to the more elusive narrative device of free indirect discourse. Stream of consciousness, or "interior monologue," carried with it the implication that subjectivity was at the center of Joyce's modernist project, an affirmation of the self that was acclaimed in Western liberal circles but drew criticism as a symptom of alienation or bourgeois individualism from the left. As late as Franco Moretti's *Modern Epic* (1996), stream of consciousness is still center stage, aligning Joyce squarely with modes of interiority attributed by commentators such as Georg Simmel to the metropolis.[11] Joyce, on this reading, is the very model of a modern European, with his Irishness featuring at most as past history, a nightmare from which the cosmopolitan hero is trying to awake. Yet, as several critics have cogently argued, as early as the "Aeolus" chapter in *Ulysses*, there is a parting of ways with subjectivity and a gradual opening out into more public, socially contested linguistic domains facilitated by free indirect discourse.[12] In this colloquy of voices, Joyce's stylistic innovations arise out of a deep, protracted engagement with the culture that produced him, a society that experienced seismic shifts not only in language but in the forms of life or habitats within which words acquire meaning.

In a revealing exchange during the early critical reception of *Ulysses*, the Irish critic Ernest Boyd took issue with Valery Larbaud's celebrated pronouncement that with Joyce's masterpiece, "Ireland is making a sensational re-entrance into high European literature."[13] Boyd's pique was understandable: as a leading figure of the Irish Revival, he perceived Larbaud as writing out the enormous contribution made by Yeats, Synge, and others to establishing Ireland's literary reputation on the world stage.[14] Boyd may also have been provoked by the implicit religious bias in Larbaud's association of Joyce with the achievements of pre-Reformation Irish Christianity, signaling, in effect, the demise of Anglo-Irish hegemony and the reemergence of Irish Catholicism (however deformed in Joyce's treatment) as a dominant cultural presence in Ireland.[15] The initial recognition of Joyce's genius in Ireland, Boyd was not slow to point out, derived not from his Catholic or Nationalist contemporaries but from Yeats, AE, Synge, and Moore—and, if somewhat belatedly, Boyd himself.[16] Boyd's aim was to rescue Joyce from his "prematurely cosmopolitan reputation," the prejudice that his standing in world literature was damaged by locating him in the formative context of the Irish Revival: "To the Irish mind no lack of appreciation of James Joyce is involved by some slight consideration for the facts of Ireland's literary and intellectual evolution, and the effort now being made to cut him off from this stream of which he is a tributary is singularly futile."[17]

Yet for all his insistence on reclaiming Joyce for Ireland, Boyd, in keeping with Yeats's prescriptions at the beginning of the Revival, sees this primarily in terms of content and Irish themes, not as a matter of *form*. As Boyd sees it, Joyce derived his technical innovations in *Dubliners* from French naturalism—an influence shared, as we shall see, with George Moore—and even the audacious experimentalism of *Ulysses* also had its provenance in "Jules Romains and the *Unanimistes*" and German expressionism: "With *Ulysses*, James Joyce has made a daring and valuable experiment, breaking new ground in English for the future development of prose narrative. But the 'European' interest of the work must of necessity be largely technical, *for the matter is as local as the form is universal.*"[18] In this formulation, it is possible to detect outlines of the "provincial cosmopolitanism" (in Boyd's own phrase) that was to dominate criticism for decades to come. Such Irishness as Joyce's work possesses is primarily of local interest and operates solely at the level of subject matter; the source of Joyce's true modernist innovations at the level of form and style lies elsewhere.

It was in fact Larbaud who contested these limitations, portraying Joyce's achievement (in his careful wording) as Ireland's *reentry* into Europe and the world at large, not as a debut on the world stage. On this reading, Joyce's modernism did not emerge fully formed in exile but drew considerably on forces that were latent in Irish culture, waiting their moment of articulation. For recent commentators such as Anne Chevalier, this challenge to the metropolitan basis of modernism is but another distortion on Larbaud's part: "One constantly notes a systematic distortion [in Larbaud]: cosmopolitanism springs up on every occasion—long before the author [Joyce] physically goes away to Paris, Zurich, Trieste and Rome, determining influences, right in Ireland, breathe internationalism."[19] That Ireland could have been the smithy in which Joyce forged some of the key innovations of modernism is beyond the comprehension of Boyd and Chevalier—a perception, it might be added, that prevailed in much early Joyce criticism but has been challenged by critics inside and outside Ireland in recent decades. To be sure, Ireland provided no shortage of raw material in the eyes of early critics, but these restraints were viewed as nets that held Joyce back, rather than braids of the "strandentwining cable[s]" (*U* 3.37) that connected his work to modernism. For Fritz Senn, by contrast, these links were already apparent in "the complex and allusive style" of Joyce's earliest published prose, placing it on a continuum with "the later convoluted intricacies of *Ulysses* and *Finnegans Wake*." It was this that led Hugh Kenner to "concede the baffling fact that Joyce was a potential modernist before he left his native city at 22": "He had commenced to write about his [modernist] subject while in Dublin. He took it with him into exile and continued to write about it. His devices, as they accreted by expressive necessity, gathered themselves around it."[20] It is not, therefore, that Ireland was outside the modern: rather, its imbrication in the modern from the outset, like that of other colonial dependencies, helped to secure the cosmopolitan reach of the metropolis within the "differential" spaces of the world system.[21]

If the technique of stream of consciousness is accorded pride of place in Joyce's formal innovations, then there indeed is a case for arguing that his modernism emerges on the European mainland—though, as we shall see, variants of interior monologue were already evident in Ireland through George Moore's experiments in the early 1880s, which predated the more celebrated use by Édouard Dujardin in 1886 and 1887.[22] But if the more socially attuned device of free indirect discourse is also given due recognition as a source of Joyce's stylistic breakthroughs, then the linguistic ferment of nineteenth-century Irish literature also contributed to the innovations that Joyce distilled into modernist form. It is almost a commonplace in criticism to attribute the truncated development of the nineteenth-century novel in Ireland to its endless, if not futile, search for *form*: "The history of the Irish novel," wrote Thomas Flanagan, "is one of continuous attempts the represent the Irish experience within conventions that were not innately congenial to it. . . . The best of them, which seek to move beyond these forms, make their strongest points and exist most vividly through indirection, symbol, allusion, and subtle shifts in point of view."[23] Not least of the conventions prompting "subtle shifts in point of view" was mastery of Standard English, the precondition of narrative authority in mainstream English fiction. In the hands of early nineteenth-century novelists such as John and Michael Banim, Gerald Griffin, or William Carleton, narrative command of Standard English was stilted and wooden, lacking the assurance of writers such as Jane Austen for whom English was a native tongue, steeped in centuries of tradition.[24] As Wolfgang Zach states:

> A greatly inhibiting factor in this was, of course, that most of the [Irish] authors still wrote with the English market in mind. Thus we

find, for example, that Irish novelists usually shrink from speaking in a recognizable "Irish" voice in the authorial parts of their books, opting rather for a "genteel" English narrator, while experimenting with various techniques to represent the language of Irish peasants in their dialogues.[25]

Standard English for Irish writers functioned, in Jacques Derrida's terms, as an "other" rather than a "mother" tongue,[26] and its use was something to be explained rather than taken for granted, like the fine diction assumed by the servant Nelly in *Wuthering Heights*. That dialogue rather than third-person narration was the natural condition of Irish fiction is clearly evident in Gerald Griffin, who, as his brother relates, tended to write the story in dialogue first before struggling to raise it to the condition of impersonal, third-person narration: "He used to point out the best novels as containing a large proportion of dialogue, and requiring very little aid from narrative, and the most impressive scenes in them as highly dramatic in character."[27] The incongruity of deploying elegant diction or a matter-of-fact tone to describe the scenes of violence, horror, or superstition with which Irish fiction abounded was soon apparent, and as the century progressed (or regressed), it was as if, bearing out Carlyle's worst fears of Celtic contamination, the King's English itself gradually became infected by the idioms of Irish lowlife. As David Gilligan observes, even at an early stage the novels of the Banim brothers became a force field of clashing linguistic registers, in which "the language of dialogue of low life, of field, street, and tavern is often set in a subversive relationship to this high literary style and parodies it":

> In novels such as *The Boyne Water* low life characters such as Rory na Chopple, in all probability a South Armagh horse thief, emerge to plague the formal tone and structure of the book. The Banims seek to control and censor this peasant voice which intrudes upon their sense of Victorian rectitude and an awareness of the English reading public. The other voice can be sublime or crude in its expressions [as when Rory, in despair at the Battle of the Boyne, laments,] "'Mostha, aye, Shamus-a . . .' using a vulgar, cruel and unmerited Irish expletive, recollected to this day but rather unsuited to our pages, 'Shamus-a . . . is gone sure enough.'"[28]

Aware of the capacity of "the humourous jargon of the lower classes of Irish" to unmask pretensions to propriety in the Banims' grim tale "Crohoore of the Billhook" (1826), a contemporary reviewer in the *Edinburgh Review* advised: "Should the reader be deterred by the interspersion of

Irish and phrases not at least English through the dialogue, let him turn to the tale of John Doe, where he will meet with less of these interruptions a story to our taste far more interesting."[29]

The dilemma facing Irish fiction was that when first-person narration is given the vernacular voice, as in Maria Edgeworth's *Castle Rackrent* (1800), it forgoes all claims to reliability; when, on the other hand, narration secures the authority of Standard English, it has already crossed over to the other side — sometimes in the overt persona of informer, as in William Carleton's "Wild Goose Lodge" (1830) or *Rody the Rover; or, The Ribbonman* (1845), where diction itself amounts to apostasy. The moderate tone of Standard English curbed local enthusiasms in the regional novels of Walter Scott, establishing the narrative middle — or higher — ground that purported to resolve internecine conflict: by contrast, as James Cahalan has observed, "the Irish hero more often moves beyond an initial moderation and passivity into partisanship. . . . [I]nstead of moving from one side to the middle, the Irish hero generally moves from the middle to the nationalist side" — for better or worse.[30] The protracted struggle to devise innovations in form appropriate to the turbulence of Irish culture was the task facing the novel, and it is in this sense that "the introduction without warning of snatches of conversation, of prolonged dialogue," into the narration, which Ernest Boyd takes as central to Joyce's technique, was the disruptive condition of nineteenth-century Irish fiction itself, providing unstable precursors of Joyce's breakthroughs into form.[31] There is no doubt that, as D. A. Miller contends, free indirect discourse was often deployed in the nineteenth-century novel to reaffirm the monological authority of the master narrative, mimicking idiomatic voices of characters all the more to put them back in their places.[32] But as Brian McHale emphasizes, "no one who has investigated the FID [free indirect discourse] phenomenon could fail to be astonished at [any] reduction of it to an unequivocal instrument of monologism" — particularly, it might be added, in a postcolonial context. On this reading, the dominant narration "does not subvert the characters' authority in order to secure its own, but the other way around, secures the characters' authority at the risk of subverting its own":

> FID, far from securing monologic authority, can introduce local turbulence into textual monologism. Problematic and equivocal, so elusive that we are sometimes unable to say for certain that it is even present in a given instance, let alone specify its function, FID can increase the centrifugal force of the text, its tendency to fly apart in multiple voices or traces of voice, even in the face of the centripetal authority of the nineteenth-century novelistic narrator.[33]

Vernacular Idioms and Free Indirect Discourse

Wild primates not stop him frem at rearing a writing in handy antics.
JAMES JOYCE (*FW* 229.1–2)

Maria Edgeworth's pioneering *Castle Rackrent* is widely acclaimed as the first attempt to compose a novel in dialect, a descent into the lower register of Hiberno-English justified by the first-person narration of the old retainer, Thady Quirk. Dialogue becomes, as it were, the condition of narration itself, but as we have noted, deviation from Standard English comes at a cost: the chronic unreliability of the narrator, and the danger of constant incomprehension by the English reader (at whom the novel was primarily addressed). Damage limitation in *Castle Rackrent* required a more authoritative narrative scaffolding thrown around the novel in the form of explanatory footnotes, translated idioms, and—when all else was lost—a "Glossary" and commentary at the end. The disparity in levels of authority is responsible for the much commented-on irony of the novel, the introduction of marginalized or vernacular voices invariably bringing a patronizing or condescending tone toward the upstart or lowlife characters who insinuate themselves into narrative authority. In a notable ethnographic shift, irony in the novels of Edgeworth's contemporary Sydney Owenson tended to be directed *at the outsider*—the visiting Englishman, the uninitiated traveler, the returned exile—who is not *au fait* with the inside story, the occluded culture of the native inhabitants. The Standard English of Owenson's narrative voice is interspersed with French and Latin tags (hallmarks of sophistication) but also with local idioms, flagged, as Volosinov noted, through the use of italics or inverted commas. The spare eloquence in Owenson's *Patriotic Sketches* (1807) of an old woman complaining about the high rate of rent for her miserable cabin attests to the collision of two languages in the one charged voice:

> "Surely it is too much to pay for *a shed to break one's heart under!*" So energetic, so expressive is the Irish language, that those of the lower order, who borrow the idiom of their English from that of their native tongue, frequently say more in a single sentence than volumes could express.[34]

As the sympathy of impersonal narration extends to a character, particularly in a Gaelic context, it picks up the resonances of the voice. In Owenson's (by then Lady Morgan) *The O'Briens and the O'Flahertys* (1827), the protagonist Murrogh O'Brien is greatly moved reading an ancient manuscript containing the annals of his Gaelic past: "It had touched a nerve in his heart, which vibrated painfully to the impression. Twice he had passed his hand across his humid eyes, and pshaw'd and pished away his womanish sensibility"; likewise, when a description of Galway mentions two society gossips stationed permanently at a window, the narration drops inverted commas as it catches their idioms: "No little voteen picked her way to mass in the morning or mall in the evening; no drydum was given by the dowagers of one sex, nor jorum of punch by the dowagers of the other; not a pair of Connemara stockings was sold in the Four-ways, nor a basket of fish disposed of in the Cladagh, to the cadgers of Galway and Tuam, without their knowledge and commentary."[35]

The opening sentence of the Banim brothers' *The Bit o'Writin'* (1865) addresses the problem of vernacular idioms, leading to several pages of exposition before the story even starts: "On a fine morning in the month of May, Murty Meehan was occupied 'threnching his little pee-aties.'"[36] Glossing the meaning of "threnching his little pee-aties" to signify both Murty's meager claim to his produce and its status as a term of endearment, the narration digresses: "The French people would understand the term, in the double sense mentioned, better than the English. But to a portion of the rather unfigurative community for whose edification we write, it seems incumbent to explain why Murty Meehan applied to his fine sprouting plot of potatoes the epithet 'little.'"[37] Explanatory material of the kind hitherto confined to footnotes intrudes into the main narrative, leading to an aside of almost eight pages: the implication here is that any idiomatic term may contain such concentrated subtexts, as if discordant voices introduce other "volumes" and multiple narratives, derailing the linear progression of the tale.

As vernacular energies gathered political momentum through the protracted Land Wars of the nineteenth century, the idiomatic voice slipped through the nets of dialogue and other modes of containment (italics, quotation marks) to usurp passages in the descriptive narration itself, bearing witness to the increased capacity of a culture to control its own enunciation. In Charles Kickham's *Knocknagow* (1877), the colorful language of the locals is, for the most part, subordinated to the Standard English of the master narrative, but at certain moments when strong peasant characters assert their presence, the narrative exposition takes on (often understated) vernacular inflections. When the hero of the novel, Mat Donovan ("Mat the Thrasher") is taken to task over working (or not working) on the Sabbath, local speech patterns are recapitulated in the narration: "'Wisha, Mat,' she continued, 'how long you're about makin' thim couple uv brooms.' . . . Mat Donovan, we are bound to confess, would not have thought it a mortal sin *to cut the makings* of a broom on the Sabbath" (italics added).[38] When another local, Phil Lahy, is introduced, it is on similar idiomatic terms:

> Billy Heffernan, on reaching his own door, was about bidding his companion good-night, when it occurred to him that Phil might take it into his head to pay a visit to Jack Delany's forge. . . . Phil Lahy had the look of a martyr who was slaving from year's end to year's end to keep a roof over the heads of his wife and children. . . . At certain seasons, too, he was wont to take sudden fits of industry, which usually lasted half an hour at a time, and evinced themselves in "digging the haggart"; and 'twas wonderful how often the handle of the spade would get loose. (*K* 160–62)

The vernacular phrase signaled in "digging the haggart" could be extended to many of the other buried colloquialisms in the description: "might take it into his head"; "look of a martyr who was slaving from year's end to year's end"; "wont to take sudden fits of industry," not to mention the "'twas wonderful" at the end. The manner in which vestiges of dialogue seeped into the narration can be partly attributed to the indeterminacies of the voice itself, which oscillate, as Emer Nolan has pointed out, between objective third-party narration aimed at strangers—the more authoritative mode throughout—and a more oral-based "we" addressed to a seemingly familiar audience and implicated in the action.[39] When Mat Donovan sings a sentimental English ballad, the narrative speculates on the various reasons for such an inappropriate choice, and notes that the priest, Father Hannigan, mistakenly believes it is an Irish song:

> For some reason or all of these reasons, or for some reason unknown to *us*, this song, as *we* have said, was popular in a high degree. . . . And Mat the Thrasher's song *reminds us* that at the very last wedding *we* had the honour of being invited to in the neighbourhood of Knocknagow. . . . [W]hen *we*, at the suggestion of the bride's father, went to escort Father Hannigan back to his place at the mahogany table . . . he laid his hand impressively on *our* shoulder and said in a whisper: "That's a fine thing!" "Why, that," we replied, "is the *English* sentimental song—'Oh no, we never mention her.'" . . . So the music as well as the words of this much abused lyric has been a puzzle to *us*. (*K* 156–57, italics added)

It is not made clear who "us" and "we" refer to in the midst of what is otherwise an impassive, third-person narration, other than to suggest the momentary control of the narrative by the lowly rural subjects normally confined to dialogue, as is clear in a later marriage sequence. When the local beauty, Bessy Morris, dressed in a white jacket, catches the eye of Mat Donovan and others during Ned Brophy's wedding festivities, it is not to everyone's satisfaction, particularly a stout young lady with yellow kid gloves: "This young lady regarded Bessy with *sulky looks* because a certain young man from the mountain *would keep gadding after* the white jacket, though the yellow-gloved hand and four hundred pounds were at *his service for the asking*" (italics added). When the narration turns to the bride, Mrs. Ned Brophy, it is to highlight that she was also the subject of many advances from prospective suitors:

> Matches innumerable had been proposed and rejected, and "made" and "broke off" for one reason or another, in her case; which gave her very little concern, as she knew there was wherewithal in the old saucepan to secure her a husband—or rather "a nice place"—sooner or later. (*K* 236–37)

"Made," "broke off," and "a nice place" are marked as reported speech, but "wherewithal in the old saucepan," borrowed from an earlier idiomatic exchange, eases itself into the narrative without being reported as such.

Free indirect discourse was used by Jane Austen, Gustave Flaubert, Henry James, and others to ventriloquize the inner thoughts of characters, and thus operated primarily at a psychological level: by contrast, in *Ulysses*, as Gerald Bruns notes, this technique is "situated less in a specific consciousness (the narrator's, Bloom's) than in the already given world of worn expressions which serves as the narrator's lexicon. That is to say, in effect, that the narrator exists as a mind fabricated out of other minds."[40] This lexicon draws on the tendency in the nineteenth-century Irish novel to use what Russian linguists referred to as *skaz*, the disruption or appropriation of narrative authority by colloquially inflected speech.[41] For Boris Eichenbaum, the association of *skaz* with storytelling, as in the fiction of Nikolai Gogol, Nikolai Leskov, and others, linked it to the folktale but also implied a performative use of language based on "aural" properties: improvisation, intonation, gestures, mime, accent. It was the challenge of transposing these extratextual effects into written form, the "phonetic projection" of the voice onto the page, that prompted many of the experimental techniques in the vernacular modernism that emerged in the European peripheries of Ireland and Russia. Though formalist critics such as Eichenbaum tried to identify specific linguistic markers, internal to the text, to signify the presence of such

effects, interpretation in the last resort, as Brian McHale notes above, depends on factors "outside" the work.[42] A text employing *skaz* is more like
a musical score, which depends for its realization on those sufficiently
attuned to its resonances, and hence for all its objective literary properties, "the factor of utterance, of the artistic-vocal performance, as it
were, deforms the objective nature of a literary work in its own peculiar and individual way."[43] To some extent, this is stating the obvious:
understanding the "Cyclops" chapter of *Ulysses*, for example, is greatly
enhanced when it is performed in a Dublin accent, or, even more specifically, the inner-city Coombe accent that Joyce himself relished. For Pier
Paulo Pasolini (as described by Gilles Deleuze), "the richer a language is
in dialects, the more it allows free indirect discourse to flourish, or rather
instead of establishing itself on an 'average level' it is differentiated into
'low language and high language.'"[44]

   What is important to grasp is that this does not undermine the universality of the work, for it is precisely by means of free indirect discourse
that the local finds expression in the wider world, and the nuances of the
utterance are relayed in textual form. It is for this reason that I. R. Titunik
equates *skaz* not just with orality or residual idioms themselves but also
with the operation of this technique at one remove, the transformation
of dialogue into narration, and reported into *reporting* speech.[45] That the
same problem arises of recognizing its existence—there are no objective
markers for identifying irony, submerged voices, or shifts in point of view
in free indirect discourse—does not take away from its central role in
bringing voices in from the periphery to furnish new vernacular modern-
isms.[46] As John Paul Riquelme writes of Joyce, in terms that could apply
to Joyce's account of the Maamtrasna trial:

> The ambiguous merger of voices makes it difficult, even impossible,
> for the reader to distinguish between the cunningly combined voices
> of character and narrator. Because the technique requires the reader
> to translate third person into first and to attempt discriminations,
> however difficult, between the merged voices, it necessitates the
> reader's active recreative rendering of the narration. The reader per-
> forms the text of narrated monologue with a special kind of involve-
> ment because of the device's unusual nature.[47]

   The manner in which direct speech dissolves into indirect discourse,
leaving it unclear whether such a transition even takes place, is evident
in a passage from Emily Lawless's *Grania* (1886), dealing with the life of
a young spirited woman on the Aran Islands. At a climactic moment in
the novel, the romantic yearnings of the eponymous heroine, Grania, at

last find expression when her insensitive lover, Murdough, places his arm around her on a boat trip and they kiss for the first time. While Grania is lost in romantic reveries, the less than enamored Murdough indulges in pipe dreams of his own—a fanciful scheme to use his seafaring skills as a pilot to make money, narrated in a faltering free indirect discourse:

> Profiting by the cessation of his labours, Murdough presently pulled out his pipe, lit it—though not by the phosphorescence—sucked at it for a few minutes, and, thus refreshed, embarked upon a new disquisition upon the great advantages to be gained by being a pilot. Yes indeed, it was himself ought to have been one, so he ought; and if he had been a pilot, it is the best pilot upon the three islands he would have been—by God! yes—the very best! It was out beside the Brannock rocks—the farthest rocks of all—he would have stopped mostly, and stopped, and stopped, and stopped, no matter what storm might be blowing at the time, and waited until a ship came. And the very minute a ship came in sight—a real big ship, that is, from the East Indies, or, maybe, America, or, better still, California— then he would have rowed out to her all by himself. He would not have taken anyone with him, no, for he did not want to be sharing his money with anyone, but he would have rowed and rowed, out and out, till he got into the middle of the big Old Sea.[48]

There, he muses, he would more or less cajole the captains of the "big ships" into paying him handsomely to act as a guide through the treacherous waters:

> And he would have said that he did [know the waters], and no man better, nor so well, not on all the islands, nor on the Continent, nor in Dublin itself—"And if you do not want me, and if you will not pay me my full big price, it is not I that will go with you, no, not one half foot of me. And if I do not go with you, it is in upon the rocks you will go this night, my fine captain, you and all your poor men— yes, indeed, upon the rocks this night and be drowned every one of you—for there is no other man on Inisheer, no, nor on any of the islands, that dare bring you into Galway upon such a night, only myself alone." (G 225)

The narrative transitions in the first passage are apparent when the third person narration ("Profiting by the cessation of his labours . . .") shifts, almost imperceptibly, into what appears to be interior monologue ("Yes, indeed, it was himself ought to have been one . . ."), but then breaks into the actual speech of the second passage quoted ("'And if you do not want me . . .'"). The transformation into overt speech is, in fact, misleading, for he has been speaking all along, literally thinking out loud—except he is so engrossed in his musings, and Grania in the rapture of their first kiss, that she does not hear a word of what he says: "Grania, however, never uttered word or syllable. She hardly looked at him, could not have told afterwards what he had been talking about, or what had passed them by. They took to their oars again after half an hour, and rowed slowly home-ward, past the western extremity of the smaller island" (G 226).

In a story contemporary with *Knocknagow*, May Laffan's "The Game Hen" (1879), this kind of narrative double-voicing is transferred to the city, to Commons-lane, a slum district of Dublin. Private life hardly exists in Commons-lane, in keeping with its rural counterpart, as "life is conducted mainly out of doors, and everything seems in a way pub-lic property."[49] Past secrets are hard to conceal, and when a new woman, Honor Walsh, with a small child and a baby, moves into the lane, her neighbors Mrs. Dowling and Mrs. Carmody are determined to figure out where she comes from. The narrative for the most part is in Standard English, but as the story unfolds, it opens up to different voices like the gossip of the community itself.

> Mrs Dowling, on seeing that the newcomer was burdened with a new baby, came forward and offered to relieve her of it, while she made some preparation for passing the night. *She could not well refuse, and then came the inevitable questions: Her husband? Yes; he was a sailor, gone on a long voyage; she did not know when he would be home.* (FTC 114, italics added)

"She could not well refuse" seems to articulate Mrs. Dowling's thoughts, but the next lines—"and then came the inevitable questions: Her hus-band? Yes; he was a sailor, gone on a long voyage; she did not know when he would be home"—ventriloquize Honor Walsh's inner life, as if the narrative voice changes midsentence. Like private and public life in the lane, inner and outer speech, as well as different voices, cross-cut each other. When a character from a house of ill fame at the corner of the street, Peggy, is recognized by Honor as someone from her hidden past, the detachment of the third-person narrative is also unsettled as Honor disavows all knowledge to her inquisitive neighbors:

> She turned away abruptly towards her own door, trembling from head to foot, her colour coming and going at every word. "No; only she reminds me—I don't know her. I never saw her before." She

barely waited to finish her answer, and heedless of their entreaties, beat a hasty retreat into her cabin. . . . Mary Kennedy; it was none other. Mary Kennedy herself! The unfortunate woman she had heard spoken of as Peggy. Good God! Could it be true; William Kennedy's sister here! It was useless to try to hide herself. Here she thought she might have been safe; it was the far side of Dublin from where the country people resorted . . . and yet this was the sister of the only man who—. She looked wildly around her as if her own thoughts were a source of additional terror. (*FTC* 117–18)

Here the "neutral" narration is intercepted, midsentence, by Honor's own voice as she struggles with the shock of recognizing the sister of the man (William Kennedy) who betrayed her. Her mental life appears to assail her from the outside, becoming an "additional terror" forcing her to look "wildly around her." It is striking that the scene in question represents an intrusion of the countryside into city, as if modernist techniques are precipitated by the visitations of a dark rural past on the present. When Honor regains her composure, her voice is still not confined to dialogue but remains lodged in the narrative: "[S]he was self-possessed, and ready with her answers. She had made a mistake: the girl's face was so like someone she knew; never saw her before in her life" (*FTC* 119)." "Never saw her before in her life" is a barely disguised report of direct speech ("Never saw her before in *my* life!"). When one of the neighboring women, Mrs. Carmody, attempts to explain who "Peggy" is, the narrative again seems to pick up Honor's (or another local) voice:

> "Ye know she's wan of them charackters lives in the big old house in the corner, an' a shame an' disgrace to the place it is." This was from Mrs Carmody, a *very dragon* of censoriousness, and who was only half-satisfied with Mrs Walsh's disclaimer. A curious feeling seized Honor Walsh, and kept her silent for a moment. . . . Who was she [Honor herself, with her secret past] to cast a stone at her? If they only knew! (*FTC* 120, italics added)

Dialectical Modernism

In Lawless's and Laffan's fictions, the layering of voices and deletion of quotation marks around dialogue prefigure the advanced fictional techniques of George Moore. As Ernest Boyd noted, it is in the fiction of Moore that the intersection of French naturalism and Flaubertian techniques with Irish idioms takes a distinctive turn through a shift from tentative interior monologue to free indirect vernacular discourse.[50] In Moore's experimental novella "Mildred Lawson" (1888), the first story in his book *Celibates* (1895), the young eponymous socialite rejects a staid bourgeois life in England and a doomed relationship with a sickly English artist, Ralph Hoskin, to take up painting and a bohemian life in France. Moore's prose renders Mildred's inner life through a succession of random, impressionistic thoughts that remain inchoate, as in her confused responses to Ralph's declaration that he would kill himself out of love for her: was she appalled or was she secretly flattered by his suggestion? In this early version of stream of consciousness, it is already possible to identify an issue central to modernist explorations of subjectivity: which thoughts register the "real" self, as against those that simply pass through consciousness but are "out of character"? For the most part, however, Mildred's inner life is rendered in free indirect discourse, in third-party narration colored by her own turns of phrase. It is as if, like Gabriel Conroy in "The Dead," she has to look from the outside — as in a mirror — to see herself at all:

> Mechanically, as if in a dream, she opened a bandbox and put her hat away. She smoothed her soft hair before the glass. Her appearance pleased her and she wondered if she were worth a man's life. *She was a dainty morsel, no doubt*, so dainty that life was unendurable without her. But she was wronging herself, she did not wish him to kill himself.[51]

It may have been precisely these intonations of voice that attracted James Joyce to Moore's novella at a moment when he was on the verge of his own innovations in narrative style. In December 1904, Joyce wrote to his brother Stanislaus that he was "setting about (with the aid of the Director Francini) the translation into Italian of 'Celibates' for a big publisher in Florence."[52] Joyce was working on *Stephen Hero*, and in the next letter wrote to his brother to send him the last of three stories he had published in the *Irish Homestead*:[53]

> Please send me the "Irish Homestead" containing my story and the Xmas no. At the end of the week I send you Chaps XII. XIII. XIV. I am now at Chap XV. And have begun the Italian version of "Mildred Lawson." I wish you to write at once about these chapters.[54]

The issue of the *Irish Homestead* requested contained the story "After the Race," a story Joyce did not consider entirely successful for reasons that may have had to do with its lack of a suitably modulated narrative voice, inflected by dialogue.[55] The lack of dialogue in Joyce's own life was beginning to take its toll, and he urged Stanislaus to write more often: "I expect you to write to me much oftener than you do. You know I have no one to talk to. Nora, of course, doesn't care a rambling damn about art. When she read 'Mildred Lawson' she said Moore did not know how to finish a story."[56]

In "Mildred Lawson," free indirect discourse often assumes an ironic tone in which a character's subjective states or words are turned against him or herself, but in other stories of Moore's, the device attests less to the superiority of the omniscient narrator over a character's flawed vision, as in Austen or Flaubert, than to uncertainties that leave the reader also in the dark. In "A Faithful Heart" (1892), the respectable Major Shepherd leads a double life through his secret marriage to a woman below his station who has borne his child, but when it transpires that his sisters may know of his clandestine life, the idioms in his own voice come through as he "turned on his heel and left the house":

> As he walked towards Branbury he asked himself if it were possible they knew anything about Charlotte Street [where his secret wife lived]; and as he approached the town he looked about nervously fearing *lest some friend might pop down on him*, and after some hesitation, decided to take a long detour so as to avoid passing by the house of some people he knew.[57]

At this early point in the story, the reader does not know his secret, but when it is revealed, the distress induced by his paltry contribution to his wife's upkeep, a mere three pounds per week, is captured by the plaintive tones of her voice in the otherwise impersonal narration: "By strict economy, however, Mrs Shepherd managed to *make two ends meet*. . . . Hers was a kind-hearted simple nature, that misfortune had brought *down in the world*' (*IMK* 133, italics added).[58]

It is in Moore's Irish stories that the colloquial turn in free indirect discourse acquires a new importance, the voice of culture and history, rather than that of omniscient narration, putting subjectivity in its place. In the story "The Voice of the Mountain" (1904), the main character, Dan Coogan, takes to the woods of the Hill of Howth at night to find his voice: "There was a wistfulness in the distance, and it seemed to steal into his heart, and to draw him out of himself, out of the self he had known always, into another self, a second self" (*IMK* 182). Under this persona he walks further into the woods, and when he encounters a "Druid Stone," or dolmen, a great boulder resting on four upright stones, the vernacular further impinges on the narration:

He had heard this stone had been an altar and that the Druids came there to worship the sun, but he had not listened to these stories, *they had gone in one ear and out through the other* as wind goes through a crack in the door. But now these stories were *like music in his ears* and the earth he had cared for only to plant potatoes in and that he had thought good for nothing else . . . seemed to whisper everything he needed to know [of the terrors of Irish history]; the blood that had been shed seemed his blood; the wrongs that had been done seemed his wrongs, and he learned all these things through that night on the hill. (*IMK* 182–83, italics added)

What passes before his mind's eye is an unfolding of the Irish past, as if history itself has entered inner life: the time of the Druids, the Danes and Brian Boru's driving them out of Ireland, the Norman invasion at the behest of a traitor, the Siege of Limerick and the flight of the Wild Geese: "When the dawn began the outlines of the coast seemed to enclose his life, and the mountain seemed to whisper a message, and in their message were the names of Emmet, Wolfe Tone, Mitchell [*sic*] and Stephens" (*IMK* 182) — an interaction with the past not unlike Stephen Dedalus's vision of history on Sandymount strand in the "Proteus" chapter in *Ulysses* (*U* 3.300–309).[59] Dan's peculiar behavior of taking to the woods and neglecting the farm he is due to inherit endangers his prospects of marriage, but he pleads with Mary, his intended, that there are voices addressing him, and not just from the national past: "Someone is calling me. Mary, I cannot help myself. It is as if someone is calling me from beyond the sea" (*IMK* 185). This is taken to mean the lure of emigration, and Mary resigns herself to travel abroad to America — or perhaps even Australia or New Zealand, which are also discussed. It is when he states that Africa is calling him that even his mother begins to have doubts:

"Was it a fairy," said his mother, "that told you to go to Africa last night when you were at the top of the hill?"

"No, mother, I saw no fairy; and you may think me mad if you like and Mary may think me mad if she likes."

He turned to go out the door, but Mary stopped him.

"I don't think you mad. I will go to Africa with you if you think better of Africa than America."

He looked at her tenderly, like one who appreciates a sacrifice and is not able to accept it. (*IMK* 186)

But it turns out that Mary will not be accompanying him, for at that moment "a footstep was heard on the door and the priest came in with a paper in his hand. 'There's war in Africa,' he said, 'or there will soon be. The Boers have broken out, and they say they are going to drive the English into the sea'" (*IMK* 186). The voices from the distant past have merged with a distant call from beyond the sea, or even the future. When Dan joins the Boers' war effort, Mary reassures herself that she need "not look in the newspapers for news of Dan": "She knew that she would be the first to have news if anything were to happen to him. She knew that she would see him in the hillside" (*IMK* 187).

It is the breaking of the idiomatic "in one ear and out through the other" (*IMK* 182) into the already tentative third-person narration that opens Dan's inner life to the stories of the past and distant places, including the most important one: the memory of the Wild Geese, the Irish who went abroad to fight the British on foreign fields. In Moore's landmark Irish story collection, *The Untilled Field* (1903), the soundings of the vernacular voice are no less pronounced, emphasizing Bakhtin's description of *skaz* as constituting not simply a character's voice but "a voice socially distinct, carrying with it precisely those points of view and evaluations necessary to the storyteller": "What is introduced here, in fact, is a storyteller, and a storyteller, after all, is not a literary person; he belongs in most cases to the lower social strata, to the common people (precisely this is important to the author) — and he brings with him oral speech."[60] The opening sentence of the first story in *The Untilled Field* signals this colloquial turn with a light touch: "Pat Phelan's pigs were ready for Castlebar market, but so were his bullocks, and *he was of a mind* to send his son James with the bullocks to Westport fair where they *would fetch* a higher price. But James was *set on* staying at home to help Catherine with the churning, and his son Pat was *a bad hand* at a bargain" (italics added).[61] In the second story, "Home Sickness," the emigrant James Bryden returns to Ireland to marry a local woman and make a success of his homecoming: "He was going with his father-in-law to a fair. His father-in-law was *learning him* how to buy and sell cattle. And his father-in-law was saying that the country *was mending*, and that a man might become rich in Ireland *if he only had a little capital*" (*UF* 31, italics added). As if under pressure from these idioms, localisms are sometimes overtly flagged as they veer toward cliché — "The printer's ink was hardly dry, as the phrase runs, when other paragraphs had appeared saying that Father McCabe was considering still another journey to America" (*UF* 195). For the most part, however, the colloquial inflections are no less pronounced for being almost imperceptible: Father McCabe "fell to thinking how much money he would need to go away *on the sly*" ("Fugitives," *UF* 196, italics added). The story "The Wedding Feast" begins almost in midflight: "And everywhere Kate [Kavanagh] went her gown was being talked about—the gown she was to be married in, a grey silk that had been bought at a rummage sale. *They were all at her*" (*UF* 59, italics added). Later, the narrative relates of another character: "Alert as a bee she sprang from her chair, for she was thinking of the work that was waiting for her as soon as she could rid herself of that *bothering old slut Mary*, who'd just as lief sit here all the morning talking of the Kavanaghs" (*UF* 61, italics added).

In her valuable introduction to the Oxford edition of *A Portrait of the Artist as a Young Man*, Jeri Johnson writes: "'The Uncle Charles Principle' writ large is the stylistic principle of *Portrait*. The lexicon, the sentence structure, the diction, follow those of the protagonist, the artist of the title . . . but by retaining the third-person narrative, Joyce displaces the potentially stifling narcissistic egoism that such proximity might produce":

> Character here exists at the intersection between interiority and exteriority, between the idiolect of the character (that private interior language of individualism) and the third-person narrative (that exterior frame itself significant of the ostensible objectivity of the outer world), neither wholly private, nor entirely public.[62]

The displacement of egoism and the individual is not produced solely by the "objectivity of the outer world" but also by the *cultural* idiolects that infuse both subjective and objective worlds with the "dialect of the tribe" of early twentieth-century Dublin. As Frank Budgen remarked, "it is not by way of description that Dublin is created in *Ulysses*"; instead it is cast through the accented eye of its characters, and Dublin "must grow upon us not through our eye and memory, but through the minds of the Dubliners we overhear talking to each other."[63] For Fredric Jameson, it is the "'peculiarity' of Joyce's narrative content" that "determines a certain number of formal results": "[E]ncounters in Joyce are already (or perhaps I should say, still) linguistic: they are stories, gossip, they have already been assimilated into speech and story telling while taking place, so that . . . the need to invent a new speech in order to render the freshly revealed, non-linguistic contingencies of modern life" is "short-circuited" in Joyce.[64] The use of quotation marks—"perverted commas," as Joyce called them (*JJL* III, 99)—to circumscribe dialect or dialogue is dispensed with so that all the text is, in effect, in quotation marks, even the seemingly neutral prose of Standard English. Whereas the concept of *skaz* is oriented "towards the idiosyncrasies of oral speech, preferably in dialect,"[65] in Joyce's hands, it is Standard English itself that is regional and idiosyncratic, as is evident in the *reductio ad absurdum* of the "Ithaca" chapter in *Ulysses*, whose legal/scientific literalism is no more to be taken at face value than the poker face that goes with it.[66]

As if bearing in mind Derrida's injunction to deploy an "other" rather than a "mother" tongue, Joyce "others" Standard English itself, wresting it from the great tradition of the English novel over which it presided as a mother tongue. Jonathan Rée has usefully compared the forms of life in a speech community to a linguistic commons, subject to various acts of enclosure by disparate groups and speakers,[67] and in this light, Joyce's practice, in keeping with his family background, can be seen as a mode of linguistic Whiteboyism, resisting enclosures of language, whether by dominant groups or egotistical subjects.[68] As Mikhail Bakhtin wrote in a related context:

> Language is not a neutral medium that passes freely and easily into the private property of the speaker's intentions; it is populated— overpopulated—with the intentions of others. Expropriating it, forcing it to submit to one's own intonation and accents, is a difficult and complicated process.[69]

One of the consequences of Joyce's mastery of free indirect discourse is to realign it as a literary device from the subjective/objective (psychological) axis on which it conventionally turned toward the politics of language in colonial Ireland. Though the "free" aspect of the technique may be interpreted as imparting a new freedom to the vernacular voice, there is nothing inherently emancipatory in the deployment of the device: as finessed by Flaubert and others, it was often used to put down marginal or dissident voices, giving them a hearing all the more to highlight their inadequacies or shortcomings.[70] In these cases, the authority of the master narrative(s) eventually prevails, albeit established obliquely through irony, parody, or condescension—as in the translator's response during the Maamtrasna trials. By contrast, as Joyce's ironic reworking of this legal language in turn shows, other uses of the technique set out not to denigrate demotic speech but to enable previously silenced voices to break into, or to upstage, dominant or consensual narrative forms. Vernacular is not simply popular, if by that is meant some form of consensus: rather it contests the ossification of the popular into received wisdom, the claim of the popular on stability or even the *authority* of common usage. For James Maddox, *Ulysses* is driven by "its novelistic concern with character and plot on the one hand and its meta-novelistic concern with narrative authority on the other."[71] It is this rejection of undue deference, whether toward Standard English or the clichés of popular parlance, that is worked back into Joyce's politics of style. As Emer

Nolan has suggested of this verbal energy, it may even be that because the best lines are given to certain characters such as the Citizen or Molly Bloom, the sheer force of speech often overturns the rudiments of narrative control, sweeping all before it.[72] Notwithstanding systematic attempts to establish the presence of free indirect discourse on purely textual grounds, or through identifiable linguistic markers, the presence of the technique in the last instance can only be detected — or *performed* — by the reader, the "reading out loud" stressed by Volosinov that locates meaning as much outside as inside the text. That its presence may not always be discerned, however, is clear from the manner in which it escapes even the vigilant ear of Hugh Kenner in his own classic account of the "Uncle Charles Principle." Discussing the presence (or absence) of "ghostly idioms" in Bloom's and Stephen's coming together in the "Eumaeus" chapter of *Ulysses*, Kenner writes:

> Next we learn of the hope that they "might hit upon some drinkables in the shape of a milk and soda or a mineral," and there rises within each reader a ghostly schoolmaster to protest that drinkables are not for hitting, and liquids proverbially have no shape: moreover by what appeal to absent idiom does "a mineral" become the shape of a drinkable?[73]

What Kenner misses here (unless irony is doubling on the "ghostly schoolmaster") is that the term "mineral" is often used as shorthand ("mineral water") to describe a soft drink, a ghostly idiom familiar to Irish ears and, indeed, on other occasions, to Kenner himself.[74]

CHAPTER 4

"Ghostly Light"

VISUALIZING THE VOICE IN JAMES JOYCE'S
AND JOHN HUSTON'S "THE DEAD"

"Do you hear what I'm seeing . . . ?"

JAMES JOYCE (*FW* 193.10)

In one of the few biographical glimpses of James Joyce's relationship to film, Lucie Noël, the wife of his literary executor, Paul Léon, relates how the writer often asked her to accompany him to the cinema. One such film was the controversial *Ecstasy* (1933), in which the beautiful Austrian actress Hedy Lamarr was shown swimming in the nude, and in which there was also, as Noël recounts, "a very realistic love scene between horses":

> The film was quite erotic and I was quite embarrassed, because I had to explain much of the action to Joyce. . . . At that time his eyesight was really bad, and every few minutes he would ask, "What are they doing now?" I would try to tell him in as general a way as I could, and he would say, "I see," obviously amused by my fumbling explanation. But we both thought it was a very fine picture.[1]

Listening to the words, however "fumbling," of his companion, Joyce did not answer "I understand" or "I follow" but "I *see*," as if words were sufficient by themselves to enable him to view the world—even the world as flesh.[2] It is perhaps not coincidental that this verbal "gaze" is grounded in female speech, for such were the cadences of a woman's voice in Joyce's acoustic imagination that they resonated in optical form. The sonorous, reciprocal qualities of language for Joyce possessed the erotic allure of the image but without its voyeuristic associations, and it is this visualization of the voice, as we shall see, that John Huston sought

4.1 John Huston, *The Dead* (1987). Still of Gabriel (Donal McCann), Lily (Rachael Dowling), and Gretta (Anjelica Huston). Private collection.

to evoke on the cinema screen in his memorable film adaptation, *The Dead* (1987).

W. B. Yeats's "masterful images"—or what Christian Metz termed "scopic regimes"—do not come easily to individuals in Joyce's fiction, and not just because of bad eyesight, whether on the part of the author or the characters themselves.[3] In *A Portrait of the Artist as a Young Man*, Stephen's experience of sexual pleasure with a prostitute seems to elude the nets of vision. In a moment of rapture, we are told that he "closed his eyes" as the sensuality of the word merged with the other senses: during the kiss "he read the meaning of her movements," and the "dark pressure of her softly parting lips . . . pressed upon his brain as upon his lips as though they were the vehicle of a vague speech . . . softer than sound or odour" (*P* 107–8). It is not just Stephen who "surrenders" here; the image itself falls under the aural and olfactory spell of language. This dispersal of vision becomes a permanent condition of the colonial city, as experienced by Stephen on his futile amorous expeditions through its streets. When the unattainable "E—C—" rejects Stephen's sexual overtures later in *Portrait*, he seeks consolation for her shattered image in half-remembered snatches of female speech and song:

Rude brutal anger routed the last lingering instant of ecstasy from his soul. It broke up violently her fair image and flung the fragments on all sides. On all sides distorted reflections of her image started from his memory: the flowergirl in the ragged dress with damp coarse hair and a hoyden's face who had called herself his own girl and begged his handsel, the kitchengirl in the next house who sang over the clatter of her plates with the drawl of a country singer the first bars of *By Killarney's Lakes and Fells*. (P 239)

It is not just that "E—C—" has scorned his advances: she has taken an authority figure into her confidence, entrusting her inner life and such "innocent transgressions" as she has ventured to "the latticed ear of a priest": "To him she would unveil her soul's shy nakedness" (P 240). Nakedness is again exposed through the medium of language: for Stephen, the most radiant, erotic vision is filtered, or rather intensified, through speech, even if, in this case, the darkened auditorium belongs to the censorious gaze of the confessional rather than "the occasion of sin" that was cinema.

It is not, then, as if the graphic and the visual do not feature prominently in Joyce, for, as was evident from the earliest critical responses to his work, the cinematic nature of his prose and narrative techniques was already such as to place him among the preeminent literary exponents of the new twentieth-century technologies of vision. What is at stake in Joyce's engagement, however, is a resistance to *spectacle*, if by that is meant the drive toward pure opticality or "ocularcentrism," cleansing the doors of perception of all extravisual components to do with language, narrative, history, or, indeed, the other senses.[4] According to Guy Debord, spectacle ensures a one-way flow between the viewer and the image: "The spectacle is the existing order's uninterrupted discourse about itself, its laudatory monologue. . . . [T]his 'communication' is essentially *unitlateral*": "But the spectacle is not identifiable with mere gazing, even combined with hearing. It is that which escapes the activity of men, that which escapes reconsideration and correction by their work. It is the opposite of dialogue."[5] Joyce's writing is visual throughout, but the modes of experience he is interested in, and the ones that lend themselves to his distinctive modernist sensibility, are those that question the sovereignty of sight and seek to recast vision through the reciprocity of a *dialogical* imagination. In the *Phenomenology of Perception* (1945), Merleau-Ponty did much to dethrone the centrality of the eye, arguing that the returned gaze, the mingling of sight with other senses, and the carnality of the body as it moves through space and time are crucial in negotiating our experience of the external world. Joyce takes this a stage further, showing that eyesight is embedded not only in the erotics of the body but also in the texture of language and history, in a *politics* as well as a phenomenology of perception. In the world of the young Stephen Dedalus, even the most elementary responses to the visual environment, such as color, are already refracted through the prism of politics, in this case, the divisions in Irish society precipitated by the fall of Parnell in the early 1890s. That sight acquires certain "intonations" is due to the fact that its precocious — and troubled — entry into history is inflected by the human voice, as is clear from Stephen's dawning awareness of both language and the impressions of the senses in the opening pages of *Portrait*. The difficulty for pictorial representations, and particularly for cinematic adaptations, is how to orchestrate the image to register these subtle modulations of the voice. Through a brief discussion of one motif in *Portrait* and a more extended analysis of John Huston's cinematic adaptation of "The Dead," it is possible to glimpse how images can capture the cadences of a voice, and by extension, the somatic effects of history, whether registered in the tonalities of speech or through the spectral traces of peripheral vision.

The Politics of Perception

> Lying about what I see, you might say, is knowing what I see and saying something else. Supposing I said it just consists of saying to myself "this is red" and aloud "this is green."
>
> LUDWIG WITTGENSTEIN, "Notes for Lectures
> on 'Private Experience' and 'Sense Data' "

In an early scene in *Portrait*, the young Stephen Dedalus arrives home for Christmas from the wintry cold of Clongowes College and experiences the warm glow of the dining room:

> A great fire, banked high and red, flamed in the grate and under the ivytwined branches of the chandelier the Christmas table was spread. They had come home a little late and still dinner was not ready; but it would be ready in a jiffy, his mother had said. They were waiting for the door to open and for the servants to come in, holding the big sides covered with their heavy metal covers. (*P* 25–26)

It is not too difficult to imagine a camera evoking this scene on film: indeed, it is the stuff of sentimental Christmas cards and Dickensian evocations of seasonal cheer. If we attend closer to the description, however, it may be this archetypal image that is the problem, for it is largely of our own making, and not in the prose itself. Joyce, practicing

his own "scrupulous meanness," is very sparing on the specific details
of the scene, mentioning the only two features of the room that catch
Stephen's eye: the fire, flaming in the grate, and the ivy on the chandelier. The distinguishing feature here is one of color, a contrast between
red (of the fire) and *green* (of the ivy) that recurs on several occasions
when the narrative is sifted through Stephen's visual sensibility: "But
Clongowes was far away; and the warm heavy smell of turkey and ham
and celery rose from the plates and dishes and the great fire was banked
high and red in the grate and the green ivy and holly made you feel so
happy" (*P* 28).

Why, then, is the chromatic range of Stephen's perception so disposed
as to alight on the colors of red and green whenever they enter his field
of vision? If we revert to the account of his earliest sensory experiences
at the beginning of the book, we are told of his aunt Dante that she "had
two brushes in her press. The brush with the maroon velvet back was for
Michael Davitt and the brush with the green velvet back was for Parnell"
(*P* 3–4). That the colors associated with Michael Davitt (1846–1906) and
Charles Stewart Parnell (1846–91) — the towering figures of the Land
League and the Irish Nationalist movement at the end of the nineteenth
century — become the organizing codes of Stephen's universe is clear in
the account given of his geography book when he moves to Clongowes
as a small boy:

> There was a picture of the earth on the first page of his geography:
> a big ball in the middle of clouds. Fleming had a box of crayons,
> and one night during free study he had coloured the earth green
> and the clouds maroon. That was like the two brushes in Dante's
> press, the brush with the green velvet back for Parnell and the brush
> with the maroon velvet back for Michael Davitt. But he had not told
> Fleming to colour them those colours. Fleming had done it himself.
> (*P* 12)

For Stephen, it is as if Fleming gives an objective confirmation of his
highly colored vision of the world.[6] Politics, and the fraught narratives
of the nation under the charismatic leadership of Parnell and Davitt,
are not confined to current affairs or the public sphere but, in keeping
with Vygotsky's account of internalization, frame the child's emerging
inner life, shaping the very contours of his consciousness: "It pained him
that he did not know well what politics meant and that he did not know
where the universe ended" (*P* 14). In the opening lines of *Portrait*, the
primordial basis of this elementary color scheme is traced back to "baby

tuckoo's" (Stephen's) lisping response to the plaintive ballad sung to him
by his father:

> O, the wild rose blossoms
> *On the little green place*
> He sang that song. That was his song.
> *O, the green wothe botheth.* (*P* 3)

In the father's version, red and green are separated, but the infantile crav-
ing for order and unity is so pronounced that Stephen fuses them together
through the force of language and music, as if the world — whether physical or political — would fall apart were these colors sundered. This impulse surfaces again at Clongowes when Father Arnall's division of his
classroom into the white and red factions of the "War of the Roses" induces a reverie on whether roses might come in other colors: "Lavender
and cream and pink roses were beautiful to think of. Perhaps a wild rose
might be like those colors and he remembered the song about the wild
rose blossoms on the little green place. But you could not have a green
rose. But perhaps somewhere in the world you could" (*P* 9).

The War of the Roses was an internecine war, and the catastrophic impact of the fall of Parnell, and the defection of Davitt from the Parnellite
camp, on the young Stephen precipitates a civil war, as it were, in his sensorium. The devastating news of the death of Parnell comes to him when
he is lying in the sick bay of the college in a semidelirium:

> —He is dead. We saw him lying on the catalfaque.
> A wail of sorrow went up from the people.
> —Parnell! Parnell! He is dead!
> They fell upon their knees, moaning in sorrow.
> And he saw Dante in a maroon velvet dress and with a green velvet
> mantle hanging from her shoulders walking proudly and silently past
> the people who knelt on the water's edge. (*P* 25)

This is the passage that precedes Stephen's return home from college,
when on entering the dining room he sees the "great fire, banked high
and red" and the "ivytwined branches of the chandelier," which made
"you feel so happy" — as if the surge of desire for healing the wounds
of the Parnell split is such that the red and green are magically united
again in the glow of Christmas. The happiness, however, is short-lived,
for the tumultuous row that breaks out at the Christmas table as a fren-
zied Dante sides with the church against the "uncrowned king" reduces
the family friend, Mr. Casey, to sobs of pain:

—Poor Parnell! He cried loudly. My dead king!

He sobbed bitterly and loudly.

Stephen, raising his terrorstricken face, saw that his father's eyes were full of tears. (*P* 39)

Given the importance of the leitmotif of color in the early sections of Joyce's *Portrait*, it is clear that in the account of Stephen's arrival home from Clongowes, the spare descriptive detail is not simply a matter of narrative economy but is central to understanding the framing perspectives of Stephen's vision. How, then, might a camera be expected to highlight these "signatures" of the visible (*U* 3.1–2), giving them pride of place in the mise-en-scène?

One could perhaps envisage—borrowing from the artificial luster of Christmas advertisements—a point-of-view shot from Stephen's position, using lighting, color, and compositional techniques to compose the shot so that the eye would be drawn immediately to the fire, and then, perhaps with a slight tilt of the camera, to the chandelier. But, even at that, more would be included in the domestic interiors than is necessary for Joyce's prose—a visual surplus that may inundate the underlying anxieties behind Stephen's stifled and highly selective vision. As Seymour Chatman writes of Jean Renoir's adaptation of Maupassant's story "A Country Excursion," discussing a scene in which the excursion cart passes over a bridge:

The number of details in Maupassant's sentence is limited to three. . . . Thus the reader learns only those three and can only expand the picture imaginatively. But in the film representation, the number of details is indeterminate, since what this version gives us is a simulacrum of a French carriage of a certain era, provenance, and so on. Thus the number of details that we could note is potentially large, even vast. In practice, however, we do not register many details.[7]

Chapman proceeds to make a distinction between the capacity of language to *assert* a statement and the more limited capacity to simply *name* a quality or present it. "The cart was tiny: it came over the bridge" corresponds to the former, an assertion. "The green cart came onto the bridge" corresponds to the latter, in which greenness is not asserted but included as an incidental detail. In this latter case:

The greenness of the cart is not asserted but slipped in without syntactic fuss. It is only named. Textually, it emerges by the way. Now, most films seem to be of the latter textual order: it requires special effort for films to assert a property or relation. The dominant mode is presentational, not assertive. A film doesn't say, "This is the state of affairs." It merely shows you that state of affairs.[8]

It is this latter use of filmic language that corresponds to Joyce's practice, for it is precisely as throwaway details, or incidental references, that the narrative voices and sensibilities structuring the novel reveal their barely discernible presence. Over and above the more familiar uses of montage and parallel editing in *Ulysses* that are usually taken to exemplify its cinematic qualities, Joyce's visual effects, paradoxically, are often most in evidence when his prose is at its most acoustic, if by that we mean the kind of peripheral vision that best serves to register the intonations of a voice. Voice, in this case, has to do with the multiple framing perspectives through which the story is told, and is less concerned with mimetic realism than with the cultural and subjective intonations given to our everyday world. In Joseph Strick's film version of *A Portrait of the Artist as a Young Man* (1977), attention is paid to period detail to give a reasonably accurate rendering of a late nineteenth-century upper-bourgeois household, but Joyce's fiction is not interested in inert surroundings so much as in the points of view of those who inhabit them. As Robert Stam argues:

> Less important than a film's "accuracy" is that it relay the voices and the perspectives—I emphasize the plural—of the community or communities in question. . . . [A]n appeal to voice over image, *or better in conjunction with image*, disputes the hegemony of the visible and the image-track by calling attention to sound, voice, dialogue and language.[9]

This emphasis on the voice takes effect when the image is at its most optical, as when, for example, the tinctures of red and green are initially picked up in the mise-en-scène of Strick's *Portrait* on Stephen's arrival home. The episode opens with a shot of young Stephen knocking at the front door and being welcomed by his parents, followed by a cut to the dining room depicting his father (T. P. McKenna) and Mr. Casey (Desmond Perry) imbibing whisky in front of a mirror placed over a sideboard. The mirror is garlanded with holly and red berries, recalling perhaps the earlier evocation of the room in Stephen's imagination at Clongowes: "There were holly and ivy round the pierglass and holly and ivy, green and red, twined round the chandeliers" (*P* 18). There is no red fire banked high, but during the Christmas dinner, Stephen's mother (Rosaleen Linihan) is dressed in maroon and framed against closed curtains

of a matching color. These items are surrounded by a surfeit of other details, but it is not clear that this by itself is sufficient for the film to lose
sight of the Parnellite color-coding threaded through the narrative. The
failure to relate the mise-en-scène to a narrative voice, and to the emotional coordinates of Parnell and Davitt that orchestrate Stephen's moral
universe, is clear, however, from the fact that Simon Dedalus (a Parnellite) wears a red/maroon cravat (aligning him with Davitt) while, equally
at odds with Joyce's text, Dante (Maureen Potter) is dressed in green,
which would ally her with her arch-enemy Parnell (though admittedly
she is imagined by the young Stephen as wearing, in addition to maroon,
"a green velvet mantle" [P 25] at the dead Parnell's homecoming, before
he realizes her utter antagonism to the deposed leader). The muted Parnell subtext is given a literal textual expression — it is introduced through
intertitles, silent-movie fashion, at the beginning of the film, and discussed out loud by priests when Stephen is in the sick bay — but it is not
relayed visually as it is in Joyce's acoustic imagination. Politics remains in
the public sphere, narrowly conceived, whereas the underlying impulse
of Joyce's narrative suggests that it is part of the innermost structures of
feeling of the characters in the Dedalus household. In Chatman's terms,
the Parnell theme is *asserted* in the film — often crudely — but not "slipped
in" through the modality of the visible; by contrast, Joyce, though narrating in language, makes words perform the work of images, displaying
the details that matter most through the nuances of the voice.

So far from the image achieving its effects in film at the expense of
voice and intonation, it may be the camera's very ability to attend to
throwaway details, and the surfaces of things, that relays the intonations
of inner speech — often, indeed, while departing from a literal or pedan-
tic fidelity to the original work. This is of interest not just for literary
narration but for cinema itself, for, as Stam suggests, the ultimate test
of an adaptation of a literary work lies not in a scrupulous adherence to
the letter of the original but more in fidelity to its spirit — or spirits, if by
that we mean the colloquy of voices or perspectives that frame the story,
giving it its emotional and tonal coloring. While recourse to voice-over,
or other overt verbal devices, provides one obvious method of registering these narrative viewpoints, it is when these are conveyed through
"the look" of a film, and its optical qualities, that the voice finds its most
evocative tonal effects. Through editing and camera movements, set de-
sign, pictorial composition, lighting, color-coding, costume, and other
techniques, the visual architecture of a film may ventriloquize unspoken
or absent voices, the image functioning, as Paul Willemen suggests, as an
echo chamber of inner speech.[10]

Even with subjective camera, as Chatman notes above, there is always more included in the shot than could possibly be noticed by the character, and it may be precisely this quality of cinema that appealed most to Joyce's distinctive narrative styles. Though uniquely attuned to the idioms of a character's voice, the narrative is seldom confined to their consciousness, the pervasive use of free indirect discourse suggesting, as with the cinematic image, something beyond the singular self. This dual vantage point, as Weldon Thornton argues, belongs to the authorial voice, but

> rather than expressing either a traditional "omniscient author" or a distinct persona/character, simulates the social or collective psyche that Stephen constantly, implicitly participates in, thus illustrating the inextricable interrelatedness of "individual" and "social," conscious and unconscious. . . . Perhaps the most distinctive feature of Joyce's presentation of his characters' psyches both in *Portrait* and in *Ulysses* is the persistent merging of figural consciousness and exposition . . . of individual psyche and collective psyche.[11]

For a negotiation of this merging between the figural and the literal, the individual and collective psyches, we may turn to Joyce's story "The Dead," and to John Huston's attempt to visualize the colloquy between inner and outer worlds in his film *The Dead* (1987).

"The Dead": The Voice from below the Stairs

With the singing of the "The Lass of Aughrim" and its powerful effect on Gretta, it is ultimately the Irish folk song, representative of "low" culture, which created the strongest effect on a character.

RAPHAËLLE COSTA DE BEAUREGARD

In Huston's film, it is as if the image comes into its own when it is haunted by occult speech. Throughout the film, off-screen, inaudible voices bear witness to one of the underlying themes of the story: the capacity of unrequited sorrow to assume a palpable, almost otherworldly force in the minds of the living. The facility with which the cinematic image evokes these voices is evident in its relaying of the overlooked, the cast-off objects or indeed people at the margins of the action. It is fitting, therefore, that it is the voice of the servant, Lily (Rachael Dowling), with all her hesitations and infelicities, that introduces the action in Joyce's story. Huston's achievement was to find visual expression for this tremulous voice and, by linking it to other characters and events, gesture toward what may be called the cultural underworld of "The Dead," the elusive and shadowy forces caught in the hinterland of a servant's story.[12]

Joyce's story "The Dead" is unusual in that a servant's voice is not only heard but, in its different idiomatic frequencies, assumes a narrative intensity that will not go away, despite the best attempts of other controlling voices to silence it. The servant's voice is that of Lily, the maid in the Misses Morkan's household, but her idiomatic English is not only heard in the first person but also breaks through the feigned detachment of the third-person free indirect discourse that opens the story: "Lily, the caretaker's daughter, was literally run off her feet" (*D* 175). According to Clive Hart, "This sloppy, market-place use of 'literally' is Lily's language; or perhaps we should say that the language of the story is attracted into Lily's linguistic aura."[13] "Sloppy" this language may be, in that it is no doubt Lily who empties the slops of the Morkan household each day, but it is far from being inaccurate or inappropriate, and Hart is correct to insist that the story thereafter resonates with the echoes of her voice. What we learn from Lily's colloquial voice is not just that she is extremely busy but also that the literal has lost contact with the ground she walks on in more ways than one, as it merges with the figural in her consciousness. It is in this sense that the rest of the story is indeed attracted into her "linguistic aura," for it is the contested ground between literal and imaginative truth that will come to preoccupy the minds of those present at the Morkans' party as the events of the night unfold. The second sentence of the story is again inflected by Lily's voice, concerned as it is with such commonplace details as unadorned spaces and malfunctioning doorbells: "Hardly had she brought one gentleman into the little pantry behind the office on the ground floor and helped him off with his overcoat, than the wheezy hall-door bell clanged again and she had to scamper along the bare hallway to let in another guest" (*D* 175). We suspect that it is Lily who is wheezy and out of breath, thus foreshadowing the fate of the bronchial Michael Furey at the end of the story. Since Lily's voice introduces the story, the problem facing a prospective filmmaker is how to attract the image into the vernacular idioms of her speech; how, that is, to filter the mise-en-scène through the minds of characters who are not, at first sight, even the main focus of the story.

At one point in Huston's film, a guest at the dinner, Mr. Grace (Sean McClory), takes to the floor to recite one of the many party-pieces that punctuate the action. The recitation in question, "Broken Vows," is, Mr. Grace explains, a translation by Lady Gregory from the Gaelic original, "Donall Óg," and relates a tale of love and betrayal in which a young woman is seduced by a lover who promises her unimaginable riches and happiness, only to abandon her in her hour of need. As the verses he recites express it:

> You promised me a thing that is not possible;
> That you would give me gloves of the skin of a fish;
> That you would give me shoes of the skin of a bird
> And a suit of the dearest silk in Ireland.
>
> My mother said to me not to be talking to you,
> Today or tomorrow or on Sunday.
> It was a bad time for telling me that,
> It was shutting the door after the house was robbed.[14]

The poem, as critics of Huston's film were not slow to point out, is an interpolation in Joyce's original story, and is thus, like the ghost of Michael Furey, something of an uninvited guest at the party. But its centrality in the screenplay, and its eerie premonition of what is to come, are made clear from the mention of the name "Gregory" in relation to the translator of the work. In the context of what is to emerge later in the night, this also alludes to the name of the ignoble seducer, Lord Gregory, who betrays the "Lass of Aughrim" in the haunting ballad of that name sung at the end of the party. As the young peasant "Lass" stands in the rain and snow with her baby in her arms, she pleads at the door of Lord Gregory's castle to be admitted, and for the father to acknowledge his paternity of her baby (*D* 211):

> *O, the rain falls on my heavy locks,*
> *And the dew wets my skin;*
> *My babe lies cold* [within my arms:
> Lord Gregory, let me in].[15]

In keeping with the textual ghosts of Joyce's style, the mention of Lord Gregory is occluded from the verse fragment in the story (printed in italics in the original), and remains in the shadows. Nor are the reverberations of the name "Lord Gregory" confined to the ballad. In Irish popular memory, Lady Gregory's husband was the author of the notorious Gregory clause in the Poor Law Act of 1847 that was responsible for the eviction of thousands of destitute peasants during the Great Famine of 1845–48.[16] The Lass of Aughrim, it would seem, was not the only victim to be thrown onto the roads by a callous Lord Gregory (Aughrim in County Galway is only a short distance from Lord Gregory's estate), and the ironic inclusion of his widow's translation of a lament from the Irish introduces a disturbing political undertow to the personal narratives of many of those present at the Misses Morkan's party, particularly those whose "people," as Gabriel Conroy notes, are from the west of Ireland. Lily dispenses potatoes "wrapped in a white napkin" (*D* 198) at the dinner, and keeps three especially for Gabriel, as if to remind him of the west of Ireland he is so keen to dislodge from his own cultural memory.

In Huston's film, this is prefigured in the opening scenes when Lily complains of her difficulty in watching the potatoes and answering the hall door as the guests arrive. Lily's west-of-Ireland resonances are hinted at by her three-syllabic idiomatic pronunciation of Gabriel Conroy's (Donal McCann) name — "Mr. Con-o-roy" — when she proceeds to the pantry to help him take off his overcoat on his arrival at the party: the extra syllable is a faint echo of its Gaelic version ("Con-air-e").[17] In the original story, this is characteristically off the page — Gabriel merely "smiled at the three syllables she had given his surname" (*D* 177) — thus creating the precedent for a series of extratextual presences that will haunt the night's proceedings — not least the words of "The Lass of Aughrim" that fade into ellipses. The plight of the abandoned peasant girl in "The Lass of Aughrim:" is foreshadowed as Gabriel first recalls Lily as a child "nursing a rag doll" and, attempting to sound a friendly note, asks her jocularly, in a scene reenacted in the film, "I suppose we'll be going to your wedding one of these fine days with your young man, eh?" (*D* 177), only to be met with a rejoinder from the beleaguered girl ("said with great bitterness"): "The men that is now is only all palaver and what they can get out of you." (*D* 178) "Gabriel coloured," we are told in the story, "as if he made a mistake. . . . It had cast a gloom over him which he tried to dispel by arranging his cuffs and the bows of his tie. . . . He had taken up a wrong tone" (*D* 178–79). Gabriel's mistake lies in his failure to grasp where Lily's voice is coming from: it would seem that she has been emotionally bruised (perhaps by a would-be suitor) and responds to his words accordingly. "There's that Lily," says her employer, Aunt Kate (Helena Carroll). "I'm sure I don't know what has come over her lately. She's not the girl she was at all" (*D* 181). In Joyce's fiction, the voices that matter are often barely audible and, in an important sense, are not entitled to speak or, at least, are not used to being heard. Lily, we are told, got on well with her three mistresses, "but the only thing they would not stand was back answers." As Margot Norris suggests, "[W]e are prompted here . . . to think of the text of 'The Dead' as a narration itself unwilling to allow a series of back answers that nevertheless disrupt it."[18] Hence, when Lily breaks into speech directly in the text, it has the effect of unsettling Gabriel and, indeed, the night's proceedings in the Morkan household.

Lily's voice—articulating her barely concealed plight—acts as a narrative thread bringing together many of the seeming loose ends in the story: Lady Gregory's translation of "Broken Vows," Lord Gregory and the experience of eviction, the ballad "The Lass of Aughrim," and both Gretta Conroy's and Lily's (figural) association with the west of Ireland. But if the grain of this voice—and its tonal echoes in the lives of other characters in the story—is relayed through the idiomatic inflections of Joyce's prose, Huston's task in his film adaptation was to ventriloquize these through the visual medium of cinema. In "The Cinema of Poetry," Pier Paolo Pasolini suggested that while cinema has no grammatical equivalents of linguistic idioms, the use of stylistic markers involving framing and composition, camera movement, focus, editing, and so forth allows it to produce a visual equivalent of free indirect discourse. By means of such techniques, the "look" of the camera simulates the "disoriented, disorganized beset by details state of mind of the protagonist," visualizing other voices or presences:

> The intense moments of expression in the film are, precisely, those "insistences" of the framing and the montage-rhythms, whose structural realism . . . is charged . . . till it explodes in a sort of technical scandal. *Such an insistence on details, particularly on certain details in the digressions, is a deviation in relation to the system of the film: it is the temptation to make another film.*

It is as if other points of view or voices are impinging on the action, threatening to throw it off course by "the obsessive attachment to a detail or a gesture."[19] That such forces are at work in Joyce's "The Dead" is clear from a mysterious narrative agency at the Misses Morkan's party, which seems to interrupt or cut across a character's train of thought, giving it an emphasis other than what the character intended. Hence in Gabriel Conroy's final grief-laden exchanges with Gretta in their hotel bedroom, as R. Brandon Kershner describes it:

> Another voice constantly mitigates the effect he intends, as when "a kinder note than he had intended went into his voice" or "he tried to keep up his tone of cold interrogation but his voice when he spoke was humbler and indifferent" or even when a "strange friendly pity for her entered his soul." [This] second inner voice, the one associated with [Michael] Furey and the ghosts, has begun to creep into his thought and his speech, causing him to pull his conversational punches.[20]

Early in Joyce's story, Aunt Julia enters the room "looking behind her at something": "What is the matter, Julia? asked Aunt Kate anxiously. Who is it?" (*D* 184). It turns out to be Gabriel ushering Freddy Malins in, but, as Eithne O'Neill has suggested, Huston's film picks up on a more general uncertainty whereby "cinematic representation in *The Dead* deals less with what is featured on the screen, than with what must lie elsewhere."[21]

The challenge presented to a film version of "The Dead" is how to visualize the ghostly voices and presences that haunt the Morkan household—a challenge that also faces film adaptations of other classic ghost stories. In the opening scenes of William Wyler's *Wuthering Heights* (1939), the camera follows Lockwood (Miles Mander) through a swirling snowstorm, accompanied by a few strains of "Cathy's Theme," the signature melody of the film. "The camera is more than an observer," writes John Harrington; "it is a *participant*."[22] As Lockwood seeks refuge from the storm in the Heights and encounters Heathcliff (Laurence Olivier) and Nelly (Flora Robson) in its shadowy interiors for the first time, the camera focalizes the action through his eyes, by means of point-of-view shots and camera angles within his field of vision. When he is shown to his decrepit bedroom, however, the association of the camera with Lockwood is disrupted. Hearing an ethereal voice outside the clattering window, he goes to investigate and reaches out through a broken windowpane, only to be seized by an unseen hand. That this is no dream is demonstrated by a sudden reverse shot of Lockwood's frightened face from outside the window, orchestrated by intensified strains of "Cathy's Theme," evoking the point of view of another "presence": "We watch Heathcliff from the position from which Cathy's spirit called out," writes Harrington,[23] and the association of this position with "Cathy's Theme" hints that the opening scene, in which the camera tracks Lockwood stumbling through the moors accompanied by the theme, may also have been through the eyes of a ghost.

In the opening scene of Huston's *The Dead*, silhouetted dancers move gracefully on the shades of the first-floor windows of number 15, Ushers Island (fig. 4.2). This may simply be a neutral establishing shot conveyed by an omniscient camera, but it may also suggest the point of view of someone standing in the street, excluded from life's feast. Citing Jean Mitry, Gilles Deleuze points to the "semi-subjective" nature of certain cinematic images, relaying "the anonymous point of view of someone unidentified among the characters": "The camera does not simply give us the vision of the character and his world; it imposes another vision in which the first is transformed and reflected."[24] On the night of the

4.2 John Huston, *The Dead* (1987). Still of opening shot from street. Private collection.

Misses Morkan's party, this "someone unidentified" may be the ghost of Michael Furey. When his image is conjured up by Gretta's plaintive words in the hotel room at the end of Joyce's story, it seems to slip its psychological moorings to emerge in the dim light of the room, and to present itself to Gabriel's anxious eyes: "The tears gathered more thickly in his [Gabriel's] eyes and in the partial darkness he imagined he saw the form of a young man standing under a dripping tree" (D 224). In Huston's screenplay, it was intended to show the ghost:

EXT. A TREE IN THE COUNTRYSIDE
A young man, standing under a dripping tree.

DISSOLVE TO:
Other dark and mysterious shapes seen through a watery lens. (DS 119)

However, this literalization of Gabriel's twilight state of mind was wisely deleted in the final cut, for the true mystery of Michael Furey is that he does not belong to content but takes shape as "form": "Other forms were near" (D 224). The camera does not show a ghost for it is a ghost itself. Cinema, writes Alan Cholodenko, "become[s] not only a host for the spectres it images but is itself a ghost, a second spectre."[25]

Much of Huston's stylistic achievement in *The Dead* derives from the manner in which absences, constantly oscillating between the inner and outer worlds, are evoked by visual style and camera movements. When Aunt Julia (Cathleen Delany) sings "Arrayed for the Bridal" in a faltering voice reminiscent of Maria in "Clay," the camera is set adrift and moves slowly up the backstairs to explore the keepsakes and bric-a-brac of the Morkans' past in bedrooms — porcelain angels, faded photographs, old war medals, ornamental glass slippers, a needlework sampler, a crucifix with beads — akin to the mementoes locked in a drawer that prompt Stephen's ghostly memory of his dead mother in *Ulysses* (*U* 1.255–79).[26] This somnolent camera could be a journey into Julia's psyche, a transition between inner and outer states that recalls Eisenstein's scheme for a "polyphonic image" that would emulate "the dissolution of the distinction between subject and object undertaken in the novels of Édouard Dujardin and fulfilled in *Ulysses*":

> [R]acing visual images over complete silence. Then linked with polyphonic sounds. Then polyphonic images. Then both at once. Then interpolated into the outer course of action, then interpolating elements of the outer action into the inner monologue. As if presenting inside the characters the inner play, the conflicts of doubts, the explosions of passion, the voice of reason, rapidly or in slow-motion, marking the different rhythms of one and the other.[27]

The mementoes evoked in Julia's mind are redolent of imperial nostalgia, displaying the extent to which Catholic middle-class households in Joyce's Dublin had taken empire to heart — a theme relayed throughout the story in the account of Patrick Morkan's truncated ride to the Fifteen Acres to see a military review, the dance at the party (a quadrille called "Lancers"), Gabriel's writing for the Unionist *Daily Express*, and, perhaps more obliquely, Aunt Kate's attachment to the "sweet English tenor voice" of Parkinson. When the action shifts again to another song heard on a stairs, "The Lass of Aughrim," it provides the setting for the reemergence of a lost love, and the remnants of a discarded culture that may lie outside empire but are no less part of modernity.

When Mr. Grace performs his recitation "Broken Vows" in Huston's film, the camera focuses at first on the speaker as his words, in the stage directions of the screenplay, cast "a spell" over his hearers. There follows an edit to a pensive Gabriel, but when the camera cuts to Gretta (Anjelica Huston), "a strange aura seems to surround her" as she passes into a rapt state: "It is almost as if she were in a trance. Though her gaze is inward, an enigmatic beauty pours from her like that of a fine unsentimental picture of the Annunciation" (*DS* 35, 37). At this point, the camera

begins to move slowly of its own accord along the line of young women
who are also transfixed by the recitation, thus picking up an important
suggestion in Joyce's original story that the impact of "The Lass of Aughrim" is not confined to Gretta's personal story but touches on a shared,
cultural memory of a vestigial past: "O, Mr D'Arcy, cried Mary Jane, it's
downright mean of you to break off like that when we were all in raptures
listening to you" (D 212). When the focus switches back to Mr. Grace, he
has, "despite being a corpulent middle-aged academic ... somehow managed to transform himself utterly into the spirit of the young speaker,"
the forlorn peasant girl of the poem. This is visually evoked in the composition of the shot as the recitation reaches its final stanzas, for the editing
not only homes in on the central players of the story but also catches the
unobtrusive entry of Lily into the corner of the frame:

> You have taken the east from me,
> You have taken the west from me,
> You have taken what is before me
> And what is behind me;
>
> You have taken the moon,
> You have taken the sun from me,
> And my fear is great
> You have taken God from me.

As Mr. Grace invokes "the east," the camera cuts to a taciturn Gabriel,
devotee of all that lies in that direction (Britain, Belgium, Europe), who
reacts with a suspicious glance toward Gretta (fig. 4.3). With the invocation of "the west," the focus shifts to Gretta, who appears to be lost in a
world of her own, her eyelids closed as if to protect a slumbering world
within (fig. 4.4). At the precise moment Mr. Grace utters the words "and
what is behind me," Lily emerges in the dark space of the stairs in the
background of the shot, accompanied by the muffled sound of footsteps
and the faint rustle of clothes. Standing in the half-light on the backstairs,
Lily presages Gretta's reverie on the main stairs later in the night as she
listens to "The Lass of Aughrim"—a connection picked up in the stage
directions for the screenplay, as Gabriel shifts his gaze from Gretta to
Lily: "GABRIEL. Slightly baffled by the look on his wife's face. There is
movement behind him. He looks round. It is Lily" (DS 38). As Mr. Grace
reaches the last despairing lines of "Broken Vows," Lily steps out of the
frame of the stairway into the room, as if responding on cue to the voice
of the young abandoned peasant girl in the ballad (fig. 4.5).

4.3 John Huston, *The Dead* (1987). Still of Gabriel (Donal McCann), recitation scene: "You have taken the east from me." Private collection.

4.4 John Huston, *The Dead* (1987). Still of Gretta (Anjelica Huston), recitation scene: "You have taken the west from me." Private collection.

4.5 John Huston, *The Dead* (1987). Still of Mr. Grace (Sean McClory) and Lily (Rachael Dowling), recitation scene: "You have taken what is before me / And what is behind me." Private collection.

Joyce's "The Dead" is structured throughout by tripartite divisions—the three wise men of the Epiphany, the three Morkan sisters, and, not least, the emotional triangle that unfolds at the end of the story. Huston extends this to the three occasions on which Gretta relapses into a trancelike state. The rendition of "Broken Vows" induces the first trance, and as the applause for the recitation snaps Gretta out of her reverie, the camera cuts immediately to Lily, who informs Aunt Kate, in a quivering voice, that the goose will be ready in half an hour:

> LILY. And, Mam . . . I've just put fresh towels in the toilet.
> AUNT KATE. Good girl, Lily.
> Lily turns away, a preoccupied look on her wan face. Aunt Kate looks
>   after her. Something is definitely not right with the girl. (*DS* 38)

In this sequence, the image hints at Lily's inner world as well as Gretta's, bringing the matrix of associations bound up with the servant's story into the emotional aura of Gretta's past. As if to underscore this connection, Gretta is again lost in her thoughts during the meal when Aunt Kate pays nostalgic homage to a forgotten singer, Parkinson, only for the spell to be broken once more by Lily's voice over Gretta's shoulder, announcing that the pudding is ready to be served. Gretta's and Lily's profiles are framed against one another in eye contact, as the mention of Parkinson's sweet tenor voice foreshadows another lost tenor voice, that of Michael

4.6 John Huston, *The Dead* (1987). Still of Gretta (Anjelica Huston) and Lily (Rachael Dowling) at table. Private collection.

Furey—a set of visual affinities drawn in Joyce's story through the description of both Lily's and Gretta's heads as lit by gaslight (*D* 177, 213), linking both in turn with Michael Furey's job in the gasworks in Galway, as will be discussed below. Notwithstanding Gretta's middle-class airs, her background may not be too different from that of the servant girl: her idiomatic English and the fact that, as a "country cute" (*D* 187) Galway girl, she insinuated herself into Gabriel's affections explain the "sullen opposition" (*D* 187) of Gabriel's mother to their marriage. It is Lily once again who introduces the third reverie, helping Gabriel to put on his galoshes in the hallway until the strains of "The Lass of Aughrim" transfer his attention from the girl at his feet to his wife on the stairs (fig. 4.6).

In an early exchange in Joyce's story, it is reported that the word "galoshes" makes Gretta somehow think of the New Christy Minstrels (*D* 181), but the unvoiced word ("gollywog") that links them remains off the page. Nevertheless the silence is communicated, for Aunt Kate, with "brisk tact," seeks to change the subject and move the conversation on. When Gabriel apprehends Gretta listening to the ballad on the stairs, his immediate response is to translate sound into spectacle, and music into the still formality of an image:

> He asked himself what is a woman standing on the stairs in the shadow, listening to distant music, a symbol of. If he were a painter he would paint her in that attitude. Her blue felt hat would show off the bronze of her hair against the darkness and the dark panels of her

skirt would show off the light ones. *Distant Music* he would call the picture if he were a painter. (*D* 211)

As if lifting the silence of a still life, Huston's achievement is to create an acoustic image, infusing the film at key moments with the sound at the top of the stairs. In a backstage sequence shot during rehearsals in Lilyan Sievernich's documentary on the making of the film, *John Huston and the Dubliners* (1987), we catch "Lily" in silhouette looking in at the night's proceedings through a lace-curtained window—an uncanny reenactment of the establishing shot from the street that opened the film. As soon as Lily glides out of the shot, the camera moves toward the window and occupies her position, as if framing the action from her point of view. Like the movements of a camera, the labor of the servant is all but invisible, and, as if in mutual sympathy, the camera, the ghost, and the servant collude at several points in Huston's *The Dead* to bring out the "illuminated cadences" (*D* 211) of the image, the words through which, like Joyce at the cinema, we view the world of both the living and the dead.

Ghostly Light: Specters of Modernity

Will o' the wisp. Gas of graves.

JAMES JOYCE (*U* 6.73–54)

In an early essay on James Clarence Mangan, Joyce wrote that "in those vast courses which enfold us and in that great memory which is greater and more generous than our memory, no life, no moment of exaltation is ever lost" (*OCPW* 60). This observation dates from a period in which, despite all his skepticism toward the occult and spiritualism, he retained an interest in key Theosophical concerns such as cyclical history and the pursuit of arcane, hermetic knowledge.[28] One particular aspect that held an enduring fascination was the possibility of world memory, an "akasic" medium, as described in *Ulysses*, that records "all that ever anywhere wherever was" (*U* 7.884). Such a medium is still memory, but it is not just psychological, isolated within individual skulls. In Ireland, this spectral memory was grounded in conjunctions of the old and the new— the old Gaelic, pre-Famine order reconstituted in the byways of urban life and of which, indeed, Mangan was the last literary representative in Joyce's eyes: "Those whom the flames of too fierce love have wasted on earth become after death pale phantoms of desire" (*OCPW* 81). It is difficult not to see in this a presentiment of "The Dead," for while the "shade" of Michael Furey is clearly lodged, at one level, in Gretta Conroy's unconscious, it also has a transsubjective element, impinging on Gabriel's consciousness as if it had an (after)life of its own.[29] It is not that Joyce comes down decisively on one side or the other, designating ghosts as either psychic states or ethereal beings, but that certain traces of memory have a force independent of the minds that recall them. Their haunting is *cultural*, in the deepest sense, requiring a (re)connection with a world, exemplified by Gretta Conroy's and Michael Furey's upbringing in the west of Ireland, which colonial modernity had consigned to oblivion. One of the achievements of John Huston's *The Dead*, deriving perhaps from his residence in Galway, is to bring out this latent cultural uncanny of Joyce's story, depicting the "ingenuous insularity" and "hospitality," as Joyce described it (*JJ* 254), of an urbane, middle-class Dublin for whom life on the western seaboard is as strange as any paranormal phenomena. Instead of vanishing in the name of progress, many anachronistic features of peripheral cultures remain in the shadows of brightly lit cities or echo through the silences of empty streets.

In the closing sequence of "The Dead," Gabriel Conroy and his wife, Gretta, are shown to their room in the Gresham Hotel on O'Connell Street by a sleepy porter, who has lit a candle for the purpose. There is a faint disturbance in the air as they begin their ascent, for the porter has to halt "on the stairs to settle his guttering candle. They halted too on the stairs below him" (*D* 217). When they enter the room, "the unstable candle" is placed on a toilet-table, but its services are not required:

> The porter pointed to the tap of the electric-light and began a muttered apology but Gabriel cut him short.
> —We don't want any light. We have light enough from the street. And I say, he added, pointing to the candle, you might remove that handsome article, like a good man.
> The porter took up his candle again, but slowly for he was surprised by such a novel idea. (*D* 217)

The Gresham Hotel had proudly proclaimed its modernity to the Dublin public with advertisements announcing the installation of electric light and an electric elevator, but there appears to have been a power shortage on the night of the epiphany.[30] Fifty years earlier, it was unlikely the light from the street would have illuminated a room in the Gresham, as a witness to an official inquiry claimed he could not even read his watch at the foot of the gas lamp outside the hotel.[31] In the latter half of the nineteenth century, however, Dublin began to showcase its metropolitan status with the introduction of more extensive gas lighting in the city center in the 1870s, followed by electric light on a small scale in 1892, generated by a power station in Fleet Street. The major drive toward electrification did not take place until the completion of the massive Pigeon House power station between 1899 and 1903, which facilitated the introduction of electric trams and the more widespread use of electric lighting. The *Irish Times* complained, however, that there was still not sufficient power to generate a twenty-four-hour supply, electricity being cut off at midnight, and it is perhaps Joyce's memory of this desultory detail that accounts for the outage when Gabriel and Gretta enter the Gresham.[32] Gas lighting at the turn of the century had extended to several thousand lamps throughout the city, but, for all its modernity, it is barely able to keep the shades of the past at bay as events unfold on the night of the Misses Morkan's party. As the porter leaves the room and Gabriel turns the lock:

> A *ghostly light* from the street lamp lay in a long shaft from one window to the door. Gabriel threw his overcoat and hat on a couch and crossed the room towards the window. He looked down into the street in order that his emotion might calm a little. Then he turned and leaned against a chest of drawers with his back to the light. (*D* 217, italics added)

It is as if the movement of air that disturbed the candle (if not the electricity) on the stairs has made way for gaslight, and later, for an "air" of a different kind, that of the ballad "The Lass of Aughrim," associated with Michael Furey, who worked in the gasworks in Galway.[33] In some early editions of *Dubliners*, "ghostly" is printed as "ghastly," a mistake to be sure, but one that in its own Joycean way catches the eerie manifestations of "gas," "air," and "light" in the story. For Buck Mulligan in *Ulysses*, the Holy Ghost is little more than "a gaseous invertebrate" (*U* 9.487), and if Michael Furey is the third person in another trinity, it is perhaps fitting that he assumes this airy form.[34]

Earlier in the night, the associations between air and gaslight are established when Lily opens the door and helps Gabriel off with his overcoat:

> A light fringe of snow lay like a cape on the shoulders of his overcoat and like toecaps on the toes of his goloshes; and, as the buttons of his overcoat slipped with a squeaking noise through the snow-stiffened frieze, a cold fragrant air from out-of-doors escaped from crevices and folds. (*D* 177)

The release of air from the overcoat is picked up by three senses — sound, smell, and touch (if we include feeling the chill) — and no sooner has it made its presence felt than Gabriel's attention is drawn to Lily's voice and her appearance, illuminated by the light in the pantry: "She was a slim, growing girl, pale in complexion and with hay-coloured hair. The gas in the pantry made her look still paler" (D 177). This is the first mention of "gas" in the story, signaled by the escape of cold, wintry air, and the Gaelic inflections, as we have seen, of Lily's pronunciation of Gabriel's name. Later on, when the guests are leaving the party after the performance of "The Lass of Aughrim," Mr. Darcy walks out of the pantry and engages with Gabriel and others in some mild banter about his head cold, and the need "to be very careful of his throat in the night air" (D 213). Michael Furey, we discover at the end, was not so careful of his throat when he sang in the night air, and as if with this in mind, the next lines turn to Gabriel, who now sees Gretta in the same kind of light that had illuminated Lily:

> Gabriel watched his wife who did not join in the conversation. She was standing right under the dusty fanlight and the flame of the gas lit up the rich bronze of her hair which he had seen her drying at the fire a few days before. (D 213)

Gretta seems lost in her thoughts, and then suddenly turns to Mr. Darcy:

> —Mr Darcy, she said, what is the name of that song you were singing?
> —It's called *The Lass of Aughrim*, said Mr Darcy, but I couldn't remember it properly. Why? Do you know it?
> —*The Lass of Aughrim*, she repeated. I couldn't think of the name.
> —It's a very nice air, said Mary Jane. I'm sorry you were not in voice tonight. (D 213)

What begins as air in the physical sense — "cold fragrant air" — turns gradually into an acoustic, cultural medium, which is no less physical but which carries a component that cannot be reduced to sonic effects alone. This is, of course, no more than the resonances of music, language, and the human voice, but in fact the mystery of how something can be heard, over and above what is *literally* present, mere sound waves, became an issue of central importance in modernist investigations of mind and matter, and of the indeterminate zones where outer and inner worlds collide. Such investigations were greatly enhanced by the rise of new technologies, which carried energy — heat, magnetism, light and sound waves — in a manner that was closer to magic in the popular imagination than to the dull laws of science, conventionally understood. The capacity of the wireless, for example, to send human communication on Hertz waves

through an apparently invisible medium came to resemble thought
transference itself, a new modernist mode of telepathy. As Helen Sword
has commented, much was made of the numerous

> historical and thematic parallels between the rise of spiritualism in
> the late nineteenth century and the simultaneous development of
> new communications technologies. . . . [A]s radios became an in-
> creasingly affordable household item, the notion that the dead can
> communicate via "etheric vibrations," using a special frequency un-
> detectable by the living, became a commonplace.[35]

Joyce was to make considerable use of such parallels with regard to photography and film in *Ulysses* and, indeed, radio and television in *Finnegans Wake*, but in "The Dead," such "etheric vibrations" emanate from the
more elementary technologies of city streets and domestic lighting. In
one sense, this runs counter to conventional understandings of the perceived antagonism between technology and tradition, especially in the
case of superstition or folklore. As Patricia Lysaght writes in her study of
the banshee in Ireland:

> It is generally said the ghosts and fairies disappeared when elec-
> tricity was introduced and . . . [i]t is not difficult to understand why.
> . . . Lights from the window of a house would . . . enable people ap-
> proaching it to see the something which had attracted their attention
> was not a death messenger. Light from lampposts and other outside
> lights, which have become increasingly common, even in small vil-
> lages and private houses in the country, will no doubt have dispelled
> many an image, which might otherwise have impressed itself an ob-
> server's mind as a banshee or a some supernatural being.[36]

In making his case for the connection between Joyce's story and the
old Irish legend of King Conaire, John V. Kelleher notes that one of the
motifs in the legend is that sleep should not take place in a house in
which light can be viewed from without: "Thou shalt not sleep in a house
from which firelight is manifest outside after sunset, and in which light
is manifest from without."[37] The nimbus emanating from street lamps
and lighted windows was offset by shadows and darkness, evocatively
captured in the cityscapes of the late Victorian painter Atkinson Grimshaw (1836–93), whose illuminated streets at night, glistening with rain
or suffused with fog and silhouettes, take on an air of mystery akin to that
of Joyce's Dublin: "The lamps were still burning redly in the murky air
and, across the river, the palace of the Four Courts stood out menacingly

against the heavy sky" (*D* 214). What Marina Warner writes of the science of optics and light in relation to the greater realism induced by stage technology and the magic lantern also applies to gas and electric light in general:

> Optics developed tools that probed the unseen in an effort at rationality, and their use could be seen as a struggle to subdue the uncanny. But the character of the faculties involved was itself interwoven with imagery and symbolism, because the devices that amplified the mind's faculties were modeled on pre-existing ideas of the inner eye, the organ of envisioning, and they also reproduced mental imagery, and projected phantasms, dreams, and memories from the dark chamber of the mind into the light of day.[38]

Just as the streets were dark with something more than night, as Raymond Chandler might have it,[39] so also the city resonated with something more than sound. That sound extends beyond its own physical—or sensory—boundaries is constantly suggested in "The Dead," as the ear picks up noises that are virtually inaudible, or would not be noticed by others. Gabriel's buttons slip through his frozen overcoat with a "squeaking noise" (*D* 159), which acts as a prelude for his detecting the three syllables with which Lily pronounces his name (but which as readers we do not hear). As the Conroys ascend the stairs to the hotel room on returning from the party, the silence is such that "Gabriel could hear the falling of molten wax into the tray and the thumping of his own heart against his ribs" (*D* 217). The latter is understandable, albeit a sound from within; if the "falling" of the wax is audible, however, it is perhaps because it is partly coming from within as well, in the manner of the "falling" snowflakes that bring the story to an end.

Following Gretta's sorrowful recollections of Michael Furey, Gabriel is thrown in on himself but is brought to his senses by a faint sound: "A few light taps upon the pane made him turn to the window. It had begun to snow again. He watched sleepily the flakes, silver and dark, falling obliquely against the lamplight" (*D* 225). It is as if sound imbues the natural world with agency, the action of the snowflakes also reenacting Gabriel's earlier tapping on the window with his fingers to compose himself before his speech. As the shading of sound into light indicates, moreover, the phrase "light taps" also plays on "the tap of electric light" whose failure has permitted the gaslight, or its ghostly shade, to infiltrate the room. "A vague terror" seizes Gabriel when he discovers that Michael Furey had died out of love for Gretta: while standing in the rain at the back of the house in Galway where Gretta was staying, her young lover had produced his own taps on a window, the gravel thrown up at Gretta's bedroom to attract her notice: "I can see his eyes as well as well!" she says in a sobbing voice. "He was standing at the end of the wall where there was a tree" (D 223).[40]

Air passes from sound into voice—the cold air of the night into the air of a song—but then is transmuted into *light*. When the first notes of "The Lass of Aughrim" reached him, Gabriel "stood still in the gloom of the hall, trying to catch the air that the voice was singing and gazing up at his wife": "The voice, made plaintive by distance and by the singer's hoarseness, *faintly illuminated* the cadence of the air with words expressing grief" (D 211). If the air in this passage is physical, then perhaps it may be "illuminated"; but if it belongs to music, as "cadence" would suggest, then some indiscernible kind of sensory transfer or synaesthesia has taken place—"Hear? . . .'Tis optophone which ontophanes" (*FW* 13.13, 15), as it is transmuted in *Finnegans Wake*. In *Portrait*, Stephen and Cranly are overtaken by the sound of a servant singing, which recalls "the *touch* of music" from another female voice in a choir during Easter Week: "[A]ll hearts were *touched* and turned to her voice, *shining* like a young star, *shining* clearer as the voice intoned the proparoxyton and more faintly as the cadence died" (P 266, italics added). As Marina Warner has noted, the association of "air" as the principle of life and breath with music took on particular currency during the Baroque era: "This synaesthetic equivalent between air and music gives the words 'aria' and 'air,' which began in the same period to describe tunes and songs of especial, emotive potency."[41] In "The Dead," it is notable that it is not an aria of the kind discussed at length over the dinner table that inspires Gretta, but a homespun national air, sung in the "old Irish tonality" (D 211). As she recalls the memory of Michael Furey, Gretta's own voice seems suspended between the visible and invisible:

> —I suppose you were in love with this Michael Furey, Gretta, he [Gabriel] said.
> —I was great with him at that time, she said.
> Her voice was *veiled* and sad. (D 221)

"Veiled" can be understood as a visual metaphor to mean something concealed through sound, but it is the fact that it is more than a metaphor that adds to its precision in the context. As the psychoanalysts Nicolas Abraham and Maria Torok show, the melancholic inability to mourn involves acts of concealment in which the lost object is hidden away, preserved through "encryptment," though part of what is hidden is the pain of betrayal or abandonment that led to the loss. In this case, the suffering of the survivor is recast as devotion to the lost object, the subject who inflicted the pain of loss in the first place:

> Freud is surprised that melancholics show no shame at all for the horrible things for which they blame themselves. Now we can understand it: the more suffering and degradation the [love] object undergoes (meaning the more he pines for the subject he has lost), the prouder the subject can be: "he endures all this because of me." . . . Melancholics embody their phantom object in everything that the phantom, frantic with grief, endured for them.[42]

"Phantom" is used here, Nicholas T. Rand points out, "in the medical sense of 'phantom limb syndrome,'" in which pain is still felt long after its source is missing.[43] Metaphor is not only a figure of speech but a way of responding to what cannot be named, what is veiled from both sight and sound. In this sense, Gretta's voice is veiled throughout, a mode of "extra" sensory perception in which the senses give way to one another under the pressure of events. Metaphors, as a rule, articulate experiences that exist "in the head" and do not literally correspond to reality, but the ventriloquism of Joyce's free indirect discourse confounds subjective and objective narration, leaving it unclear whether something belongs to inner experience or emanates from an indistinct, external world. As Rand writes again of Abraham and Torok's idea of a "foreign presence" in a voice, extending to a collective past:

> Abraham likens the foreign presence to ventriloquism and calls it a "phantom," a "haunting," or a "phantomatic haunting." The concept of the phantom redraws the boundaries of psychopathology and extends the realm of possibilities for its cure by suggesting the existence within an individual of a collective psychology comprised of several generations, so that the analyst must listen for the voices of one generation in the unconscious of another.[44]

According to John Paul Riquelme, Joyce's use of language throughout "The Dead" carefully contrives situations in which "the narrator's [objective] perspective and character's have been subtly mingled and merged . . . by a style that mediates between an internal and external view":

> The style signals the merger because it uses the third person, an ostensibly *external* view, to present not only what occurs *within* the character (in words that appear to mimic the character's language), but also . . . [the] act of hearing something that apparently lies *out-*

side . . . . [This] is not just a matter of reading semantically. It involves
also recognizing the ambiguous relations of literal to figurative, part
to whole, internal to external, living to dead, and narrator to character that enable the sentence's words to carry implications they might
not carry in other contexts.[45]

As a telling example, Riquelme cites the merger between Gabriel's
"swooning" and the "faintly" falling snow in the cadences of the final
sentence: "His soul swooned slowly as he heard the snow falling faintly
through the universe and faintly falling, like the descent of their last
end, upon all the living and the dead" (*D* 225). This blurring of inner
and outer worlds, literal and figurative, goes back to the opening sentences of the story in which Lily's voice, ventriloquized through free indirect discourse, testifies to a world in which the literal is merged with
the metaphorical. As we have seen, the "free indirect image" may inform
the style of cinema itself, the "spectral" powers of the camera as a narrative medium allowing it to move effortlessly through walls and doors,
to position itself unobserved in rooms, to merge past and present, or to
bend the material world to the emotional states of its inhabitants.

The difficulty for cinema as a visual medium lies in the impossibility
of "pure" subjective narration of the kind that is easily achieved in literature. In the case of the horror or haunted film, the gap between camera
and subject-position, between narrator and character, is prised open in
a more manipulative way to unsettle not only characters in the movie
but spectators in the audience. When the camera moves stealthily along
the dimly lit privet hedges of suburbia in John Carpenter's *Halloweeen*
(1978), coming to rest outside an illuminated ground-level window, the
fear is that this is not just a film technique, a means of intensifying the
atmosphere, but the point of view of the killer spying on his vulnerable
teenage victims. The threat assumes an overt physical presence in the
monster film, but it may be that haunted cinema is at its most effective
when the source of terror is kept off-screen, as in classic films such as *The
Uninvited* (dir. Lewis Allen, 1944) or *The Innocents* (dir. Jack Clayton,
1963).[46] As Gary J. Svehla writes: "Unlike vampires, Frankenstein mon-
sters, and creatures from black lagoons, the substance of ghost cinema
resides well within the domain of the human psyche and solutions are
never as easy as a wooden stake through the heart."[47] Svehla is correct to
emphasize the link with the "domain of the human psyche," but haunting
cannot always be reduced to this, or to the recesses of a particular character's mind. Such an approach rules out the possibility that the haunting
may derive from *another* "character," emanating from an unrequited past
that is not psychologically internalized, or contained within memory.[48]

For Svehla, ghosts and hauntings "often become metaphors representing the external manifestations of a character's inner tumoil ... and once these psychological demons have been exorcized, the external ghost also vanishes."[49] But what if it is not so easy to distinguish between metaphor and external reality, or if metaphors have the force of presences— however off-stage or liminal—in peoples' lives? This, it could be argued, is the state of affairs that pervades the Misses Morkan's party and its aftermath, the condition that is general all over the world of Joyce's and Huston's story.

In one of the earliest discussions to address the spectral elements in "The Dead," Janet Egleson Dunleavy argued that it is

> a ghost story that features a veritable Who's Who of Irish dead who walk unseen through the substructure, perceived only in the subconscious of the Misses Morkans' living guests. . . . Perversely unwilling to reveal themselves that they may be given their due, these spirits nevertheless become malevolent when treated with disrespect.[50]

Egleson Dunleavy is at pains to establish that the "ectoplasmic" disturbances of the text cannot be attributed to narrative techniques alone, to Joyce's virtuosity in handling multiple perspectives in a story. Polyphony is not merely a literary technique but hints at presences that "cannot be ranked as multiple point-of-view narrators (because they are not given full responsibility for telling the tale) but who can be described as characters," over and above the more overt personages in the story.[51] Four such "personalities" are identified by Egleson Dunleavy, by virtue of their distinctive voices or narrative idioms, and while such an exercise in characterization ultimately fails to be persuasive, the suggestion that certain acoustic or visual effects extend beyond the psychologies of individual characters does point to the possibility of "shades" or forces that have not yet passed into memory. As Riquelme and others have observed, it is vital for Joyce's story that the narrative voice in the final paragraph does not belong to Gabriel alone, since that would confine it to precisely the kind of enclosed, subjective world that is contested throughout the story. Yet it is this aspect of Huston's adaptation that drew some opprobrium in critical responses to the film, mainly on account of the introduction of a sonorous voice-over, enunciated by Gabriel, to accompany the final images. As Franz Stanzel remarked:

> The shift from third to first person reduces the dimension of meaning from near-universal validity to Gabriel's subjectively limited personal view. Such a procedure, probably induced by the necessities of

4.7 John Huston, *The Dead* (1987). Still of ruins of Round Tower. Private collection.

the camera art, throws light on the difficulty, if not the impossibility, of rendering in the medium of film the precarious equilibrium between figural and narrative voices achieved in the story through free indirect style.[52]

Gabriel indeed utters the words, but it does not follow that everything on the screen is confined to his consciousness.[53] The images summoned up are both related to, and yet at one remove from, his mind as the camera travels not just across the snowbound countryside but through memorials of the Irish past before it reaches the graveyard where Michael Furey lies buried. The ruins that loom in silhouette on the screen — a castle, a round tower, an ancient abbey — are themselves "external manifestations" of memory in national iconography, and they provide a crucial, *cultural* mediation for the transcendental impulse toward the universal that is often noted at the end of Joyce's story. In this, Huston is not departing from the spirit (if such is the appropriate word) of the text, for the ghosts that haunted Joyce belonged not to the séances of late Victorian spiritualism but to the "broken lights" (*P* 195) of Irish myth and tradition — a class apart from the spiritual exhaustion of Ouija boards and table turning in London (or Dublin) drawing rooms (fig. 4.7).

One of the criticisms directed at Huston's version of "The Dead" is that it is *too* Irish, implicating a story of deep personal grief in submerged narratives of political loss of the kind that Joyce (so this account goes) clearly rejected in his own life. Commenting on the insertion of Lady Gregory's translation of "Broken Vows" into the night's performances,

Clive Hart writes: "Joyce would have hated the introduction into his story of a passage of Celtic Revival literature—especially, I believe, a passage from a writer for whom he had so little respect."[54] It is true that much of Joyce's animus against the Revival had to do with its Anglo-Irish leadership, and the "nativist" leanings of urban literati intent on re-creating the western seaboard in the image of Romantic Ireland. What is often overlooked, however, is that during the period of the composition of "The Dead," such hostilities to the romanticism of the Revival derived from modernizing *nationalist* sympathies on Joyce's part, as in his support for Sinn Fein protests against the Abbey's staging of Synge's *Playboy of the Western World*.[55] From this perspective, Molly Ivors's enthusiasm for an excursion to the Aran Islands can be seen as reclaiming the west of Ireland for a modernizing project in keeping with the resurgent energies of Joyce's own generation. Galway is not an out-take from modernity (though some Revivalists may have imagined it thus): Michael Furey, after all, was employed in the gasworks, and on visiting Galway himself, Joyce wrote of its new suburbs that one has to close one's "eyes to this unsettling modernity just for a moment" to see "the shadows of history" in the city (*OPCW* 197).[56] On the same visit in 1912, Joyce continued his journey westward to Clifden in Connemara, not to praise the scenery but to interview (unsuccessfully, as it turned out) Marconi at his new wireless station on Derrygimlagh bog, outside the town—an excursion that found its way into *Finnegans Wake*.[57] Galway's connections to mainland Europe were evident again in an encounter with Danish fishermen, whose presence prompts a turn toward the Irish past in Joyce's mind, if not in theirs:

> They were out on the ocean for the summer fishing and made a stop at Aran. Silent and melancholic, they look as if they are thinking of the Danish hordes that burned the city of Galway in the eighth century and of the Irish lands which, as legend has it, are included in the dowries of Danish girls; they look as if they are dreaming of re-conquering them.[58]

So far from Molly Ivors being "a flat character" in "The Dead," as the critic Allen Tate charged, she is central to the imaginative spaces prepared in the text for the opening up of Gretta's buried past and the ghostly visitation of Michael Furey. As Tate himself concedes: "[Molly Ivors] stands for the rich and complex life of the Irish people out of which Gabriel's wife has come, and we are thus given a subtle dramatic presentation of a spiritual limitation which focuses symbolically, at the end of the story, upon his relation to his wife."[59] It is all the more inexplicable, then, to find Tate concluding, in one of the most-cited critical observations on the story, that "no preparation" is made for Michael Furey's "sudden" appearance at the end, thus introducing a structural flaw in the continuity of the narrative on Joyce's part.[60] In fact, as we have seen, the semantic charge attached to words such as "air," "snow," "cold," "tap," "gas," and "light"; the thematic allusions linking Lily and Molly Ivors to Gretta's west-of-Ireland affiliations; the topographical resonances of Aughrim and the political associations of the monuments of "King Billy," Wellington, and Daniel O'Connell—all carry intimations from the outset of events that were to unfold later in the night, albeit with a touch as light as the snowflakes tapping on the windowpane.[61]

It is not Huston, therefore, who introduces a nationalist undertow to Joyce's text: rather he gives a "visual tonality" to nuances in the story that open up modernity to its own excluded voices. In marked contrast with the nostalgia of the Revival, there is no romantic regression, no attempt to escape from the world of gas, electricity, galoshes, light opera, connections to the Continent, or the wider world. As several critics have noted, the story ends with an invocation of the universal as well as the local, as the journey westward toward Galway, like the snow that is general all over Ireland, moves out into a wider, unbounded space. For Bruce Robbins, this recourse to weather, whether figural or literal, is part of a linguistic shift beyond "place" and the "national," signaled by the introduction of "universe" into the final reverie:

> This is not just a moment of alternative nationalism. The snow that is general all over Ireland cannot help but stand for patterns of weather and ecology which are notoriously impossible to restrict within one's national borders, even those of an island—which the Republic of Ireland notoriously both is and isn't. The phrase about the snow being general that Gabriel repeats as he sinks into unconsciousness is a phrase from the newspapers, but he adds to it the words "the universe," words which are not in the newspapers. The impulse to detach and re-bond by forgetting can and does work on more than one scale.[62]

The irony here is that for Joyce, even the weather bears the imprint of nationality: "The rain is falling on the islands and on the sea," Joyce wrote of Aran and Galway Bay. "It is raining as it can rain only in Ireland" (*OCPW* 205). This observation comes at the end of Joyce's essay "The Mirage of the Fisherman of Aran," where he envisages moving out into the wider world from a particular location, Galway, a "journey westward" (*D* 225) that would be possible once again if the city were regenerated as the port of global importance it was before colonial rule. Holding a map of proposed trade routes spreading out from the harbor, Joyce closes his essay with an echo of the mystical journey outward at the end of "The Dead," complete with its image of a "lily" flourishing:

> In the twilight, we cannot make out the names of the ports, but the lines that start from Galway, branching and extending outwards, recall the symbol placed next to the arms of his native city by the mystic, perhaps even prophetic Dean of the Chapters: *Quasi lilium germinans germinabit et quasi terebinthus extendens ramos suos* [It will flourish like a lily growing and like a terebinth tree spreading its branches]. (*OCPW* 205)[63]

Just as the wider world radiates out from a place on the periphery, so also the otherworld carries traces of locality in the Irish imagination. Part of the undoubted appeal of Theosophy and "world memory" was that it afforded the prospect of a unified cosmic consciousness beyond the ruin and fragmentation of modernity, but as W. B. Yeats wryly noted, even the otherworld occasionally speaks in a national accent: "If one question the voices at séance they take sides according to the medium's nationality":

> All spirits for some time after death, and the "earth-bound" as they are called, . . . those who cannot become disentangled from old habits and desires, for many years, it may be centuries, keep the shape of their earthly bodies and carry on their old activities. . . . [S]hould I climb to the top of that old house . . . where a medium is sitting among servant girls . . . the apparition will explain that, but for some family portrait, or for what it lit on rummaging in our memories, it had not remembered its customary clothes or features, or cough or limp or crutch.[64]

As Jacques Derrida concludes of the ghost's sensitivity to location, not to mention the vernacular: "A phantom can thus be sensitive to idiom. Welcoming to this one, allergic to that one. One does not address it in just any language. . . . Haunting implies places, a habitation, and always a haunted house."[65]

CHAPTER 5

"Pale Phantoms of Desire"

SUBJECTIVITY, SPECTRAL MEMORY,
AND IRISH MODERNITY

The economic and intellectual conditions of his homeland do not permit the individual to develop.

JAMES JOYCE, "Ireland, Island of Saints and Sages"

One of the notable yet strangely neglected aspects of the formation of modern Ireland is the absence of individualism as a driving force in the Cultural Revival. "More often than not, say the Irish themselves, we go in groups, in cliques, in separate leagues; with us individualism has not yet come forth from its Limbo, and the community is still the dominant fact."[1] Though Max Weber linked individualism and the Protestant Ethic with the rise of capitalist modernity, it is not difficult to see why these forces failed to contribute to the self-images of a resurgent Irish culture: indeed, notions of freedom and self-determination in Ireland may be seen as defining themselves *against* these ideals, identifying them with British colonialism and Protestant Ascendancy in their various manifestations. In a highly charged controversy in the early years of the Revival, Sir Horace Plunkett's claim that Irish modernity was hampered by the lack of self-reliance and the work ethic was countered by a trenchant riposte from Monsignor Michael O'Riordan, based in Rome, who argued that the example of Continental Catholicism, and in particular Belgium, showed that countries could enter the modern world without taking the utilitarian Protestant route.[2] The irony of the controversy was that Plunkett was no believer in the gospel of egoism but looked to the energies of the co-operative movement and the "associative character of the Celt" to forge a distinctive collective vision of an Anglo-Irish future at odds with Anglo-Saxon individualism. It was left to James Connolly and other Irish radicals to push this collective ideal in a syndicalist or socialist direction, but in the fiction of James Joyce, new modes of subjectivity received

their most complex cultural articulation. As Patricia Waugh writes of the
more overt socially constituted self-images of postcolonial societies, that
challenged immanent notions of the psyche or "inner" essentialism:

> For those marginalized by the dominant culture, a sense of iden-
> tity as constructed through impersonal and social relations of
> power (rather than a sense of identity as the reflection of an inner
> "essence") has been a major aspect of their self-concept long before
> post-structuralists and postmodernists began to assemble their cul-
> tural manifestos.[3]

It is not surprising that the ideal of the self-contained bourgeois individual was contested during the Revival, given what John Wilson Foster
has termed the "eclipse of self" in the Irish fiction of the period. Central
to the displacement of the individual was the impact of the epic, and the
old Irish sagas, on the formation — or deformation — of character in the
Irish novel. "Although we might speak of self-reliance and self-sacrifice
in the stories of the Ulster cycle, there is in the old heroic romances little
sense of what we moderns mean by self: there is small portrait of the
hero's inner life, and almost no overt psychology."[4] It is not that there
are no emotions: rather, as one scholar observes, "the characters are not
made to *say* what they feel" but, in a theatrical fashion, "*show* it by a blow,
a leap, or by the king at a moment of elation waving his crown in the air"
(*FLR* 14).[5] Dialogue augments this process, "promot[ing] action rather
than revealing character" (*FLR* 17–18). Such prepsychological conceptions of character worked their way from the epic form into the novel,
leading Wilson Foster to attribute the arrested growth of realist fiction
to a deficit in explorations of inner life:

> Perhaps this absence of psychology in the ancient stories metamor-
> phosed, given the persistence among the people of the old manu-
> script and folk stories, into the aversion to psychology and that pref-
> erence for a ritualistic approach to character (though the Church's
> distrust of psychology is probably a factor too) that are features of
> modern Irish literature and that have hindered the growth of a strong
> novel tradition. (*FLR* 14)

What needs to be explored at the outset, however, is the limitations
of psychological conceptions of the subject, according to which personal identity depends on an anterior psychic or mental conception of
the self, sundered from the body or the interactions of social life. As Joel
Pfister has argued, a comparativist approach to culture, shorn of West-

ern claims to universalism, provides little evidence that the self is compromised by a lack of a pregiven interiority, still less by the absence of
modes of self-absorption cut off from the material world: "Numerous
anthropologists have recognized that Western cultures tend to be far
more preoccupied with distinctly 'psychological' notions of selfhood
than many non-Western societies. Not all cultures have spawned whole
industries consecrated to the exploration and advertising 'inner space.'
For these cultures, the psychological—at least as many Americans generally understand it—simply isn't meaningful."[6] Nor is this solely a characteristic of "premodern" societies: Pfister cites Joel Kovel's observation
that "'within our culture, introspection signifies participation in a particular class and social relation"—that is, the milieu of a white middle- or
upper-class identity.[7] This is not to say, of course, that non-Western cultures or, indeed, working-class people, lack inner life or self-reflection:
rather, consciousness and agency may owe more to intersubjectivity or
collective solidarity than to the psychological adjustments of individualism. The crucial point is that neither emotional depth nor intellectual complexity is dependent on the invention of the psychological in
its dominant Western guise. While collective ideals and group solidarity
conjured up scenarios during the Cold War of the pod-people in *Invasion
of the Body Snatchers* (1956), not least of the anomalies of modern American individualism is that it coexists with the conformity of mass culture,
the more familiar pod-people who inhabit the shopping malls in George
Romero's *Night of the Living Dead* (1968), or who subscribe to the myth
of choice in consumer society. Conceptions of freedom and inwardness
central to individualism draw on disciplinary regimes of emotional control, largely effected through an internalization of authority figures and
power structures specific to Western capitalist modernity, and it is for
this reason, Gayatri Chakravorty Spivak argues, that Marx opposed the
bourgeois individual not with a proletarian or subaltern self cut from
the same cloth but with a "divided and dislocated subject whose parts
are not continuous or coherent with each other."[8] For the anthropolo-
gist Michelle Rosaldo, the assumption that there is a universal "precul-
tural inner space within which external cultural controls—once taken
'inside' in various forms, like mechanisms of guilt or shame—do their
managerial work" is a construct of the West, re-creating human diversity
in its own preconceived self-image.[9] It is not so much that the dispersed
subaltern "subject" lacks or lags behind the unifying structures of the
Western ego but that it challenges them, offering possibilities of different
modes of subject-formation than the self-contained individual of capitalist modernity. As Elleke Boehmer writes of such anticolonial appropria-
tions of modernity in the margins:

Anti-colonial nationalisms, that is to say, took over the premises of modernity (individualism, state-organized politics, and social improvement), yet adapted or married these to both native and other imported forms of knowledge for anti-colonial purposes.[10]

This is not to diminish the importance of personal agency, still less the distinctiveness of human persons, but to question whether the retreat into interiority—the psychological processes of internalization or introjection in their dominant Western guise—constitutes the highest conception of the self. For Wilson Foster, the stunting of character and inner life captured in Joyce's fiction derives from the dead weight of an outworn culture—the Irish past, and its ramifications in cultural nationalism. Custom and ritual are the sources of this sclerosis, the lingering ties with Irish folklore and, indeed, the west of Ireland, preventing the urban middle-class sensibility of characters such as Gabriel Conroy in "The Dead" from achieving the sophistication that comes from holidays on the Continent, or writing for newspapers such as the *Daily Express*. The Misses Morkan's party exemplifies "the sterility of ritual and despotism of custom that exist by virtue of their own momentum and in which Gabriel participates before he sees himself as a dupe of convention and transcends in vision [i.e., in inner life] its demands" (*FLR* 158). That every conversation in "The Dead" finds its way back to loss and the "faithful departed" ensures that the dinner party is, in effect, "a funeral ceremony with its ritual dancing, ceremonial feast, formal speech, and ritual singing" (*FLR* 146). These testify to a moribund respect for dead generations and "the required submission to one's forefathers": "Implicitly championed in Miss Ivors' exalting of the Gaelic Irishry, these ancestors will not willingly release their grip on the living, as Gabriel discovers when he tries—with some snobbery—to rescue his wife from the demanding echoes of her Connacht background" (*FLR* 158). Ritual on this reading becomes little more than a matter of "mere gesture and rote," stifling "real communion with others" for Gretta Conroy, recalling that other self-contained creature of habit, Mr. Duffy in "A Painful Case."

As the example of Mr. Duffy shows, what is at stake here is not ritual or custom but their collapse into routine and conformity, the decanting of meaning from once expressive actions into "the strange impersonal voice which he recognised as his own, insisting on the soul's incurable loneliness. We cannot give ourselves, it said: we are our own." (*D* 107) In this sense, it may not be the connection with the past but an accelerated break with it that lies at the heart of the paralysis diagnosed by Joyce in *Dubliners*. Reading Wilson Foster's analysis, it is useful to recall Freud's distinction between mourning and melancholia, the latter consisting in a pathological attachment to a lost object that is dead and gone. For Freud, the successful "working through" of mourning is effected through the psychic work of internalization, introjecting the lost object and disassociating it from its traces in the material world. By contrast, melancholia resides in a compulsion to repeat the past, thereby seeming to engage in futile attempts to "act out" or restore what has been lost. As Dominick LaCapra summarizes Freud's distinction:

> In acting-out one has a mimetic relation to the past which is regenerated or relived as if it were fully present rather than represented in memory and inscription. In psychoanalytic terms, the acted-out past is incorporated rather than introjected, and it returns as the repressed. Mourning involves introjection through a relation to the past that recognizes its difference from the present and enacts a specific performative relation to it that simultaneously remembers and takes at least partial leave of it.[11]

LaCapra is careful to point out that Freud avoids a clear-cut distinction between mourning and melancholia, accepting that notions of closure or a complete cure were as illusory as any compensatory objects induced by a refusal to let go. Mourning itself may be in no position to let go of melancholia, even as it detaches grief and loss from their more acute pathological fixations. For this reason, LaCapra contends that working through can never be a purely intellectual or private process but always requires public forms and a renewal of cultural attachments, i.e., precisely the work of relational ties and ritual. As if with *Dubliners* in mind, he asks:

> Does modern society have suitable public rituals that would help one to come to terms with melancholia and engage in possibly regenerative processes of mourning, even if in extremely traumatic cases an idealized notion of full recovery may be misleading? . . . To be effective, mourning apparently requires a supportive or even solidaristic social context.[12]

Jacques Lacan also points to the breakdown in ritual or social codes as requiring expiation by the ghost. The ghost represents a collective, not an individual, "madness," in that it is not only seen by others but is also occasioned by a rent in the connective tissue of society—"that image which can catch the soul of one and all unawares when someone's departure from this life has not been accompanied by the rites that it calls for."[13] In a sense, instead of being a symptom of madness, the ghost may be a saving grace: "This explains the belief we find in folklore in the very close association of the lack, skipping, or refusal of something in the satisfaction of the dead, with the appearance of ghosts and specters in the gap left by the omission of a significant rite" (*DH* 39). Lacan goes on to note the suppressions of ritual in *Hamlet*, including the burial of Polonius in secret and the priest's condemnation of the suicidal Ophelia being given a Christian burial. It is "insufficient mourning" that produces haunting, and hence the importance of the symbolic register—"the level of the logos"—with which ritual works through community:

> The work of mourning is accomplished at the level of the logos: I say logos rather than group or community, although group and community, being organized culturally, are its mainstays. The work of mourning is first of all performed to satisfy the disorder that is produced by the inadequacy of signifying elements to cope with the hole that has been created in its existence, for it is the system of signifiers in their totality which is impeached by the least instance of mourning. (*DH* 38)

With the grounding of psychology in scientific method in the nineteenth century, the determination to exorcize the ghost took on a new lease of life, culminating in the identification of hysteria by Jean-Martin Charcot and other neurologists as the pathology underlying the witchcraze in Shakespeare's era, that of the early modern period. Informed by reason and a spirit of tolerance, the medicalization of the occult sought to establish "that many of the women brought to court and condemned to death on charges of witchcraft or possession by the devil were not culpable at all, but simply ill."[14] To believe in magic or unworldly hallucinations was not only wrong but *irrational*: it was to become a case for treatment. But already it is clear there is a problem with this formulation, for it was not only witches but also prosecutors who were in the grip of pathology, the fervor of the witch-hunters more than matching that of their hapless victims. What needs to be explained, Paul Hirst and Penny Woolley contend, is not just the persistence of archaic superstitions but "how men, apparently rational and able to conduct their lives to their own satisfaction, could believe in witchcraft. Those men are not merely members of a primitive tribe but Luther or Bodin" (the latter one of the founders of modern law).[15] As Derrida argues, exorcism is not always an escape from the effects of the ghost but may give the ghost even greater effect.[16]

It could be argued that while the witch-hunter still believed in the forces of darkness he was opposing, this does not apply to modern attempts to explain away such phenomena in the name of science. From a reductionist psychological approach, self-deception rather than heresy conjures up the ghost, but as Oliver Sacks notes, it is not just a matter of error or cognitive illusion so much as the psyche itself giving way under acute stress. In a survey of widowhood reported in the *British Medical Journal*, W. D. Rees discovered that of nearly three hundred bereaved interviewees, almost half experienced fully fledged apparitions of their dead loved ones: "Rees considered these hallucinations to be normal and even helpful in the mourning process."[17] The ghost attests not to "some dissociation or disconnection" in the neural system but to breakdowns in the social system or everyday life — injustice, guilt, tragedy, suffering, or other existential impasses not lending themselves to easy explanations.[18] This applies with greater force to "premodern" or non-Western cultures that have "not yet learned that hallucinations are considered (in our culture) 'abnormal,'" but whose rituals and entire life-worlds may be endangered.[19] There is nothing abnormal in an intelligent person steeped in such cultures working through mourning and melancholia by means of visions or collective dreams, as in Native American or, for that matter, Irish vernacular culture. Instead of signifying mental instability, it may be the annihilation of such worldviews, whether through ethnocide or "social death," that leads to psychological disintegration.[20] So far from going over the edge, the ghost, as Lacan reminds us, may be a way of keeping madness at bay.

Outcast from Life's Feast

All spirits in fact are not, as far as psychic communications are concerned, spirits at all, are only memory.

GEORGE YEATS, writing to W. B. Yeats

In accounting for the absence of individualism in Irish society, Sir Horace Plunkett identified, among other factors, the persistence of superstition, the tendency to look to otherworlds for what should be generated by the mind. But what if the experience of history has left no shortage of material for mourning but has prevented the development of an inner life to act as a haven for loss, or the sedimentation of grief? Such are the conditions of cultural hauntings, according to Nicolas Abraham and Maria Torok, and the persistence of the spectral in the modern world derives from a literal failure of memory, that is, from the inability to transfer disruptive events from external reality into the psyche, where they can be *acted upon*, rather than painfully — or traumatically — reenacted. Due to the absence of introjection, painful events are negotiated instead through a process of "incorporation" in which material or corporeal aspects are still part of the experience, if only by virtue of being lodged somatically in physical or tangible form. Rituals lend themselves to such performances, the festivities of eating and drinking associated with wakes in peasant societies, for example, signifying "the communion of survivors through the partaking of food. The communion here means . . . we will bury the deceased in the ground rather than in ourselves."[21] The physical dimension of ritual allows an acknowledgment of loss without letting go of the past, just as it also gestures towards language or symbolic form without letting go of the material world:

> [A]cting out the fantasy of incorporation . . . symbolizes both the impossibility of introjecting the loss and the fact that the loss has already occurred. Eating the corpse [symbolically] results in an exorcism of the survivor's potential tendency for psychic incorporation after a death. (*SK* 130)

But what happens when society is de-ritualized, and trauma and suffering impinge on a psyche that persists in looking outward rather than inward in the disorientation that follows loss? In these circumstances, lost "objects" (persons, events, things) hover in an indeterminate zone between inner and outer life, assuming the "encrypted" form of revenants or hauntings from the past. In the opening story of *Dubliners*, "The Sisters," Old Cotter's misgivings about discussing the death of the paralysed Father Flynn in front of children leads the young boy's uncle Jack to change the subject by turning attention to food:

> "Mr. Cotter might take a pick of that leg of mutton," he added to my aunt.
> "No, no, not for me," said old Cotter. My aunt brought the dish from the safe and put it on the table.
> "But why do you think it's not good for children, Mr. Cotter?" she asked.
> "It's bad for children," said old Cotter, "because their minds are so impressionable. When children see things like that, you know, it has an effect." (*D* 2–3)

As if in response to the anxiety, the young boy gorges himself with food, but it is precisely this ingestion and the "unfinished sentences" that give rise to the ghost:

I crammed my mouth with stirabout for fear I might give utterance to my anger. Tiresome old red-nosed imbecile!

It was late when I fell asleep. Though I was angry with old Cotter for alluding to me as a child, I puzzled my head to extract meaning from his unfinished sentences. In the dark of my room I imagined that I saw again the heavy grey face of the paralytic. I drew the blankets over my head and tried to think of Christmas. But the grey face still followed me. (D 3)

In a significant break with Freudian orthodoxy, Abraham and Torok contend that the past in question need not have originated with the self but may be "transgenerational," emanating from the lives of other people through the mechanisms of collective memory. For Freud, anxieties always emerge from *within*, but for Abraham and Torok—as in the case of trauma generally—the disturbance is located in the public, physical world, and the difficulty lies precisely in introjecting it, assimilating it into consciousness. When a lost object is introjected, a gap is left behind in reality; in the case of incorporation, however, the gap is in the psyche itself: "Incorporation is the refusal to introject loss. The fantasy of incorporation reveals a gap in the psyche: it points to something that is missing just where introjection should have occurred" (SK 127). Though the refusal to accept—to introject—loss is associated by Freud with melancholia, for Abraham and Torok, the unassimilated loss congeals into a "physical" *imago* or charged object, which instills a strange kind of hope:

> Not being able to remove repression and thus remaining unfulfilled, the long-contained hope is cornered in a desperate dilemma: deadly renunciation or fallacious triumph. Regression permits the latter, substituting fantasy for the real thing, magic and instantaneous incorporation for the introjective process. (SK 117)

It is in this sense that the spectral involves a breakdown of language and signification itself, inasmuch as the boundaries between outer and inner worlds, *literal* and *figurative* meaning, are suspended: "The fantasy of incorporation merely simulates profound psychic transformation through magic: it does so by implementing literally something that has only figurative meaning" (SK 126). Situations removed from the objective world through the power of figurative language are reinstated in experience through a process of "*demetaphorization* (taking literally what is meant figuratively) and *objectification* (pretending that the suffering is not an injury to the subject but instead a loss sustained by the love object)" (*SK* 126–27).

In Joyce's story "A Painful Case," there is a vivid realization of the links between the spectral, loss, and modernity, and of the cross-over between the literal and the metaphorical, as the emotional armor with which Mr. Duffy has insulated himself from the lives of others is pierced by a chance glimpse of a story in a newspaper. Mr. Duffy is an individual immune to intimacy, and when he is befriended by a lonely woman, Mrs. Sinico, whose husband is away at sea, it can only come to grief. Such release as he experiences with his new friend comes from sharing the experience of listening to music, its physical vibrations allowing minds to meet on the home ground, as it were, of the body: "The dark discreet room, their isolation, the music that still vibrated in their ears united them. This union exalted him, wore away the rough edges of his character, emotionalized his inner life" (*D* 107). In a moment of rapport in a restaurant, Mrs. Sinico reaches across a table to touch her friend's hand, but his incapacity for affection is such that he construes it as a violation, and withdraws into himself.

Some years later, Mr. Duffy is reading the *Dublin Evening Mail* propped up as usual against the carafe of water during his evening meal when his eyes alight on the report of an inquest into the death of the woman whom he had befriended, and then callously rejected, four years earlier. His sense of shock is visceral. Mrs. Sinico, it is reported, was killed in a railway accident while trying to cross the tracks at Sydney Parade station under the influence of alcohol. It has taken Mr. Duffy several years to catch up with the consequences of his actions, and, as in the case of Mrs. Sinico, what hits his body is a delayed reaction to an earlier submerged event. It is not, however, as if the event is retrieved as a memory: rather, as in the Freudian concept of *Nachträglichkeit* or "belatedness," it has the force of actuality, coming across as if experienced for the first time.[22] It has been buried in the sensorium rather than in the ground, which it is to say it has not been buried at all. That Mr. Duffy's body acts as a barrier to emotion is clear from the various ills that beset even the routine of eating and ingestion. On a desk in his room in Chapelizod, he keeps a sheaf of papers in which he jots down occasional notes and on which, "in an ironical moment, the headline of an advertisement for *Bile Beans* had been pasted on the first sheet" (*D* 103–4). In the restaurant, it is as if the advertisement comes back to haunt him in a failure not only of introjection but of incorporation, as his first response to the story in the newspaper while eating his evening meal is a stultifying loss of appetite: "[T]he cabbage began to deposit a cold white grease on his plate. The girl came over to him to ask was his dinner not properly cooked. He said it was very good and ate a few mouthfuls of it with difficulty. Then he paid his bill and went out" (D 109). Mr. Duffy does not read the newspaper story in full until he retreats to his room, but the impact on his memory assumes a palpable form, assailing him from the outside:

> As the light failed and his memory began to wander he thought her hand touched his. The shock which had first attacked his stomach was now attacking his nerves. He put on his overcoat and hat quickly and went out. The cold air met him on the threshold: it crept into the sleeves of his coat. (D 112)

The ghostly gesture recapitulates the scorned touch of her hand years earlier. As in the case of the cold air emanating from Gabriel's overcoat in the "The Dead" that intimates spectral traces of Michael Furey, the cold air in Chapelizod meets Mr. Duffy at the door and creeps into his clothes. By the same token, the sordid details of Mrs. Sinico's death, and the state of abjection to which she had been reduced by alcohol, seem to enter Mr. Duffy's nervous system as physical matter, and to allay his turmoil, he sets out on a journey to the Phoenix Park, the scene of some of their affectionate meetings:

> He entered the Park by the first gate and walked along under the gaunt trees. He walked through the bleak alleys where they had walked four years before. She seemed to be near him in the darkness. At moments he seemed to feel her voice touch his ear, her hand touch his. He stood still to listen. Why had he withheld life from her? Why had he sentenced her to death? He felt his moral nature falling to pieces. (D 113)

Walking through the park, memories of Mrs. Sinico press on him with the force of her original bodily presence, so that even the echoes of her voice are transmuted into touch.[23] As J. F. Lyotard points out, traumatic repetition acquires spectral form not because an event literally repeats itself but because of its *belated* quality, the feeling that something belonging to another situation has not taken place until now: "[a] feeling, it seems, born of nothing that can be verified in the present situation in a perceptible, verifiable, or falsifiable way, and which therefore points to an elsewhere that will have to be located outside this situation, outside the present contextual situation, imputed to a different site than this one."[24] In this light, Mr. Kernan's view in *Ulysses* of a more genial accommodation between past and present through "a kind of retrospective arrangement" (*U* 10.783) takes on a darker cast, as the assumption of a secure vantage point in the present from which to view the past is thrown into question, and arrangements, retrospective or otherwise, are not always available at will. It is not that an event has come down unmediated from the past: rather, mediation itself is the problem, the medium converting what has been displaced as content into form.[25]

The tendency, in certain aspects of Freud's thinking, to "interiorize trauma, as if the external trauma derived its force entirely from internal psychic processes," comes back to haunt Mr. Duffy:[26] the medium of memory itself acquires a semitangible form, to remind him that there were indeed other voices beyond his own. This "falling to pieces" brings Mr. Duffy to his senses—such as they are—but rather than provide a psychic resolution, it staves off the integration of this traumatic episode into his already overintegrated sense of self. Mr. Duffy does not lack an inner life: his problem is that he is locked into it, with no sense of openness toward others: "[A]s he attached the fervent nature of his companion more and more closely to him, he heard the strange impersonal voice which he recognized as his own, insisting on the soul's incurable loneliness. We cannot give ourselves, it said: we are our own" (*D* 107). Inner life becomes a vault, a crypt entombing its contents as if in a separate space from the self. For all his isolation, he is not even his own best company, and is in some senses a stranger to himself: "He lived a little distance from his body" (*D* 104) and had the habit of writing notes about himself in the third person, as if seeing himself solely from the outside. The conflation of inner and outer worlds is such that the landscape of the Phoenix Park seems to accuse and look back at him, in the guise of furtive lovers seeking to escape his gaze: "He knew that the prostrate creatures down by the wall were watching him and wished him gone. No one wanted him: he was outcast from life's feast" (*D* 113). Mr. Duffy is a thoroughly modern sensibility and certainly considers himself—by virtue of his reading of Hauptmann and Nietzsche—to be in advance of what passes for thinking among the common herd. Routine has replaced ritual as the means of punctuating everyday life, yet for all his intellectual grasp of his predicament—displaying "an exactitude which was the product of a leisure not within their [working people's] reach" (*D* 107)—he is part of a dislocated post-Famine culture in which the individual has no recourse to a permeable inner life to safely deposit internalized objects. Excluded from life's feast, he has only his conscience to chew on, as if this is lodged in the body rather than the mind: "He gnawed the rectitude of his life" (*D* 113). Putative psychic entities, memory traces, are never fully extricated from sense experience, and under the pressure of pain, they acquire a tactile presence akin to hauntings. One of the difficulties of Irish literature, as Eleanor Hull wrote during the Revival, is

> the curious feeling that we are hung between two worlds, the seen and the unseen; that we are not quite among actualities, or rather, that we do not quite know where the actual begins or where it ends. Even in dealing with history we may suddenly find ourselves wafted away into some illusory spirit world with which the historian seems to deal with the same sober exactness as in dealing with any fact of ordinary life.[27]

According to Sir William Wilde, writing in the mid-nineteenth century, the modern world of print culture was destined to dispel such archaic forces, since "nothing contributes more to uproot superstitious rites and forms than to print them."[28] Mr. Duffy's ethos, however, is that of the newspaper, advertising, and the tram, and yet he is still prone to disturbances from an unsettled past. In *Ulysses*, as we shall see, Bloom's stifled mourning over the death of his son, Rudy, eleven years earlier produces a similar effect: an apparition that may be an optical illusion induced by the phantasmagoria of new media technologies and yet is also an "out of mind'" experience, a reminiscence so painful that it cannot be contained within the psychic boundaries of the self. As Kimberly Devlin notes, Bloom's "envisioning of dying and death is matter-of-fact and non-superstitious,"[29] and yet as he leaves Glasnevin Cemetery at the end of "Hades" his mind recalls that the "last time I was here was Mrs Sinico's funeral" (*U* 6.995–96). No wonder the place will "[g]ive you the creeps after a bit. I will appear to you after your death. You will see my ghost after death. My ghost will haunt you after death" (*U* 6.999–1001).

Dominant models of anthropology in the early twentieth century turned on evolutionary models of progress in which *ontogeny* (the stages of child or individual development) recapitulated *sociogeny* (the developmental stages of society). On such schemes, influenced by Comte, Spencer, and Freud, primitive societies and children shared common mentalities, characterized by animism, play, sympathetic magic, and prerational worldviews in general. This, of course, underlined the importance of taking a firm, guiding hand with innocents abroad, ensuring that premodern peoples were relieved of adult responsibilities such as self-determination and autonomy until socialized into normal, i.e. Western, modes of behavior. Central to this model was the tendency to look to pathology and mental illness—the irrational, not merely the nonrational—to explain away beliefs in apparitions, delusions, hallucinations, and other outbreaks of superstition among primitive peoples. One of the major contributions of modern anthropology was to explode these prejudices as themselves superstition and wishful thinking in relation to the superiority of Western thought. As Claude Lévi-Strauss argued, there is nothing unstable or irrational about the savage mind: were it otherwise, all of human history up to the modern period would thus be pathologized (as indeed Freud seemed to suggest). While open to philosophical interrogation, it does not follow that cultural differences, whether in time or space, point to mental breakdown: to dismiss all departures from contemporary Western mores as being not only wrong but mentally deficient is the mark of a madness itself.

There is an important corollary to Lévi-Strauss's argument, however: while it makes no sense to automatically pathologize (whatever about morally or philosophically disputing) practices that belong to other cultures or eras, the destruction of those life-worlds may produce pathologies that inflict far greater damage on cultures than premodern or even superstitious practices. This is, in effect, the condition of Joyce's Ireland: characters are cut adrift from a Gaelic past but are also at odds with a coercive imperial progress that impels them toward the future. To the extent that the liminal experiences charted by Joyce reactivate attachments to a submerged culture, as in the case of Gretta in "The Dead," the "supportive or even solidaristic social contexts" identified by LaCapra as essential for coming to terms with trauma are called into existence. This, as we have seen, is not the west of Ireland idealized in romantic primitivism but the Galway that included the gasworks where Michael Furey worked. By contrast, the precarious manner in which individualism and interiority rested on the perilous supports of colonial modernity reduced inner life to ressentiment, and characters to little more than shadows of themselves. Such transcendence as appears at the end of "The Dead" is brought about not through Gabriel's retreat into interiority but by his escape from the secluded self, "the shameful consciousness of his own person" (*D* 221). It is not a psychic but a physical journey that is required: "[T]he time had come for him to set out on his journey westward" (*D* 225), a spectral quest that pays its respects to both the living and the dead.

"All Becoming Shades": Photography, Haunting, and History

One of the central tenets of imperial views of progress was that all beliefs in the supernatural were not equal in the eyes of the Lord, and some were more rational than others. The belief in rational—or "natural"—religion found its most influential proponent in Sir James Frazer, whose monumental *The Golden Bough* (1890–1915) sought to trace the evolution of the spirit from primitive myth and superstition to an inner faith consistent with modernity. For Frazer, it was as if the pilgrim's progress through the ages took the form of a thoroughly dematerialized spirituality, eschewing all outward shows of worship or signs of divinity in the quest for inwardness. On this developmental logic, *magic* represented the most primitive response to the otherworld, a means of bending both the natural and supernatural "by the sheer force of spells and enchantments," as if the gods were at the mercy of the designs of the wizard or sorcerer.[30] This is succeeded by *superstition*, which restores to deities their sovereignty over mortals but which sees worship as an attempt to propitiate or influence their power. This phase survived into the modern era under the guise of Catholicism and similar ritual-based religions, for while "the intelligent and thoughtful part of the community" had seen through this cajoling of the gods, this was not true of "the dull, the weak, the ignorant, and the superstitious, who constitute, unfortunately, the vast majority of mankind":

> One of the great achievements of the nineteenth century was to run shafts down into this lower mental stratum in many parts of the world, and thus to discover its substantial identity everywhere. It is beneath our feet—and not very far beneath them—here in Europe at the present day, and it crops up on the surface of the heart of the Australian wilderness and wherever the advent of a higher civilization has not crushed it underground. This universal faith, this Catholic creed, is a belief in the efficacy of magic. (*GB* 53–54)

It is only in the modern era that *religion* in the true sense emerges, its just claim to reason deriving from its abandonment of magic and credulity. Grasping the empirical methods of science, "shrewder intelligences" came to see that "magical ceremonies and incantations did not really effect the results they are designed to produce," and that the gullible "had been pulling at strings to which nothing was attached." But everyone, unfortunately, had not the same firm grounding in reason, for even in these islands, the forces of irrationality lay barely concealed beneath the topsoil of common sense:

> We seem to move on a thin crust which may at any moment be rent by the subterranean forces slumbering below. From time to time a hollow murmur underground or a sudden spirit of flame into the air tells of what is going on beneath our feet. Now and then the polite

world is startled by a paragraph in a newspaper which tells how in Scotland an image has been found stuck full of pins for the purpose of killing an obnoxious laird or minister, [or] how a witch has slowly been roasted to death in Ireland. (*GB* 54)

The Irish "witch" in question was Bridget Cleary, a young married woman who was burned to death on suspicion of being a fairy-changeling by her husband, father, and other family members in County Tipperary in 1896. The true scandal of the event was not just its misogynistic cruelty but the fact that it took place in the shadow of modernity: a recently built slated cottage complete with Singer sewing machine (on which Bridget Cleary partly earned her living); a young woman (the victim) who eschewed peasant clothing for fashionable garments; her husband, Michael Cleary, the most educated of the perpetrators of the murder; and a nearby town, Clonmel, serviced by markets, railways, gas lighting, and newspapers, among other signs of improvement. It was not the trappings of modernity that came across in contemporary expressions of outrage, however, but the eruption of savagery and barbarism in the Irish countryside: "Among Hottentots one would not expect to hear of such an occurrence," as the coroner said to the jury in the subsequent trial.[31]

The assumption that savagery is enmeshed with superstition, and that both are residues of a distant past, or alien practices in distant lands, is a legacy bequeathed by Victorian Social Darwinism to evolutionary anthropology. While Darwin was preoccupied with the survival of the fittest, anthropologists and theologians were more concerned, as Mary Douglas describes it, with "the lingering survival of the unfit," and cultural fossils left over from other eras.[32] In his sharply critical comments on *The Golden Bough*, Ludwig Wittgenstein sought to demystify such genealogies of fear and addressed precisely the legacies of the Celts, derived from ancient practices such as the burning of humans during the Fire Festivals of Bealtaine. Though "surviving," according to Frazer, in the relatively harmless form of festive bonfires in the modern era, such rituals still contained a "deep and sinister" element deriving from a belief that such fires were originally occasions of human sacrifice, mainly involving witches. For Wittgenstein, writing in the late 1940s in the aftermath of the Holocaust,[33] there is no need to impute distant origins to horror: the threat lies not in the past but in what it says to us, or about us, in *the present*. Apprehending sinister rituals, such as throwing effigies of humans onto fires, we are justified in fearing the worst, without any need to fall back on prehistoric cruelty: "It is not simply the thought of the possible origin of the Beltane Festival that carries with it the impression but rather . . . the enormous *probability* of this thought," the realization

that humans in any period are capable of such acts.[34] To say that practices have something in common is not to say one derives from the other:
"[A]ll these practices show that it is not a question of the derivation of
one from the other, but of a *common spirit*."[35] Though particularly attuned
to ethnographic differences and the fallacious judging of other cultures
solely by our own standards, Wittgenstein insisted that we are not so different that violence and irrationality lie on one side, and progress and
truth on the other. "The point here," in Brian Clack's words, "is that savagery is not something alien to us—something from another age or a distant continent—but is dormant and within us."[36] Clack, however, construes Wittgenstein as echoing Frazer's sentiments on this point, citing
Frazer's lament, quoted above, on the eruption of "residual" savagery in
the modern world.[37] But there is a crucial difference: Wittgenstein sees
the savage *within* modernity, whereas Frazer attributes it to archaic elements in outlying regions. These survivals have to be stamped out by the
brute force of the civilizing process, if contemporary Unionist reactions
to the burning of Bridget Cleary were to be believed. As the *Dublin Evening Mail* (Mr. Duffy's reading matter in "A Painful Case") remonstrated,
linking events in Tipperary to the Maamtrasna murders in Connemara
over a decade earlier:

> We trust that as many as are convicted of assisting in the torment of
> Bridget Cleary will be met with a punishment as exemplary as that
> which overtook the savages of Maamtrasna. It is a lying claptrap that
> says "Force is no remedy." Force is sometimes the only remedy for
> an evil.[38]

Contrary to Frazer's view, superstition is not bound up with primordial violence or even primitivism, any more than fairy-lore among the
peasantry is bound up with romanticism or Celticism. Such imputations
are projections of the modern mind, seeking to attribute "otherness"
to demons largely of its own making. So far from being exotic or even
occult, the customs and lore surrounding fairies were grounded in everyday concerns of rural societies, and much of the capacity of supernatural beings to wreak havoc on mortals had to do with violations in this
world. Instead of representing anarchy or irrationality, the supernatural
often functioned, as in *Macbeth* and *Hamlet*, as one of the last sanctions
against injustice, particularly against those who appeared to have got-
ten away with their crimes.[39] Folklore also contained its own reflexive or
critical elements even among the rural poor, as in the response of Mary
Battle, the old servant working for W. B. Yeats's maternal family in Sligo,
to the burning of Bridget Cleary. Discussing the use of cruelty in exor-

cism, Yeats noted that the aim was "to make the body uncomfortable for its tenant" (an interesting metaphor in itself)—but not to go too far. However, such limits, he ruefully noted, were not always respected, as the case of Bridget Cleary demonstrated:

> A man actually did burn his wife to death in Tipperary a few years ago, and is no doubt still in prison for it. My uncle, George Pollexfen, had an old servant Mary Battle, and when she spoke of the case to me, she described the man as very superstitious. I asked what she meant by that and she explained that everybody knew that you must only threaten, for whatever injury you did to the changeling the fairies would do to the living person they carried away. . . . The Tipperary witch-burner only half knew his own belief. "I stand here in the door," said Mary Battle, "and I hear them singing over there in the field, but I have never given in to them yet."[40]

Mary Battle is, as it were, distinguishing ordinary decent superstition from its rebarbative versions, but is also attributing violence to the exorcist, to the forces intent on purging all traces of unorthodox otherworldly influences. It is striking that Frazer diminishes the role of modernity itself in stoking the witch-burning craze in early modern Europe, attributing it to a continuation of ancient barbaric rituals: "Hence when we remember the great hold which the dread of witchcraft has had on the popular European mind of all ages, we may remember that the primary intention of *all these fire-festivals* was simply to destroy or at all events to get rid of all the witches."[41] It is perhaps with this in mind that Wittgenstein was led to conclude uncharitably that "Frazer is much more savage than most of his savages": the conviction with which modernity sought to exorcize its demons is as murderous as that of its diabolical counterparts.[42] One of the ironies of the sudden emergence of witch-burning in Tipperary at the end of the nineteenth century is that there was, due to the absence of a successful Reformation, no tradition of witch-hunting in Ireland.[43] Instead of being demonized, folk or vernacular practices had coexisted in the Irish countryside alongside "respectable" religion, and indeed may have been given a new lease of life by the suppression of a Counter-Reformation Catholicism under the Penal Laws throughout the eighteenth century. As the Rev. Michael P. Mahon wrote of the coming of Christianity in his book *Ireland's Fairy Lore* (1919):

> [St. Patrick] approached the people with preconceived respect and though he destroyed their ancient beliefs and pagan practices he made no attempt to obliterate these things forever as historical tra-

ditions. He allowed these "humanities" to live on, and, as a matter of fact, is not Europe indebted to the "humanities" of Greece and Rome for its education, and very largely for the language in its mouth?[44]

Virtually none of the conditions outlined by Keith Thomas in his magisterial study of the decline of magic in seventeenth- and eighteenth-century Britain prevailed in late nineteenth-century Ireland, except perhaps two: the legacy of the Reformation at one remove, and official hostility toward such primitive beliefs and practices.[45] For Thomas, the consolidation of Protestantism, the Puritan rejection of ritual (and its connection with magical rites), and the growth of psychological and spiritual interiority were key religious factors in banishing fairies, ghosts, and the otherworld—though in Wales, some commentators attributed the disappearance of fairies to their flight from the zealousness of Methodist preachers and teetotalers.[46] At a social level, the gradual disenchantment of the natural world by science and technology coincided with new measures of control over the environment, the rationalization of economic activity, and a growing sense of security in matters relating to life and death after the English Civil War.[47] The corresponding accelerated rate of change in Ireland, however, had to await the nineteenth century, and it occurred under radically different modes of uneven development that departed in significant ways from what happened in mainland Europe, or, for that matter, Britain. Physical well-being in relation to life and death, for instance, was hardly assured in mid-nineteenth-century Ireland, where economic rationality found its expression in the catastrophe of the Great Famine. A fundamental transformation took place in Irish agriculture after the Famine, but the individualism of peasant proprietorship was tempered by familial ties and collective national ideals, as well as the historical grievances that precipitated the Land War. A "Devotional Revolution" occurred in the Catholic church, but instead of repudiating ritual, it promoted a greater emphasis on orthodox devotional and liturgical practices—the intoxicating ceremonies of incense vividly evoked in passages of Joyce's Portrait.

The reforms in post-Famine Catholicism were determined to root out the more ribald practices associated with "pagan" vernacular culture, particularly the libidinal excesses at wakes and patterns, but as Patricia Lysaght notes, "the clergy, who were largely responsible for education were not, on the whole hostile to folk beliefs: they seem to have either tolerated them or pretended they did not exist."[48] This, it is safe to assume, is the outward conformity that enables a certain laxity in Mrs. Kernan's belief system in Joyce's story "Grace," as described above.[49] It was perhaps this that led Stanislaus Joyce to write to his brother James in

1905 that he was not at all impressed with the debunking of miracles in Renan's rationalist approach to the *Life of Jesus*:

> Another thing I object to strongly is his explanation of miracles. Unless the miracle is of such a nature as to suggest some simple explanation I don't think we should argue about it. One might as well reason against superstition. If country people believe they hear the banshee or that if they break a looking-glass they will have seven years bad luck, why should they not believe these as well [as orthodox Christianity]? Aren't they Christians? Are we to expect them to be fastidious, to have a taste in nonsense?[50]

According to theories of the disenchantment of modern life, late nineteenth-century Ireland was simply catching up with early seventeenth-century England, but there is, of course, a critical difference: the latter was *proto-* or early modern, whereas Ireland was firmly located *within* the modern world system. If fairy folk trooped the back roads of the Irish countryside, or indeed the back-alleys of Dublin, this was not despite of, but in keeping with, Ireland's uneasy position within colonial modernity. This was nowhere more evident than in the introduction of media technologies in Ireland, and particularly the fascination with photography and the magic lantern that, in the eyes of some commentators, was even responsible for one of the showcases or "displays" of the Devotional Revolution, the apparitions at Knock in 1879.[51]

"Beyond the Spectrum": Magic Lanterns, Projection, and Melancholia

The eerie capacity of photography to depict the contents of the mind — memories of the past, fleeting impressions, figures of desire — in an external medium already had given photography an occult aura in the nineteenth century, as befits the term "medium."[52] The development of the new cultural form coincided with the growth of spiritualism that followed the mass outpourings of grief in the aftermath of the American Civil War, the Franco-Prussian War of 1870, and the Paris Commune.[53] At the end of the century, as noted in chapter 4, the discovery of hidden phenomena in nature — radioactivity, x-rays, hertz waves — led to speculation that vital forces of the kind that could only be captured by the camera, the wireless, the telephone, or the phonograph might permeate the physical world. The apprehension of ghosts, spirits, and otherworldly presences had hitherto been limited to sense experience; now the advent of the new technologies opened the doors of perception "beyond the spectrum" to answer the deepest yearnings produced by loss and human mortality. As Edward L. Gardner, one of the leading adepts of the Theosophical Society, explained:

> Well within our human octave there are degrees of density that elude ordinary vision. Just as there are many stars in the heavens recorded by the camera that no human eye has seen directly, so there is a vast array of living creatures whose bodies are of that rare tenuity and subtlety from our point of view that lie beyond out normal senses. Many children and sensitives see them, and hence our fairylore—all founded on actual and now demonstrable fact.[54]

It is against this background that R. Brandon Kershner interprets the sad ghostly manifestation of Bloom's deceased son, Rudy, at the end of the "Circe" chapter in *Ulysses* as, in effect, a photograph, a product of the macabre interaction between photography, death, and the paranormal. One of the more intriguing hypotheses in the debates surrounding technology and the occult was that photographs may have been in a position to relay "images of dead people preserved in memories of the living, or other images from their imaginations, mentally projected onto the photographic plate" by a kind of mental x-ray, and it is this weight of sorrow that is picked up by Joyce in *Ulysses*.[55]

Certainly, the death of Rudy immediately after his birth eleven years earlier was weighing heavily on Bloom's mind on the day of 16 June 1904. As the hearse carrying Bloom and other mourners at Paddy Dignam's funeral passes through Ringsend in the "Hades" chapter, Bloom's eyes alight on Stephen Dedalus, "a lithe young man, clad in mourning, a wide hat" (*U* 6.39–40). Simon Dedalus, who is also in the funeral carriage, fails to catch sight of his son, and when Bloom draws his attention to the missed opportunity, Mr. Dedalus can only express his exasperation at the company his son is keeping, in particular "that Mulligan cad" (*U* 6.49). Bloom reflects on his response—"Noisy selfwilled man. Full of his son"(*U* 6.74)—but then, as if prompted by an unspoken sorrow, suddenly changes heart: "He is right. Something to hand on. If little Rudy had lived. See him grow up. Hear his voice in the house. Walking beside Molly in an Eton suit. My son. Me in his eyes. Strange feeling it would be" (*U* 6.74–78). The traumatic loss of Rudy, who died eleven days after birth, left a void in the lives of Bloom and Molly that extended to their sexual relations, as if intimacy itself were blighted by the tragedy. Thoughts of Rudy recur when the cortege passes the Rotunda maternity hospital at the corner of Rutland (now Parnell) Square:

White horses with white frontlet plumes came round the Rotunda corner, galloping. A tiny coffin flashed by. In a hurry to bury. A mourning coach. Unmarried. Black for the married. Piebald for bachelors. Dun for a nun.

—Sad, Martin Cunningham said. A child.

A dwarf's face mauve and wrinkled like little Rudy's was. Dwarf's body, weak as putty, in a whitelined deal box. Burial friendly society pays. Penny a week for a sod of turf. Our. Little. Beggar. Baby. Meant nothing. Mistake of nature. If it's healthy it's from the mother. If not from the man. Better luck next time.

—Poor little thing, Mr Dedalus said. It's well out of it. (*U* 6.321–31)

When Bloom crosses paths with Stephen Dedalus once more at the end of the day in the phantasmagoria of Nighttown, the painful loss again catches up with him. Following the violent attack on Stephen by Private Carr, Bloom goes to the aid of "Simon Dedalus's son" (*U* 15.4808), and the rush of unrequited paternal care for the abandoned son recalls Rudy with a new intensity:

(Against the dark wall a figure appears slowly, a fairy boy of eleven, a changeling, kidnapped, dressed in an Eton suit with glass shoes and a little bronze helmet, holding a book in his hand. He reads from right to left inaudibly, smiling, kissing the page.)

BLOOM
(Wonderstruck, calls inaudibly) Rudy!

RUDY
(gazes, unseeing, into Bloom's eyes and goes on reading, kissing, smiling. He has a delicate mauve face. On his suit he has diamond and ruby buttons. In his free left hand he holds a slim ivory cane with a violet bowknot. A white lambkin peeps out of his waistcoat pocket.) (*U* 15.4956–59, 4965–67)

Much of this vision corresponds to spirit photography, as Kershner suggests, and a projected image indeed features earlier in "Circe" in a slide show of Bloom's dream of a Zionist home "at Agendath Netaim in faraway Asia Minor": *"The image of the lake of Kinnereth with blurred cattle in silver haze is projected on the wall"* (*U* 15.986–87). This time, however, the figure materializes on the wall without any apparent technological medium, but that it seems to exist outside Bloom's mind is suggested by the "independent" maturation of the boy in the intervening eleven years, and his movements of reading, smiling and kissing the book. Bloom responds as if to a real emanation: "(*wonderstruck, calls inaudibly*) Rudy!" (*U* 15.4952). Though their eyes meet, the boy does not see him, and throughout nothing is heard: both the young boy's reading and Bloom's cry are inaudible. "Through the ghost of the unquiet father," Stephen remarks of *Hamlet*, "the image of the unliving son looks forth" (*U* 9.380–81), but in this case, the son is not reflected in Bloom's eyes, thus vanquishing the primordial desire for the returned look that pervades *Ulysses*.

Much of the pathos of this apparition derives from what Abraham and Torok associate with an acute failure to mourn: the memory of the lost loved one is not as they were when they died, but how they would be in the present had they continued to live. In the case of a young boy whose ten-year-old sister died when he was eight, the analysts noted several years after that "the boy gave as his own the age his sister would have been" and stole clothes for her as if she were maturing into adolescence: " 'Yes,' he said, explaining his thefts, 'at fourteen she would have needed a bra.' "[56] It is at this point that the distinction between introjection and incorporation as psychic and somatic defences against loss acquires a new poignancy. If in *introjection* the dead person is gradually removed from the outside, material world to an interior, psychic space, it follows that there is less pathological attachment to physical reminders of the person: though certain charged objects may still retain an aura of the loved one, they do not function as surrogates for, or "missing pieces" of, the departed. This process, however, is not always possible, and in cases of trauma or acute grief, the loss may be too profound or too tangible to pass into memory. Instead of introjection, *incorporation*, as noted above, is the most that can be achieved, according to which the external, physical reality of the loved one is never fully renounced. "*Incorporation results from losses that for some reason cannot be acknowledged as such*" (*SK* 130): as a result, all traces or objects, including the body itself, are debarred from symbolic appropriation, particularly through language. Caught between inside and outside worlds, loss and desire, memory is *encrypted*, both in the sense of resisting meaning and of being "entombed," buried alive, as it were, within the grieving body:

> In these special cases the impossibility of introjection is so profound that even our refusal to mourn is prohibited from being a language. . . . The words that cannot be uttered, the scenes that cannot be recalled, the tears that cannot be shed—everything will be swallowed along with the trauma that led to the loss. Inexpressible mourn-

ing erects a secret tomb inside the subject. Reconstituted from the memories of words, scenes, and affects, the objectal correlative of the loss is buried alive in the crypt as a full-fledged person, complete with its own topography. (*SK* 130)

It is not, therefore, that the vision of Rudy represents a projection on Bloom's part of an internal loss onto an external medium: rather, the memory was never fully introjected in the first place, in keeping with a disjunctive Irish culture in which waking rituals, communal memory, and haunting were at most "incorporated" rather than internalized within modernity. Rudy's appearance is bound up with the Victorian psychic shadowlands between photography and the occult, but it is also ethnographically grounded in Irish communal responses to death, the coexistence of vernacular folklore with urban modernity, and even the prosaic matter-of-factness of Bloom's outlook on life. "Bloom considers himself a man of science," writes Brandon Kershner, "but always remains aware of the wealth of folk beliefs that survived even in urban, twentieth-century Ireland."[57] In "Ithaca," the question is asked what pastimes (if any) might figure in Bloom's dreams of bungalow bliss in a suburb suitably removed "not less than 1 statute mile from the periphery of the metropolis":

What syllabus of intellectual pursuits was simultaneously possible?
Snapshot photography, comparative study of religions, folklore relative to various amatory and superstitious practices, contemplation of the celestial constellations. (*U* 17.1588–91)

In the apparition at the end of "Circe," Rudy appears as "a fairy boy of eleven, a *changeling*, kidnapped" (*U* 15.4957, my italics), an allusion to the "kidnapping" of Bridget Cleary by the little people and her replacement by a "changeling," and several related cases of fairy abduction in nineteenth-century Ireland, discussed above. Earlier in *Ulysses*, when Stephen's morning reverie on Sandymount strand evokes communal memories of Dublin's multilayered, ancient past, he imagines himself to be a changeling, carrying shards of memory across the centuries as if embodying Beckett's "scraps of an ancient voice in me not mine":[58]

Galleys of the Lochlanns ran here to beach, in quest of prey, their bloodbeaked prows riding low on a molten pewter surf. Dane vikings, torcs of tomahawks aglitter on their breasts when Malachi wore the collar of gold. A school of turlehide whales stranded in hot noon, spouting, hobbling in the shallows. Then from the starving cagework

city a horde of jerkined dwarfs, my people, with flayers' knives, run-
ning, scaling, hacking in green blubbery whalemeat. Famine, plague
and slaughters. Their blood is in me, their lusts my waves. I moved
among them on the frozen Liffey, that I, a changeling, among the
spluttering resin fires. I spoke to no-one: none to me. (U 3.300–309)

Another incarnation of the undead, this time of Stephen's dead mother,
is recalled soon after: "He comes, pale vampire, through storm his eyes,
bloodying the sea, mouth to her mouth's kiss" (U 3.397–98). It is this
manifestation of grief, including the bite of remorse — "Agenbite of
inwit" (U 1.481) — that comes to Stephen's lips when, at the end of the
day, Bloom attempts to revive him after the British soldier Private Carr's
attack. Bending over the insensate Stephen, Bloom "brings his mouth
near the face of the prostrate form" and calls his name, as he does Rudy's
a moment later:

Stephen! (*There is no answer. He calls again.*) Stephen!

STEPHEN
(*frowns*) Who? Black panther. Vampire (U 15.4928–30)

The "vampire" in question refers to another pervasive revenant in *Ulysses*,
the ravaged ghoul of Stephen's dead mother, who preys on his guilt over
his failure to kneel at her bedside and make his peace with the Catholic church in her last hours. Originating as a torment — or nightmare —
recalled by Stephen earlier in "Telemachus" and "Proteus," the vampire owes its return in "Circe" less to the Gothic genre than to a Gaelic
love song collected by Douglas Hyde in the west of Ireland, on which
Stephen superimposes the image of "pale vampire . . . mouth to mouth"
(U 7.522–25).[59] Stephen also slurs lines of W. B. Yeats's poem "Who Goes
with Fergus," which he had sung to his dying mother, and which he had
also recalled earlier in the day in the Martello tower when her memories came back to haunt him. As Kershner points out, this has its own
mythic resonances: Stephen "is drunkenly muttering Yeats's 'Who Goes
with Fergus?' a lyrical invitation to join the hosts of Faerie, so as to become immune to human 'hopes and fear' as well as 'love's bitter mystery,'
precisely, it seems, what Rudy has done, willingly or not" — a recourse to
folk culture that again affirms the coexistence of otherworlds with the
bleak modernity of Dublin's red-light district.[60]

In the controversies that surrounded the use of spirit photography
to afford glimpses of the otherworld, skeptics frequently countered that
"magical" apparitions were little more than technical effects achieved

through double exposures, superimpositions, or interference with the photographic plate. Some of the examples of fraud and trickery achieved notoriety, as in the medium Ada Emma Deane's nebulous photographs of Armistice Day 1924, which showed faces of a large number of dead soldiers in a long exposure taken during the two minutes of silence at the commemoration. Publication of the spectral photographs was peremptorily halted when journalists recognized the faces of many well-known living boxers and soccer players among the ghostly visages, leading to worries of fines for infringement of copyright. The unseemly commerce between mass culture and the spirit world was evident once more when the mysterious head of an American Indian appeared in another photograph Deane had taken of her "spirit guide," which turned out to be identical with a portrait on the cover of the popular *My Magazine* a short while earlier.[61] While the technique of superimposition was adduced to expose the impostures of spiritualists by certain modernist sensibilities, the real mystery, according to Walter Benjamin, was superimposition itself, the capacity of the distracted mind moving through city streets to apprehend layers of time and multiple pasts in the one cultural frame. As Howard Eiland describes this fascination on Benjamin's part:

> The flaneur moves through a peculiarly stratified space and time—one could say, peculiarly haunted. As he goes about the city, drawn by the incidental, he feels that "far-off times and places interpenetrate the landscape and the present moment." . . . [H]e experiences an uncanny thickening and layering of phenomena, an effect of superimposition, in which remembered events or habitations show through the present time and place, which have suddenly become transparent, just as in film an image may bleed through one or more simultaneously perceptible, interarticulated images in multiple exposure.[62]

The mystery of superimposition, montage, and related film techniques is that effects worked out in a new technological medium reappear in — or are incorporated into — the sensorium of the city dweller, exposed like a photographic plate to the myriad pasts of his or her surroundings. The camera does not only affect the psyche: like a surgeon, it also cuts into or "penetrates" the body, even if it leaves the illusion of "an equipment-free aspect of reality" behind.[63] In the moment of its usurpation by modernity, the past returns in relational form, in the new structures of experience afforded by the mass media and the phantasmagoria of city streets. Responding to Max Horkheimer's insistence on the finality of history, the fact that "past injustice has occurred and is completed . . . [t]he slain are really slain," Benjamin replied that "what science has 'determined,' remembrance can modify. Such mindfulness can make the incomplete (happiness) into something complete, and the complete (suffering) into something incomplete."[64] It may be true that certain brute facts cannot be undone, but for Benjamin, others are far from over, such as the triumphs enjoyed by the victors of history: energies of "confidence, courage, humour, cunning, and fortitude, [with] effects that reach far back into the past . . . constantly call into question every victory, past and present, of the rulers."[65] In their analysis of the inability to mourn, Abraham and Torok note that the materialized image—the "imago"—need not lapse into melancholic despair: "The imago, along with its external embodiment in the object, was set up as the repository of hope; the desires it forbade would be realized one day" (SK 116). In the apparition, or imago, of his dead son, Rudy,[66] Bloom views the tragedy of his Jewish family life through the palimpsest of the Irish cultural past, both of which have undergone transformations under new media technologies. In Irish tradition, a fairy changeling never grew: refracted through Joyce's modernist lens, however, Rudy changes through time as if the otherworld itself enters history, projecting alternative futures for those living in the shadows of the past. As the returned gazes between Bloom and Stephen in "Eumaeus" discussed in chapter 1 suggest, it may be that Rudy becomes a repository of hope, the mutation of the ghost over time evolving into the "I, a changeling" (U 3.308–9) of a "son" in whose eyes Bloom can at last see himself.[67]

CHAPTER 6

"Spaces of Time through Times of Space"

HAUNTING THE "WANDERING ROCKS"

Joyce with his own material can do what no painter can within the limits of colour and flat surface. . . . He can build up his picture of many superimposed planes of time.

FRANK BUDGEN, *James Joyce and the Making of "Ulysses"*

On one of his forays into the Irish countryside, J. P. Mahaffy, distinguished provost of Trinity College, Dublin, and no friend of James Joyce, missed a train because the time on the clock outside the station differed from that on the clock inside. When he took one of the locals (or "aborigines," as he might have referred to them) to task for this affront to efficiency, he received the timely answer: "If they told the same time, they'd be no need to have two clocks!"[1]

Even the clocks, as well as the trains, failed to run on time in this outpost of modernity. This resistance to synchronicity (if it can be so elevated) questions one of the key assumptions in theories of modernity, namely, that new technologies in transport and mass communications work their way inexorably through traditional communities, transforming the experience of time and space out of all recognition. According to conventional understandings of modernity, the vagaries of local memory were abolished by the advent of railways, the postal system, the wireless telegraph, the telephone, and, above all, the greater accuracy and availability of clocks and watches. In his study of the culture of time and space at the beginning of the modern era, Stephen Kern argues that this realignment of a sense of time affected all forms of public experience: what was left of diversity and contingency retreated into psychological space, exiled, as Hegel said of religion under modernity, to the private lair of the skull.[2] But what if it is not possible, as we have seen, to make such a clear-cut division between inner and outer worlds in the first place? In

INJUSTICE TO IRELAND.

Is it there,yez are, ye two-faced Lyin' Blaguard wid yer mane Blarney
about the Sun ; no Sun ivir riz anywhere, afore it did in Ould Ireland !
England afore Ireland ! nivir !! Hurroo !! !

6.1 "Injustice to Ireland." Postcard: Private collection.

Joyce's *Ulysses* there are indeed different senses of time, but it is not at all clear that they require a clear separation of public and private experience. Instead, the difference occurs *within* these zones, as different temporalities and relationships to place cut across the routines of everyday life in Dublin, 16 June 1904.

In opening the city to competing, unresolved temporalities, the experience of disjunctive or "allochronic" time, *Ulysses* makes a significant departure from the new modalities of space and time that were coming to define modernity in the metropolitan center. For the proponents of modernity, in Foucault's account, the onset of the twentieth century saw the triumph of the "determined inhabitants of space" over "the pious descendants of time."[3] Long before Foucault, Joseph Frank proposed his influential thesis on the "spatialization" of form in the modern novel, according to which the unfolding of time through narrative is flattened out by, and converted into, the coordinates of the spatial imagination.[4] The modern novel, on this reading, approximates to the flat two-dimensional plane of a modernist painting, or — more germane to *Ulysses* — to the layout and composition of the newspaper, in which events are related to each other, not through the linear progression of an overarching narrative, but solely on the grounds that they all took place on the same day.[5]

The recourse to spatial form in modern culture represents an attempt to register, in artistic terms, one of the most pervasive features of the machine age: the experience of *simultaneity*. The new transport and communications systems brought widely separated regions and different cultures into contact with a rapidity previously unimaginable. This process was greatly facilitated by the International Meridian Conference convened in Washington in October 1884 that sought to universalize time by establishing Greenwich as the zero meridian in a longitudinal grid of twenty-four worldwide time zones. Through the narrative techniques of crosscutting and parallel action, transverse time was incorporated into the syntax of early cinema, providing the cue for the innumerable chases and last-minute rescues that enthralled popular audiences. According to Arnold Hauser, "the new concept of time, whose basic element is simultaneity and whose nature consists in the spatialization of the temporal element, is expressed in no genre so impressively as in this youngest art." Hauser goes on to argue that of the key modernist writers, none is more cinematic than Joyce:

[Joyce] pushes the spatialization of time even further than Proust, and shows the inner happenings not only in longitudinal but also in cross-sections. The images, ideas, brainwaves and memories stand

side by side with sudden and absolute abruptness; hardly any consideration is paid to their origins, all the emphasis is on their contiguity, their simultaneity. The spatialization of time goes so far in
Joyce, that one can begin the reading of *Ulysses* where one likes, with
only a rough knowledge of the context. . . . The medium of the novel
in which the reader finds himself, is in fact wholly spatial, for the
novel describes not only the picture of a great city, but also adopts
its structure to some extent, the network of its streets and squares,
in which people stroll about, walking in and out and stopping when
and where they like.[6]

But a question arises here: is Dublin, or for that matter the Ireland out of
which Joyce emerged as a writer, to be defined solely, or even primarily,
in terms of space as conceived by high modernism? Certainly there have
been studies of geographic and topographical relationships in Joyce, but
it is not clear that they assume the sovereignty of space in Joyce's imagination, as if Dublin were simply another metropolis like Paris, Berlin,
or Boston. In *Ulysses*, Robert M. Adams writes, "Joyce does not seem to
have an antiquarian's eye for old Dublin,"[7] but is it the case that Joyce's
Dublin is confined to the extended present, which modernists claimed
to be the product of the spatializing drive of painting and of cinematic
form? Is the past simply erased and, thereby, are the disparities of time
removed from the public sphere to the domain of what Edmund Husserl
referred to as "internal time-consciousness"?

"The Past and Its Phantoms"

> *Francis was reminding Stephen of years before when they had been at*
> *school together in Conmee's time. . . . You have spoken of the past and its*
> *phantoms, Stephen said. Why think of them? If I call them into life across*
> *the waters of Lethe will not the poor ghosts troop to my call?*
>
> JAMES JOYCE (*U* 14.1110–14)

According to Stephen Kern, "the highpoint of simultaneous literature" in
the modern novel is *Ulysses*: "In *Ulysses*, he [Joyce] improvised montage
techniques to show the simultaneous activity of Dublin as a whole, not a
history of the city but a slice of it out of time, spatially extended and embodying its entire past in an extended present."[8] Echoing what is virtually
a critical consensus, Kern points to the "Wandering Rocks" episode as
the most vivid example of spatial form. Indeed, if we are to believe Stuart
Gilbert, it is a microcosm of the novel as a whole.[9] In this episode, the
action (such as it is) takes place in nineteen sections (or cross-sections),

VERY REV. JOHN CONMEE, S.J.

6.2 Rev. J. Conmee, SJ (1895).
From Very Rev. J. S. Conmee, SJ,
Old Times in the Barony (1895;
Dublin: Carraig Books, 1976).

connecting by spatial contiguity and temporal coincidence a series of random and seemingly inconsequential activities happening all over Dublin. As Kern observes, several narrative devices are deployed to convey this effect: multiple accounts of an action in different sequences; recurrence of the same object in different places; cross-cutting and eventual convergence of movement to suggest the linear temporal flows and spatial interrelatedness of the city, and to provide points of juncture for all that was happening.

In the light of these coordinates, the narrative shifts in the "Wandering Rocks" episode may be examined, particularly as they affect that punctilious man of the clock, "the superior, the very reverend John Conmee S.J." (*U* 10.1) (fig. 6.2). The episode begins with Father Conmee resetting his "smooth watch" (well worn from regular use, we conclude) as he leaves the presbytery near Belvedere College to walk to the orphanage at the O'Brien Institute in Donnycarney, to secure admission for the late Paddy Dignam's son (motivated not just by compassion but also, as we shall see in chapter 7, by a concern to prevent him falling into the hands of Protestant "soupers"). No sooner has he left the presbytery than he passes a one-legged sailor begging for alms, before crossing Mountjoy Square, where he encounters the wife of a prominent Home Rule parliamentarian:

He walked by the treeshade of sunnywinking leaves: and towards him came the wife of Mr David Sheehy M.P.
—Very well, indeed, father. And you, father? (*U* 10.16–18)

This brief exchange — an answer to an unvoiced question — introduces the kind of narrative ellipsis that acts as a stylistic marker of the chapter: the tendency for things to happen off the page, whether in the form of unspoken words, unseen presences, or actions that occur in "off-screen" space.[10] As Conmee proceeds on his errand of mercy, he gives a letter to a young boy to post in the pillarbox at the corner of Fitzgibbon Street, an action followed by an almost imperceptible shift in location that disrupts the coherence of the spatial field:

> Master Brunny Lynam ran across the road and put Father Conmee's letter to father provincial into the mouth of the bright red letterbox. Father Conmee smiled and nodded and smiled and walked along Mountjoy square east.
>
> Mr Denis J. Maginni, professor of dancing &c, in silk hat, slate frockcoat with silk facings, white kerchief tie, tight lavender trousers, canary gloves and pointed patent boots, walking with grave deportment most respectfully took the curbstone as he passed lady Maxwell at the corner of Dignam's court.
>
> Was that not Mrs M'Guinness?
>
> Mrs M'Guinness, stately, silverhaired, bowed to Fr Conmee from the farther footpath along which she sailed. And Father Conmee smiled and saluted. How did she do? (*U* 10.52–65)

Everything in the episode up to this point has been within Father Conmee's range of vision, so we would expect the colorful Mr. Maginni and Lady Maxwell to be on his route alongside Mrs. M'Guinness. In fact, the mention of Dignam's Court, close to O'Connell Street, indicates that they are a considerable distance away. The unity of space and vision has already begun to disintegrate.[11]

Father Conmee's walk quickly takes him to North Strand Road, where he passes Corny Kelleher totting figures as he chews a blade of hay in O'Neill's funeral establishment, before making his way to Newcomen Bridge, where he steps on board the Dollymount tram. The description of boarding the tram is repeated, as in a double take, thus signaling another variant on spatial form identified by Kern, viewing the same scene from a different perspective:

> On Newcomen bridge the very reverend John Conmee S.J. of saint Francis Xavier's church, upper Gardiner street, stepped on to an outward bound tram.
>
> Off an inward bound tram stepped the reverend Nicholas Dudley

C.C. of saint Agatha's church, north William street, on to Newcomen bridge.

At Newcomen bridge Father Conmee stepped into an outward bound tram for he disliked to traverse on foot the dingy way past Mud Island. (*U* 10.107–14)

The boarding of the tram is replayed again in more abbreviated form in the next section of the chapter ("Father Conmee stepped into the Dollymount tram on Newcomen bridge" (*U* 10.213–14), where it coincides with Corny Kelleher's relieving himself of the contents of his mouth, but also with another arclike action: "Corny Kelleher sped a silent jet of hayjuice arching from his mouth *while* a generous white arm from a window in Eccles Street flung forth a coin" (*U* 10. 221–23, italics added). This is the only explicit use of the preposition "while" in a crosscutting context, so central to the narrative techniques of early cinema ("Meanwhile, back at the ranch . . ."), but its implicit presence underlies the unfolding of simultaneous action throughout the entire chapter. Apart from the visual resemblance, then, what has the gesture of throwing the coin to do with Corny Kelleher? We learn in the following section that a one-legged sailor has ambled up Eccles Street, where a woman, whom we later take to be Molly Bloom, throws him a coin (*U* 10.251–52). Though we are not expressly told, it is safe to presume that the one-legged sailor who crops up in Eccles Street is, in fact, the same character Father Conmee has encountered a short while earlier on leaving the presbytery (*U* 10.7–8).

Other items that catch Conmee's attention, however, prove to be more enigmatic, and their interrelations take us far from the initially secure coordinates of his gentlemanly stroll through the north side of Dublin just before he steps on the tram:

Moored under the trees of Charleville Mall Father Conmee saw a turfbarge, a towhorse with pendent head, a bargeman with a hat of dirty straw seated amidships, smoking and staring at a branch of poplar above him. It was idyllic: and Father Conmee reflected on the providence of the Creator who had made turf to be in bogs whence men might dig it out and bring it to town and hamlet to make fires in the houses of poor people. (*U* 10.101–6)

The language of Conmee's reflections is taken from his nostalgic pamphlet on his native County Westmeath, *Old Times in the Barony* (1895), which he "thought of" a little later. But what connects Westmeath with the turfbarge?[12] The cultural (and mental) geography of the episode be-

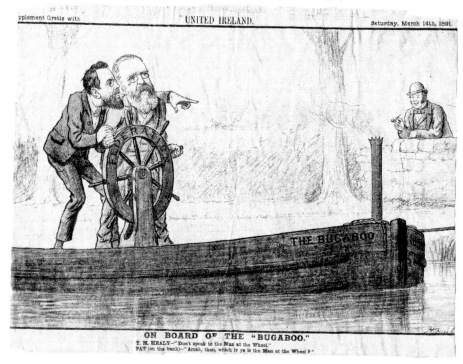

pplement Gratis with

" UNITED IRELAND.

Saturday, March 14th, 1891.

ON BOARD OF THE "BUGABOO."
T. M. HEALY—"Don't speak to the Man at the Wheel."
PAT (on the bank)—"Arrah, then, which iv ye is the Man at the Wheel P "

6.3 "On Board of the *Bugaboo*." From *Freeman's Journal*, 14 March 1891. Private collection.

comes apparent if we revert to a moment earlier in the day, recounted in the "Hades" chapter, in which Leopold Bloom sits in the hearse (supplied by O'Neill's funeral establishment, Corny Kelleher's workplace) as Paddy Dignam's funeral wends its way across the city to Glasnevin Cemetery. Crossing the Royal Canal at Crossguns Bridge in Phibsborough, we get the following description: "Water rushed roaring through the sluices. A man stood on his dropping barge, between clamps of turf. On the towpath by the lock a slacktethered horse. Aboard of the *Bugabu*" (*U* 6.439–41). Is the legendary *Bugabu* recalled by Bloom the same barge perceived by Father Conmee later in the day (fig. 6.3)?[13] Shari and Bernard Benstock think so, equating the two bargemen in their directory of Joyce characters:[14] just as it is highly improbable that there were two one-legged sailors in the same vicinity that afternoon, likewise it is improbable that there were two bargemen with straw hats on turfbarges on the Royal Canal. There is no way of definitively settling whether the turfbarges establish a *spatial* link between the two episodes, but as we shall see, they are linked through a measured *temporal* connection that augments the intricate simultaneity of the action.

As the hearse passes the barge at Crossguns Bridge, Bloom's thoughts turn to his fifteen-year old daughter, Milly, who has taken up a job as a photographer's assistant in Mullingar, County Westmeath:

> Their eyes watched him [the man on the barge]. On the slow weedy waterway he had floated on his raft coastward over Ireland drawn by a haulage rope past beds of reeds, over slime, mudchoked bottles, carrion dogs. Athlone, Mullingar, Moyvalley, I could make a walking tour to see Milly by the canal. Or cycle down. Hire some old crock, safety. . . . Perhaps I will without writing. Come as a surprise, Leixlip, Clonsilla. Dropping down lock by lock to Dublin. With turf from the midland bogs. Salute. He lifted his brown straw hat, saluting Paddy Dignam. (*U* 6. 442–46, 449–52)[15]

Bloom's desire to pay a surprise visit to his daughter perhaps is motivated by his worries about her sexual precocity. These fears may not be entirely groundless, for her suitor, Alec Bannon, has boasted that he has procured what he euphemistically refers to as "a cloak" to protect her from "wetting" on their amorous trysts at Lough Owel, near Mullingar (*U* 14.771–84). Bloom's anxieties about Milly are enmeshed with his distress over his wife's adultery with Blazes Boylan; Bannon, it transpires, also sings Boylan's risqué ditty about "Those Lovely Seaside Girls," and when in "Circe" Bloom is taunted about Molly's infidelity by Bello, the brothel owner, in the midst of the sexual delirium of the Nighttown episode, he imagines he sees his wife on their first encounter years ago:

> I see her! It's she! The first night at Mat Dillon's! But that dress, the green! And her hair is dyed gold and he . . .
>
> BELLO
>
> (*Laughs mockingly*) That's your daughter, you owl, with a Mullingar student. (*U* 15.3162–66)

"Owl," it would seem, is here a particularly appropriate term of abuse, given the location (Lough Owel) of Bannon's seduction of Milly.

As Father Conmee reaches the Malahide road toward the end of his walk, he encounters a young man, later identified as Lynch, coming through a gap in a hedge with a young woman who "with slow care detached from her light skirt a clinging twig" (*U* 10.201–2). ("Twig?" it is recalled later in "Oxen of the Sun": "Bold bad girl from the town of Mullingar. Tell her I was axing at her. Hauding Sara by the wame. On the road to Malahide . . ." [*U* 14.1493–96]). Just before this incident, the priest's thoughts turn to the Malahide of long ago, and it is this that expressly calls to mind his pamphlet about life in the midlands. This is then followed by a strange, abrupt cut to a new paragraph rendered in the same present tense as the "objective" description of Conmee's perambulations:

> Those were old worldish days, loyal times in joyous townlands, old times in the barony.
>
> Father Conmee, walking, thought of his little book *Old Times in the Barony* and of the book that might be written about jesuit houses and of Mary Rochfort, daughter of lord Molesworth, first countess of Belvedere.
>
> A listless lady, no more young, walked alone the shore of lough Ennel, Mary, first countess of Belvedere, listlessly walking in the evening, not startled when an otter plunged. Who could know the truth? Not the jealous lord Belvedere and not her confessor if she had not committed adultery fully, *eiaculatio seminis inter vas naturale mulieris*, with her husband's brother? (*U* 10.159–69)[16]

The first sentence of the last paragraph appears to usher in a revenant from another time, the shadowy, tragic figure of the first Countess of Belvedere, who underpins (or undermines) the narrative logic linking Belvedere College, Father Conmee, the turfbarge, Bloom, Mullingar, Milly, Molly's adultery, and the "nature lessons" of Lynch and the young woman on the road to Malahide.[17] In 1743, Mary Rochfort had been locked away by her husband, Lord Belvedere, on his estate near Lough Ennell (Joyce drops the second *l*) at Mullingar, for an alleged adulterous liaison with Arthur Rochfort, the lord's younger brother. Belvedere College, which Joyce had attended and where Father Conmee once acted as prefect of studies, was built by the countess's son, and was said to be haunted by her. This sad story of betrayal and revenge loomed large in Joyce's imagination, as is clear from as early as 1906 when he first conceived of writing a story about Ulysses. In a letter to Stanislaus, he states, "I thought of beginning my story Ulysses, but have too many cares at present," and then he mentions another possible venture:

> You remember the book I spoke to you of one day in the Park into which I was going to put William Dara and Lady Belvedere? Even then I was on the track of writing a chapter of Irish history. I wish I had a map of Dublin and views and Gilbert's history.[18]

6.4 Mary Rochfort, Lady Belvedere. From Leo Daly, *Titles* (Mullingar: Westmeath Examiner, 1991). Private collection.

The story was of sufficient importance to the overall conception of *Ulysses* for Joyce to feel compelled in late 1921, in one of his last-minute queries when the novel was at the printers, to check again about its historical accuracy in a letter to Belvedere College (*JJL* III, 49–50). But as Eoin O'Mahony has pointed out, his correspondent Father Doyle did not provide accurate information on the story. He confused Belvedere House on Lough Ennell with the family mansion at Gaulstown, miles away (fig. 6.4).[19]

Does the cutaway to Lady Rochfort's walking by Lough Ennell represent a sudden intrusion of the historical past upon the present, thereby radically disturbing the temporal/spatial logic in the chapter — or can it be accounted for solely as a subjective *memory* on Father Conmee's part, in keeping with Kern's demarcation between public and subjective time? Clearly it is precipitated by Father Conmee's meditations on history, and his musings on the confessional (even though Lady Belvedere was not a Catholic) further suggest it is in the mind. But it is not quite as clear-cut as this: there are indications from subsequent "apparitions" in the chapter that Mary Rochfort's appearance may not be an entirely subjective phenomenon, and that the reverberations of her transgression and punishment persist into the present. Just as there are two descriptions side by side of Father Conmee's boarding the tram at Newcomen Bridge, one objective, the other indicating his state of mind, and likewise two descriptions of the "same" bargeman on the canal, so also there are *two* consecutive descriptions of the countess walking by Lough Ennell—the second filtered perhaps through Father Conmee's free indirect discourse, but the first using terminology that escapes his purview and that appears in a later section:

(1) "A listless lady, no more young, walked alone the shore of lough Ennel." (*U* 10.164–65)

immediately followed by:

(2) "Mary first countess of Belvedere, listlessly walking in the evening, not startled when an otter plunged. Who could know the truth?" (*U* 10.165–66)

The first "listless lady, no more young" is apparently linked to a mysterious woman who was involved in court proceedings in Dublin on 16 June 1904, for later in the chapter, we read of a court case in Dublin on that day in which

[a]n elderly female, *no more young*, left the building of the courts of chancery, king's bench, exchequer, and common pleas . . . (*U* 10.625–66, italics added)

In the Benstocks' directory, this woman is identified in turn with a woman mentioned in an earlier passage in the chapter:[20]

Lawyers of the past, haughty, pleading, beheld pass from the consolidated taxing office to Nisi Prius court . . . and heard rustling from the admiralty division of king's bench to the court of appeal *an elderly female* with false teeth smiling incredulously and a black silk skirt of great amplitude (*U* 10.470–75, italics added)[21]

These latter two women are considered identical, yet the "semantic ghost" (to use Fritz Senn's insightful term) of the phrases "no more young" and "an elderly female" links them both to the anachronistic "listless lady" at Lough Ennell—establishing affinities of the kind suggested by the two descriptions of Father Conmee boarding the tram, or the manner in which the appearance of the *Bugabu* in "Hades" prefigures the barge perceived by Father Conmee.[22] If Lady Belvedere has slipped through the nets of Father Conmee's consciousness, her listless walking is no longer a memory but a spectral emanation of the past, prefiguring a haunting of the law (divorce?) courts in modern Dublin.[23]

The point here is not that the truth can be finally ascertained ("Who could know the truth?" [*U* 10.166]), but that if we adhere to a register of simultaneity, it is essentially *undecidable*. Father Conmee, priding himself on his virtue amid all the intimations of sexual misbehavior and secrecy in the past, is comically sexualized and transported back into "old times" in the barony—"Don Juan Conmee walked and moved in days of yore" (*U* 10.173)—and then to his time in Clongowes, which comes across as both a memory and a reenactment of the past in the present:

> Fr Conmee, reading his office, watched a flock of muttoning clouds over Rathcoffey. His thinsocked ankles were tickled by the stubble of Clongowes field. He walked there, reading in the evening, and heard the cries of boy's lines at their play, young cries in the quiet evening. He was their rector: his reign was mild.
>
> Fr Conmee drew off his gloves and took his rededged breviary out. An ivory bookmark told him the page.
>
> Nones. He should have read that before lunch. But lady Maxwell had come. (*U* 10.184–92)

At one moment Father Conmee is on the Malahide road; the next moment he has traveled back in time to his period as rector at Clongowes, but whether the latter is a subjective memory on his part or a narrative shift to another time remains unclear as intrusions from the past disrupt the apparently homogeneous space/time axis of the present. The sins of the flesh are not confined to the past, moreover, for it is at this point that Father Conmee meets the young couple (with links to Mullingar related later in the "Oxen in the Sun" passage quoted above) emerging from a tryst in the fields:

> A flushed young man came from a gap of a hedge and after him came a young woman with wild nodding daisies in her hand. The young man raised his cap abruptly: the young woman abruptly: bent and with slow care detached from her light skirt a clinging twig.
>
> Father Conmee blessed both gravely and turned a thin page of his breviary. *Sin*:

—*Principes persecuti sunt me gratis: et a verbis tuis formidavit cor
meum.* (*U* 10.199–205)²⁴

That the logic of spatial form eventually collapses amid the counter-
flows of time in "Wandering Rocks" is finally evident as the episode draws
to a close with the slow procession of the viceregal cavalcade through the
opposite side of Dublin. Mimicking Conmee's walk, the procession too
crosses a canal, albeit under the gaze of the racialized face (white face,
black mask) of the performer Eugene Stratton grinning from a poster:

> In Lower Mount street a pedestrian in a brown mackintosh, eating
> dry bread, passed swiftly and unscathed across the viceroy's path.
> At the Royal Canal bridge, from his hoarding, Mr. Eugene Stratton,
> his blub lips agrin, bade all comers welcome to Pembroke township.
> (*U* 10.1271–5)

The difficulty here is that it is the *Grand* Canal Bridge that adjoins
Lower Mount Street, not the *Royal* Canal. A poster of Eugene Stratton
is noticed by Father Conmee earlier in the chapter, but it is at Annesley
Bridge, rather than at Newcomen Bridge on the Royal Canal: "From the
hoardings Mr Eugene Stratton grimaced with thick niggerlips at Father
Conmee" (*U* 10.141–42). It may be that there is an "edit" across the city
to this hoarding, except that the Royal Canal has no spatial relation to
the Pembroke township.²⁵ Just as everything in the chapter seems to con-
verge, as in a D. W. Griffith film, things fall apart. Both space and time are
out of joint. Whatever the truth of the ghost in Belvedere College, Mary
Rochfort herself haunts the pages of *Ulysses*, introducing disturbances
from the past into the spatial logic of a city defined by the regulated circuits of both church and state.

The Parallax View

*Some differences of opinion exist as to whether the Free State is, indeed,
free. There can hardly be freedom which ignores the laws of space and
time and the profound implications of these, to which we have only recently awakened.*

J. F. MCCABE, "Irish Time," *Dublin Magazine*

The breakdown of simultaneity in Joyce's Dublin, the dislocation of synchronicity by aberrant senses of time, is nowhere more evident than
in the phenomenon of *parallax*, which Hugh Kenner and others have

6.5 Timeball, Ballast Office, Westmoreland Street, Dublin (c. 1900). Private collection.

identified as one of the key organizing (or disorganizing) motifs in the novel.[26] As Bloom approaches the Ballast Office (fig. 6.5) on Westmoreland Street from O'Connell Bridge in the early afternoon, he does his best to put painful thoughts of Molly's impending rendezvous with Blazes Boylan out of his head:

> Mr Bloom moved forward, raising his troubled eyes. Think no more about that. After one. Timeball on the ballast office is down. Dunsink time. Fascinating little book that is of Sir Robert Ball's. Parallax. I never exactly understood, There's a priest. Could ask him. Par it's Greek: parallel, parallax. (*U* 8.108–12)

A short time later, Bloom realizes he has made a mistake and that it is not in fact one o'clock:

> Now that I come to think of it that ball falls at Greenwich time. It's the clock is worked by an electric wire from Dunsink. Must go out there some first Saturday of the month. If I could get an introduction to professor Joly or learn up something about his family. That would do to: man always feel complimented. Flattery where least expected . . . lay it on with a trowel. Cap in hand goes through the land. Not go

in and blurt out what you know you're not to: what's parallax? Show
this gentleman the door. (*U* 8.571–9)

As Bloom understands it, the timeball on top of the Ballast Office registers Greenwich Mean Time as an aid to shipping and for communications with England, but the clock on the front of the building registers
Irish (Dunsink) time, which was twenty-five minutes behind London, as
established at the Washington Conference in 1884.[27] So while modernity
sought to standardize time to facilitate synchronic timetabling at a global
level, the imperial connection and the need to facilitate shipping from
Britain imposed another time scale on Irish society, undermining that
simultaneity. Perhaps this explained the double standards of the rural
railway station where J. P. Mahaffy missed his train.

Though Bloom's musings on parallax lead him into abstract speculations on astronomy (prompted by Sir Robert Ball's famous handbook
on astronomy, *The Story of the Heavens* [1885], which Bloom has on his
shelf), discrepancies in time were in fact a bitterly contentious political issue in Ireland at the turn of the century, and particularly during the
1914–21 period when Joyce was writing *Ulysses*. In August 1916 — as if in
retaliation for the Easter Rising four months before — the British government passed the Time (Ireland) Act, which abolished Dublin (Dunsink) mean time and replaced it by what Father R. S. Devane described
as "English or Greenwich Time." "So," according to Devane, "by a few
lines of a British Act we lost our own Irish Time, conferred on us by an
international congress, and, shall I say, an Irish sun was replaced by an
English sun":

> It was not asked for by the Irish people, nor were they consulted as
> to whether they desired it or not. As a matter of fact the nation was
> too upset at that time to think of anything but arrests, raids, shoot-
> ings and executions. This was the period immediately following the
> Rising of Easter Week, and fourteen of the leaders of the Rebellion
> had been executed the previous week. It is unnecessary to recall the
> mental state and strain of this country during these awful days to
> anyone who lived through. It was at this unforgettable time Daylight
> Saving was imposed on Ireland.[28]

Nor was the alteration of Hibernian time restricted to twenty-five minutes. In 1907, following the innovation of Daylight Saving Time to facilitate early morning factory schedules in Britain, another hour was lopped
off the Irish clock, thus leading to the incongruous situation in late 1916

where as many as four different time scales could have been operating in Ireland:

(1) Dunsink Time (11:35 a.m.)
(2) Greenwich Mean Time (12:00 p.m.)
(3) Summer Time (Ireland) (12:35 p.m.)
(4) Summer Time (England) (1:00 p.m.)

This was one step too far for patriotic Irish sentiments, and for those sympathizing with the plight of farmers of the Irish countryside who had to rise almost an hour and a half earlier to facilitate their British working-class counterparts. Stating that for rural dwellers an early September morning was now little different than a cold December one, another priest, the Rev. C. Mangan, remonstrated:

> Why should the body of the people be penalized by having to rise prematurely and to grope in the dark for a match which has a way of not being easily found on such occasions, and to face all the rawness of the elements on a winter's morning before the sun has come to shed his mellow influence on them, and to use artificial light for the preparation and taking of their morning meal to suit the fanciful convenience of a few? . . . The whole thing is utter retrogression. . . . [I]t is due to no honest desire to benefit any Irish interest, but rather to the insufferable arrogance of the ruling caste in England and its complacent garrison in Ireland. There is a suspicion that it was motivated by a desire to check the national sentiment which the people might have in distinct Irish time.[29]

Ten years later the matter was still unresolved, provoking J. F. MacCabe in the *Dublin Magazine* to note that the conflict was indeed one of different tempos and rhythms in the life of the nation. His comment raised wider questions about economic development and the insertion of Ireland into global modernity. Drawing on the social-distributivist critiques of industrial capitalism advanced by G. K. Chesterton and Hilaire Belloc, MacCabe pointed out that both agricultural labor and the Irish factory floor involved elements of craft and skill that did not answer to the automated routines of mass industrial production:

> Some differences of opinion exist as to whether the Free State is, indeed, free. There can hardly be freedom which ignores the laws of space and time and the profound implications of these, to which we

have only recently awakened. . . . It cannot be disputed that the imposition of "Summer Time" on Ireland was a definite invasion of our
national habits of thought, work and outlook. It was, and is, the product of English town and industrial life.[30]

Ireland had broken free in name from British rule, yet not only Irish
human beings but even Irish cattle were still held captive by the work
disciplines of British industry:

The beginning of all these things is, necessarily, our own time stan-
dard. In itself it is an indication of our own separate, Irish entity. . . .
It would also convenience our Irish cows and help our harvesters. . . .
So let us blaspheme neither space nor time but combine them for
Irish purposes.[31]

Notwithstanding the distributivist diction, MacCabe was drawing attention to a key issue relating to decolonization under capitalist modernity: whether the cultural logic of development in the West—in particular, the work ethic, time-discipline, Taylorism, automation—provides the
only successful mode of entry into the modern world system. As Fredric
Jameson argues, there is only one world system, and to that extent a "singular modernity," but there are "alternate historical paths" leading into,
traversing, and indeed traducing this global network of capital.[32] What
may be anachronistic or dead weight in one society need not be so in another, and still less need it be a form of romantic regression. A famous advertisement by the Irish Development Authority in the 1980s, designed
to attract "high-tech" international investment to Ireland, showed a sepia
photograph of a grim Victorian factory, with the caption "MISSING THE
INDUSTRIAL REVOLUTION WAS THE BEST THING THAT EVER HAP-
PENED TO THE IRISH."[33] Of course, Fordism, not to mention sweatshop
labor, is still very much part of late capitalism, but it does not follow that
this is due to the intrinsic logic of modernity, as against the expansionist
policies of accumulation of particular capital formations in the West.[34]
As Dipesh Chakrabarty argues, taking issue with E. P. Thompson's attri-
bution of "time-discipline" to the structural logic of market economies:

Even if . . . a place like India suddenly and unexpectedly boasted
human beings as averse to "laziness" as the bearers of the Protestant ethic are supposed to be, we would still . . . never know for sure
whether this condition . . . was a genuinely universal, functional
characteristic of capital, or whether world capitalism represented a

forced globalization of a particular fragment of European history in which the Protestant ethic became a value. A victory for the Protestant ethic, however, global, would surely not be a victory for any universal.[35]

Flashbacks and the Public Sphere

As soon as montage intervenes . . . the present becomes past: a past that, for cinematographic and not aesthetic reasons, is always in the present mode (that is, it is a historic present).

PIER PAOLO PASOLINI, "Observations on the Long Take"

At one point in his analysis of the psychic life of (Western) capitalism, Chakrabarty cites Max Horkheimer's famous dictum: "Machinery requires the kind of mentality that concentrates on the present and can dispense with memory and the straying imagination."[36] In the interests of calibration, uniformity, and built-in obsolescence, part of this process was to remove the discontinuities and fragmentation of time under modernity from public space—political or economic—onto the psyche, an inner life re-created in the image of the new culture industries. The paradox here, however, is that by virtue of the pressures placed on the past, modernity also created ways of reactivating it in the present, with new internal shocks of dislocation. The issue here is not only "survivals" from another era, as in the practice of herding cattle through the streets of Dublin, which the mourners at Paddy Dignam's funeral momentarily glimpse on their way to Glasnevin (*U* 6.386–405). This "residual" practice is itself a product of capitalist modernity, for the cattle are being exported on the hoof to Britain, leading to the crushing of an independent Irish agricultural policy: "That doctrine of *laissez faire* which so often in our history. Our cattle trade. The way of all our old industries. Liverpool ring which jockeyed the Galway harbour scheme" (*U* 2.234–36). The anachronistic presence of cattle in the metropolis, moreover, prompts one of Bloom's imaginative exercises in city planning, utilizing the most advanced transport technologies: "I can't make out why the corporation doesn't run a tramline from the parkgate to the quays, Mr Bloom said. All those animals could be taken in trucks down to the boats" (*U* 6.400–402). As Chakrabarty points out, to speak of "survivals" in this context is misleading as it suggests stagist or stadial theories of progress in which anachronisms could "be seen as leftovers from an earlier period, still active, no doubt, but under world-historical notice of extinction."[37] As Bloom's utopian scheme indicates, however, the days of this residual practice are not numbered, since the imperial policy of exporting cattle on the hoof only awaits new technological improvements not only to persist into, but also to add greater efficiency to, the present.

It is in this jarring sense that the instabilities of time in Joyce's Dublin inhabit public space and coexist with, or may even be actively produced by, the dislocations of colonial modernity. "Time shocked rebounds, shock by shock" (*U* 2.316–17), according to Stephen, anticipating Pier Paolo Pasolini's argument that with the introduction of cinematic montage, past and present are juxtaposed in hitherto unthinkable ways.[38] In the very sundering of the past from the present, cinema also created — or articulated — ways of reliving memory with an unprecedented, almost visceral immediacy. It is not, moreover, as if this is simply a cinematic or literary device, operating at the level of *representation*, while life carries on regardless, oblivious to such innovations in the art world. As the work of film scholars such as Miriam Hansen and Mary Ann Doane shows, some of the most radical changes brought about by new mass-media technologies of modernity consist precisely of the restructuring of our senses and frames of knowledge.[39] The psychological diagnosis of trauma — or "shell shock," as it was initially called — in World War I, with its symptomatology of flashbacks, nightmares, and broken narratives, coincided with the appearance of flashbacks and the aesthetics of shock in early cinema: "The term flashback implies the cinematic possibility of literally reproducing or cutting back to a scene from the past and hence expresses the idea that the trauma victim's experiences are exact 'reruns' or 'replays' of the traumatic incident."[40]

The reappearance of such painful experiences is disturbing, but in early Irish cinema, it is not clear, as in the case of Father Conmee, whether flashbacks are taking place in the head or are spectral emanations from the past. In the first Irish feature film, *The Lad from Old Ireland*, shot on location in Ireland for the American Kalem Company in 1910, the male hero, Terry (Sidney Olcott), emigrates to America to seek his fortune and is shown on the deck of the ship overcome by loss, pining for his sweetheart, Aileen (Gene Gauntier). She suddenly appears beside him, superimposed on the deck of the ship (fig. 6.6). Is this a flashback, an attempt to visualize his memory or inner life, or is it an apparition in the "external" world? Terry apparently thinks the latter, for he reaches out to physically embrace her — at which point she vanishes into thin air. As Maureen Turim argues of the early phase of cinema, before 1910:

Flashbacks in this period are extremely difficult to distinguish from "vision" scenes that are meant to be understood as imaginary, or actions that happen simultaneously, but are "seen" by a character in no

6.6 Sidney Olcott, *The Lad from Old Ireland* (1910). Still sequence of Terry and Aileen on deck. Private collection.

position to observe them. . . . A 1914 text called *Playwriting for the Cinema: Dealing with the Writing and Marketing of Scenarios*, gives us a section on "visions" but none on flashbacks. It suggests abandoning the superimposition for the sequential presentation of dreams punctuated by fades-in and -out, a preference presented as more economical for producers.[41]

This latter scenario corresponds to Joyce's interpolations of Mary Rochfort/Lady Belvedere in "Wandering Rocks," except—crucially—there are no fades-in or -out to signal their imaginary status.[42] As Jo Anna Isaak observes of the anomalies in time in Joyce's modernism, the various characters in *Ulysses* move around not just in various spaces but also through different time frames, or "chronotopes," which overlap and interpenetrate each other. Clock time, psychological time, and political time are sedimented in the buildings and streetscapes encountered by the various characters:

> Numerous planes of space and time have been superimposed. What distinguished this technique from the common novelistic technique of flashback is that Joyce, concerned with surface and texture, is not so much interested in entering the past as he is in having segments of the past (or the future) overlap upon the present.[43]

There is no regression in time here, but the past is not abolished either. As Isaak notes, in the use of cinematic flashbacks there is a clear separation of *now* and *then*: what we find in Joyce is *unannounced* flashbacks, or rather "flash-cuts," in which the pressure of the past forces its way into the present.

In the course of teaching his history lesson in "Nestor," Stephen reflects that the past is over but it is not done with, and may contain narratives whose time has yet to come—"Or was that only possible which came to pass?" (*U* 2.52). The realm of possibility is opened up rather than closed down by the contingency of fact, and draws on the unrequited past as much as the unknown future. It is not that such possibilities remain in "thought" only but that the boundaries between inside and outside, past and present, come apart in Joyce's Dublin. The alternative histories with which *Ulysses* abounds (many of which point to genealogies of an independent Ireland, such as Galway's strangled harbor scheme) were still part of a contested *public* sphere in Ireland, resisting relegation to a private, psychological space. Through increasingly clear lines drawn between inner and outer worlds, public and psychological space, the new mass media infiltrated not only the conscious but also the unconscious, leaving little space beyond the reach of art. The allocation of trauma, or related notions of "involuntary memory," to private experience belied the fact that under colonial modernity, such experiences were bound up with dislocations in the public sphere. Whatever about the ahistorical triumph of space over time in metropolitan modernism, in *Ulysses* space is continually at odds with temporal powers. As Stephen muses: "Fabled by the daughters of memory. And yet it was in some way if not as memory fabled it. . . . I hear the ruin of all space, shattered glass and toppling masonry, and time one livid final flame. What's left us then?" (*U* 2.7–10).

CHAPTER 7

"Famished Ghosts"

BLOOM, BIBLE WARS, AND "U. P: UP"
IN JOYCE'S DUBLIN

> *Soup, joint and sweet. Never know whose thoughts you're chewing.*
> *. . . Famished ghosts. Ah, I'm hungry.*
>
> JAMES JOYCE (*U* 8.717–18)

One of the traumatic aspects of the "nightmare of history" in *Ulysses* is that the past is not confined to dream but may visit its terrors again on the present. One such nightmare wakes up Denis Breen in a panic attack in "Lestrygonians," as reported by his wife to Bloom on Westmoreland Street:

—Woke me up in the night, she said. Dream he had, a nightmare. Indiges.
—Said the ace of spades was walking up the stairs.
—The ace of spades! Mr Bloom said.
She took a folded postcard from her handbag.
—Read that, she said. He got it this morning
—What is it? Mr Bloom asked, taking the card. U. P.?
—U. p: up, she said. Someone taking a rise out of him. It's a great shame for them whoever he is.
—Indeed it is, Mr Bloom said.
She took back the card, sighing.
—And now he's going round to Mr Menton's office. He's going to take an action for ten thousand pounds, he says.
She folded the card into her untidy bag and snapped the catch. (*U* 8.251–64)

Bloom's exchange with Mrs. Breen (and the bare stirrings of indigestion) is preceded by an encounter with a YMCA proselytizer outside

Graham Lemon's in Lower O'Connell Street, dispensing throwaways announcing that salvation is nigh: "Elijah is coming. Dr John Alexander Dowie restorer of the Church of Zion is coming!" (*U* 8.13–14). Crossing O'Connell Bridge, Bloom notices seagulls foraging for scraps of food in the Liffey— *"the hungry famished gull / Flaps o'er the waters dull"* (*U* 8.62–63)—and throws the leaflet into the water to see if they would rise to the bait: "He threw down among them a crumpled paper ball. Elijah thirtytwo feet per sec. is com. Not a bit. The ball bobbed unheeded on the wake of swells, floated under by the bridgepiers. Not such damn fools" (*U* 8.57–59). The presentation of spiritual salvation in the guise of food signals one of the abiding themes of "Lestrygonians": the specters of famine and "souperism" that followed the linking of food relief with proselytism during the Great Famine. "Good Lord, that poor child's dress in flitters. Underfed she looks too. Potatoes and marge, marge and potatoes. It's after they feel it" (*U* 8.41–42). On Bachelor's Walk, Bloom spots one of the destitute Dedalus sisters hovering around Dillon's auction rooms: "Must be selling some furniture" (*U* 8.29). When the starving Dedalus sisters, Katey and Boody, reappear later in the "Wandering Rocks" chapter, they are living off pea soup provided by the Sisters of Charity home in Gardiner Street, and Bloom learns in the early hours of the following morning in the cabman's shelter that Stephen Dedalus also has not eaten since "the day before yesterday" (*U* 16.1777).

Bloom's intermittent memories of the Famine and its ghoulish legacy in Ireland are touched off, literally, by the potato he carries around with him all day as a talisman of sorts, and which he confirms is in his pocket as he leaves his house for the butcher's at the beginning of "Calypso." As he approaches Davy Byrne's for a midday lunch, Bloom turns to thoughts of religious conversion, food, and disease, prompted by memories of the emaciation associated with Soyer's famous soup kitchen in the Phoenix Park during the Great Famine:

Suppose that communal kitchen years to come perhaps. All trotting down with porringers and tommycans to be filled. Devour contents in the street. . . . My plate's empty. After you with our incorporated drinkingcup. Like sir Philip Crampton's fountain. Rub off the microbes with your handkerchief. Next chap rubs on a new bunch with his. Father O'Flynn would make hares of them all. Have rows all the same. All for number one. Children fighting for the scrapings of the pot. Want a souppot as big as the Phoenix park. . . . Hate people all around you. . . . Soup, joint and sweet. Never know whose thoughts you're chewing. . . . Famished ghosts. Ah, I'm hungry. (*U* 8.704–6, 710–15, 718–19, 730)[1]

The point of ghosts is to remind us that the past may materialize in the present, and that far from being distant memories, chronic hunger, disease, and sectarian wars still stalked Ireland at the turn of the twentieth century. The sensitivity of radical nationalists toward the condescension of aristocratic charity was captured by D. P. Moran's mockery of fawning "Castle Catholics," who caught "the Vice-Regal microbe" of snobbery.[2] The very facility with which the air carried pestilence was attributed by Arthur Griffith to reckless afforestation carried out by the British, leading also to skepticism about anti-TB measures proposed by the Castle administration, on the grounds they were designed to destroy Irish trade by tainting exported goods as contaminated.[3] The fact that the Women's National Health Association was founded by the wife of the Lord Lieutenant, Lady Aberdeen (also known as "Lady Microbe"), led to accusations by Alice Milligan that it was a cover for new forms of modern souperism.[4] It was not, therefore, as if famine were past history: the ominous threat of crop failure and widespread starvation on the western seaboard in 1898 prompted Maud Gonne and James Connolly to visit the counties of Mayo and Kerry, and to coauthor a pamphlet indicting the cult of private property that presided over famine.[5] It was in this context of bitterness and suspicion that Brian O'Higgins penned another satire on the political contagion of microbes, exposing what he considered British plans to induce a new famine to solve the Irish question.[6]

Though much emphasis has been placed in Joycean scholarship on the rise of the confessional state and Catholic nationalism, less attention has been devoted to the Bible wars mounted by evangelical Protestantism. Ultra-Protestantism and militant Unionism were far from negligible forces in Ireland—and particularly Dublin—at the turn of the twentieth century, not least because, ultimately, they had the power of the state on their side (albeit a Tory administration embarrassed at times by sectarian excesses). This strand of Anglo-Irish politics, which refused to accept the decline of the Ascendancy in the aftermath of the Land War, and which strongly resisted Home Rule, was given forceful expression in the Irish Unionist Association's *Notes from Ireland* and the newssheet of Frederick Trench, Third Baron Ashtown, *Grievances from Ireland*.[7] No stranger to paranoia of the kind that besets Denis Breen in *Ulysses*, Ashtown published an alarmist tract, *The Unknown Power*, in 1908, which saw in the Ancient Order of the Hibernians an Illuminati-type conspiracy embracing everything from Whiteboyism, Ribbonism, and the Molly Maguires to Michael Davitt, Parnell, and John Redmond.[8] As Patrick Maume describes this paranoid style:

Lord Ashtown was part of an ultra-Protestant sub-culture still preaching modernization through Protestant evangelisation and speaking for groups affected by the breakdown of traditional structures of Anglo-Irish ascendancy. In the eighteen-nineties this sub-culture was visibly represented in Dublin by missionary groups, such as that headed by the former Catholic priest Thomas Connellan, publisher of a monthly called *The Catholic*.[9]

On leaving Davy Byrne's, Bloom walks along Duke lane quietly ruminating on his lunch of Gorgonzola cheese, bread, and burgundy wine, and turns into Dawson Street:

> Mr Bloom turned at Gray's confectioner's window of unbought tarts and passed the reverend Thomas Connellan's bookstore. *Why I left the church of Rome*. Birds' nest women run him. They say they used to give pauper children soup to change to protestants in the time of the potato blight. Society over the way papa went to for conversion of poor jews. Same bait. *Why we left the church of Rome*. (*U* 8.1069–74)

No sooner have thoughts on religious proselytism run through Bloom's head than he spots a blind stripling attempting to cross over to the other side in a more literal, pedestrian manner:

> A blind stripling stood tapping the curbstone with his slender cane. No tram in sight. Wants to cross.
> —Do you want to cross? Mr Bloom asked.
> The blind stripling did not answer. His face frowned weakly. He moved his head uncertainly.
> —You're in Dawson street, Mr Bloom said. Molesworth street is opposite. Do you want to cross? There's nothing in the way. (*U* 8.1075–81)

There was nothing in the way to prevent the blind man crossing to the other side of the street, but the same could not be said for the owner of bookstore Bloom had just glimpsed, the Rev. Thomas Connellan (1854–1917) (fig. 7.1), author of the appropriately titled *Hear the Other Side*, one of the most combative apostate tracts in late nineteenth-century and early twentieth-century Ireland.[10] For the most part, Connellan has drawn a blank in detailed exegeses of "Who's Who" in Joyce's work, a situation not helped by the misprinting of the passage relating to him in early editions of *Ulysses* to read confusingly: "*Why I left the Church of Rome? Birds' Nest*. Women run him."[11] Robert M. Adams, in *Surface and*

Photo. by ... Rev. Thomas Connellan.   Chancellor. Dublin.

OLS B-9-480 No. 11

7.1 Rev. Thomas
Connellan. From Rev.
Thomas Connellan, *Hear
the Other Side,* 12th ed.,
revised and enlarged
(Dublin: Office of *The
Catholic,* 1908). Trinity
College Library, Dublin.

Symbol (1962), was the first to note that the version as printed made little
sense and, drawing on the fair-copy Rosenbach manuscript of *Ulysses*
and the original publication in the *Little Review,* suggested the correct
reading now incorporated into the Gabler edition.[12] This version is warranted not only on the textual grounds adduced by the editors but also,
as we shall see, by the extratextual evidence concerning Connellan that
Joyce drew on in his composition of the passage.[13]

As Gifford and Seidman point out, though the sentiments expressed in
Why I Left the Church of Rome apply to Connellan, the actual author was a
Canadian apostate priest, Charles Chiniquy, who published his pamphlet
in 1883.[14] That Chiniquy's publication was on sale in Connellan's bookstore, and advertised in his newspaper along with other attractions such
as *Walled Up Nuns,* may explain its springing into Bloom's mind as he is
passing by (though it hardly explains how it sprang up in Joyce's head in
Zurich, thirteen years later). Four years after the publication of Chiniquy's book, Father Thomas Connellan prepared for his own dramatic
conversion experience by staging his death by drowning in Lough Ree on

the River Shannon, near the town of Athlone, County Westmeath. James Joyce was not the first Irish novelist to be fascinated by Connellan's story. In 1905, George Moore's *The Lake* fictionalized the staged drowning of a priest named (much to Joyce's delight) Father Oliver Gogarty, whose obsession with a young teacher whom he drove from the parish, Norah Glenn, leads to his own farewell to the priesthood.[15] Father Gogarty's "drowning" in *The Lake* takes place within sight of "Kilronan Abbey," the name of a ruin near Connellan's homeplace that the young priest had written about as a local historian before his defection from the Catholic church.[16]

Thomas Connellan was born in Geevagh, County Sligo, in 1854 and was ordained a priest for the Diocese of Elphin in 1880. A curate of exceptional ability, he officiated in the bishop's palace at Sligo for four years before moving first to Strokestown, County Roscommon, then to Roscommon town, and finally to St. Peter's Church, Athlone. His ability to turn a phrase was soon evident in a series of articles published in the *Irish Ecclesiastical Record* on both local history and topics of wider historical interest. In an article on Mary Stuart and Elizabeth Tudor, he refers to Henry VIII as "England's Bluebeard" and cites the zeal of the convert John Knox and "the angry tide of the Reformation" in Scotland as the main factors that brought Mary Stuart to her doom:

> [Knox] had been a priest, but after a little experience found it more convenient to cast aside his religious vows and marry a wife. Like all renegades, he had an unconquerable hatred for the Church that cast him out. Rude, unpolished, uncultivated with a tongue rarely equalled in coarse scurrility except by his master Martin Luther.[17]

Parts of this pen-picture could have been written later about Connellan himself, though his style was far from being unpolished, uncultivated, or even humorless. In his autobiographical *Hear the Other Side*, he outlines how among the student population at Maynooth, "the sanctimonious scoundrel, with face expressive as a time-worn tombstone; with eyes fixed upon the ground as if eternally measuring six feet for a grave; with hypocrisy personified in his gait, and speaking in his voice—he will be a success, not alone in Maynooth, but in his after life as a priest" (*HTOS* 13). Connellan's initial years of service at the bishop's palace at Sligo, under the formidable Bishop Laurence Gillhooly (1819–95), proved a turning point:

> Never had Eastern despot, Russian Czar, or Japanese Mikado, a more obsequious set of courtiers. The bishop laid down the law on all ques-

tions—politics, morals, economy, geography—and the retinue assented in chorus. He had a method of testing whiskey; he could detect the real aroma of coffee; as a judge of wine he spoke with a tone of infallibility. In fact, he seemed an animated encyclopedia, a star of the first magnitude, while we, poor satellites, merely turned on our feeble rushlights occasionally to bring out our leader's brilliance by contrast. (*HTOS* 16)

Though Connellan points out that the possession of George Eliot's *Adam Bede* or *The Mill on the Floss* would have merited expulsion from Maynooth, the bishop's spelling of literature with a double *t* did not lessen his infallibility: "when convinced of his mistake, [he] protest[ed] that 'litterateur' was in his head" (*HTOS* 18). A series of confrontations with church authorities led eventually to Connellan's radical break with the faith, as he recounts in his memoir:

Tuesday, September 20th, 1887, was my last day on the Shannon. . . . After breakfast my parish priest had a talk with me about certain schools of which I had charge, and then I walked out of St. Peter's forever. I had sent a Gladstone bag containing a secular suit of clothes to the boat, and determined at any risk to have done with my old life. . . . [Having] deposited my secular clothes in some underwood, and pushed into the river[,] I then undressed, dodged a fisherman for a little, and having plunged into the water swam ashore. . . . No baptism by water had ever wrought a more wonderful regeneration than had that plunge into the sun-lit Shannon. (*HTOS* 77)

Not without wry humor, Connellan goes on to quote at length his obituaries in the *Westmeath Independent* and the *Roscommon Messenger*, testifying to the exhaustive search for his body, the great esteem in which he was held by his parishioners, and "a most mysterious" factor: although his clothes were stacked in the boat, his gold watch and purse were missing. "The load of sufferings and care which I had carried for years remained with my clerical garb in the boat" (*HTOS* 78), he writes, but some material possessions were clearly too valuable to be left behind, even in the interests of committing the perfect disappearing act (fig. 7.2.)

Connellan began his new life as a born-again Christian in London before returning to Dublin in 1889, where he established his own evangelical mission at 51B Dawson Street. With his characteristic energy, he published a proselytizing newspaper provocatively called *The Catholic* and, joined by his brother and a coterie of converts (fig. 7.3), began his

7.2 Lough Ree, County Westmeath, the scene of Rev. Thomas Connellan's disappearance. From Rev. Thomas Connellan, *Hear the Other Side* (Dublin: Office of *The Catholic*, 1908). Trinity College Library, Dublin.

Photo. by]   GROUP OF WORKERS, ALL CONVERTS.   [Brook Smith, Dublin

7.3 Rev. Thomas Connellan with a group of converts. From Rev. Thomas Connellan, *Hear the Other Side* (Dublin: Office of *The Catholic*, 1908). Trinity College Library, Dublin.

work of winning over lost souls. It is in this context that his name is first associated with the Bird's Nest orphanage in Dun Laoghaire and related institutions in Dublin, run by the redoubtable Mrs. Smyley. "As regards Catholic Homes for destitute children there seems to be only two," wrote the Rev. Joseph Keating in his pamphlet *"Souperism"* (1914), "to balance nine or ten proselytizing institutions run by the notorious Smyly [*sic*] family and its connections."[18] An article in *The Catholic* in December 1891 entitled "Daily Schools for Orphans" reported that Protestant homes were thriving and that voluntary contributions would be greatly received by Mrs. Smyley, 35 Fitzwilliam Street, Dublin.[19]

The bewilderment of Connellan's former parishioners can well be imagined when word reached them that their deceased curate had not only come back from the dead but was born again in another sense. As if returning to the scene of the crime, Connellan revisited Athlone to bring his spiritual mission to the heart of the Irish countryside. On September 15, 1892, the *Westmeath Nationalist* carried the following headline and story:

PROSELYTISM IN ATHLONE—A NEFARIOUS AGENCY
AT WORK—CATHOLICS INSULTED—
POPULAR INDIGNATION

Intense indignation was aroused in Athlone on Thursday morning by the discovery that during the night a gang of "Soupers" had been at work in the town. Every dead wall was placarded with handbills, in which the Catholic religion, its ceremonies, doctrines and practices were shamefully traduced and ridiculed. Sheaves of those precious leaflets were also found thrust into letter boxes, and one or two copies of a pamphlet by the apostate priest "Father" Connellan, were also, (so we are informed), brought to light.[20]

An accompanying editorial under the heading "Mrs. Smyley's Home–Bird's Nest" warns readers "of the attempt to introduce the methods of Mrs. Smiley [*sic*] into Athlone":

MRS SMYLEY'S HOME—BIRD'S NEST

In another column we give a brief account of the attempt to introduce the methods of Mrs. Smiley [*sic*] into Athlone. The clique responsible for the outrage will be surprized to hear that their self-sacrificing modesty and love of retirement has not succeeded in hiding them from the popular gaze. They are known and will probably soon be exposed.[21]

These and related incidents provide the basis for the correct emendation by Robert Adams of the passage in *Ulysses* to read: "Mr Bloom turned at Gray's confectioner's window of unbought tarts and passed the reverend Thomas Connellan's bookstore. *Why I left the church of Rome.* Birds' nest women run him." It was no doubt through his association with Mrs. Smyley, highlighted in *The Catholic*, that Joyce made the link between the apostate priest and the "Birds' nest women" that orchestrated his campaigns.

Extratextual sources add new complexities to textual meanings, but the question then arises, which has been raised earlier: how did Joyce acquire this information? Even allowing for the perception that, like Bishop Gilhooly, "he seemed an animated encyclopedia," it strains credibility that the *Westmeath Nationalist* was avidly read by the young Joyce at the age of ten, still less that he remembered it in Zurich twenty-five years later. Thomas Connellan's Dublin-based *The Catholic* is a more likely source as it carried advertisements, as we have seen, for Mrs. Smyley's "Daily Schools for Orphans," noting that "while the schools were working, no child in Dublin need be without food, education, or knowledge of the Saviour."[22] Joyce's bemusement with George Moore's *The Lake* may have further whetted his interest (including the fact that Father Gogarty in the novel escapes to "Joycetown"), but one of Leo Daly's most interesting suggestions is that Joyce's trip to Mullingar with his father in the summer of 1900 may have filled in some of the background knowledge. Thomas Connellan's brothers James and Patrick moved—perhaps because of local pressures due to the scandal caused by the defrocked priest—from Sligo to Mullingar, where they ran a bar, restaurant, and grocery beside the courthouse. The bar, as a prominent Nationalist Party establishment, was almost certainly a stopping-off point for Joyce's father, whose work on the voting register in the courthouse was the occasion of their visits to Mullingar. Over and above these factors, the general notoriety attached to Bird's Nest institutions was such as to lead to a subgenre of captivity narratives in Catholic Truth Society literature, which could hardly have escaped Joyce's notice. In the pious tract *Rescued!* the young heroine overhears the opening gambit of a well-dressed evangelical proselytizing in a cabin in terms that evoke the Rev. Thomas Connellan: "But you haven't heard the other side, my very dear friend. Wait till I have pointed out to you the errors of Rome, and then I think you'll agree with me that the Papists are really idol-worshippers."[23]

All these suggestions relating to Joyce's acquaintance with Thomas Connellan and the moral panic surrounding Bird's Nest institutions are, of course, "off the page" and amount to little more than circumstantial

evidence. Nevertheless, they are sufficient to indicate that the basis for
Adams's correct interpretation of the Thomas Connellan paragraph lies
not only in genetic criticism and the Joyce archive, however valuable, but
also in sources we can be reasonably sure that Joyce never consulted: the
dusty files of the *Westmeath Nationalist* for the year 1892, or Connellan's
more obscure pamphlets. Historical references to extratextual factual details are often cited as one of the few ways to stabilize meaning in the
semantic hall of mirrors that is *Ulysses*, but as Derek Attridge points
out, rather than controlling the mass of fragmentary detail, "Joyce's
major texts *allow* meaning to arise out of that mass by the operation of
chance."[24] Instead of "fixing" interpretations, recourse to the factual, to
the historical record, opens up more questions than it can answer.[25]

"Doublin Up"

*This allegation—known as souperism . . .—caused lasting acrimony, and
inflamed relations between Protestant and Roman Catholic clergy during
relief operations, contributing to a mutual paranoia, and perhaps acceler-
ating the post-famine "devotional revolution."*

MELISSA FEGAN, *Literature and the Irish Famine, 1845–1919*

It is during Stephen's visit to Mullingar in *Stephen Hero* that the motif
of death through drowning is introduced in Joyce's fiction, the tragedy
on this occasion taking the form of the body of a female inmate from
Mullingar Mental Asylum who was recovered from the Royal Canal. A
recent drowning incident in Dublin Bay near Sandymount features at
the beginning of *Ulysses* in "Telemachus," and the theme is taken up in
"Nestor," when Stephen thinks of Milton's "Lycidas":

> *Weep no more, woful shepherd, weep no more*
> *For Lycidas, your sorrow, is not dead,*
> *Sunk though he be beneath the watery floor.* (U 2.64–66)

"Lycidas" comes again to Stephen's mind in "Proteus," along with passages relating to drowning from *The Tempest* and Ophelia's death in
Hamlet (U 3.470–88). In "Telemachus" and "Eumaeus," Buck Mulligan's
saving of a man from drowning plays on this theme, but it is also related to "metempsychosis," the possibility of resurrection exemplified
by the controversial "reappearance" of the lost Tichborne Claimant, believed dead from drowning, to reclaim his estate in England in the mid-
nineteenth century.[26] Connellan's return represents an equally dubious
case of rebirth through drowning, but the residues of souperism, fam-

ished ghosts, and return from the sea also recur in relation to vestiges of Stephen's dead mother. When Bloom seeks the return of his talismanic potato in "Circe," it is on the grounds that "it is nothing, but still, a relic of poor Mamma" (*U* 15.3513): earlier it transpires that the "shrivelled potato" (*U* 15.289) is among her mementoes. Stephen's haunting by his dead mother recalls the cannibalism of the Famine ("Ghoul, Chewer of Corpses" [*U* 1.278; also *U* 15.4214]) as well as the "Agenbite" of remorse, while her grisly specter insists that his starving sister Dilly "make you that boiled rice every night after your brainwork" (*U* 15. 4201–2). The death of Stephen's mother, with "the ghostcandle to light her agony" (*U* 1.274), is equated in "Proteus," as we have seen, with the figure of the undead, the vampire, who emerges from the sea: "In sleep the wet sign calls her hour, bids her rise. Bridebed, childbed, bed of death, ghostcandled. OMNIS CARO AD TE VENIET. He comes, pale vampire, through storm his eyes, his bat sails bloodying the sea, mouth to her mouth's kiss" (*U* 3.396–99). That the recurring past belongs not just to personal memory but to history is clear from the indictment of the potato through its association with Sir Walter Raleigh, "who brought from the new world that . . . killer of pestilence by absorption" (*U* 15.1356–57), sentiments echoed by the macabre chant of the "Daughters of Erin" in "Circe," linking the potato once again with religion: "Potato, Preservative against Plague and Pestilence, pray for us" (*U* 15.1952).

When the chorus of "Irish Evicted Tenants" (*U* 15.1183) is summoned up to bring Bloom face-to-face with his hidden past in "Circe," it is in the company of other victims of sectarian wars in Dublin, "Artane Orphans" (run by Christian Brothers) and "Girls of the Prison Gate Mission" (a Protestant Magdalene laundry). In the "Wandering Rocks" section, as we have seen, the efforts of another priest with both Athlone and Mullingar connections, "the superior, the very reverend John Conmee S.J.," formerly of Belvedere College, are charted, as he journeys to the O'Brien Institute at "Artane" to arrange for the custodial care of the son of the deceased Paddy Dignam in a Catholic orphanage—before the soupers get their hands on him.[27] In the phantasmagorical setting at the beginning of "Circe," Bloom is discovered consorting with prostitutes by Mrs. Breen, whom he had met earlier in the day on Westmoreland Street in "Lestrygonians" (and who is also, as Josie Powell in her premarriage days, an old flame of Bloom's). Bloom pleads ingenuously that his intentions are honorable as he is on a Bird's Nest mission, saving lost souls from "haunts of sin": "Rescue of fallen women. Magdalen Asylum. I am the secretary. . . ." (*U* 15.402). A short time later, Mrs. Breen's unhinged husband, Denis, comes on the scene, still smarting from the prank in which he was the recipient of the provocative postcard carrying the cryptic message: "U. p:

U. P. UP.

Vengeance, " quick as lightning and true as steel,"
has overtaken the grabbers of the Caledonian Games'
Society. In March their annual meeting for the election of officers was held. Mr. A. Morrison-Miller, the
father of the Society, was elected Hon. Sec., for the
third time. About the middle of May an extraordinary
treble-whip meeting was held. Twenty-six, out of between sixty and seventy members, attended, and the
votes of twelve of these unceremoniously deposed Mr.
Miller, without rhyme or reason. I asked the reason
why, and got no answer till this week. To keep up
appearances, they skirled about for a while, and resolved to hold their annual sports on the 1st of August, the day being a general holiday. But the hour for
work came round—that hour of shams' " black arch
the key-stone "—and the now dismayed sons of Scotia
resolved to have a feed instead of the sports. Accordingly, they announced by circular that a pic-nic party
was being organised for the 16th of July. A United
Presbyterian (I don't know how long he is married)
laughed when I gave him the top of the " Ray," and
he heartily endorsed the opinion expressed by an educator of youth and the proprietor of Helptheboys Hall.
The C.G.S. has died a sudden and unprovided death.
R.I.P.

7.4 "U. P. UP," *Celtic Times* (1887). Private collection.

up." Later in the "Cyclops" chapter, one reflexive meaning of the initials
is intimated by a pun, as Breen passes by the pub on his demented quest
to sue the perpetrators of the joke:

> Look at him, says he [Alf Bergen]. Breen. He's traipsing all around
> Dublin with a postcard someone sent him with U. p: up on it to take
> a li . . .
> And he doubled up. (*U* 12.257–59)

"Doubled up" is literally the condition of the letters on the postcard, and
the ridicule of the barflies rouses the attention of both the citizen's dog
and the citizen himself in the corner of the bar.

Not least of the ironies here is that the citizen may be responding to
his own joke, since the enigmatic letters "U. P. UP" appeared as a heading
on one of Michael Cusack's (aka "the Citizen") own columns in the *Celtic
Times* in 1887 (fig. 7.4). More than perhaps any other puzzle in *Ulysses*—
with the possible exception of the mysterious "man in the mackintosh"

at Paddy Dignam's funeral—"U. p: up" has been subjected to an endless array of interpretations, ranging from sexual innuendo to the plausible existence of a pseudo-Ulysses (the sailor Murphy as "Ulysses Pseudo-angelos," i.e., UP) and to a form of baseball notation. Given the emphasis on proselytism, evangelical wars, and hunger in "Lestrygonians" when the initials first appear in the text, and then the reemergence of the enigmatic message in "Cyclops" in the presence of the citizen, it is worth relating the context of the earlier appearance of the initials/letters in 1887.[28]

The *Celtic Times* was established in Dublin in 1887 by Michael Cusack and a Scottish expatriate socialist, A. Morrison-Miller, to promote pan-Celtic sporting and cultural alliances linking Ireland, Scotland, and Wales (fig. 7.5). Morrison-Miller had already organized a series of Caledonian Games in Dublin that acted as a catalyst for the founding of the Gaelic Athletic Association in 1884, but the attempt to spread the Celtic Revival among Scottish circles in Dublin soon met with opposition. In May 1887, a Presbyterian faction expelled Morrison-Miller from the Caledonian Games Society he had founded, much as Cusack and, indeed, Parnell were deposed by their erstwhile colleagues in the organizations they had helped to establish.[29] Cusack's colorful gossip column "Harmonic Rays" for 18 June 1887 carries the following entry:

U. P. UP

Vengeance, "quick as lightning and true as steel," has overtaken the grabbers of the Caledonian Games' Society. In March their annual meeting for the election of officers was held. Mr. A. Morrison-Miller, the father of the society, was elected Hon. Sec., for the third time. About the middle of May an extraordinary treble-whip meeting was held. Twenty six, out of between sixty to seventy members, attended, and the votes of these unceremoniously deposed Mr. Miller, without rhyme or reason. I asked the reason why, and got no answer till this week. *To keep up* appearances, they skirled about for a while, and resolved to hold their annual sports on the 1st of August, the day being a general holiday. But the hour for work came around—that hour of shams' "black arch the key-stone"—and the now dismayed sons of Scotia resolved to have a feed instead of the sports. Accordingly, they announced by circular that a pic-nic party was being organized for the 16th of July. A United Presbyterian (I don't know how long he is married) laughed when I gave him the top of the "Ray," and he heartily endorsed the opinion expressed by an educator of youth and the proprietor of Helptheboys Hall. The C.G.S has died a sudden and unprovided for death. R.I.P.[30]

·Let· Native· Industries· Literature· Arts· &· Pastimes· Flourish·

The Celtic Times

VOL. I.—No. 42.   DUBLIN, SATURDAY, OCTOBER 15, 1887   [Registered for Transmission Abroad.]   PRICE 1D.

£100 | The Proprietor of this Paper has Assured every Purchaser in the General Accident and Employers' Liability Assurance Association, Ltd., in the sum of | £100
(See Conditions on 4th page.)

IRELAND'S RESOURCES

AND

TRUE ECONOMY.

Amongst all thickly-populated peoples the essential requisite of progress is peace. Indeed, civilization implies peace—peace that acknowledges duties and respects rights. Progress in science and art cannot occur in the midst of turmoil and war. Men must be assured of the reward of their industry before they engage in toil or in the expenditure of their money. To be a citizen of a state is to conform to laws in which you had a voice either of approval or disapproval. It is to be one of a community that have agreed to perform their several duties and to enforce their several rights. Each citizen preserving his individuality and enforcing to the limit all those rights which do not injuriously affect his fellow, and at the same time exhibiting his brotherhood by conforming to those duties which are deemed requisite for the national liberty and well-being.

In a properly administered Commonwealth, the prosperity of the State simply tells of the ensuring to each individual the fruit of his labour in peace. This, in sparsely populated countries, is not so difficult a task, but when population increases and machinery replaces hand labour, the exact proportioning to each person their fair share of the blessings which flow from a just and strong government is a task which requires familiarity with the labours of each and wisdom in apportioning the awards.

Again, machinery may so change pre-existing relations, that the total social condition undergoes a revolution. The introduction of steam as a motive power for ocean ships and railways, so changed the value of agricultural produce, that the Land Laws had to be changed, and more security in his employment, and a less tax on his labour, were of necessity conceded to the farmer. In applying improved methods to their legitimate ends, want of proper forethought may seriously diminish the value of the improvement. The reckless extravagance with which our earlier railways were planned and made, has injuriously kept up the high carriage rates which so lamentably cripple trade in this country. Who can look on the suspension folly of the Boyne suspension bridge, at Drogheda, and not regret the lack of wisdom that literally threw tens of thousands of pounds into the sea, and ultimately placed the station in the most unsuitable and inconvenient position for the traders and passengers, and, by an extravagant outlay, produced charges that are almost prohibitory to trade on one of our principal railways.

To fail to avail ourselves of opportunities and improvements is almost as bad as to use them unwisely. No city is so excellently situated for water carriage on both sides of the river than Dublin, and yet the canals that connect the city with almost every town of importance in the country, are comparatively unused, the Ulster canal being absolutely unused for years. And this principally results for want of a proper motive power on the water, or from a want of proper adaptation of the motor power. Difficulties lie in the way of steam-propelled boats, and electricity, which could be so easily generated at many of the Irish waterfalls, is untried. Goods are slowly dragged along, and the country trader prefers to pay a higher rate by rail and be first in his local market with the wares, whereas, by electric-lit and electric-driven boats, travelling by night as well as day, the goods could be carried more safely, less expensively, and almost as quickly as by railway car. Holland does not fail to utilise her canal system, and yet we in Ireland make no move to utilise an unrivalled canal system.

Along with the drawback of slowness there is the difficulty from the natural opposition of railways who own in some cases and compete in others with the canals. Such interference with a system which would benefit trade should not be allowed to exist, and in such a case a combination of the traders and artisans, speaking through their town councils and city corporations, should demand from the State redress for the injury that railway capitalists inflict on the country. One of the facts necessary to be kept well before us is, that, owing to the free communications between peoples, foreign competition can only be defeated by intelligent combination between capitalists and workers, or by properly organised co-operation. Of the two, we would prefer the latter but we wish either rather than neither. Both demand a full recognition by the individual of his rights and duties, and in either case he must learn that his folly or wisdom injuriously or beneficially affects his fellow-worker. The complete body of workers is what the characaer of the individuals composing make it. If the individuals in an industrial league are sober, intelligent, and skilful workers, their league will soon attain distinction, and their work will quickly become recognised as good and reliable.

Now, our primary object is the promotion of this intelligent and skilful work by sober, industrious men. It is workers who make a country great. Intelligent handicraftsmen are a great wealth to a nation. The work of a good artisan reflects the man, and tells of his characteristics better than any photograph, for the photograph of his mind is in his work, which may be called his psychograph, or soul-writing. Such a worker finds labour no toil, and he delights in the excellence of his work. He interferes not with his fellow-man, and has a word of encouragement for every beginner. Such men speak with authority when the time to redress an evil comes ; and such men, when combination is necessary, do combine intelligently, with a determinate object and with a definite plan.

In many trades difficulties arise between the workers and the capitalist, and many processes of several trades are positively injurious to health, and should be either altered or at least lessened in their health-injuring properties, and in attempting to carry out modifications to benefit the worker our hope lies in support of sober, intelligent workers. It is the sober-thinking, industrious men that raise a state to a high standard of civilization.

PETTICOATS DOWN TO MY KNEES.

When my first lessons in life I began to know,
Spry as a chick newly out of the shell,
Nothing I longed for so much as a man to grow,
Sharing his joys and his sorrows as well.
Now that the high tide of life 's on the slack again,
Pleasure's deep draught drained down to the lees,
Dearly I wish that I had the days back again
When I wore petticoats down to my knees.

Well do I mind the day I donned trouserzens,
My proud mother cried, " We 'll soon be a man ? "
Little we knew what Fate has in store for us ;
Truth, it was then my troubles began.
Cramped up in clothes little comfort or ease I find,
Crippled and crushed, almost frightened to sneeze ;
Oh ! to have back my old freedom and peace of mind,
When I wore petticoats down to my knees.

Now must I walk many miles for an appetite,
And after all may journey in vain.
Oh ! for the days when, howe'er you might wrap it tight,
My school lunch was ate at the end of the lane.
Now scarce a wink of sleep on the best of nights,
Worried in mind and ill at my ease ;
Headache not heartache ne'er troubled my rest of nights,
When I wore petticoats down to my knees.

Gone are the days I thought girls were nuisances,
Petting and coaxing and ruffling your brow ;
Now Love, the rogue, runs away with my few senses,
Vainly I wish they would fondle me now.
Idols I worship, with order unspeakable,
But none of all half so fitted to please
As the poor boys, full of sawdust and breakable,
When I wore petticoats down to my knees.

Little I cared then for doings political,
The ebb or the flow of the popular tides ;
Europe might quake in a crisis most critical—
I had my bread buttered well on both sides.
Now must I wander for themes for my puny verse,
Over earth's continents, islands and seas ;
Small stock I took of affairs of the universe
When I wore petticoats down to my knees.

Life is a puzzle, and Man is a mystery,
He that would solve them a wizard need be.
Precepts lie thick on the pathways of history—
This is the lesson that time has taught me.
Man ever longs for the dawn of a golden day,
Visions of joy in futurity sees.
Ah ! he enjoyed life's crown in the olden day,
When he wore petticoats down to his knees.

DREOILIN.

Industries.

THE IRISH INDUSTRIAL LEAGUE.

THE DUBLIN PAVING WORKS.

SERIOUS CHARGE AGAINST A CORPORATION OFFICIAL.

THE RE-ORGANIZATION OF THE LEAGUE.

THE CHRISTMAS CARD INDUSTRY.

An important meeting of the League was held on Tuesday last, at 75, Aungier Street, Mr. Joseph Foley presiding. Amongst the letters read was the following important communication from Mr. J. Hutchinson, the general secretary of the Irish National Foresters :—" DEAR SIR—Having read

7.5 Front page, *Celtic Times* (15 October 1887). Private collection.

In this "death notice," "U. P." refers to "United Presbyterian" and the attempts of this faction to "keep up" appearances — "U. P. UP" — while carrying on what is deemed their sectarian anti-Irishness under the guise of a picnic in the park. Interestingly, the circular canceling the games was issued by "H. M. Macintosh, Hon. Sec." Three weeks earlier, in a column entitled "The Reason Why," Cusack implicated the *Irish Times* in the underhand move against Miller, singling out the editor, James Carlyle, for special rebuke:

> For ingratitude and treachery it would be hard to beat the records of some Irishmen. I very much fear the Caledonians in Dublin have cut the record. After three years of arduous and fruitful labour, the founder of their society has been removed from the position to which he had been re-elected a few weeks before. Is the staff of *The Irish Times* trying to grab the work of Mr. Miller's hands, much as the *Freeman* tried to grab the work of my hands? Answer at once, Mr James Carlyle, manager of *The Irish Times.* You signed the circular calling the meeting. . . . Read Carleton's "Rody the Rover," and you will find that we ought to be very careful to avoid those practices which by little and little qualify us to out-Judas Judas.[31]

Still dwelling on the cryptic postcard in "Lestrygonians," Bloom's thoughts turn to the Scotsman James Carlyle as the inspiration behind the *Irish Times*'s attempts to attract a Catholic, provincial readership, while they also hint at the possible Scottish elements of the postcard through its origins in the Scotch house:

> U. p: up. I'll take my oath that's Alf Bergan or Richie Goulding. Wrote it for a lark in the Scotch house I bet anything. Round to Menton's office. His oyster eyes staring at the postcard. Be a feast for the gods.
> He passed the *Irish Times.* There might be other answers lying there. Like to answer them all. Good system for criminals. Code. At their lunch now. . . . Enough bother wading through fortyfour of them. Wanted, smart lady typist to aid gentleman in literary work. I called you naughty darling because I do not like that other world. Please tell me what is the meaning. (*U* 8.320–28)

Bloom's mention of "code" refers to the telegraphese he employed in the classified advertisements section of the *Irish Times* to strike up a clandestine romantic exchange with a female correspondent. The problem with the covert form was that it attracted forty-four replies, many of them sincere and far from romantic fodder, including one from the real-life Lizzie

Twigg, protégé of A.E. (George Russell), whom he spots a short time later walking on Grafton Street with the famous poet ("Her stockings are loose over her ankles. I detest that" [U 8.542]). By carrying advertisements aimed at the Catholic population, the *Times* had increased its circulation while still deferring to the Protestant Ascendancy—a shrewd move on the part of James Carlyle, to Bloom's way of thinking:

> Best paper by long chalks for a small ad. Got the provinces now. Cook and general, exc. cuisine, housemaid kept. Wanted live man for spirit counter. Resp. girl (R.C.) wishes to hear of post in fruit or pork shop. James Carlisle made that. Six and a half per cent dividend. Made a big deal on Coates's shares. Ca' canny. Cunning old Scotch hunks. All the toady news. Our gracious and popular vicereine. (U 8.334–39)

On the letters page of the issue of the *Celtic Times* that carried "U. P. UP," Cusack announced that the paper was not able to carry "one-tenth part of the correspondence received relative to [the cancellation of the] Caledonian Games in Dublin" but printed a few protests from irate readers. One of the them, under the heading "The Bun and Lemonade Society," was sent by a correspondent, James A. Caird, who finished his letter as follows: "Since the C.G. and S.A. [Caledonian Games and Sports Association] of Ireland has changed its policy, I respectfully submit that it also change its name, and suggest that it be henceforth known as the The Scotch Anti-Irish Bun and Lemonade Society. This action will tend to preserve the luster of the short but glorious career of the C.G. and S.A."[32] As he passes the *Irish Times* office, it seems Bloom's thoughts also turn to the provision of food along methodical religious lines, with his reflections on Mina Purefoy's marriage:

> Poor Mrs Purefoy! Methodist husband. Method in his madness. Saffron bun and milk and soda lunch in the educational dairy. Y. M. C. A. Eating with a stopwatch, thirtytwo chews to the minute. And still his muttonchop whiskers grew. (U 6.358–61)

It is not, moreover, as if codes and secret communications were confined to clandestine, erotic affairs. The intense sectarian wars in Dublin led to the founding in 1903 of the undercover Catholic Association, which aimed to protect Catholic business interests against a perceived imbalance of Protestant economic power: "Catholics are three fourths of the people, the Protestants are three fourths of the upper classes": "In all nations having even a tincture of civility, there is some generally understood ideal of respectability; here in Ireland the Protestants represent that ideal, and our poor people had only two practical courses open to them, either to copy Protestant society, or to crawl into it."[33] The association attracted leading lights among the Catholic elite, with Edward Martyn acting as chairperson and the O'Conor Don among its ranks.[34] Its pretensions to respectability were ridiculed by its Protestant critics, not least the Rev. Thomas Connellan, who saw it as severely restricting its membership: "Indiscreet Roman Catholics are to be carefully excluded. So are drunkards, which condition must have greatly limited the scope of enquiry in Irish provincial towns."[35] One feature of the association, however, drew vitriolic condemnation from its critics: the recourse to encryptment and secret codes in communications among members. Not without a certain delight, Connellan reprinted the guidelines: let "a constant flow of streams of communication," the association advised, be "added, when useful, by private personal dispatches, and the use of a telegraphic code for expediency and privacy."[36] When the archbishop of Dublin, William Walsh, prohibited the organization, opponents were quick to point out that this was not on account of its sectarian methods but had a more base motivation: support for Catholic charities by wealthy Protestant donors was endangered by introducing religious zealotry into the commercial world.[37]

It is perhaps in this context that Denis Breen takes grave offense at the encrypted message on the postcard sent to him, and not only because of its sexual innuendo: it also pokes fun at his holier-than-thou religious leanings. When Breen shuffles past Barney Kiernan's looking for a detective to identify the writer of the card, Joe Hynes asks Alf Bergan if he was the perpetrator of the joke: "Was it you did it, Alf? says Joe. The truth, the whole truth and nothing but the truth, so help you Jimmy Johnson" (*U* 12.1038–39). This refers to a Scottish Presbyterian evangelical preacher, the Rev. Jimmy Johnson, author of *Learning to Float; or, Saved by Faith* (1869), *The Lily in the Pool; or, A Pure Life in a Polluted World* (1870), and *Learning to Walk in the Paths of Righteousness* (1889).[38] Denis Breen's religious piety is held directly up to overt ridicule when Bloom's expression of sympathy for the predicament of his wife, Josie (Powell) Breen, married to such a half-wit, serves only to draw the ire of the others in the bar:

> Begob I saw there was trouble coming. And Bloom explaining he meant on account of it being cruel for the wife having to go round after the old stuttering fool. Cruelty to animals so it is to let that bloody povertystricken Breen out on grass with his beard out tripping him, bringing down the rain. And she with her nose cockahoop after she married him because a cousin of his old fellow's was pew-

opener to the pope. Picture of him on the wall with his Smashall
Sweeney's moustaches, the signior Brini from Summerhill, the eye-
tallyano, papal Zouave to the Holy Father, has left the quay and gone
to Moss street. And who was he, tell us? A nobody, two pair back and
passages, at seven shillings a week, and he covered with all kinds of
breastplates bidding defiance to the world. (U 12.1060–69)

Given Breen's sanctimonious snobbery and religious posturings, a card
accusing him in effect of apostasy in the manner of Thomas Connellan,
or "elevation" to the condition of being a United Presbyterian (to "out-
Judas Judas"), would seem designed to bring him to the point of apo-
plexy. Breen is encountered for the last time in "Circe" in the company
of Hely's sandwichboard-men, shuffling their way through the street of
Dublin, as if he has also been reduced to a set of initials (U 15.479–85).[39]
That the experience of proselytism touches on Bloom's own family history is clear from his father Virag's conversion into the Protestant church
by the Society for Promoting Christianity among the Jews: "Society over
the way papa went to for conversion of poor jews. Same bait" (U 6.1073–
74). Bloom, of course, reverses this trend, formally renouncing Protestantism to adopt Catholicism to marry Molly in 1888, but as his parting
shot in the next sentence indicates — "*Why we left the church of Rome*"
(U 6.1075) — his lacklustre conversion would leave a lot to be desired by
the standards of the religious wars conducted in Joyce's Dublin.

CHAPTER 8

"Haunting Face"

SPECTRAL PREMONITIONS AND
THE MEMORY OF THE DEAD

Swarming city, city filled with dreams
Where the spectre in broad daylight accosts the passerby

BAUDELAIRE, "The Seven Old Men"

As Bloom walks along Grafton Street by the Provost's House at Trinity College in "Lestrygonians," his eyes alight on the brother of Charles Stewart Parnell (fig. 8.1), on the other side of the street:

> The sun freed itself slowly and lit glints of light among the silverware opposite in Walter Sexton's window by which John Howard Parnell passed, unseeing. There he is: the brother. Image of him. Haunting face. Now that's a coincidence. Course hundreds of times you think of a person and don't meet him. Like a man walking in his sleep. No-one knows him. Must be a corporation meeting today. They say he never put on the city marshal's uniform since he got the job. (*U* 8.499–56)

Charles Stewart Parnell had been in Bloom's mind a moment earlier as, passing Trinity College, he recalled the anti–Boer War demonstration in December 1899 protesting the awarding of an honorary degree to Joseph Chamberlain, one of the architects of the war (fig. 8.2). Bloom ponders the absence of charismatic leadership in Ireland since the fall of Parnell, and the lack of conviction in the demonstrators, who would most likely become tomorrow's "magistrates and civil servants":[1] as a leader "you must have a certain fascination: Parnell. Arthur Griffith is a square-headed fellow but he has no go in him for the mob. Or gas about our lovely land" (*U* 8.462–64). That John Howard Parnell's appearance on the street follows Bloom's thoughts of his famous brother has an air of the uncanny: the manifestation of something in the real world as soon

8.1 John Howard Parnell (late
nineteenth century). Irish School.
Standfast Ireland HGS Private
Collection. Photograph courtesy
of Whyte's Gallery, Dublin.

as one thinks of it. The ghost might be considered a mental entity that
has taken on an external appearance, or perhaps the opposite: memories that are too present or powerful to be relegated to inner life. In the
case of Parnell, such was the traumatic fallout from his death little more
than a decade earlier that many of his loyal followers refused to accept
his death. As a recently defeated member of Parliament, Parnell's brother
was a poor substitute for the "great man":

> Look at the woebegone walk of him. Eaten a bad egg. Poached eyes
> on ghost. I have a pain. Great man's brother: his brother's brother. . . .
> That's the fascination: the name. . . . Still David Sheehy beat him for
> south Meath. . . . Simon Dedalus said when they put him in parlia-
> ment that Parnell would come back from the grave and lead him out
> of the house of commons by the arm. (*U* 7.507–19)

Not the least of the ghosts haunting *Ulysses* is the specter of Parnell, and
that his "apparition" is prompted by the mobilization of anti–Boer War
sentiments indicates that the spirit of the nation itself has come back
from the grave, even if the true successors to the "Chief" have not yet
materialized.

In an essay on the impact of ressentiment on inner life, the German
philosopher Max Scheler noted an unusual phenomenon in personal
encounters: the experience of being struck by a resemblance in a face
to someone we cannot recall. A face comes across as familiar, or even

Le Petit Journal

Le Petit Journal
Le Supplément Illustré

SUPPLÉMENT ILLUSTRÉ

Huit pages : CINQ centimes

ABONNEMENTS

Dixième année

DIMANCHE 31 DÉCEMBRE 1899

Numéro 476

EN IRLANDE
Manifestation contre M. Chamberlain

8.2 Pro-Boer demonstration against Joseph Chamberlain outside Trinity College, Dublin. *Le Petit Journal*, 31 December 1899. Photograph courtesy of Professor Donal McCracken, University of Natal, South Africa.

friendly, but we are unable to pin down the person it evokes, the missing term, as it were, of the relation that shapes our response:

> Thus we may be struck by the particular resemblance of one face to another which we cannot picture, but have to seek in our memory. The awareness of a relation here determines the conscious appearance of the second term. There is, indeed, phenomenal proof that there are pure experiences of relatedness, which select and actualize their terms only afterwards. The specific contents then come to occupy the still indeterminate places of a previously given relation.[2]

Scheler uses this example to support his argument that the world presents itself to us not just as discrete objects, or things, but also as *relations*, or forms: relations, moreover, that impress themselves upon us even in the absence of some of their terms. Manifestations of the uncanny along these lines feature repeatedly in *Ulysses*, not least in the case of resemblances between known people and faces never actually seen—in several cases, the face of Jesus. In "Hades," the caretaker at Glasnevin relates a story concerning two drunks who went to visit the grave of a friend, Mulcahy, one drunk spelling out the name on the grave while the other "was blinking up at the statue of Our Saviour the widow had got up": "*Not a bloody bit like the man*, says he. *That's not Mulcahy*, says he, *whoever done it*" (*U* 6.726–31). Later, in the "Aeolus" chapter, the bearded face of William Braden, editor of the *Freeman's Journal*, also recalls the face of Jesus to Red Murray, though Bloom considers the resemblance closer to "Mario the tenor": "Yes, Red Murray agreed. But Mario was said to be the picture of Our Saviour" (*U* 7.49–55). The ghostly trace left by a missing person appears once again in "Cyclops" when Alf Bergin reports having seen Paddy Dignam on Capel Street before entering Barney Kiernan's. His story is quickly cut short with the news of Dignam's death:

> —Is it Paddy? says Joe.
> —Yes, says Alf. Why?
> —Don't you know he's dead, says Joe.
> —Paddy Dignam dead! says Alf.
> —Ay, says Joe.
> —Sure I'm after seeing him not five minutes ago, says Alf, as plain as a pikestaff.
> —Who's dead? says Bob Doran.
> —You saw his ghost then, says Joe, God between us and harm. . . .
> —Dead! says Alf, He's no more dead than you are.

—Maybe so, says Joe. They took the liberty of burying him this morning anyhow. (*U* 13.318–33)[3]

Max Scheler's account of the everyday uncanny in which an experience of an object or event recalls something lost, half-remembered, or unseen underlies the spectral politics of Joyce's Dublin. "It is a proven phenomenal fact," writes Scheler, "that the relation between two terms (for example, colours, sounds, faces, etc.) can be contained in the perception of one of those terms alone."[4] For all the physicality of the city and the hard-edged clarity of Joyce's prose, there is a recurring sense, as we have noted, of something offstage, a relationship to presences and absences vaguely apprehended by those walking the streets. At times, it is as if the city itself is a face wherein people may read strange matters, albeit of the most mundane kind. In "A Painful Case," physiognomy yields insights into both the character of an individual and the appearance of the city, one recalling the countenance of the other: "Mr Duffy abhorred anything that betokened physical or mental disorder. A medieval doctor would have called him saturnine. His face, which carried the entire tale of his years, was of the brown tint of Dublin streets" (*D* 104). The often commented-on photographic or cinematic nature of Joyce's style conveys an image of Dublin akin to that of Eugène Atget's photographs of Paris, as described by Walter Benjamin. In "After the Race," Dublin "wore the mask of a capital" (*D* 39); the Paris of Atget's photographs, famously devoid of human figures, is compared by Benjamin to "an actor who, disgusted with his profession, wiped off the mask and then set about removing the make-up from reality too."[5] Removing the makeup still leaves the face, however, whose expressive features do not simply lie in the eye of the beholder but are intrinsic to its recognition as a face.

A properly human response to a face, according to Scheler, does not take the form of some subjective element added to a primary perception of skin and muscle; a face is perceived as a face from the outset, even by barely conscious infants. By the same token, as we have seen, Joyce's fiction conveys how the most primordial responses to the material world, as in "baby tuckoo's" registering of his environment in the opening pages of *Portrait*, are imbued with interpersonal and cultural significance. Inhabitants of the city do not simply see bricks, mortar, and technology; rather, their lives and histories are bound up with objects, to the extent that at times the objects appear to be speaking or looking back. In the offices of the *Freeman's Journal*, Bloom picks up on the rhythms of the printing press as if it, and not just the newspaper, is speaking: "Sllt. Almost human the way it sllt to attention. Doing its level best to speak.

That door too sllt creaking, asking to be shut. Everything speaks in its own way. Sllt."(*U* 7.176–78). The city itself wears a countenance, much as a face exhibits emotions in Merleau-Ponty's account: "Anger, shame, hate and love are not psychic facts hidden at the bottom of another's consciousness: they are types of behavior or styles of conduct which are visible from the outside. They exist *on* this face or *in* those gestures, not hidden behind them."[6] It is, of course, vital to preserve the difference between responding to a human face and to material objects, but the issue does not turn on the distinction between animate and inanimate worlds. As Scheler points out, societies historically experienced their entire lifeworlds, both human and nonhuman, through affective ties. What has to be learned under modernity is the painful lesson of *disenchanting* the environment, reducing it to its mere physical and abstract properties, often at odds with the lived texture of everyday life.[7] The forced acceleration of this process, perhaps, lies at the basis of the "paralysis" that besets Joyce's Dubliners, manifested in the semicomatose responses of many characters to life-defining, human situations. Yet the very fact that elements of this "unlearning" are overdetermined in Ireland, as part of a colonized, imposed modernity, means they are not fully internalized or taken to heart. The city, in one sense, has been culturally cleansed by the march of progress, but the "inner life" of the streets still exists "*on* this face or *in* those gestures," *on* this site or *in* that building, though in a manner not always obvious to the detached spectator or, for that matter, to the surveillance regimes of Dublin Castle. What the folklorist Henry Glassie writes of the "volumes" (in the multiple senses of the word) of domestic spaces applies to the public arena as well, in that objects themselves become part of our material environment through relational ties or attachments: "Build the walls of anything, deck them out with anything, but do not change the arrangement of the rooms or their proportions. In those volumes—bounded by surfaces from which a person's senses rebound to him—his psyche develops: disrupt *them*, and you can disrupt *him*."[8]

It is for this reason, according to Walter Benjamin, that the visage presented by the city is not the expressive portrait of romanticism, removing accidental tics and surface qualities to reveal the hidden soul within; instead, the physiognomy of the city lies precisely in the accidents themselves, "the tiny spark of contingency, of the here and now, with which reality has, so to speak, seared its object."[9] Instead of a city posing for its picture, Dublin presents itself much as Molly does in the photograph Bloom shows to Stephen toward the end of *Ulysses*: "As for the face it was a speaking likeness," but as she had not "posed for the ensemble," the photograph did not display her charms to maximum effect, "her stage presence being, frankly, a treat in itself which the camera could not at all do justice to" (*U* 16.1445–60). It is the incidental features of the photograph, however, that catch Stephen's eye — "her full lips parted," a copy of the ballad "In Old Madrid" on the piano, "Lafayette of Westmoreland street" as the name of the studio — and, as if picking up on such details, Bloom is also drawn in the end to the way in which the materiality of the medium itself intrudes of the sensuality of Molly's image, its "slightly soiled" nature "creased by opulent curves" (*U* 16.1431–34, 1465). For Benjamin, the capacity of the photograph to catch reality off guard is such that "the very creases in people's clothes have an air of permanence," and it is this claim on the future that gives the most transient of objects an occult or dreamlike quality: "All this is in its origins more native to the camera than the atmospheric landscape or the soulful portrait." Accordingly, Benjamin says, "[p]hotography reveals in this material the physiognomic aspects of visual worlds which dwell in the smallest things, meaningful yet covert enough to find a hiding place in waking dreams."[10] To depict the city at face value is not to animate it but to bring out the sense in which thoughts and waking dreams, conventionally stored away in the mind, slip their inner moorings and find hiding places in the material environment. Joyce, wrote Ezra Pound in his landmark review of *Dubliners* in 1914, "deals with subjective things, but he presents them with such clarity of outline that he might be dealing with locomotives or builders' specifications."[11] Pound may have been thinking of "A Painful Case," for at the end of this story, as Mr. Duffy's past catches up with him over his callous treatment of Mrs. Sinico, the very rhythms of "a goods train winding out of Kingsbridge Station" seem to echo his troubled inner speech, reminding him from the outside of something he had buried within.[12]

In *Persons and Things*, Barbara Johnson observes how a literary language that refuses detached descriptions of objects and locations "brings the whole surrounding world into the speech event," transforming the environment into an "I-thou" rather than a detached "I-it" relationship. *Apostrophe* is the figure most appropriate to this situation, and it is striking in "Lestrygonians" how much of Bloom's inner conversation is directed at the self as second person, "you" as both subject and addressee of narration: "Course hundreds of times you think of a person and don't meet him" (*U* 8.504–5).[13] While the reader is also implicated in the "you" in question, it is hardly the anonymous reader as defined by the abstract market or the estrangement of mass society. Johnson quotes John Stuart Mill's famous dictum that "eloquence is heard; poetry is overheard," but one of the problems posed by Joyce's writing is how difficult it is to overhear it, to pick up on a conversation without participating, even at one

remove, in the exchange. Joyce's early epiphanies take the form of "reve-
lations" from casual eavesdropping, as if the most transient passerby is
addressed or summoned as a witness to the commonplace. Recounting
Joyce's protracted efforts to publish *Dubliners* in England, Joseph Kelly
notes that "English readers, apparently, were little more than eavesdroppers on his conversation with his compatriots," and it is this encryptment
of everyday life, a withholding in the guise of realism, that gave unprecedented access to the inner life of a society. In his review of *Dubliners*,
Pound noted that "Mr Joyce's merit, I will not say his chief but his most
engaging merit, is that he carefully avoids telling you a lot that you don't
want to know." The difficulty, particularly in the case of *Ulysses*, was that
this reticence also applied to what readers *wanted* to know, as if much of
the text remained in the background despite the surfeit of explicit detail:
"No, not tell all" (*U* 11.876), as the narrative advises in "Sirens." Pound
proceeded to commend address to a universal reader, as against the kind
of national audience "used to the promotion of Irish peasant industries":

> [Joyce] accepts an international standard of prose writing and lives
> up to it. . . . He gives us Dublin as it presumably is. . . . That is to
> say, the author is quite capable of dealing with things about him, and
> dealing directly, yet these details do not engross him, he is capable of
> getting at the universal element beneath them.[14]

Though correct about "the universal element," Pound is mistaken in his
assumption that Joyce's meticulous attention to the local somehow ob-
scured this effect. It was the demand by printers to erase local names that
led to the delay in publishing *Dubliners*, Joyce's obdurate attachment to
actual names and places proving nonnegotiable in the editing (or cen-
sorship) process. Pound, however, had put his finger on one of the stylistic keys to Joyce's prose: endless details, local allusions, and historical
events function as *elements* in Scheler's or Glassie's relational forms outlined above, repeatedly pointing to something beyond, in the manner of
John Howard Parnell's ghostly visage.

"Grim Spectres": Shadows of the Invincibles

If history happens off the page in much of Joyce's writing, this obliquity
derives from the condition of Dublin itself as a colonial city. As critics
such as Enda Duffy and Kimberly Devlin have pointed out, panoptical
surveillance was the order of the day, and there was no shortage of eavesdroppers or native informants to fill in the blanks in police intelligence:

"Never know who you're talking to. Corny Kelleher he has Harvey Duff in his eye. Like that Peter or Denis or James Carey that blew the gaff on the invincibles" (*U* 8.441–43). Joyce's writing can be seen as emulating the kind of knowledge that attempts to slip through the nets of church and state—if not through the small print of textuality itself. "Politically," Peter Costello writes, "Joyce was a Fenian, and something of the Fenian outlook remained with him into his later years."[15] In his notes for the "Cyclops" chapters of *Ulysses*, Joyce wrote: "State: monster fed with our blood, must be starved . . . police provoke crimes or disappear, armies war," a set of remarks preceded by "Fenian tells secret—shouts; Gestures of fenian cause tornado." That secrets are communicated through the most inconsequential forms and gestures is intimated earlier in the notes when Joyce encodes the banalities of pub conversation with the clandestine signs of agrarian secret societies such as the Ribbonmen and Whiteboys, designed to establish who is in the know and who is not:

Q. what are your opinion of the times
A. I think the markets are on the rise
Q. Foreign wars is the cause of it
A. It's the Russian's wish to tyrannize
Q. What is the age of the moon? <Ribbonmen>
A. Really I don't know
Q. R. Hand rubbed over brow
A. Left hand down the pocket < Kilts, scratch arse quicker>
R. hand to knee
Thumb in breeches' pocket.[16]

In the Christmas dinner scene in *Portrait*, Simon Daedalus points to the portrait of his grandfather on the wall to establish the family's insurgent genealogy: "Do you see that chap up there, John? he said. He was a good Irishman when there was no money in the job. He was condemned to death as a whiteboy" (*P* 37). This textual underworld was carried over into Joyce's own lifetime through his father's associations with the Fenian and Land League organizer John Kelly ("John Casey" in *Portrait*) and the Fenian revolutionaries Joseph and Patrick Casey, cousins of James Stephens, one of the founders of the Fenian Brotherhood.[17] The aim of the ill-fated Clerkenwell bombings in 1867 was to spring Joseph Casey and Colonel Richard Burke from jail, and Joseph (still living in exile in 1903) was the personal contact given to Joyce by his father on his first visit to Paris, an encounter memorialized in *Ulysses* through Stephen's recall of the fictive Kevin Egan: "Lover, for her [Ireland's] love, he prowled

with colonel Richard Burke, tanist of his sept, under the walls of Clerkenwell and, crouching, saw a flame of vengeance hurl towards them in the
fog. Shattered glass and toppling masonry" (*U* 3.246–49).

In a city subject to the rival panopticons of both church and state,
where even the most casual remark could attract suspicion, it is not surprising that cultural codes, slang, and idiolects evolved to prevent easy
access to communication. For all the city's quaint reputation as an over-
sized village where everybody knew everybody else,[18] the public sphere
was not an open arena, characterized by transparency and instant acquaintance. Conversations were more like overlapping frames, with the
"gnomon" (signaled on the opening page of "The Sisters"), the parts unsaid or withheld, remaining intelligible only to those receptive to the
codes—and often carrying the risk of being lost in translation even
among intimates, because of their "half-said" status.[19] This had the effect
of excluding unearned familiarity, the social equivalent of the sentimen-
tality Stephen Dedalus decries as enjoyment "without incurring the immense debtorship for a thing done" (*U* 9.550–51). In his "Subject Notebook" of 1917, one of the earliest extant sources for the writing of *Ulysses*,
Joyce lists two books germane to the kind of clandestine communication
required in political circles: *The Irish National Invincibles and their Times*
(London: Chatham and Co., 1896), by Patrick J. P. Tynan (or "Number One," as the title page declares); and *Twenty-Five Years in the Secret
Service: The Recollections of a Spy*, by Major Henri Le Caron (London:
W. Heinemann, 1892).[20] Le Caron's infiltration of the innermost circles
of the Fenians, not revealed until the Parnell trials of 1888, served as a reminder to the next generation of the importance of secrecy and opacity
in securing underground networks against informers. Patrick J. P. Tynan's sprawling tome on the Invincibles amounts to a virtual parody of
an insurgent handbook, top-heavy with notes, asides, and appendices
and written in an overblown fustian that would not have been out of
place in the "Cyclops" or "Eumaeus" chapters (fig. 8.3).[21] No doubt it
proved of immense interest to police intelligence, but the rambling style
of the book, dense telegraphese, surfeit of detail, facsimile holographs,
Kafka-like initials for characters, and abundant stories with loose ends
hardly made for easy reading in Dublin Castle. It is as much an exercise in obfuscation as revelation, for, as Malcolm Brown notes, "something is wrong in the tone":[22] the arch, knowing style betrays a self-
consciousness of giving too much away under the pretext of candor, as
well as providing the impression of an inside track on one of the crimes
of the century.

Recalling the tense atmosphere in Dublin on the night of the assassination of the state secretary, Lord Frederick Cavendish, and his assistant

THE IRISH

NATIONAL INVINCIBLES

AND THEIR TIMES

BY

PATRICK J. P. TYNAN
["NUMBER ONE"]

ENGLISH EDITION
WITH APPENDICES AND INDEX

COPYRIGHT

LONDON
CHATHAM AND CO.
1896

TRADE SUPPLIED BY
SIMPKIN, MARSHALL, HAMILTON, KENT AND CO., LTD.

P. J. P. TYNAN—"NUMBER ONE."

8.3 Title page from Patrick J. P. Tynan, *The Irish National Invincibles and Their Times* (London: Chatham and Co., 1896). Private collection.

secretary, Thomas Burke, in the Phoenix Park on 6 May 1882 by the Invincibles, Tynan evokes a sense of foreboding, akin to the purple prose of a Gothic shilling-shocker:

Night's shadow had scarce fallen when hark! the alarm and the panic. The grim spectre of death has come among them. There are mounted orderlies riding in hot haste, carrying messages to the regimental commanders in the different barracks of the now fully excited city. These orders are to the British colonels to have their men under arms all night. They know not what to expect. There is an unseen foe in their midst that bodes no good to British rule in Ireland. They begin again to realise that they are quartered in a hostile city, among as yet an unconquered people. "When the truth cannot be clearly made out, what is false is increased through fear." The very absence of knowledge magnified British terrors. . . . As one walks through the streets of the city, one cannot help marking the pallid faces of the police who execute British misdeeds upon the mere Irish. Note how nervously and carefully they tread their way, as if some mystic foe

was about to spring upon them from some unseen hiding-place. (*INI*
260–61)

The sensational impact of the Phoenix Park assassinations on a Saturday
afternoon prompted the first publication of Sunday newspapers in Ireland, an extension of print culture offset by communal codes in which
the facial and physical mannerisms picked up where print left off:

> Various opinions were expressed and debated by these good citi-
> zens. Among the small Sunday gatherings of the people, groups of
> men who had just come from divine service in their churches could
> be heard to express themselves approvingly of the tragic deed of the
> night before. Though in some cases they spoke guardedly, yet *the*
> *smile of joy that lighted up their faces and flashed from their eyes*, re-
> vealed the depth of their feelings. There are peculiar mannerisms
> by which Irishmen convey their real sentiments to each other, even
> though their tongues speak differently. This gift is not possessed by
> any other people. It is born of the long ages of slavery which has so
> eaten into their souls that even the best and bravest and most daring
> of the race unconscious to themselves, are its possessors. (*INI* 262,
> italics added)

Not surprisingly, Dublin pubs and bar life became the first targets of suspicion and reprisal. "Any visitors to the Dublin taverns were placed under
temporary arrest and their persons searched, the police carefully reading
every scrap of printed or written matter found, seizing anything which
their imaginations could distort into suspicious documents, and taking
the names and addresses of the men arrested. To carry this out effectually
was a very difficult task, where these employees of the alien power had
reason to suspect nine-tenths of the inhabitants of a city with over two
hundred thousand inhabitants" (*INI* 265–66).
    Tynan's inflated diction does not go so far as to suggest that "nine-
tenths of the inhabitants of the city" were in on the Phoenix Park conspiracy, but the Coercion Acts introduced by Dublin Castle certainly affected the public at large. For Tynan, the codes of a counterpublic sphere
consist not in what is expressly said but in the "peculiar mannerisms"
that light up the face or a flash in the eyes, and a nonverbal—or barely
verbal—language often "unconscious to themselves." It is this kind of
fragmented, half-spoken communication that surfaces in the late-night
setting of "Eumaeus" when Bloom and Stephen encounter one of the Invincibles, James Fitzharris, or "Skin-the-Goat," as the keeper of the cabman's shelter at Butt Bridge, holding his own with other equally disrep-

utable members of the "submerged tenth" (*U* 16.1226) of the population. Stylistically, the chapter bears all the hallmarks of Tynan's voice, leading Colleen Lamos to conclude, in relation to both the sexual and political underworlds of the chapter:

> Knowledge circulates in "Eumaeus" by means of indirection and innuendo, as the possession of insiders, concealed like a dangerous weapon and revealed through circumlocutions, oblique clues, or inadvertent slips of the tongue. Both sexual perversion and subversive political conspiracy function as open secrets, officially non-existent and privy only to the initiated.[23]

That the clandestine world of the Invincibles is not far from the minds of the makeshift crew in the shelter is clear when a story related by the globetrotting sailor Murphy about a knifing in Trieste prompts another character to recall it was the expert use of knives in the Phoenix Park murders that encouraged the belief "it was done by foreigners" (*U* 16.591). This speaker was "evidently quite in the dark" (*U* 16.589) as to the company in the shelter, and in a passage (discussed in chapter 1 above) that could have been lifted from Tynan, Bloom and Stephen communicate the faux pas through their eyes, their own inside track:

> At this remark passed obviously in the spirit of *where ignorance is bliss* Mr B. and Stephen, each in his own particular way, both instinctively exchanged meaning glances, in a religious silence of the strictly *entre nous* variety however, towards where Skin-the-Goat, *alias* the keeper, not turning a hair, was drawing spurts of liquid from his boiler affair. His inscrutable face which was really a work of art, a perfect study in itself, beggaring description, conveyed the impression that he didn't understand one jot of what was going on. Funny, very! (*U* 16.593–600)

The hermetic world of the Invincibles was hardly an open secret in Dublin—notwithstanding Skin-the-Goat's subsequent presence on the streets—but the inscrutability of the public sphere has less to do with nativism than with knowledge getting into the wrong hands. This became clear with the breaches of intimacy that brought about the fall of Parnell ten years later, "when the facts, to make matters worse, were made public with the usual affectionate letters that passed between them full of sweet nothings" (*U* 16.1362–64). Open secrets were subject to damage limitation in sympathetic circles, but the exposure of intimacy in newspapers to adversarial parties turned private affairs into public persecution, the

staples of the gutter press: "First it was strictly Platonic till nature intervened and an attachment sprang up between them till bit by bit matters
came to a climax and the matter became the talk of the town till the stag-
gering blow came as a welcome intelligence to not a few evil disposed,
however, who were resolved upon encompassing his downfall though
the thing was public property all along though not to anything like the
sensational extent that it subsequently blossomed into" (U 16.1364–70).
Rumors, moreover, did not end with Parnell's death, for such was the in-
consolable grief among his followers that stories began to circulate about
his return from the grave:

> One morning you would open the paper, the cabman affirmed, and
> read: *Return of Parnell*. He bet them what they liked. A Dublin fusi-
> lier was in that shelter one night and said he saw him in South Africa.
> . . . Dead he wasn't. Simply absconded somewhere. The coffin they
> brought over was full of stones. He changed his name to De Wet, the
> Boer general. (U 16.1297–98, 1305–36)

Levelheaded Bloom is, of course, skeptical at first, and rehearses the
physical details of Parnell's death in his mind to convince himself of his
passing. Revenants from the past, he reflects, share a common feature
with murder in that both testify to a need to return to the scene of the
crime: "And the identical same with murderers. You had to come back.
That haunting sense kind of drew you. To show the understudy in the
title role how to" (U 16.1331–33). As in *Hamlet*, the problem with coming
back is that a usurper has taken one's place, and it is this that links Parnell's revenant to another narrative of return, the controversy surrounding the Tichborne Claimant that threw the British inheritance system
into crisis in the mid-nineteenth century:

> Still as regards return. You were a lucky dog if they didn't set the
> terrier at you directly when you got back. Then a lot of shillyshally
> usually followed, Tom for and Dick and Harry against. And then,
> number one, you came up against the man in possession and had
> to produce your credentials like the claimant in the Tichborne case,
> Roger Charles Tichborne, *Bella* was the boat's name to the best of his
> recollection he, the heir, went down in, as the evidence went to show,
> and there was a tattoo mark too in Indian ink, lord Bellew, was it, as
> he might easily have picked up the details from some pal on board
> ship and then, when got up to tally with the description given, intro-
> duce himself with: *Excuse me, my name is So and So* or some such
> commonplace remark. (U 16.1339–49)

In 1854, the heir to the vast Tichborne estate in England, Roger Charles Tichborne, drowned when the ship *Bella* sank off the coast of Brazil, but in the absence of clear proof his grief-stricken mother refused to accept his death. She placed advertisements in newspapers worldwide pleading for his return home to claim his rightful inheritance, and in due course a rogue claimant presented himself in the person of a larger-than-life figure, Thomas Castro, from Wagga Wagga, Australia, also believed to be one Arthur Orton, a butcher who hailed originally from Wapping. The capacity to discern the face of a missing loved one in the face of another was central to the bitter legal dispute surrounding the case, for on being "reunited" with the impostor in Paris, Lady Tichborne claimed to recognize her son (it helped that, feigning illness, he met her in a darkened room and kept his back to her). The claimant returned to lay claim to the ninth-richest estate in Britain, but not without bitter opposition from the rest of the family and, indeed, the aristocracy. In the subsequent court case, Tichborne was defended by the maverick Irish lawyer Edward Kenealy, who had defended Chartists and Irish revolutionaries in the "Angel Street" conspiracy two decades earlier in the 1840s. The absence of a "tattoo mark too in Indian ink"(*U* 16.1345) bearing the initials "R C T," drawn on the arm of the real Roger Tichborne by his friend Lord Bellew, proved decisive in swinging the case against the pretender. The claimant, though, enjoyed massive popular support against British aristocratic interests, leading to the most serious street rioting in London since the Gordon Riots. "As in earlier radical movements," Iain McCalman notes, "charismatic Irish oratory and leadership style gave moral coherence, purpose, and identity to the Tichborne movement," thus anticipating in turn later Irish popular agitation of the Parnellite era and, indeed, pro-Boer demonstrations.[24]

The association of the rise, fall, and reappearance of the "Uncrowned King" with return from the sea not only evokes the hapless Tichborne claimant but also recapitulates the central theme of the *Odyssey*: the disappearance and eventual return of the lost hero.[25] The mysterious returned sailor in "Eumaeus," E. B. Murphy, acts as a counterpart to Bloom's wandering, constituting a pseudo-Ulysses (or "Ulysses Pseudo-angelos")[26] home from the sea. The motif of returning from the sea, or, even stronger, the possibility of rebirth through drowning, runs through *Ulysses* (as we have noted in chapter 7), and in the guise of Parnell as the leader of a lost nation, the ghost amounts to a return of the oppressed. As in the Tichborne case, claimants to Parnell's throne had to come "up against the man in possession and had to produce [their] credentials," only to be found wanting. It is precisely mourning over the fate of the nation that prompts the initial (mis)recognition of the "haunting face" of

Parnell in that of his less illustrious brother earlier in the day on Grafton Street.

Hope and Melancholia

Cast in the shadow of the Tichborne claimant, Parnell's ghost marks a shift in the politics of recognition: the transformation of a lost face into an anticipation of the future. At one level a symptom of profound grief, the transference of a long-lost face to that of another makes it clear that vestiges of the past still await their moment, like the missing elements in Scheler's "relation of resemblance." In Scheler's example, the lost (or forgotten) face is not visualized, or present in the mind making the comparison; it awaits completion, and may even be activated in the present or the future. In a crucial sense, the gap opened up in memory avoids regression or endless repetition. Indeed, the image of the past, the missing term of the resemblance, may be transfigured when it eventually comes to light. In this notion of recurrence with difference, of incomplete pasts opening new vistas on the future, the underlying narratives that frame the theme of metempsychosis in *Ulysses* are evident: "history repeating itself with a difference, after the burial of a mutual friend when they had left him alone in his glory after the grim task of having committed his remains to the grave" (*U* 16.1525–28).

Thoughts of the apparition of Parnell in "Lestrygonians" were originally prompted not only by Bloom's thoughts of the dead leader but also by recollections of a pro-Boer demonstration outside Trinity College, in which cries of "Up the Boers! Three cheers for De Wet" (*U* 8.434–35) resonated in Bloom's memory. When the rumor surfaces in "Eumaeus" that Parnell may have absconded to South Africa and reinvented himself as Christiaan De Wet—"He changed his name to De Wet, the Boer general" (*U* 16.1305)—the possibility arises that the lost face is transformed into the new face of resistance to empire, and that W. B. Yeats's exhortation on the death of Parnell, "Mourn—and then Onward," is taking effect (figs. 8.4 and 8.5). Bloom recalls that one of the reasons for Parnell's death after a last outdoor public meeting in the rain was his failure "to change his boots and clothes after a wetting" (*U* 16.1316) (the condition of the drowned Tichborne claimant)—which can perhaps also be envisaged as a "De-Wetting" in the event of the leader's "return" from South Africa to Ireland. Within a few years, the "pale and angry ghost of Parnell" acted as the presiding spirit of Patrick Pearse's essay "Ghosts," written in the months leading to the 1916 rebellion.[27]

In Carlos Fuentes's novel *Terra Nostra* (1975), a character, Valerio Camolio, explains his creation of a "Theatre of Memory" in which alter-

8.4 Charles Stewart
Parnell. From T. P.
O'Connor and R. M.
McWade, *Gladstone-
Parnell and the Great
Irish Struggle* (London:
J. S. Robertson, 1886).
Private collection.

8.5 General Christiaan De Wet, from *Black & White*, 13 September
1902. Private collection.

native pasts are staged as trial runs for the future: "The images of my theater bring together all the possibilities of the past, but they also represent all the opportunities of the future, for knowing what was not, we shall know what demands to be: what has not been, you have seen, is a latent event awaiting its moment to be."[28] This holding on to what might have been is central to Judith Butler's essay "Violence, Mourning, Politics," in which she questions Freud's view that coming to terms with grief involves letting go of the past, a process in which mourning allows us to move forward by overcoming the backward look of melancholia. In Freud's account, successful mourning effects a transfer in which grief for the lost object is free to redirect itself at will towards a new source of attachment, thus implying "a certain interchangeability of objects as a sign of hopefulness, as if the prospect of entering life anew made use of a kind of promiscuity of libidinal aim." Butler is not convinced that the libido is free-floating in this way; rather, it is itself a creation of its previous attachments: "I do not think that successful grieving implies that one has forgotten another person or that something else has come along to takes its place, as if full substitutability were something for which we might strive" (PL 21). Butler takes issue with amnesia as a condition of "moving on," arguing that forgetting, even if it were possible, comes at a heavy psychic cost and is at odds with working through profound loss and desolation. In keeping with Scheler's relational ethics, Butler writes that in grieving, we do not just lose a person but are in danger of losing a *relationship* as well, a relationship of which we also form a part:

> It is not as if an "I" exists independently over here and then simply loses a "you" over there, specially if the attachment to "you" is part of what composes who "I" am. . . . On one level, I think I have lost "you" only to discover that "I" have gone missing as well. At another level, perhaps what I have lost "in" you, that for which I have no ready vocabulary, is a *relationality* that is composed neither exclusively of myself nor you, but is to be conceived as *the tie* by which those terms are differentiated and related. (PL 21, first italics added)

Holding on to ties in the face of loss leaves one part of the relationship open, but it is this incompleteness that enables new attachments, rather than cutting them off. The refusal to let go in melancholia is less a pathology of regression than a force that may lead to new solidarities, as in the transfer of loyalties form Parnell to De Wet, from the cause of Ireland to the cause of the Boers fighting empire thousands of miles away.[29] Instead of shutting down the past, traumatic memory has the potential to act as an ethical resource, providing glimpses of alternative futures. In "Wandering Rocks," one of the few individuals who feels under no obligation to view the viceregal procession is the "ghostbright" John Howard Parnell, playing chess unconcernedly in the DBC restaurant in Dame Street:

—Is that he? Haines asked, twisting round in his seat.

—Yes, Mulligan said. That's John Howard, his brother, our city marshal.

John Howard Parnell translated a white bishop quietly and his grey claw went up again to his forehead whereat it rested. An instant after, under its screen, his eyes looked quickly, ghostbright, at his foe and fell once more upon a working corner. (*U* 10.1048–52)

The apparition of the "haunting face" that presented itself to Bloom earlier in Grafton Street arose from uncertainty over what belongs to the mind—"thoughts" of Parnell or De Wet—and what takes place in the outside world. This transsubjective zone is, in a sense, all over the place, Dublin itself, as we have seen, taking on the countenance of a face, with its laments as well as desires for unrealized futures. Broken circuits of knowledge are to be expected in societies with sundered public spheres, in which political, cultural, and religious identities are under threat, and even the pleasantries of everyday speech have a second life as encrypted codes. Joyce's response to the city refuses to dissociate intimacy from harsh realities and, through the "strandentwining cable" (*U* 3.37) of modernist form, extends this inner history to the world at large. For Max Scheler, once a value—in all its particularity or specificity—is discovered or disclosed, it is there potentially for others: "Anything in our experience which can be put into words is always something which, having been singled out by common language, must also be accessible to others" (*NS* 352). The mimetic view of art is to reproduce what is already given; the workshop of Dedalus, by contrast, forges a new consciousness, releasing the future from the foregone conclusions of the past—"Teems of time and happy returns. The seim anew" of *Finnegans Wake* (*FW* 215). Ghosts are best seen as premonitions, reminding us of "infinite possibilities" that have yet to unfold:

They are not to be thought away. Time has branded them and fettered they are lodged in the room of the infinite possibilities they have ousted. But can those have been possible seeing that they never were? Or was that only possible which came to pass? Weave, weaver of the wind.

—Tell us a story, sir

—Oh, do, sir. A ghoststory. (*U* 2.49–50)

NOTES

Abbreviations

References to the publications below appear in the text and endnotes as abbreviations, followed by page number.

TEXTS BY AND ABOUT JOYCE

D James Joyce, *Dubliners* [1914], introduction and notes by Terence Brown (London: Penguin, 1993).

FW James Joyce, *Finnegans Wake* [1939], ed. Seamus Deane (London: Penguin Classics, 2000).

JJ Richard Ellmann, *James Joyce* (Oxford: Oxford University Press, 1965).

JJ I Richard Ellmann, *James Joyce*, new and rev. ed. (Oxford: Oxford University Press, 1982).

JJCH I *James Joyce: The Critical Heritage, 1902–27*, ed. Robert H. Deming (London: Routledge and Kegan Paul, 1970).

JJCH II *James Joyce: The Critical Heritage, 1928–41*, ed. Robert H. Deming (London: Routledge and Kegan Paul, 1970).

JJL I *Letters of James Joyce*, I, ed. Stuart Gilbert (New York: Viking Press, 1966).

JJL II *Letters of James Joyce*, II, ed. Richard Ellmann (New York: Viking Press, 1966).

JJL III *Letters of James Joyce*, III, ed. Richard Ellmann (New York: Viking Press, 1966).

JJQ *James Joyce Quarterly*

JJSL *Selected Letters of James Joyce*, ed. Richard Ellman (London: Faber and Faber, 1975).

K Charles Kickham, *Knocknagow; or, The Homes of Tipperary* [1879] (Dublin: James Duffy, 1944).

OCPW *James Joyce: Occasional, Critical, and Political Writing*, ed. Kevin Barry, trans. Conor Deane (Oxford: Oxford University Press, 2000).

P James Joyce, *A Portrait of the Artist as a Young Man* [1916], ed. with introduction by Seamus Deane (London: Penguin, 1992).

SH   James Joyce, *Stephen Hero*, ed. with introduction by Theodore Spencer (London: Paladin, 1991).

SL   *Selected Letters of James Joyce*, ed. Richard Ellmann (London: Faber and Faber, 1997).

U   James Joyce, *Ulysses* [1922], ed. Hans Walter Gabler (New York: Vintage, 1986). References appear as chapter number plus line number.

UA   Don Gifford and Robert J. Seidman, *"Ulysses" Annotated: Notes for James Joyce's "Ulysses"* (Berkeley and Los Angeles: University of California Press, 1988).

OTHER TEXTS

CV   Ludwig Wittgenstein, *Culture and Value*, trans. Peter Winch (Oxford: Black-well, 1998).

DH   Jacques Lacan, "Desire and the Interpretation of Desire in Hamlet," in *Literature and Psychoanalysis: The Question of Reading: Otherwise* (Baltimore: Johns Hopkins University Press, 1982).

DS   Tony Huston, *The Dead: A Screenplay* (Los Angeles: Liffey Films, 1986).

FLR   John Wilson Foster, *Fictions of the Irish Literary Revival: A Changeling Art* (Dublin: Gill and Macmillan, 1987).

FTC   May Laffan, *Flitters, Tatters and the Counsellor; The Game Hen; Baubie Clark* (Leipzig: Barnard Tauchnitz, 1881).

G   Hon. Emily Lawless, *Grania: The Story of an Island* (London: Smith and Elder, 1892).

GB   Sir James George Frazer, *The Golden Bough: A Study in Magic and Religion* [1890–1915], ed. Robert Fraser (Oxford: Oxford University Press, 1994).

HTOS Rev. Thomas Connellan, *Hear the Other Side*, 12th ed., rev. and enlarged (Dublin: Office of *The Catholic*, 1908).

IDP   Michael Riffaterre, "Interpretation and Descriptive Poetry: A Reading of Wordsworth's 'Yew Trees,'" in *Untying the Text: A Post-Structuralist Reader*, ed. Robert Young (Boston: Routledge and Kegan Paul, 1981).

INI   Patrick J. P. Tynan ["Number One"], *The Irish National Invincibles and Their Times* (London: Chatham and Co., 1896).

IMK   *In Minor Keys: The Uncollected Stories of George Moore*, ed. David B. Eakin and Helmut E. Gerber (Syracuse: Syracuse University Press, 1985).

LD   Mary Colum, *Life and the Dream* (London: Macmillan, 1947).

NS   Max Scheler, *The Nature of Sympathy* [1912], trans. Peter Heath (New Haven: Yale University Press, 1954).

PL   Judith Butler, *Precarious Life: The Powers of Mourning and Violence* (London: Verso, 2004).

PP   Maurice Merleau-Ponty, *Phenomenology of Perception*, trans. Colin Smith (London: Routledge and Kegan Paul, 1962).

SK   Nicolas Abraham and Maria Torok, *The Shell and the Kernel: Renewals of Psychoanalysis*, ed. and trans. Nicholas T. Rand (Chicago: University of Chicago Press, 1994).

TL   Lev Vygotsky, *Thought and Language*, ed. Alex Kozulin (Cambridge: MIT Press, 1986).

UF   George Moore, "The Exile," in *The Untilled Field* [1903] (Dublin: Gill and Macmillan, 1990).

Introduction

1. As the young Joyce wrote: "Life we must accept as we see it before our eyes, men and women as we meet them in the real world, not as we apprehend them in the world of faery." James Joyce, "Drama and Life" [1900] (*OCPW* 28).

2. For discussions of Joyce, ghosts, and the otherworld, see Shari Benstock, "*Ulysses* as Ghoststory," *JJQ* 12, no. 3 (Summer 1975): 396–413; Maud Ellmann, "The Ghosts of *Ulysses*," in *James Joyce's Ulysses: A Casebook*, ed. Derek Attridge (Oxford: Oxford University Press, 2004), 83–101; Jeffrey A. Weinstock, "The Disappointed Bridge: Textual Hauntings in *Ulysses*," *Journal of the Fantastic in the Arts* 8, no. 3 (1997): 347–69; Maria DiBattista, "The Ghost Walks: Joyce and the Spectres of Silent Cinema," in *Roll Away the Reel World: James Joyce and Cinema*, ed. John McCourt (Cork: Cork University Press, 2010), 57–68; Cóilín Owens, *James Joyce's Painful Case* (Gainesville: University Press of Florida, 2008); John Gordon, "Gaslight, Ghostlight, Golliwog, Gaslight," *JJQ* 46, no. 1 (Fall 2008): 19–37, and *Joyce and Reality: The Empirical Strikes Back* (Syracuse: Syracuse University Press, 2004); Ellen Carol Jones, "History's Ghosts: Joyce and the Politics of Public Memory," *Journal of Irish Studies* 25 (2012): 3–17; Francis O'Gorman, "What Is Haunting *Dubliners*?" *JJQ* 48, no. 3 (Spring 2011): 445–56.

3. Stuart Gilbert, *James Joyce's Ulysses: A Study* (New York: Knopf, 1952), 11. Joyce remarked to Tom Kristensen: "I don't believe in any science but my imagination grows when I read Vico as it doesn't when I read Freud and Jung" (*JJ* 706). That Joyce read Frederick W. H. Myers's *Human Personality and the Survival of Bodily Death* (1903) shortly after his mother's death shows that he was at least interested in those strands of modern psychology that attempted to lend credence to belief in the otherworld. Peter Costello, *James Joyce: The Years of Growth, 1882–1915: A Biography* (London: Kyle Cathie, 1992), 212. For more on Joyce's interest in Myers, see Gordon, *Joyce and Reality*, 241–42, and Owens, *James Joyce's Painful Case*, 33–37.

4. Two German editions of Freud's works were in Joyce's library at Trieste: *The Psychopathology of Everyday Life* [1917 version] and *Leonardo da Vinci and a Memory of his Childhood* [1910]; see Michael Patrick Gillespie, *James Joyce's Trieste Library: A Catalogue of Materials at the Harry Ransom Humanities Research Center, the University of Texas at Austin* (Austin: Harry Ransom Humanities Research Center, 1986), 101–2. As Daniel Ferrer has shown, Joyce's notebooks (1925–26) for chapter XVI of *Finnegans Wake* provide evidence of attentive reading of Freud's case histories, including "Little Hans" and "The Wolf Man." Daniel Ferrer, "The Freudful Couchmare of /\d: Joyce's Notes on Freud and the Composition of Chapter XVI of *Finnegans Wake*," *JJQ* 22, no. 4 (1985): 367–82. See also Wim Van Mierlo, "The Freudful Couch Revisited: Contextualizing Joyce and the New Psychology," *Joyce Studies Annual* 8 (Summer 1997): 115–63; Luke Thurston, *James Joyce and the Problem of Psychoanalysis* (Cambridge: Cambridge University Press, 2004).

5. Edward Wakefield, cited in S. J. Connolly, *Priests and People in Pre-Famine Ireland, 1780–1842* (Dublin: Gill and Macmillan, 1982), 121.

6. Maurice Halbwachs, *On Collective Memory* [1950], ed., trans., and introduction by Lewis Coser (Chicago: University of Chicago Press, 1992), 168.

7. Frank Budgen, *James Joyce and the Making of "Ulysses"* (Bloomington: Indiana University Press, 1973), 320. Interviewed by Djuna Barnes in 1922, Joyce noted he was as interested in the influence of the conscious on the unconscious as the other way around: "I have recorded, simultaneously, what a man says, thinks, and what such seeing, thinking, saying does, to what you Freudians call the subconscious." Djuna Barnes, "James

Joyce," *Vanity Fair*, April 1922, cited in Gordon Bowker, *James Joyce: A Biography* (London: Weidenfeld and Nicholson, 2011), 299.

8. Ellmann, "The Ghosts of *Ulysses*," 86.

9. Terry Castle, "The Spectralization of the Other in *The Mysteries of Udolpho*," in *The Female Thermometer: Eighteenth-Century Culture and the Invention of the Uncanny* (New York: Oxford University Press, 1995), 120–25.

10. Tzvetan Todorov, *The Fantastic: A Structural Approach to a Literary Genre*, trans. Richard Howard (Ithaca: Cornell University Press, 1975), 33, 25.

11. For this aspect of Joyce, see Jean Michel Rabaté, *James Joyce and the Politics of Egoism* (Cambridge: Cambridge University Press, 2001), chapters 1–4.

12. Fredric Jameson, "*Ulysses* in History," in *James Joyce and Modern Literature*, ed. W. J. McCormack and Alistair Stead (London: Routledge and Kegan Paul, 1982), 139. Though seemingly focusing on the "radically objective, if that were really possible" (139), *Ulysses* also challenges this in turn, through a "great movement of dereification" which uncovers the "human and collective praxis deconcealed" in the "Ithaca" chapter.

13. Lev Vygotsky, *Thought and Language*, ed. Alex Kozulin (Cambridge: MIT Press, 1986). Subsequent references will take the form of *TL*, followed by page number, in the text.

14. David Pierce, *Reading Joyce* (London: Longman, 2008), 110.

15. Harry Levin, *Joyce: A Critical Introduction* (London: Faber and Faber, 1968), 81.

16. "To a stranger," Stanislaus Joyce wrote to James about his brother's then unpublished story "Ivy Day in the Committee Room," "your differentiations of character would seem nothing less than marvellous. And the poem—the 'turn' in this case—is entirely Irish." Stanislaus Joyce to James Joyce, 10 October 1905 (JJ II, 115).

17. Judith Butler, *Gender Trouble: Feminism and the Subversion of Identity* (New York: Routledge, 1990), 134.

18. Dorrit Cohn, *Transparent Minds: Narrative Modes for Presenting Consciousness in Fiction* (Princeton: Princeton University Press, 1978), 100.

19. Tom McCarthy, "'Ulysses' and Its Wake," *London Review of Books* 36, no. 12 (19 June 2014): 40. For the cultural structuring of interior monologue in *Ulysses*, see also Richard Begam, "Joyce's Trojan Horse: *Ulysses* and the Aesthetics of Decolonization," in *Modernism and Colonialism: British and Irish Literature, 1899–1939*, ed. Richard Begam and Michael Valdez Moses (Durham: Duke University Press, 2007), 194–98.

20. Jacques Derrida, "Theses," in *Archive Fever: A Freudian Impression*, trans. Eric Prenowitz (Chicago: University of Chicago Press, 1998), 85.

21. In Jensen's story, the ghost speaks back to Hanold. Ludwig Wittgenstein's arguments against the possibility of purely private language suggest that interior "monologue," as we shall see in relation to Molly Bloom's soliloquy in chapter 2, is itself public at its core. Ludwig Wittgenstein, *Philosophical Investigations*, trans. G. E. M. Anscombe (Oxford: Blackwell, 1958), §§243–315.

22. Contrary to naïve realism, it is striking how vividly the presence of others comes across, even if imagined, as against projections of one's own mind: citing neuroscientific research by Perrine Ruby and Jean Decety in France, John L. Locke notes that a specific region of the brain "was activated when their subjects mentally stimulated actions as they would appear *to others*, but not as the same actions would appear to the subjects themselves." John L. Locke, *Eavesdropping: An Intimate History* (Oxford: Oxford University Press, 2010), 60. As Derrida notes, even Freud felt obliged to concede a partial truth to hallucinations otherwise dismissed as monologues/projections: "He tells us

that under analysis, under psychoanalytic examination, the delusion's lack of verisimil-tude (*die Unwahrscheinlichkeit dieses Wahnes*) seems to dissipate (*scheint . . . zu zer-gehen*), at least to a large extent: 'The greater part' [*zum grössern Teile*]." Derrida, *Ar-chive Fever*, 86.

23. Bruno Latour, *On the Modern Cult of the Factish Gods*, trans. Catherine Porter and Heather Maclean (Durham: Duke University Press, 2010), 9.

24. Bruce Hood, *The Self Illusion: How the Social Brain Creates Identity* (Oxford: Oxford University Press, 2012). That the unified self is "Imaginary" is central to the psychoanalysis of Jacques Lacan, but in what follows, I argue that this process itself is historically constituted in relation to personal and cultural identity. There is no pregiven subject, any more than a mystical "spirit of the nation" presides over, or predates, na-tional identity.

25. Latour, *On the Modern Cult of the Factish Gods*, 13.

26. Ibid., 10. This was the basis of Marx and Engels's materialist critique of Max Stir-ner's "egoism": for its relation to Joyce, see Rabaté, *James Joyce and the Politics of Egoism*, chapters 1–4.

27. Shane McCorristine, *Spectres of the Self: Thinking about Ghosts and Ghost-Seeing in England, 1750–1920* (Cambridge: Cambridge University Press, 2010), 7. McCorri-stine's discussion relates more to psychological dispositions to haunting than to the self as specter: "[G]host-seeing is continuous with the idea of a mind that is haunted by itself and a subjectivity that is ghost-ridden" (7).

28. The adoption of the Voice Dialogue approach in several dozen cases of "hearing voices" in the district of Maastricht in the Netherlands resulted in "a decrease in the per-ceived 'destructiveness' of the voices, including a transformation from 'negative' to 'posi-tive' voices with increased understanding from the person, along with an increased ca-pacity (and willingness) to dialogue with the voices. No person has so far become more psychotic, and quality of life is sometimes substantially improved. A key variable in the effectiveness of this treatment appears to be whether or not the person can (or believes they can) dialogue with their voices." Andrew Moskowitz, PhD, and Dirk Corstens, MD, "Auditory Hallucinations: Psychotic Symptom or Dissociative Experience?" *Journal of Psychological Trauma* 6, no. 2–3 (2007), accessed at http://www.hearingvoicesmaastricht .eu/page12.php.

29. Stephen Ullmann, *Style in the French Novel* (Cambridge: Cambridge University Press, 1957). As Fredric Jameson notes, Flaubert saw creativity itself in these hallucina-tory terms, a process in which "forms or figures" passed "discontinuously across the field of vision" as though "somehow on this side and nearer than the objects of the visible world." Jameson, "*Ulysses* in History," 137.

30. Charles Lock, "Double Voicing, Sharing Words: Bakhtin's Dialogism and the His-tory of the Theory of Free Indirect Discourse," in *The Novelness of Bakhtin: Perspectives and Possibilities*, ed. Jorgen Bruhn and Jan Lundquist (Copenhagen: Museum Tusca-laneum Press, 2001), 80.

31. Ullmann, *Style in the French Novel*, 101–2.

32. Owens, *James Joyce's Painful Case*, 37.

33. Steven Connor, *Dumbstruck: A Cultural History of Ventriloquism* (Oxford: Oxford University Press, 2001), 79. This "indirect perception" is akin to Joyce's experience of the apparition of his dead mother described at the opening of this chapter. As noted below (at the beginning of chapter 4), Joyce's poor eyesight also disposed him to "view" films through the words of those friends who accompanied him to the cinema.

34. The capacity of the phonograph to coexist with the "undead" also features in Bram Stoker's *Dracula*.

35. Connor, *Dumbstruck*, 390–91.

36. Margaret C. Anderson, *My Thirty Years War: An Autobiography* (New York: Knopf, 1930), 247.

37. John Rickard, *Joyce's Book of Memory: The Mnemotechnic of "Ulysses"* (Durham: Duke University Press, 1998), 89–90. Rickard's valuable discussion traces how paranormal effects are elaborated through Joyce's stylistic devices.

38. Gordon, *Joyce and Reality*, 191–92.

39. For some of the issues raised by these anomalies, see Kevin Dettmar, *The Illicit Joyce of Postmodernism* (Madison: University of Wisconsin Press, 1996), 179–80, and Gordon, *Joyce and Reality*, 189–90.

40. Translation of Latin prayer for the dying: "May the glittering throng of confessors, bright as lilies, gather about you. May the glorious choir of virgins receive you" (*UA* 19).

41. As Dettmar shows, this "coincidence" was inserted in a later draft, indicating it was a studied effect. Dettmar, *The Illicit Joyce of Postmodernism*, 178.

42. Rickard, *Joyce's Book of Memory*, 94–95. Bloom eventually hears a version of the line from Stephen in "Eumeaus" (*U* 16.1764), implying that the "Sirens" occurrence is also a foreshadowing. For other "telepathic" coincidences, such as Bloom's and Stephen's agreement that drowning is the easiest form of death, see R. M. Adams, "Hades," in *James Joyce's "Ulysses": Critical Essays*, ed. Clive Hart and David Hayman (Berkeley: University of California Press, 1977), 107–10.

43. Hence Adams's verdict on the porousness of Bloom's inner life: "Bloom is a diffused personality—not merely dim and hazy around the edges, but with chunks of other personalities incorporated with his, and vice versa" (Adams, "Hades," 110).

44. Oliver Sacks, *Hallucinations* (London: Picador, 2012), 275. Sacks (275) cites William James: "The popular mind wonders how the lost feet can be felt. For us, the cases for wonder are those in which the lost feet are not felt" ("The Consciousness of Lost Limbs," *Proceedings of the American Society for Psychical Research* 1, no. 1 [July 1885]: 253).

45. Jacques Mercanton, "The Hours of James Joyce," in *Portraits of the Artist in Exile: Recollections of James Joyce by Europeans*, ed. Willard Potts (Seattle: University of Washington Press, 1979), 213.

46. Sacks, *Hallucinations*, 277, 252.

47. Ibid., 59–60.

48. Mercanton, "The Hours of James Joyce," 226.

49. Sigmund Freud, *The Psychopathology of Everyday Life*, trans. Alan Tyson (New York: Norton, 1965), 257. This, as noted above (note 4), was one of the works by Freud in Joyce's library in Trieste. Freud returns to the subject of haunting in "Delusions and Dreams in Jensen's 'Gradiva,'"[1907], reprinted in Sigmund Freud, *Art and Literature*, Pelican Freud Library (Harmondsworth: Penguin, 1985), 14: 27–119. It is the hesitations and gaps in this later essay that are subjected to critique in Derrida's "Theses" in *Archive Fever* (see note 20 above).

50. Freud, *The Psychopathology of Everyday Life*, 258, italics in original.

51. Jean Laplanche and Serge Leclaire, "The Unconscious: A Psychoanalytic Study," *Yale French Studies* 48 (1972): 119–20.

52. Hence Lacan's insistence that the unconscious is "the discourse of the Other"

(Jacques Lacan, "Subversion of the Subject and Dialectic of Desire," in *Écrits: A Selection*, Alan Sheridan [London: Tavistock, 1977], 312) and is "structured in the most radical way like a language" (Lacan, "The Direction of Its Treatment and the Principles of its Power," ibid., 234). For this reason, "the unconscious is neither primordial not instinctual" (Lacan, "The Agency of the Letter in the Unconscious, or Reason since Freud," ibid.,170).

53. As Lacan's emphasis on the role of the "mirror stage" in preparing ultimate entry into the symbolic order of language indicates, the formation of both the conscious and the unconscious turns on an awareness of others—that I not only see but am seen from the outside (as in the case of Stephen: "His father told him that story: his father looked at him through a glass"). Jacques Lacan, "The Mirror Stage as Formative of the Function of the I as Revealed in Psychoanalytic Experience," ibid., 1–7.

54. Jeri Johnson, introduction to James Joyce, *A Portrait of the Artist as a Young Man* (Oxford: Oxford University Press, 2000), xx–xxiii.

55. As Jean Laplanche points out, though "everything comes from without in Freudian theory," the primordial driving force still emanates from within: "[E]very effect—in its efficacy—comes from within, from an isolated and encysted interior." Jean Laplanche, *Life and Death in Psychoanalysis*, trans. Jeffrey Mehlmann (Baltimore: Johns Hopkins University Press, 1976), 43.

56. Mikkel Borsch-Jacobsen, *The Emotional Tie: Psychoanalysis, Mimesis, and Affect*, trans. Douglas Brick and others (Stanford: Stanford University Press, 1992), 20. Borch-Jacobsen notes further the extent to which "Freud is held prisoner by the metaphysics of the Subject": the multiplication of layers and agencies within the psyche "does much more to presume than to contradict the unity and identity of the subject: the subject can be divided only because it is first of all *one* subject" (20).

57. Morton Schatzman, *Soul Murder: Persecution in the Family* (Harmondsworth: Penguin, 1976). The historical importance of the sadistic regimes of Schreber's father is also central to Gilles Deleuze and Felix Guattari's critique of Freud: *Anti-Oedipus: Capitalism and Schizophrenia* (London: Athlone Press, 1972). For Freud's analysis, see "Psycho-analytic notes on an autobiographical account of a case of paranoia (dementia paranoids)" [1911], *Standard Edition of the Complete Psychological Works of Sigmund Freud*, trans. J. Strachey (London: Vintage, 2001), 12:3–82. According to Janet Malcolm, the break of both Schatzman and his fellow dissident psychoanalyst Jeffrey Masson with Freudian orthodoxy consisted in their seeking "corroboration in historical material for their view that we are ruled by external reality rather than by our inner demons." Janet Malcolm, *In the Freud Archives* (London: Papermac, 1997), 81. The "rather" is problematic here: historical material is, of course, mediated and encrypted in inner lives (Schreber's experience being a case in point), but is no less "external" for that.

58. As Marcia Cavell notes of Freud's assumption that mental processes are in place from the outset: "[I]n the case of the very early 'wishes' Freud invokes as essential to his theory, the conditions for assigning any specific mental content to the infant are not yet present. . . . [P]sychoanalysts underestimate the perceptual-cognitive steps necessary to form an intrapsychic representational world." Marcia Cavell, *The Psychoanalytic Mind: From Freud to Philosophy* (Cambridge: Harvard University Press, 1993), 46, 51.

59. "It was Sándor Ferenczi who introduced the term 'introjection' which he coined as the opposite of 'projection.'" J. Laplanche and J.-B. Pontalis, *The Language of Psychoanalysis*, trans. Donald Nicholson-Smith (London: Hogarth Press, 1980), 229. Freud is, of course, aware that the ego formation is a process, and that the "incorporation" of the

mother is central to this at an early oral stage, but, as Cavell notes, the "wish" to internalize the mother already presupposes a prior infantile psychic agency (if it is to be other than mere biological instinct).

60. Nicolas Abraham and Maria Torok, *The Shell and the Kernel: Renewals of Psychoanalysis*, ed. and trans. Nicholas T. Rand (Chicago: University of Chicago Press, 1994). Subsequent references will take the form of *SK*, followed by page number, in the text.

61. Wolfgang Schivelbusch, *Disenchanted Night: The Industrialization of Light in the Nineteenth Century* (Berkeley: University of California Press, 1992).

62. Connolly, *Priests and People*, 11–32.

63. Ibid., 119.

64. William R. Wilde, *Irish Popular Superstitions* (Dublin: James McGlashan, 1852), 10. For Deborah R. Davis, "thin-legged revenants" of the Famine rival earlier vernacular traditions as a source of the spectral: "In Ireland, elements of expressive culture that enable people to find meaning in ghostly manifestations draw upon religion (both pre-Christian and Christian), as well as upon economic circumstances (most poignantly the devastating nineteenth-century Famine)." Deborah R. Davis, "Famine Ghosts and the Fear Gortach: A Strand of Irish Belief," *Folklore Forum* 27, no. 2 (1996): 41.

65. Connolly, *Priests and People*, 115, 108. The burning of the "changeling" Bridget Cleary is discussed below in chapter 5.

66. Alessandro Francini Bruni, "Joyce Stripped Naked in Piazza," in Potts, *Portraits of the Artist in Exile*, 27. Francini Bruni taught English with Joyce at the Berlitz School in Trieste and was one of his closest European friends for years.

67. DiBattista, "The Ghost Walks," 58.

68. Stephen's suggestion refers to the possibility that Shakespeare himself played the ghost in the original production of *Hamlet* (*U* 9.14–69).

69. Bloom is reluctant to include Boylan among the "topnobbers"—"he can't sing for tall hats" (*U* 11.687–88)—but Molly claims that Boylan "was in a great singing voice" (*U* 18.149). Alternatively, it could be Molly's name that is on the tip of his tongue, which is how Mr. Power tactfully interprets it: "And *madame*, Mr Power said smiling. Last but not least" (*U* 6.224).

70. Drawing on traditions of "negative theology" in Joyce's writing, Colleen Jaurretche notes that the apophatic "defines that sense of presence through negation and denial." The use of language to allude to (unspoken) events off the page, or in the material world, is central to Joyce's method, as I will argue in chapter 1. See Colleen Jaurretche, *The Sensual Philosophy: Joyce and the Aesthetics of Mysticism* (Madison: University of Wisconsin Press, 1997), 13.

71. As John Rickard notes, "proleptic, dynamic modes of memory" are a feature of *Ulysses*, realizing "the continual power of the past to drive us involuntarily into the future." Rickard, *Joyce's Book of Memory*, 87. Bloom suffers from "premonitions" in his sleep (*U* 17.282), and parodic "intimations . . . effected or projected" (*U* 17.327) are received, "graven in the language of prediction" (*U* 17.340–41) relating to the fate of the horse Throwaway in the Ascot Gold Cup that day.

72. In view of this, George Sigerson's putative claim that "[o]ur national epic has yet to be written" (*U* 9.309), quoted at the outset of this introduction, may hint at a "ghost-story" after all, except in this case the haunting "predicts" the future—the writing of *Ulysses* itself.

73. Stuart Gilbert, *Reflections on James Joyce: Stuart Gilbert's Paris Journal*, ed. Thomas P. Staley and Randolph Lewis (Austin: University of Texas Press, 1993), 9.

74. Adams, "Hades," 100.

75. Enda Duffy, "Disappearing Dublin: *Ulysses*, Postcoloniality, and the Politics of Space," in *Semi-Colonial Joyce*, ed. Derek Attridge and Marjorie Howes (Cambridge: Cambridge University Press, 2000), 46.

76. While working on *Dubliners* in Rome in 1906, Joyce wrote to his aunt Josephine in Dublin requesting "tram-tickets, advts, handbills, posters papers, programmes &c" (*JJSL* 124).

77. As critics have noted, the text itself contains its own "internal" omissions, most notably Bloom's visit to the Dignam home, but knowledge of this is not "extratextual" in the manner of real events that require empirical or archival grounding.

78. Nicholas Royle, *The Uncanny* (New York: Routledge, 2003), 280.

79. Margot Norris, *Virgin and Veteran Readings of "Ulysses"* (London: Palgrave, 2012), 70. Norris is referring to knowledge gleaned intratextually from the novel, but as she points out, this also extends to "unstated" material contexts, outside the text. Norris is drawing on H. P. Grice's linguistic theory of implicature: "Most cases of implicature" depend on "factors, outside the language . . . taking account of the fact that context is often crucial to the difference between literal and intended meaning." Siobhan Chapman, "H. P. Grice," in *Key Thinkers in Linguistics and the Philosophy of Language*, ed. Siobhan Chapman and Christopher Routledge (Oxford: Oxford University Press, 2005), 111–12.

80. Jacques Derrida, *Specters of Marx: The State of the Debt, the Work of Mourning, and the New International*, trans. Peggy Kamuf (New York: Routledge, 1994), xix.

81. Seamus Deane, "Dead Ends: Joyce's Finest Moments," in *Semi-Colonial Joyce*, 23.

82. Ellmann, "The Ghosts of *Ulysses*," 96.

83. Judith Butler, *Precarious Life: The Powers of Mourning and Violence* (London: Verso, 2004), 21. Subsequent references will take the form of *PL*, followed by page number, in the text.

Chapter 1

1. Mary Colum, *Life and the Dream* (London: Macmillan, 1947), 381. Subsequent references will take the form of *LD*, followed by page number, in the text.

2. One of Joyce's favorite photographs was taken of him, by Carola Giedion-Welcker, with his back to the camera at the Platzspitz in Zurich (fig. 1.1).

3. Joyce joked that the ceaseless flow of the Liffey could extend as far as Trieste, making it the longest river in the world. James Joyce to Ettore Schmitz, 21 November 1925 (*JJL* III, 535).

4. Shane Leslie, "Review of *Ulysses*," *Quarterly Review* 238 (October 1922), cited in Herbert Gorman, *James Joyce: A Definitive Biography* (London: John Lane the Bodley Head, 1949), 295–96. This part of the quotation is omitted in the reprint of Leslie's review in *James Joyce: The Critical Heritage*, ed. Robert H. Deming (*JJCH* I, 206–11). Leslie is suggesting that because of their subsequent importance in political life, well-known personalities like Griffith do not present to the non-Irish reader the problem posed by the lesser-known real-life figures that walk the streets of Dublin in the novel.

5. For Griffith's aversion to cosmopolitanism, see his criticisms of the Irish international socialist Frederick Ryan in this light, in "The Death of Fredrick Ryan" [1913], reprinted in "Constructing the Canon: Versions of National Identity," ed. Luke Gibbons, in *The Field Day Anthology of Irish Writing*, ed. Seamus Deane, 3 vols. (Derry: Field Day; London: Faber and Faber, 1991), 2:1002–3.

6. Maurice Merleau-Ponty, *Phenomenology of Perception*, trans. Colin Smith (Lon-

don: Routledge and Kegan Paul, 1962). Subsequent references will take the form of *PP*, followed by page number, in the text.

7. Merleau-Ponty takes issue with explanations that account for the phantom limb solely in physiological terms, but equally with explanations that construe it as a psychological event, something existing entirely "in the head." A physiological explanation of a phantom arm that considers the stump as sending the same signals to the brain as the original arm fails to explain how the phantom limb persists during a local anesthetic. More to the point, and closer to the sense of place in Joyce's work, the fact that "an emotion or circumstance, which recalls those in which the wound was received, created a phantom limb in those who had none," can hardly be accounted for in terms of tissue and severed nerves. On the other hand, a psychological account that relegates it to a representation or a memory cannot "overlook the fact that the severance of the nerves to the brain abolishes the phantom limb" (*PP* 77).

8. That the body is viewed as a "gestalt" or whole is suggested by the fact that phantom limbs also occur congenitally, so are not exclusively bound up with memory of a missing limb.

9. Robert D. Romanyshyn, "Unconsciousness: Reflection and the Primacy of Perception," in *Phenomenology: Dialogues and Bridges*, ed. Ronald Bruzina and Bruce Wilshire (Albany: SUNY Press, 1982), 161.

10. Cited in Cyril Pearl, *Dublin in Bloomtime: The City Joyce Knew* (London: Angus and Robertson, 1969), 7–8. Patricia Hutchins also remarks: "The canals and little rivers with their footpaths and trees, and at low tides the wide strands of the bay, were remembered by Joyce in Pola or Trieste, beside the Zurichsee or as the light on some houses across the Seine brought back an early morning near the Pigeon House." Patricia Hutchins, *James Joyce's World* (London: Methuen, 1957), 1.

11. Laplanche and Leclaire, "The Unconscious," 128. For the relation to "phantoms," see Peter Nicholls, "The Belated Postmodern: History, Phantoms, and Toni Morrison," in *Psychoanalytic Criticism: A Reader*, ed. Sue Vice (Cambridge: Polity Press, 1996), 50–74. In trauma, there is no unmediated access to the "event," but this is not to say the event had no existence, or that it is no more than a projection of the present onto the past. Freud's point is that an "impression" is received to which an individual may be unable to react adequately at the time but which, through "an entire network of meaningful relations that integrate it into the subject's explicit apprehension of himself" (Laplanche and Leclaire, "The Unconscious," 128), enables the individual "even twenty years later . . . to grasp within his conscious mental processes what was then going on in him." Sigmund Freud, "From the History of an Infantile Neurosis" [1918], in *Case Histories II*, vol. 9 of the Pelican Freud Library, ed. Angela Richards (Harmondsworth: Penguin, 1981), 278. It is worth noting that Joyce was familiar with this publication of Freud's, which dealt with the "Wolf Man." See note 4 to the introduction above.

12. Heinrich Straumann, "Four Letters to Martha Fleischmann" (*JJL* II, 428).

13. As Roy Gottfried summarizes it, referring to Joyce's cosmopolitan literary readership, this "audience was more sophisticated, more able to see the work in a broader context. . . . It was not Catholic and parochial but secular and prominent, not Irish but international; not those who shared Joyce's past but those who shared his present profession. . . . It had wider horizons than those of religion, as these readers are part of an aesthetic view that spurned nationalism and parochialism in its allegiance to modernism." Roy Gottfried, "The Audiences for Joyce's Autobiographies," in *Joyce's Audiences*, ed. John Nash (Amsterdam: Rodopi, 2002), 80.

14. Joseph Kelly, *Our Joyce: From Outcast to Icon* (Austin: University of Texas Press, 1998), 16.

15. James Joyce to Grant Richards, 23 June 1906 (*JJL* I, 63–64).

16. Joyce to Richards, 23 June 1906 (*JJL* II, 122, italics added). Joyce's determination—or anxiety—on this score is evident in his further remark to Richards that his autobiographical novel, though "a thousand pages," has "the defect of being about Ireland" (*JJL* II, 132).

17. Seamus Deane et al. "Political Perspectives on Joyce's Work," in *Joyce & Paris 1902 . . . 1920–1940 . . . 1975*, ed. J. Aubert and M. Jolas (Lille: Publications de Universitie de Lille III; Paris: Éditions du CNRS, 1979), 106–7.

18. For the centrality of free indirect discourse to Joyce's work, see chapters 2 and 3 below.

19. A more extended discussion of parallax in *Ulysses* is developed in chapter 6 below.

20. Martin Jay, "Experience without a Subject: Walter Benjamin and the Novel," *New Formations* 20 (Summer 1993): 151.

21. Umberto Eco, *The Open Work*, trans. Anna Cancogni (Cambridge: Harvard University Press, 1989), 10.

22. Franco Moretti, "The Long Goodbye: *Ulysses* and the End of Liberal Capitalism," in *Signs Taken for Wonders: Essays in the Sociology of Literary Forms*, trans. Susan Fischer, David Forgacs, and David Miller (London: Verso, 1093), 190, 189.

23. Though inspired by the Revival, Joyce's modernism extends beyond the limited horizons of Celticism, Catholic nationalism, and Home Rule, and had more in keeping with the secular and international elements promoted by his socialist and republican contemporaries in Dublin. See Gibbons, "Constructing the Canon," in *Field Day Anthology of Irish Writing* 2:960–1020.

24. Leo Steinberg, *Other Criteria: Confrontations with Twentieth-Century Art* (London: Oxford University Press, 1972), 90. Steinberg is referring to the collages of Robert Rauschenberg in terms, as he later points out, derived from Freud and James Joyce (320).

25. Phillip F. Herring, *Joyce's Uncertainty Principle* (Princeton: Princeton University Press, 1987). According to Herring, this strategy is signaled by Joyce's use of the term "gnomon," the missing piece of a geometrical figure, in the opening paragraph of the first story in *Dubliners*, "The Sisters": "'Gnomonic' language may contain ellipses, hiatuses in meaning, significant silences, empty and ritualistic dialogue. . . . In effect, a *gnomon* may be a key synecdoche of absence, part of a general rhetoric of silence within a larger framework of language" (4).

26. The linking of Joyce's "gnomonic" or apophatic strategies to elusive local knowledge was already flagged by reviewers of *A Portrait of the Artist as a Young Man* in 1917: "Parts of the book are perhaps a little too allusive to be readily understood by the English reader. On pp. 265–6, there is an account of what happened at the Abbey Theatre, Dublin, when the Countless Cathleen, by Mr. W. B. Yeats, was put on, but the fact is darkly hidden." Unsigned review, *Everyman*, 23 February 1917 (*JJCH* I, 85).

27. Clive Hart and Leo Knuth, "Applied Thomism," *A Topographical Guide to "Ulysses"* (Colchester: A Wakes Newsletter Press, 1981), 19, 18.

28. Jonathan Culler notes that deictic language functions differently in literature: "*Now* in a poem ('now . . . gathering swallows twitter in the skies') refers not to the instant when the poet first wrote down the word, or to the moment of its first publication, but to a time in the poem, in the fictional world of its action." In the case of *Ulysses*, however, this might read that time "refers not *just* to the instant" of its occurrence, but the

instant—16 June 1904—is important nonetheless. Jonathan Culler, *Literary Theory: A Very Short Introduction* (Oxford: Oxford University Press, 1997), 31.

29. Henri Lefebvre, *Everyday Life in the Modern World*, trans. Sacha Rabinovitch (New York: Harper and Row, 1971), 98.

30. Ludwig Wittgenstein, *Culture and Value*, trans. Peter Winch (Oxford: Blackwell, 1998), 6–7. Subsequent references will take the form of *CV*, followed by page number, in the text.

31. Georges Perec, "Approaches to What?" [1973], trans. John Sturrock, in *The Everyday Life Reader*, ed. Ben Highmore (London: Routledge, 2002), 177. Stanislaus Joyce wrote of the kind of people that turned up in his brother's stories "that not only were those Dubliners below literary interest but even below human interest except for hardened philanthropic societies." Stanislaus Joyce, *My Brother's Keeper* (London: Faber and Faber, 1958), 206.

32. See Declan Kiberd, "Ulysses, Newspapers and Modernism," in *Irish Classics* (London: Granta Books, 2000), 463–81.

33. Karen Lawrence, "Joyce and Feminism," in *The Cambridge Companion to Joyce*, ed. Derek Attridge (Cambridge: Cambridge University Press, 1990), 254.

34. Wittgenstein's remark is borne out by W. B. Yeats's attempt to bring plays in dialect to native audiences in the west of Ireland: "Some countrymen in Galway, whither we carried our plays in dialect a few weeks ago, said it was no use going to see them because they showed people what could be seen on the road every day." "*Samhain*, 1908: First Principles," *Explorations* (New York: Macmillan, 1989), 231.

35. Raymond Williams, *The Country and the City* (Oxford: Oxford University Press, 1973), 243–48.

36. Max Scheler, *The Nature of Sympathy* [1912], trans. Peter Heath (New Haven: Yale University Press, 1954), 252, second italics added. Subsequent references will take the form of *NS*, followed by page number, in the text.

37. Alexander Pope, "An Essay on Criticism," in *Alexander Pope: Selected Poetry and Prose*, ed. Robin Sowerby (London: Routledge, 1988), 44.

38. This does not entail, of course, that everything can be brought to consciousness in a simplistic or literal sense: the ability to paraphrase or to stabilize meaning is in inverse proportion to the density of aesthetic form. The allusiveness and opacities of the aesthetic are thus on a continuum with everyday life (too close to it, in the eyes of many of Joyce's critics), even if the purpose is to transform the clichés and sedimented responses that pass for common sense.

39. "A Dyspeptic Portrait," *Freeman's Journal*, 7 April 1917 (*JJCH* I, 98).

40. Cheryl Temple Herr, *Joyce and the Art of Shaving* (Dublin: National Library of Ireland Joyce Studies, 2004), 15. "Enworlded," in Heideggerian terms, means a prereflective, firsthand experience of being immersed in the world.

41. Ibid., 21, italics added. Herr makes a convincing case for analyzing Joyce, in Heideggerian terms, as being primarily concerned with everyday "Being-in-the world," but immersion in the condition of the colonial city also carries with it the disabling burden of "paralysis," which Joyce seeks to challenge.

42. Mercanton, "Hours of James Joyce," 220.

43. Wittgenstein, *Philosophical Investigations*, §§14–26.

44. Robert Humphrey, *Stream of Consciousness in the Modern Novel* (Berkeley: University of California Press, 1958), 15.

45. Virginia Woolf, "The Cinema" [1927], in *Selected Essays*, ed. David Bradshaw (Oxford: Oxford University Press, 2008), 173.

46. Wittgenstein, *Philosophical Investigations*, §§19, 23, 174. See also David Kishik, *Wittgenstein's Form of Life* (New York: Continuum, 2008).

47. Norman Malcolm, *Thought and Knowledge* (Ithaca: Cornell University Press, 1977), 212; Nigel Pleasants, *Wittgenstein and the Idea of a Critical Social Theory: A Critique of Giddens, Habermas and Bhaskar* (London: Routledge, 1999), 49.

48. Walter Benjamin, "A Short History of Photography," trans. Edmund Jephson and Kingsley Shorter, in *One-Way Street* (London: New Left Books, 1979), 248–89.

49. It is in this sense that Hugh Kenner interprets David Hayman's figure of the narrator as an "arranger" in Joyce: "not the 'impersonal' author called for by Dedalian and Eliotic theory but an active participant in the shaping of the text, as vividly present often as any character." Hugh Kenner, *Ulysses* (Baltimore: Johns Hopkins University Press, 1987), 172, discussing David Hayman, *Ulysses: The Mechanics of Meaning* (Madison: University of Wisconsin Press, 1982). The active arranging by multiple narrators extends also to active readers, who are required to bring both textual and extratextual factors to bear on the novel.

50. S. Joyce, *My Brother's Keeper*, 206.

51. Michael Riffaterre, "Interpretation and Descriptive Poetry: A Reading of Wordsworth's 'Yew Trees,'" in *Untying the Text: A Post-Structuralist Reader*, ed. Robert Young (Boston: Routledge and Kegan Paul, 1981), 109. Subsequent references will take the form of *IDP*, followed by page number, in the text.

52. Ezra Pound, "*Dubliners* and Mr. James Joyce," *Egoist* 1, no. 14 (15 July 1914) (*JJCH* I, 167).

53. Roland Barthes, "The Reality Effect," in *The Rustle of Language*, trans. Richard Howard (Berkeley: University of California Press, 1989), 11–48. As Riffaterre states: "The text builds up a phantasm of history. Shift the sentence from general to particular, from nouns to names, and in terms of time or space you create an *effect of reality*" (*IDP* 109, italics added).

54. Christopher Butler, *Interpretation, Deconstruction and Ideology: An Introduction to Some Current Issues in Literary Theory* (Oxford: Oxford University Press, 1984), 48.

55. Budgen, *James Joyce and the Making of "Ulysses,"* 70. Joyce suggested that as space and time—"timeplace" (*FW* 416.24)—seem to dissolve in sleep in *Finnegans Wake*, "one should not pay particular attention to the allusions to places, historical events, literary happenings, but let the linguistic phenomenon affect one as such." Heinrich Strausmann, "Last Meeting with Joyce," in *A James Joyce Yearbook*, ed. Maria Jolas (Paris: Transition Press, 1949), 114, cited in John Bishop, *Joyce's Book of the Dark* (Madison: University of Wisconsin Press, 1986), 421–22. The irony here is that while the sonic—and dreamlike—effects of *Finnegans Wake* are indeed to the fore, conforming more closely to Riffaterre's formally sealed text, the range of extratextual allusions expands almost exponentially to the same degree, so that one never knows whether some recondite source or event is eluding attempts to decipher a passage. See Bishop, "Nothing in Particular: On English Obliterature," in *Joyce's Book of the Dark*, 42–65. The famous transcription by Samuel Beckett of Joyce's words "come in," occasioned by Joyce's response to a knock on the door while Beckett was taking down his words for *Finnegans Wake* (*JJ* 622), is emblematic of this affect, an incident possibly transposed in the text as "Sammy, call on" (*FW* 22.36–23.1).

56. Butler, *Interpretation, Deconstruction and Ideology*, 50–53. Compare this with Joyce's method in *Ulysses*, as noted by Hart and Knuth, where the kind of imprecision that surfaces at times in *Dubliners*—for example, the vagueness of a "little cakeshop near the Parkgate" in "Clay"—seldom features. Hart and Knuth, "Applied Thomism," 16.

57. At stake here is a version of Roman Jakobson's thesis that poetry gravitates toward metaphor, while prose fiction, particularly realism, turns on metonymy: "Following the path of contiguous relationships, the realistic author metonymically digresses from the plot to the atmosphere and from the characters to the setting in space and time." Roman Jakobson and Morris Halle, *Fundamentals of Language* (The Hague: Mouton, 1956), 92.

58. It is worth noting that Riffaterre sees the aesthetic work, in which the "message" is constituted by form or internal properties, as generating its own internal context: "The appropriate language of reference is selected from the message, the context is reconstituted from the message." Michael Riffaterre, "Describing Poetic Structures: Two Approaches to Baudelaire's 'Les Chats,'" in *Structuralism*, ed. Jacques Ehrmann (Garden City, NY: Doubleday, 1970), 202. It is, of course, the textual effects of *Ulysses* that send the reader to *Thom's Directory* or other sources, but the context is not decidable solely within the text. For an account of Jakobson and Riffaterre in this respect, see Robert Scholes, *Structuralism in Literature* (New Haven: Yale University Press, 1974), 12–40, and Jonathan Culler, "Riffaterre and the Semiotics of Poetry," in *The Pursuit of Signs: Semiotics, Literature, Deconstruction* (London: Routledge and Kegan Paul, 1981), 80–99.

59. John Cage, *Silence: Lectures and Writings* (Middletown: Wesleyan University Press, 1961), 99.

60. Sigmund Freud, "Mourning and Melancholia," in *On Murder, Mourning and Melancholia*, trans. Shaun Whiteside, with introduction by Maud Ellmann (London: Penguin, 2005), 203.

61. It is not, however, that events of historical importance are severed from quotidian realities. Joyce's method in *Ulysses* is to link the two, as in Bloom's return of Parnell's hat to the leader in the fracas outside the United Ireland offices in 1891 (*U* 16.1336). In this instance, a real-life event—left open by the anonymity accorded to the individual who lifted the hat in the account of the incident in Barry O'Brien's *Life of Parnell* (1898)—is exploited for fictional effect.

62. Colin McCabe, *James Joyce and the Revolution of the Word* (London: Macmillan, 1978), 28–29. As Hart and Knuth point out, in parts of *Ulysses* "the text is not entirely self-sufficient, the sense is by no means fully determined by the words alone. . . . The topography of Dublin is 'on the page' at least as much as are the meanings of the words 'priest,' 'kidney,' or 'ineluctable modality': it is part of the book's primary reference system, without which its full sense cannot be comprehended." Hart and Knuth, "Applied Thomism," 18.

63. John Kidd, "The Scandal of Ulysses," *New York Review of Books*, 30 June 1988.

64. The Captain Buller allusion may even be more complex than Kidd allows, for it is not clear that the Captain Buller of Byron Lodge was the Captain Buller who played cricket: John Simpson, "Captain Buller: that prodigious hit to square leg," in "Joyce's People," *James Joyce Online Notes*, http://www.jjon.org/jioyce-s-people/captain-buller.

65. The links between Byron and Trinity are further extended when, on bringing Stephen home to Eccles Street, Molly warms to his Byronic looks but hopes he is not at Trinity College (*U* 18.1331–32).

66. Hart and Knuth, "Applied Thomism," 19.

67. Duffy, "Disappearing Dublin," in *Semi-Colonial Joyce*, 47–48.

68. Michel Foucault, "Two Lectures," in *Power/Knowledge: Selected Interviews and Other Writings*, ed. Colin Gordon, trans. Colin Gordon, Leo Marshall, John Mepham, and Kate Soper (New York: Pantheon Books, 1980), 82. For an insightful application of this concept to Molly Bloom's soliloquy, see Carol Schloss, "Molly's Resistance to

the Union: Marriage and Colonialism in Dublin, 1904," in *Molly Blooms: A Polylogue on "Penelope" and Cultural Studies*, ed. Richard Pearce (Madison: University of Wisconsin Press, 1994), 105–18.

69. Aristotle, *The Poetics*, trans. S. H. Butcher, part 9 (New York: Dover, 1951), 17: "It is, moreover, evident from what has been said, that it is not the function of the poet to relate what has happened, but what may happen—what is possible according to the law of probability or necessity. The poet and the historian differ not by writing in verse or in prose. . . . The true difference is that one relates what has happened, the other what may happen. Poetry, therefore, is a more philosophical and a higher thing than history: for poetry tends to express the universal, history the particular."

70. This is not to rule out the possibility that chance and indeterminacy also feature in the seemingly closed world of a fictive text, as in the classic conundrum of how many children Lady Macbeth had. Elements of uncertainty pervade the lives of the fictional characters in *Ulysses*: How many lovers has Molly had? Who is the man in the macintosh? Notwithstanding the unpredictability of fictional characters, even surprises or sudden reversals have to be plausible in the end, and justified on internal textual grounds, or else they stand as textual anomalies. As Hugh Kenner famously pointed out, however, Joyce's development of character and fictional action constantly leaves gaps that are very difficult to account for solely within the text. Hugh Kenner, "The Rhetoric of Silence," *JJQ* 14 (1977): 382–94. For extended discussions of these issues, see Thomas G. Pavel, *Fictional Worlds* (Cambridge: Harvard University Press, 1986), and D. A. Miller, *Narrative and Its Discontents: Problems of Closure in the Traditional Novel* (Princeton: Princeton University Press, 1981).

71. This is the basis of Sir Shane Leslie's complaint that *Ulysses* is peopled with real-life nonentities, as against important individuals such as Arthur Griffith. While descriptions of real-life individuals are limited to what is true of them, there is no limit to what may be discovered about them: hence the difficulty in determining whether the knowledge discovered extratextually is relevant to the meaning of the text. In the eyes of Wittgenstein or Georg Perec, it is the depiction of the inconsequential that poses the greatest challenge to artistic representation—and perhaps even historical research.

72. Cage, *Silence*, 101. Cage's aesthetic is related to the advanced modernist strategy of "autonomization," as described by Fredric Jameson, according to which parts of a composition become autonomous centers, disaggregating narrative cohesion throughout the work. Fredric Jameson, *Brecht and Method* (London: Verso, 2000), 43–51.

73. Robert Martin Adams, *Surface and Symbol: The Consistency of James Joyce's "Ulysses"* (Oxford: Oxford University Press, 1967), xvii.

74. Terence Killeen, *"Ulysses" Unbound* (Dublin: Wordwell, 2005), 248. Killeen makes the point, not dissimilar to Cage's, that each episode or detail may be "conceived as a total environment (just as the whole book is in a larger framework)" (248). That important meanings may lie outside conscious deliberation runs counter to Robert M. Adams's argument elsewhere that Joyce's "imposed" totalizing designs leave little room for slippage, or for connections emerging "from a web of circumstances they unwittingly spin." Robert M. Adams, *AfterJoyce: Studies in Fiction after "Ulysses"* (Oxford: Oxford University Press, 1977), 7.

75. Derek Attridge, *Joyce Effects: On Language, Theory, and History* (Cambridge: Cambridge University Press, 2000), 119.

76. Ibid., 120–21.

77. Ann Rigney, *Imperfect Histories: The Elusive Past and the Legacy of Romantic Historicism* (Ithaca: Cornell University Press, 2001), 17–18.

78. Ruth Ronen, *Possible Worlds in Literary Theory* (Cambridge: Cambridge University Press, 1994), 41.

79. Heyward Ehrlich, "James Joyce's Four-Gated City of Modernism," in *Joyce and the City*, ed. Michael Begnal (Syracuse: Syracuse University Press, 2002), 10.

80. According to Roman Jakobson, the integration of (metonymic) *context* into a (metaphoric) *code*, subsuming the referential or "extralinguistic" aspects of language to its formal properties, is what defines the literariness of a text. As he famously expressed it, equating "the axis of selection" with metaphor, and the "axis of combination" with the metonmyic mode: "*The poetic function projects the principle of equivalence from the axis of selection into the axis of combination.* Equivalence is promoted to the constitutive device of the sequence." Roman Jakobson, "Linguistic and Poetics," in *Language and Literature* (Cambridge: Belknap Press, 1987), 71, italics in original.

81. Scholes, *Structuralism and Literature*, 7–28.

82. Ibid., 28. Scholes writes as if a "double context" were a matter of course, but clearly more formalist approaches to aesthetic form, such as those exemplified by Riffaterre above, seek to close off, or at least to diminish, this double axis of reference.

83. It is in this sense that the oscillation between text and context becomes, for Scholes, a particular achievement of aesthetic form: "Contexts in poetry . . . are multiple, and are so managed that what is background at some times is foregrounded at others. And often we find in poems the gestalt trick in which background and foreground exchange perceptual roles" (ibid., 31). Whether this is a general aesthetic principle is open to question, but it is certainly central to the narrative method of *Ulysses*.

84. Richard Kuhns elaborates on Wittgenstein's distinction between what is *shown* and what is *said*, emphasizing that putting words on the unspoken requires its own material setting: "Every talking about is at once a showing. It is as if we were to ask if we can always articulate the affective tone of what we articulate. And of course we cannot. For in articulating one set of tones, another set is articulated." Richard Kuhns, *Literature and Philosophy: Structures of Experience* (London: Routledge and Kegan Paul, 1971), 253.

85. Attridge, *Joyce Effects*, 69.

86. Peter Winch, *The Idea of a Social Science* (London: Routledge and Kegan Paul, 1958), 129–30, italics added.

87. The vocalizing of vision—"her eyes had called" (*P* 186)—is picked up again in Stephen's troubled dream at the end of *Portrait*, in which eyes perform the work of speech, and yet fail in the process: "They peer at me and their eyes seem to ask me something. They do not speak" (*P* 272). I discuss "visualizing the voice" at greater length below in chapter 4.

88. Locke, *Eavesdropping*, 102.

89. The immobilized Winnie in Beckett's *Happy Days* is aware of looks that unsettle ("Don't look at me like that!") but also wistfully desires a meeting of eyes: "Someone is looking at me still. [*Pause.*] Caring for me still. [*Pause.*] That is what I find so wonderful. [*Pause.*] Eyes on my eyes." Samuel Beckett, *Happy Days: A Play in Two Acts*, preface by James Knowlson (London: Faber and Faber, 2010), 37, 29.

90. Enda Duffy, *The Subaltern "Ulysses"* (Minneapolis: University of Minnesota Press, 1994), 15–76.

91. Ibid., 181.

92. D. A. Miller, *The Novel and the Police* (Berkeley: University of California Press, 1988), 3.

93. Ibid., 4.

94. Ezra Pound, "At Last the Novel Appears," *Egoist* 4, no. 2 (February 1917) (*JJCH* I, 83).

95. James Joyce, *Stephen Hero* (London: Paladin, 1991), 85; Andrew Gibson, *Joyce's Revenge: History, Politics and Aesthetics in "Ulysses"* (Oxford: Oxford University Press, 2002), 37.

96. Jeremiah O'Donovan Rossa, editorial in the *United Irishman* (New York), c. 25 February 1882, cited in K. R. M. Short, *The Dynamite War: Irish-American Bombers in Victorian Britain* (Dublin: Gill and Macmillan, 1979), 90–91.

97. Ibid., 65.

98. See Robert Spoo, *James Joyce and the Language of History: Dedalus's Nightmare* (New York: Oxford University Press, 1994), 81–88.

99. Arthur Conan Doyle, "A Case of Identity"[1891], cited in Moretti, "Clues," in *Signs Taken for Wonders*, 136. (The passage is slightly misquoted from Conan Doyle's original text.)

100. Ibid.

101. Though Phillip Herring writes that Joyce's "dedication to factual accuracy [is] in conflict with his uncertainty principle," elsewhere he argues more persuasively that "the attempt to solve an unsolvable problem with historical evidence and rigourous scholarship" should accompany "an awareness that this leads us into indeterminacy." Herring, *Joyce's Uncertainty Principle*, 117, 108.

102. Umberto Eco, *The Middle Ages of James Joyce: The Aesthetics of Chaosmos*, trans. Ellen Esrock (London: Hutchinson Radius, 1989), 7.

103. James Joyce, "The Shade of Parnell" (*OCPW* 196).

Chapter 2

1. Frances Hegarty and Andrew Stones, *For Dublin* (Dublin: Irish Museum of Modern Art/Nissan Art Project, 1997).

2. Irish Museum of Modern Art Press Office, "Frances Hegarty and Andrew Stones Win Nissan Art Project," 1997, http://www.imma.ie/en/page_19242.htm, accessed 6 January 2011.

3. Molly's thoughts are not related to this particular set of statues, as she makes her acquaintance with "the stranger to Dublin" in the "jews temple gardens"(*U* 18.91–92) beside the Grand Canal.

4. Donald Horne, "'Myths' of Race, Sex, Nation," in *The Public Culture: The Triumph of Industrialism* (London: Pluto Press, 1986), 109.

5. See Anne Fogarty, "'Stone Hopes': Statues and Longing in Joyce's Work," *Dublin James Joyce Journal* 1 (2008): 69–83, and Luke Gibbons, "'Where Wolfe Tone's Statue Was Not': Joyce, Monuments and Memory," in *History and Memory in Modern Ireland*, ed. Ian McBride (Cambridge: Cambridge University Press, 2001), 139–59.

6. Joyce's negative topography would thus be consistent with the "lethal histories" of cultural trauma analyzed by Nicholas Miller, in which "memorials are, in the most generic sense, never indicators of the past a such, but always of its absence and loss . . . [of] the persistence of the illegible within signification itself." Nicholas Miller, *Modernism, Ireland and the Erotics of Memory* (Cambridge: Cambridge University Press, 2002), 34.

7. James Murphy, *Abject Loyalty: Nationalism and Monarchy in Ireland during the Reign of Queen Victoria* (Cork: Cork University Press, 2001).

8. For a related narrative strategy in Joyce's fiction, mapping topography and com-

memoration onto the setting of a story following the 1903 Robert Emmet Centenary, see Cóilín Owens, "'The Charity of Its Silence': 'After the Race' and the Emmet Centenary," *Dublin James Joyce Journal* 1 (2008): 30–46.

9. Theodor W. Adorno, *Kierkegaard: Construction of an Aesthetic*, trans. Robert Hullot-Kentor (Minneapolis: University of Minnesota Press, 1989), 38.

10. Lev Vygotsky, *Mind and Society: The Development of Higher Psychological Processes*, ed. and trans. Michael Cole, S. Scribner, V. John-Steiner, and E. Souderman (Cambridge: Harvard University Press, 1978), 56–57, 89–91, 130–32. See also P. Y. Galperin, "On the Notion of Internalization," *Soviet Psychology* 5 (1967): 28–33.

11. "Piaget's Theory of the Child's Speech and Thought," in Vygotsky, *TL*, chapter 2. See also Alex Kozulin, *Vygotsky's Psychology: A Biography of Ideas* (Cambridge: Harvard University Press, 1990), and Fred Newman and Lois Holzman, *Lev Vygotsky: Revolutionary Scientist* (London: Routledge, 1993): 114–36.

12. According to Vygotsky: "The earliest speech of the child is . . . essentially social. . . . At a certain age the social speech of the child is quite sharply divided into egocentric and communicative speech. . . . Egocentric speech emerges when the child transfers social, collaborative forms of behaviour to the sphere of inner-personal psychic functions. . . . Egocentric speech, splintered off from general social speech, in time leads to inner speech, which serves both autistic and logical thinking. . . . [T]he true direction of the development of thinking is not from the individual to the socialised, but from the social to the individual" (*TL* 34–35).

13. Vygotsky, *Mind in Society*, 57.

14. The abstract logic of mathematics or the physical sciences is often taken to be universal and context-free, but as W. V. O. Quine points out, the language of science is highly context-dependent: "Thus in the physics of light, with its notoriously mixed metaphor of wave and particle, the physicist's understanding of what he is talking about must depend almost wholly on context: on knowing when to use various sentences which speak jointly of photons and of observed phenomena of light." W. V. O. Quine, *Word and Object* (Cambridge: MIT Press, 1960), 15.

15. Vygotsky, *Mind in Society*, 56.

16. Citing the work of Wendy Grolnick et al., Wertsch analyses the importance of internalization in shaping the differences between compliance to a system and assimilation of its rules. James V. Wertsch, *Voices of Collective Remembering* (Cambridge: Cambridge University Press, 2002), 121.

17. James C. Scott, *Weapons of the Weak: Everyday Arts of Peasant Resistance* (New Haven: Yale University Press, 1987); *Domination and the Arts of Resistance: Hidden Transcripts* (New Haven: Yale University Press, 1992).

18. Ernest Gellner, cited in Wertsch, *Voices of Collective Remembering*, 122.

19. The dysfunctional nature of certain forms of externalization in ressentiment is clear, for example, from its reliance on scapegoats or, at the other side of the spectrum, leadership cults.

20. Wertsch, *Voices of Collective Remembering*, 129–30. See also Orlando Figes, *The Whisperers: Private Life in Stalin's Russia* (London: Penguin, 2008).

21. For the politics of oral culture and its relationship to the aesthetic in colonial Ireland, see David Lloyd, *Irish Culture and Colonial Modernity, 1800–2000: The Transformation of Oral Space* (Cambridge: Cambridge University Press, 2011), especially chapters 2–3.

22. As the jurist Charles Fried observed, it may be impossible to know if a person can

be trusted "unless he has a right to act without constant surveillance so that he knows he can betray the trust." Charles Fried, "Privacy," *Yale Law Journal* 77 (1968): 475, cited in Locke, *Eavesdropping*, 74.

23. Mary Colum, "The Confessions of James Joyce" (review of *Ulysses*) *Freeman*, 19 July 1922 (*JJCH* I, 232). Colum notes in her autobiography, *Life and the Dream*, that this review and those of Edmund Wilson and Gilbert Seldes pleased Joyce most (*LD* 306).

24. Michael J. F. McCarthy, *Irish Land and Liberty: A Study of the New Lords of the Soil* (London: Robert Scott, 1911), 142, 119, 176. Joyce had McCarthy's *The Irish Revolution* (1912) in his Trieste library, and Stanislaus Joyce had read McCarthy's controversial *Priests and People in Ireland* (1902). See Patrick J. Ledden, "Michael J. F. McCarthy and Joyce's Dublin," *JJQ* 37, nos. 1/2 (Fall/Winter 1999/2000): 209–14.

25. Umberto Eco, *Le Poetiche de Joyce*, cited in Moretti, "The Long Goodbye: *Ulysses* and the End of Capitalism," 194.

26. Eric Hobsbawm, *Nations and Nationalism since 1780: Programmes, Myth, Reality* (Cambridge: Cambridge University Press, 1990), 78, cited in Michael Herzfeld, *Cultural Intimacy: Social Poetics in the Nation-State* (New York: Routledge, 2005), 11.

27. For "U. p: up," see chapter 7 below.

28. Colum, "Confessions of James Joyce" (*JJCH* I, 232).

29. See chapters 5 and 6 below.

30. Melvin J. Friedman, "Lestrygonians," in Hart and Hayman, *James Joyce's "Ulysses": Critical Essays*, 142.

31. Hence, as Terence Killeen notes, Joyce's odd habit of inserting strings of words in his notebooks as "textual units," functioning as "in some sense coherent entities" but which "are placed in the book in a very systematic way." Killeen, *"Ulysses" Unbound*, 258.

32. The retreat into the self, writes Nietzsche, "says No to what is 'outside,' what is 'different,' what is 'not itself.' . . . It needs, physiologically speaking, external stimuli in order to act at all—its action is fundamentally reaction." Friedrich Nietzsche, "On the Genealogy of Morals" [1887], in *On the Genealogy of Morals/Ecce Homo*, trans. Walter Kaufman and R. J. Hollingdale (New York: Vintage, 1969), 36.

33. Sophie Bryant, *The Genius of the Gael: A Study in Celtic Psychology and Its Manifestations* (London: T. Fisher Unwin, 1913), 48–50. Subsequent references will take the form of *GG*, followed by page number, in text.

34. Christopher Morley, *The Middle Kingdom* (New York: Harcourt, Brace, 1944), 108, cited in Claire Culleton, *Joyce and the G-man: J. Edgar Hoover's Manipulation of Modernism* (New York: Palgrave Macmillan, 2004), 53.

35. See Susan Bazargan, "Mapping Gibraltar: Colonialism, Time, and Narrative in 'Penelope,'" in *Molly Blooms: A Polylogue on "Penelope" and Cultural Studies*, ed. Richard Pearce (Madison: University of Wisconsin Press, 1994), 119–38.

36. Pablo del Río and Amelia Álvarez, "Inside and outside the *Zone of Proximal Development*: An Ecofunctional Reading of Vygotsky," in *The Cambridge Companion to Vygotsky*, ed. Harry Daniels, Michael Cole, and James V. Wertsch (Cambridge: Cambridge University Press, 2007), 281–82.

37. Catherine Whitley, "Gender and Interiority," in Begnal, *Joyce and the City*, 44.

38. Ibid.

39. Theodor Adorno, "Letters to Walter Benjamin," in Theodor Adorno et al., *Aesthetics and Politics* (London: New Left Books, 1977), 118–19.

40. Whitley, "Gender and Interiority," 45–46.

41. Whitley ("Gender and Interiority," 46) attributes such a stance to Karen Law-

rence ("Joyce and Feminism," in *The Cambridge Companion to James Joyce*:,196–213). Cheryl Herr brings masquerade a stage further by discerning a male drag artist in Molly: Cheryl Herr, "'Penelope' as 'Period Piece,'" in Pearce, *Molly Blooms*, 63–80. For readings of performance and masquerade as articulating key aspects of female reformulations of identity, see Judith Butler, *Gender Trouble*, and Mary Ann Doane, "Film and the Masquerade: Theorising the Female Spectator," *Screen* 23, nos. 3–4 (1982): 74–88.

42. "There is no gender identity behind the expressions of gender; that identity is performatively constituted by the very 'expressions' that are said to be its results." Butler, *Gender Trouble*, 25.

43. Jacques Derrida, "Ulysses Gramophone: Hear Say Yes in Joyce," in *Acts of Literature*, ed. Derek Attridge (New York: Routledge, 1992), 299.

44. Katie Wales, *The Language of James Joyce* (London: Macmillan, 1992), 90. Wales adds: "Molly could be imagined, in fact, as lying in bed and muttering her thoughts to herself *sotto voce*," her speech thus carrying the cadences of public idioms.

45. Miriam Bratu Hansen, "The Mass Production of the Senses: Classical Cinema as Vernacular Modernism," *Modernism/Modernity* 6, no. 2 (1999): 59–77; Wolfgang Schivelbusch, *The Railway Journey: The Industrialization of Time and Space* (Berkeley: University of California Press, 1986); Schivelbusch, *Disenchanted Night*.

46. Molly also registers the striking of church bells in the early hours: "wait theres Georges church bells wait 3 quarters the hour 1 wait 2 o clock well theres a nice hour of the night for him to be coming home at . . ." (*U* 18.1231–33).

47. Ewa Ziarek, "The Female Body, Technology, and Memory in 'Penelope,'" in Pearce, *Molly Blooms*, 279–81.

48. As in "We are flowers all a womans body" (*U* 18.1576–77). Ziarek, "The Female Body," 265.

49. Ibid., 269.

50. Herr, "'Penelope' as Period Piece," 66.

51. Kimberly J. Devlin, "Pretending to be 'Penelope': Masquerade, Mimicry, and Molly Bloom," in Pearce, *Molly Blooms*, 80–104.

52. Bazargan, "Mapping Gibraltar: Colonialism, Time, and Narrative in 'Penelope,'" 128.

53. Devlin, "Pretending to be 'Penelope,'" 96.

54. Harvey Duff is the name of the informer in Dion Boucicault's patriotic melodrama *The Shaughran* (1867).

55. Brian W. Shaffer, "Negotiating Self and Culture: Narcissism, Competing Discourses, and Ideological Becoming in 'Penelope,'" in Pearce, *Molly Blooms*, 146.

56. *For Dublin—Frances Hegarty & Andrew Stones: Nine Manifestations in Neon of James Joyce's Molly Bloom*, 23 July–31 October 1997, brochure (Dublin: Nissan Art Project/Irish Museum of Modern Art, 1997), 2.

57. Wales, *The Language of James Joyce*, 83–84.

58. Adam Phillips, "The Telling of Selves," in *On Flirtation* (London: Faber, 1996), 67.

59. Joyce, as noted above (note 4 to the introduction), owned a copy of *The Psychopathology of Everyday Life*.

60. Adam Phillips, "Contingency for Beginners," in *On Flirtation*, 13.

61. Marcel Proust, *Remembrance of Things Past: Swann's Way*, cited in Phillips, "Contingency for Beginners," 14.

62. Phillips, "Contingency for Beginners," 14.

63. George Sigerson, preface to *Bards of the Gael and the Gall* (London: T. Fisher

Unwin, 1897). See also Seamus Deane, "The Production of Cultural Space in Irish Writ-ing," *Boundary 2* 21, no. 3 (Fall 1994): 124–25.

64. The impact of this emotional recoil, and the recurrence of this rejected touch on the later haunting of Mr. Duffy, are discussed in chapter 5 below.

65. According to James Wertsch, though Vygotsky refers to inner speech as mono-logue, the "more appropriate terms for what he was studying would be 'egocentric dia-logue' and 'inner dialogue.'" James V. Wertsch, "The Significance of Dialogue in Vygot-sky's Account of Social, Egocentric, and Inner Speech," *Contemporary Educational Psychology* 5 (1980): 151, cited in J. Allan Cheyne and Donato Tarulli, "Dialogue, Differ-ence, and Voice in the Zone of Proximal Development," in *An Introduction to Vygotsky*, ed. Harry Daniels (London: Routledge, 2005), 126–27. That Vygotsky clearly allows for inner speech in external dialogue, as in coded or intimate speech, suggests that mono-logue is inner dialogue in which we are "intimate" with ourselves.

66. Deborah Parsons, *Theorists of the Modernist Novel: James Joyce, Dorothy Richard-son, Virginia Woolf* (London: Routledge, 2007), 29.

67. Charles Lock, "Double Voicing, Sharing Words," in Bruhn and Lundquist, *The Novelness of Bakhtin*, 86. As we shall see in chapter 3, it is precisely Joyce's attempt to cap-ture the social nuances of idiomatic speech in writing that extends the voice beyond the "tight bourgeois individual."

68. Joseph Valente, "The Politics of Joyce's Polyphony," in *New Alliances in Joyce Studies*, ed. Bonnie Kime Scott (Newark: University of Delaware Press, 1988), 62.

Chapter 3

1. James Joyce, "Ireland at the Bar" (*OCPW* 145).

2. Echoes of the trial appear in *Finnegans Wake*: "A child of Maam, Festy King . . . was subsequently haled up at the Old Bailey on the calends of Mars, under an incom-patibly framed indictment of both the counts" (*FW* 85.22–23, 26–28). See John Garvin, "The Trial of Festy King," in *James Joyce's Disunited Kingdom and the Irish Dimension* (Dublin: Gill and Macmillan, 1976), 157–69. For further resonances in *Finnegans Wake*, see Christine O'Neill Bernhard, "Symbol of the Irish Nation, or of a Foulfamed Potheen District: James Joyce on Myles Joyce," *JJQ* 32, nos. 3/4 (Spring/Summer 1995): 712–21.

3. The introduction of quotation marks around the English "your worship" in the Italian original accords with the convention that marks a foreign phrase: the English-language version omits internal quotation marks, in keeping with free indirect discourse, thus leaving it unclear on first reading whether the colloquialism belongs to the direct address of the interpreter to the magistrate, or the reported speech of Myles Joyce. The context indicates the latter.

4. Joyce's re-creation of features of print through gesture and intonation is clear from an exchange with Frank Budgen in which he drew attention to the importance of the last four words in the title of *A Portrait of the Artist as a Young Man*: "He underlined with his voice the last four words of the title." Budgen, *James Joyce and the Making of "Ulysses,"* 60–61.

5. James Joyce to Stanislaus Joyce, 19 July 1905 (*JJL* II, 100).

6. Dion Boucicault, "Arrah-na-Pogue," in *The Dolmen Boucicault*, ed. David Krause (Dublin: Dolmen Press, 1964), 150.

7. Though coined in relation to the linguistic tics of an individual, "idiolect" has also been applied to the distinctive speech patterns or mannerisms of community: "meaning

as determined by the most basic semantic rules common to the idiolects of members of a given community (which may or may not coincide with their conscious constructions)." Patrick Colm Hogan, *On Interpretation: Meaning and Inference in Law, Psychoanalysis, and Literature* (Athens: University of Georgia Press, 2008), 5. This would appear to be particularly the case when individuals are presented as types or stereotypes—as in the use of "your worship" in nineteenth-century Irish fiction.

8. Hugh Kenner, *Joyce's Voices* (London: Faber and Faber, 1978), 18.

9. Ida Klitgaard, "Dual Voice and Dual Style: Translating Free Indirect Discourse in *Ulysses*," *Nordic Journal of English Studies* 3, no. 3 (2004): 320.

10. V. N. Volosinov, *Marxism and the Philosophy of Language* [1929], trans. Ladislav Matejka and I. R. Titunik (Cambridge: Harvard University Press, 1973), 129.

11. Franco Moretti, *Modern Epic: The World System from Goethe to Garcia Márquez* (London: Verso, 1996), 168–232.

12. According to Karen Lawrence, "it is the obliqueness of the technique that makes free indirect discourse a more important antecedent of the radical stylistic developments in *Ulysses* than the stream-of-consciousness technique that purports to give a more direct transcription of the mental process without narrative intrusion." Karen Lawrence, *The Odyssey of Style in "Ulysses"* (Princeton: Princeton University Press, 1981), 24. See also Jean Paul Riquelme, *Teller and Tale in Joyce's Fiction: Oscillating Perspectives* (Baltimore: Johns Hopkins University Press, 1983); Michael Patrick Gillespie, *Reading the Book of Himself: Narrative Strategies in the Works of James Joyce* (Columbus: Ohio State University Press, 1989); and Kevin J. H. Dettmar, *The Illicit Joyce of Postmodernism*. These authors acknowledge their debt to the innovative textual readings of A. Walton Litz, Michael Groden, and Hugh Kenner.

13. Valery Larbaud, "James Joyce," in *Nouvelle Revue Francaise* 18 (April 1922), in "Valery Larbaud on Joyce" (*JJCH* I, 253).

14. Ernest Boyd, *Ireland's Literary Renaissance* (London: Grant Richards, 1923), 402–12.

15. John Nash, "'In the Heart of the Hibernian Metropolis'? Joyce's Reception in Ireland, 1900–1940," in *The Blackwell Companion to James Joyce*, ed. Richard Brown (Oxford: Blackwell, 2008), 108–22.

16. Ernest Boyd, "Concerning James Joyce," *New York World*, 25 January 1925 (*JJCH* I, 320–22). Joyce was not pleased at Boyd's cursory mention of him in the first edition of *Ireland's Literary Renaissance* (1916), an indication that he had no difficulty being seen as part of the Revival.

17. Boyd, *Ireland's Literary Renaissance*, 404. See also 412: "To claim for this book a European significance simultaneously denied to J. M. Synge and James Stephens is to confess complete ignorance of its genesis."

18. Ibid., 411, italics added.

19. Anne Chevalier, "A Literary Quarrel about James Joyce: Valery Larbaud versus Ernest Boyd," in *France-Ireland: Literary Relations*, ed. Guy Fehlman (Lille: University of Lille III, 1974), 232.

20. Hugh Kenner, "Notes Towards an Anatomy of Modernism," in *A Starchamber Quiry: A James Joyce Centennial Volume, 1882–1982*, ed. E. L. Epstein (London: Methuen, 1982), 15–16; Fritz Senn, "'He Was Too Scrupulous Always': Joyce's 'The Sisters,'" *JJQ* 2 (1965): 66.

21. Lloyd, *Irish Culture and Colonial Modernity*, 15–16. Lloyd draws on Henri Lefebvre's use of the term "differential space" in *The Production of Space*, trans. Donald Nicholson-Smith (Oxford: Blackwell, 1991), 52.

22. David B. Eakin and Helmut E. Gerber note Moore's use of interior monologue in the story "Dried Fruit" (1885), written two years before Dujardin's *Les Lauriers san coupés* (1887): introduction to *In Minor Keys: The Uncollected Stories of George Moore*, ed. David B. Eakin and Helmut E. Gerber (Syracuse: Syracuse University Press, 1985), 30. Subsequent references will take the form of *IMK*, followed by page number, in the text. Moore was quick to acknowledge Dujardin's formal advances in the technique, writing to him that "in 'Les Lauriers' you have discovered the form, the archetypal form, the most original in our time." *Letters from George Moore to Édouard Dujardin, 1886–1922*, trans. W. K. Magee (London: C. Paige, 1929), 40. Joyce asked Moore to write the preface for the English translation of *Les Lauriers* in 1929: Adrian Frazier, *George Moore, 1852–1933* (New Haven: Yale University Press, 2000), 455–58.

23. Thomas Flanagan, *The Irish Novelists, 1800–1850* (New York: Columbia University Press, 1959), 334.

24. Mark D. Hawthorne, *John and Michael Banim (The "O'Hara Brothers"): A Study in the Early Development of the Anglo-Irish Novel* (Salzburg: Institut für englische Sprache und Literatur, 1975).

25. Wolfgang Zach, "Blessing and Burden: The Irish Writer and his Language," in *Anglo-Irish and Irish Literature: Aspects of Language and Culture*, ed. Bridget Bramsback and Martin J. Croghan (Uppsala: Almqvist and Wiksell, 1988), 1:187.

26. Jacques Derrida, *Monolingualism of the Other; or, The Prosthesis of Origin*, trans. Patrick Mensah (Stanford: Stanford University Press, 1998), 21–43.

27. Cited in Hugh Law, *Anglo-Irish Literature* (Dublin: Talbot Press, 1926), 192.

28. David Gilligan, "Natural Indignation in the Native Voice: The Fiction of the Banim Brothers," in Bramsback and Croghan, *Anglo-Irish and Irish Literature*, 89. "Shamus-a-*Chácha*" (James the Shit) is the expletive relegated, in Joycean fashion, to ellipsis or off-the-page knowledge. For a discussion of this deletion, see Emer Nolan, *Catholic Emancipations: Irish Fiction from Thomas Moore to James Joyce* (Syracuse: Syracuse University Press, 2007), 85.

29. *Edinburgh Review*, February 1826, cited in Gilligan, "Natural Indignation," 87.

30. James M. Cahalan, *Great Hatred, Little Room: The Irish Historical Novel* (Dublin: Gill and Macmillan, 1983), 11, 18.

31. Boyd, *Ireland's Literary Renaissance*, 409.

32. Miller, *The Novel and the Police*, 25.

33. Brian McHale, "Whatever Happened to Descriptive Poetics?" in *The Point of Theory: Practices of Cultural Analysis*, ed. Mieke Bal and Inge E. Boer (New York: Continuum, 1994), 61–62.

34. Sydney Owenson, *Patriotic Sketches of Ireland, Written in Connaught* (London: Richard Phillips, 1807), 158.

35. Lady Morgan [Sydney Owenson], *The O'Briens and the O'Flahertys: A National Tale* [1827] (London: Pandora, 1988), 243, 415–16.

36. 'The O'Hara Family' [Michael and John Banim], *The Bit o'Writin'* (Dublin: James Dufy, 1865), 1.

37. Ibid.

38. Charles Kickham, *Knocknagow; or, The Homes of Tipperary* [1879] (Dublin: James Dufy, 1944), 160, italics added. Further references will take the form of *K*, followed by page number, in the text.

39. Emer Nolan writes, noting the oscillations in tone between accounts of festive occasions and more serious events such as evictions: "Multiple points of view are always brought to bear on such events." Nolan, *Catholic Emancipations*, 111.

40. Gerald Bruns, "Eumaeus," in Hart and Hayman, *James Joyce's "Ulysses": Critical Essays*, 366.

41. From the Russian *skazat*—"to tell, to relate," as in *skazka* (fairy tale), *skazanie* (legend); cited in I. R. Titunik, "The Problem of *Skaz*," in *Papers in Slavic Philology*, ed. Benjamin A. Stolz (Ann Arbor: Michigan Slavic Publications, 1977), 299.

42. See McHale, "Whatever Happened to Descriptive Poetics?," 61–62. As Volosinov notes, there are no categorical or lexical markers to clearly indicate the presence of free indirect discourse; its performative force may be most telling when it is least obvious, undetected by a tone-deaf ear. Volosinov, *Marxism and the Philosophy of Language*, 126.

43. Viktor Vinogradov, cited in Titunik, "The Problem of *Skaz*," 279.

44. Gilles Deleuze, *Cinema 1: The Movement Image*, trans. Hugh Tomlinson and Barbara Habberjam (London: Athlone Press, 1986), 73.

45. Titunik, "The Problem of *Skaz*," 292–93. Titunik tends to see narration as closing off references to extratextual factors, whereas it is such openings onto real life that constitute the signature style of *Ulysses*.

46. According to Vinogradov, it is not just the presence of colloquial idioms that signals *skaz* but "imaginative mixtures" with "written-bookish" language—the clash between high and low registers. Titunik, "The Problem of *Skaz*," 282. Molly Bloom's ventriloquizing of several voices, including her own in her confession to Father Corrigan (*U* 18.106–12), discussed in chapter 2 above, is a case in point: Father Corrigan does not seem to detect the irony in her voice.

47. Riquelme, *Teller and Tale in Joyce's Fiction*, 54. In keeping with free indirect discourse's lack of textual markers noted by Volosinov and McHale above, Saussure's student Charles Bally, the first to theorize the technique, observed that it "cannot be defined solely in grammatical terms. On grammatical terms, it often cannot be distinguished from normal authorial report, and as a result pointers like 'he thought' may be required to make it clear that a statement emanates from the character and not from the author." Roy Pascal, *The Dual Voice: Free Indirect Speech and Its Functioning in the Nineteenth-Century Novel* (Manchester: Manchester University Press, 1977), 10. It is of note that Pascal, in his pioneering study, attributes his "introduction to modern linguistics" to Nicholas Bakhtin (1894–1950), a colleague at the University of Birmingham, who may also have introduced Pascal to the writings of his then virtually unknown brother, Mikhail Bakhtin (148). Fania Pascal, Roy Pascal's wife, counted conversations with Nicholas Bakhtin among the influences that shifted Ludwig Wittgenstein's philosophy from his early logical positivism. Katerina Clark and Michael Holquist, *Mikhail Bakhtin* (Cambridge: Belknap Press, 1984), 20.

48. Hon. Emily Lawless, *Grania: The Story of an Island* (London: Smith and Elder, 1892), 223–24. Further references will take the form of G, followed by page number, in the text.

49. May Laffan, "The Game Hen," in *Flitters, Tatters and the Counsellor; The Game Hen; Baubie Clark* (Leipzig: Barnard Tauchnitz, 1881), 113. Subsequent references will take the form of *FTC*, followed by page numbers, in the text. Laffan's pioneering urban realism in Ireland is almost unknown today, according to Margaret Kelleher, but it drew appreciative contemporary responses from John Ruskin, Richard Garnett, and Dr. Thornley Stoker, and Laffan "was one of the very few contemporary novelists featured in Yeats' list of best books." Laffan's fiction, in keeping with later responses to Joyce, drew opprobrium from Catholic circles, Matthew Russell in the *Irish Monthly* condemning "tales written in a coarse, cynical spirit that commends them only to English readers."

Margaret Kelleher, "'Wanted an Irish Novelist': The Critical Decline of the Nineteenth-Century Novel," in *The Irish Novel in the Nineteenth Century: Facts and Fictions*, ed. Jacqueline Belanger (Dublin: Four Courts Press, 2005), 189–90.

50. Boyd, *Ireland's Literary Renaissance*, 410.

51. George Moore, "Mildred Lawson," in *Celibates* (London: Walter Scott, 1895), 94–95, italics added. Moore's story was published in an earlier form in 1888. In the hotel room at the end of Joyce's "The Dead," Gabriel's inner speech also cuts across his image in a mirror: "He saw himself as a ludicrous figure . . . the pitiable fatuous fellow he had caught a glimpse of in the mirror" (*D* 221).

52. James Joyce to Stanislaus Joyce, 15 December 1904 (*JJL* II, 74).

53. The stories in 1904 were "The Sisters," 13 August; "Eveline," 10 September; and "After the Race," 17 December.

54. James Joyce to Stanislaus Joyce, 28 December 1904 (*JJL* II, 4–75).

55. As John Wyse Jackson and Bernard McGinley suggest of the main character, Jimmy, in the story: "[T]he delineation of Jimmy lacks depth. Unlike other stories (notably 'Clay') the subjectivity of the character—what has been called the 'Uncle Charles Principle'—is not successfully rendered." *James Joyce's "Dubliners": An Illustrated Edition*, ed. John Wyse Jackson and Bernard McGinley (London: Sinclair Stevenson, 1995), 41. By 1903, Joyce had read Dujardin's *Les Lauriers san coupés* in Paris, but its innovative techniques, it would seem, had still not attracted his attention. For Dujardin's relation to Moore and Joyce, as well as the play of stream of consciousness in Dorothy Richardson, May Sinclair, and others, see Vicki Mahaffey, "Streams beyond Consciousness: Stylistic Immediacy in the Modernist Novel," in *A Handbook of Modernism Studies*, ed. Jean-Michel Rabaté (Chichester: Wiley-Blackwell, 2013), 35–54.

56. James Joyce to Stanislaus Joyce, 19 January 1905 (*JJL* II, 78). Joyce later writes that Nora is even more cut off by having no one to talk to but him (12 July 1905: *JJL* II, 95). Nora may have indeed been right about the flat ending of Moore's story. In a subsequent letter, 7 February 1905, Joyce objects to Stanislaus's criticisms of Nora: "You are harsh with Nora because she has an untrained mind. She is learning French, at present—very slowly. Her disposition, as I see it, is much nobler than my own, her love also is greater than mine for her. I admire her and I love her and I trust her—I cannot tell how much. I trust her, so enough" (*JJL* II, 79–80).

57. George Moore, "A Faithful Heart" (*IMK* 132, italics added).

58. It is noteworthy that in other passages Moore adds "so she said" and "the same thought came to her" to denote reporting of inner speech, but does not always feel it necessary in the case of cultural idioms: "The house was poor, and she was miserable, but *any place was good enough to suffer in*. So she said when she rose and dragged herself downstairs to do a little cooking; and the same thought came to her when she lay all alone in the little parlour, furnished with what a few pounds could buy—a paraffin lamp, a round table, a few chairs, an old and ill-padded mahogany armchair, *in which it was torture to lie*" (*IMK* 134, italics added).

59. This is discussed in chapter 5 below, 161–62.

60. Mikhail Bakhtin, *Problems of Dostoevsky's Poetics*, trans. Caryl Emerson (Manchester: Manchester University Press, 1984), 192.

61. George Moore, "The Exile," in *The Untilled Field* [1903] (Dublin: Gill and Macmillan, 1990), 1, italics added. Subsequent references will take the form of *UF*, followed by page number, in text.

62. Johnson, introduction to *A Portrait* (OUP, 2000), xxiii.

63. Budgen, *James Joyce and the Making of "Ulysses,"* 68, 70. See Valerie Bénéjam, "The Acoustic Space of Ulysses," in *Making Space in the Works of James Joyce*, ed. Valerie Bénéjam and John Bishop (London: Routledge, 2011), 55–68.

64. Fredric Jameson, *Modernism and Imperialism*, Field Day pamphlet (Derry: Field Day, 1988), 21.

65. Gary Saul Morson and Caryl Emerson, *Mikhail Bakhtin: Creation of a Prosaics* (Stanford: Stanford University Press, 1990), 153.

66. Hugh Kenner writes of the "deadly frigidity" of Father Purdon's sermon in "Grace" in *Dubliners*: "[T]he source of its coldness, we may suddenly reflect, is not the author but the preacher, whose contrivance the author's stylistic contrivance obeys." Kenner, *Joyce's Voices*, 14.

67. Jonathan Rée, *I See a Voice: Language, Deafness and the Senses: A Philosophical History* (London: Harper Collins, 1999), 371.

68. . The Whiteboy movement, one of the earliest outbreaks of agrarian insurgency in Ireland, sprang up in Munster in the early 1760s to protest against enclosures prompted by the crisis of the Seven Years' War. As noted in chapter 8 below, Simon Dedalus refers to his Whiteboy ancestors in *Portrait* (*P* 37), and Richard Ellmann notes that this corresponds to Joyce's Cork-based great-grandfather in real life (*JJ* 10).

69. Mikhail Bakhtin, "Discourse in the Novel," in *The Dialogic Imagination: Four Essays*, trans. Caryl Emerson and Michael Holquist (Austin: University of Texas Press, 1992), 294.

70. See Eric Auerbach's classic discussion of Flaubert's ventriloquism of Emma Bovary's voice in *Madame Bovary*, highlighting her deficient grasp of the world around her. *Mimesis: The Representation of Reality in Western Literature*, trans. Willard F. Trask (Princeton: Princeton University Press, 1974), 482–85.

71. James Maddox, "Mockery in Ulysses," in *Joyce's "Ulysses": The Larger Perspective*, ed. Robert D. Newman and Weldon Thornton (Newark: University of Delaware Press; London and Toronto: Associated University Presses, 1987), 147.

72. Nolan, *James Joyce and Nationalism*, 85–119.

73. Kenner, *Joyce's Voices*, 36.

74. Kenner refers to the earliest publication of Joyce's story "The Sisters" in AE's periodical, the *Irish Homestead*, "among advertisements for mineral waters and cream-separators." Kenner, "Notes Towards an Anatomy of Modernism," 15.

Chapter 4

1. Lucie Noël, *James Joyce and Paul L. Léon: The Story of a Friendship* (New York: Gotham Books, 1950), 19, cited in Thomas Burkdall, *Joycean Frames: Film and the Fiction of James Joyce* (New York: Routledge, 2001), 6. Traces of this may appear in *Finnegans Wake*: "Whervolk dorst ttou begin to tremble by our moving pictures at this moment when I am to place my hand of our true friend-shapes upon thee knee to mark well what I say? . . . I have heard her voice some-where else's before me in these ears still that now are for mine" (*FW* 565.6–8, 15–16).

2. Joyce remarked to Jacques Mercanton: "That kind of transposition—from sight to sound—I insist, is the very essence of art, which is concerned solely with the effect it wishes to obtain." Mercanton, "Hours of James Joyce," 226.

3. W.B. Yeats, "The Circus Animals' Desertion," in *Yeats's Poems*, ed. A. Norman Jeffares (London: Macmillan, 1989); Christian Metz, *The Imaginary Signifier: Psychoanalysis and the Cinema* (Bloomington: Indiana University Press, 1986), 1–65.

4. For the drive toward ocularcentrism in Western culture, and its critics, see Martin Jay, *Downcast Eyes: The Denigration of Vision in Twentieth-Century French Thought* (Berkeley: University of California Press, 1994); David Michael Levin, *Modernity and the Hegemony of Vision* (Berkeley: University of California Press, 1993).

5. Guy Debord, *Society of the Spectacle* (n.p.: Rebel Press/Aim Publications, 1987), §24, §18.

6. On these aspects of *Portrait*, see David Lodge, *The Modes of Modern Writing: Metaphor, Metonymy and the Typology of Modern Literature* (London: Arnold, 1977), 10–32, and Johnson, introduction to *Portrait* (OUP, 2000), xxiii–xxvi.

7. Seymour Chatman, "What Novels Can Do That Films Can't (and Vice Versa)," in *On Narrative*, ed. W. J. T. Mitchell (Chicago: University of Chicago Press, 1981), 121.

8. Ibid., 124.

9. Robert Stam, "Bakhtin, Polyphony, and Ethnic/Racial Representation," in *Unspeakable Images: Ethnicity and the American Cinema*, ed. Lester D. Friedman (Urbana: University of Illinois Press, 1991), 256–57.

10. For the relationship between the cinematic image and inner speech, see Paul Willemen, "Cinematic Discourse: The Problem of Inner Speech," in *Looks and Frictions* (London: British Film Institute, 1994).

11. Weldon Thornton, *The Antimodernism of Joyce's "Portrait of the Artist as a Young Man"* (Syracuse: Syracuse University Press, 1994), 109.

12. Luke Gibbons, "'The Cracked Looking Glass of Cinema': James Joyce, John Huston and the Memory of the 'The Dead,'" in "The Theatre of Irish Cinema," ed. Dudley Andrew and Luke Gibbons, special issue, *Yale Journal of Criticism* 15, no. 1 (Spring 2002): 127–48, and note 61 below, 256. For extended treatments of Huston's film, see Kevin Barry, *The Dead* (Cork: Cork University Press, 2000), and *"Dubliners," James Joyce; "The Dead," John Huston*, ed. Pascal Bataillard and Dominique Sipière (C.A.P.E.S./Agrégation Anglais; Paris: Ellipses, 2000).

13. Clive Hart, *Joyce, Huston, and the Making of "The Dead"* (London: Colin Smythe, 1988), 14. Hart is turning Joyce's earlier jibe at the "sloppy English" of D. H. Lawrence against himself. For an earlier discussion of the linguistic infelicities of modernism, see Jocelyn Brooke, "Proust and Joyce: The Case for the Prosecution," *Adam: International Review*, nos. 297–98 (1961): 5–66.

14. Tony Huston, "*The Dead*: A Screenplay" (Los Angeles: Liffey Films, 1986), 36. Subsequent references will take the form of *DS*, followed by page number, in the text. The original translation of "The Grief of a Girl's Heart/Donall Óg" is in Lady Gregory, *Poets and Dreamers: Studies and Translations from the Irish* (Gerrards Cross: Colin Smythe, 1974).

15. For a detailed historical analysis of "The Lass of Aughrim" and its many variants, see Hugh Shields, "A History of the 'Lass of Aughrim,'" in *Irish Musical Studies*, ed. Gerard Gillen and Harry White (Dublin: Irish Academic Press, 1990), 1:58–73.

16. On the Gregory Clause, see Christine Kinealy, *This Great Calamity: The Irish Famine, 1845–52* (Dublin: Gill and Macmillan, 1994), 216–227.

17. See Donald Torchiana, *Backgrounds for Joyce's "Dubliners"* (Boston: Allen and Unwin, 1986), 227. As the Irish-language scholar John V. Kelleher remarks: "[Lily's] accent is Dublin lower-class; she intrudes a vowel into his name and calls him, not 'Mr. Conroy', but 'Mr. Connery.'" "Connery" derives from the Irish "Conaire," linking the mispronunciation with the old Irish story of the Feast of King Conaire. John V. Kelleher, "Irish History and Mythology in James Joyce's 'The Dead,'" in *Selected Writings of John V.*

Kelleher on Ireland and America, ed. Charles Fanning (Carbondale: Southern Illinois University Press, 2002), 44.

18. Margot Norris, "Not the Girl She Was at All: Women in 'The Dead,'" in *James Joyce: The Dead*, ed. Daniel R. Schwarz (Boston: Bedford Books/St. Martin's Press, 1994), 193.

19. Pier Paolo Pasolini, "The Cinema of Poetry," in *Movies and Methods*, ed. Bill Nichols (Berkeley: University of California Press, 1976), 1:554. Pasolini allows for cases (e.g., Antonioni's *Red Desert*) where a character's voice takes precedence or, alternatively (e.g., Bertolucci's *Before the Revolution*), where a "contamination" takes place "between the vision [a character] has of the world, and that of the author, which are inevitably analogous, but difficult to perceive, being closely intermixed, having the same style" (553–54).

20. R. Brandon Kershner, *Joyce, Bakhtin, and Popular Culture: Chronicles of Disorder* (Chapel Hill: University of North Carolina Press, 1989), 142. In the film version of the Irish writer Dorothy Macardle's novel *The Uninvited* (dir. Lewis Allen, 1944), the ghost takes possession of one of the characters, Rick (Ray Milland), by changing a tune he is playing on the piano to a mournful melody: "Why did you change it?" his young listener Stella (Gail Russell) nervously asks, to which Rick can only reply: "It just came out that way." The spectral inspiration turns out to be Stella's dead mother (and the tune became the hit "Stella by Starlight"). See Gary J. Svehla, *"The Uninvited,"* in *Cinematic Hauntings*, ed. Gary J. Svehla and Susan Svehla (Baltimore: Midnight Marquee Press, 1996), 308.

21. Eithne O'Neill, *"The Dead* by John Huston: Memory and Screen," in Bataillard and Sipière, *"Dubliners," James Joyce: "The Dead," John Huston*, 176.

22. John Harrington, "Wyler as Auteur," in *The English Novel and the Movies*, ed. Michael Klein and Gillian Parker (New York: Frederick Ungar, 1981), 73.

23. Ibid., 75.

24. Deleuze, *Cinema 1: The Movement Image*, 72, 74. Deleuze draws on Pasolini's argument that at times this "camera-consciousness" signals the director's vision, but as Pasolini points out (note 19 above), this may also be difficult to distinguish from a character, especially an off-screen figure.

25. Alan Cholodenko, "The Crypt, the Haunted House, of Cinema," *Cultural Studies Review* 10, no. 2 (September 2004): 100.

26. "One need not believe in Irish fairies or in Catholic spirits to perceive the ghost of Mary [sic] Dedalus. She is painfully present in the 'mode of absence,' a shade negatively constituted by the remnants of a life-world once imbued with conscious meaning." Suzette A. Henke, *Moraculas Sindbook: A Study of "Ulysses"* (Columbus: Ohio State University Press, 1978), 18.

27. Sergei Eisenstein, "A Course in Treatment," in *Film Form: Essays in Film Theory*, trans. Jay Leyda (San Diego: Harcourt, Brace, 1977), 105.

28. For Joyce's interest in Theosophy, see Stanislaus Joyce, *My Brother's Keeper*, 140–41, and Ellmann, *JJ* 179–80.

29. Joyce's abiding concern with "transpersonal" memory, its connection with Theosophy, and his interest in the work of psychologists such as William James, is discussed in Rickard, *Joyce's Book of Memory*, 86–117. Rickard does not link these concerns, however, with the elements of Irish folklore and superstition that persisted within the twentieth-century city.

30. See the advertisement for the Gresham Hotel reproduced in Wyse Jackson and McGinley, *Dubliners: An Illustrated Edition*, 193.

31. Joseph V. O'Brien, *"Dear Dirty Dublin": A City in Distress, 1899–1916* (Berkeley: University of California Press, 1982), 67. See also Gordon, "Gaslight, Ghostlight, Golliwog, Gaslight," 19–37.

32. O'Brien, *"Dear Dirty Dublin,"* 68. Wyse Jackson and McGinley reproduce an advertisement from Dublin Corporation, August 1903, advising consumers that supply to new mains will be cut off at 12:00 midnight: *Dubliners: An Illustrated Edition*, 191. An account in the *Irish Times*, "Corporation Electric Lighting Scheme," 22 August 1903, noted unforeseen difficulties with laying of street mains, including extra cost of constructing the Sackville Street (where the Gresham was situated) underground substation.

33. In *Ulysses*, candlelight illuminates the apparition of Stephen's dead mother in a dream: "The ghostcandle to light her agony. Ghostly light on the tortured face" (*U* 1.274).

34. For the iconographical context of this remark and associations of the Holy Ghost with wings, air, spirits, and inspiration, see part II, "Air," in Marina Warner, *Phantasmagoria: Spirit Visions, Metaphors, and Media into the Twenty-First Century* (Oxford: Oxford University Press, 2006), 77.

35. Helen Sword, *Ghostwriting Modernism* (Ithaca: Cornell University Press, 2002), 36.

36. Patricia Lysaght, *The Banshee: The Irish Supernatural Death-messenger* (Dublin: O'Brien Press, 1996), 236–37.

37. Kelleher, "Irish History and Mythology," 47.

38. Warner, *Phantasmagoria*, 136. For the overlaps and perceived supports between technology and the "otherworld," see, in addition to Sword and Warner, Tim Armstrong, "The Vibrating World: Science, Spiritualism, Technology," in *Modernism* (Cambridge: Polity Press, 2005), 115–34; Pamela Churchwell, *Literature, Technology and Magical Thinking, 1880–1920* (Cambridge: Cambridge University Press, 2001); and Roger Luckhurst, *The Invention of Telepathy* (Oxford: Oxford University Press, 2001).

39. "The streets were dark with something more than night": Raymond Chandler, "The Simple Art of Murder" [1944], cited as epigraph to James Naremore, *More than Night: Film Noir in Its Contexts* (Berkeley: University of California Press, 1998).

40. As noted above, Huston originally filmed Gabriel's "vision" of the ghost of Michael Furey but did not include it in the final film.

41. Warner, *Phantasmagoria*, 79.

42. Nicolas Abraham and Maria Torok, "Mourning or Melancholia: Introjection versus Incorporation" (*SK* 16–37).

43. Nicholas T. Rand, editor's note to "Secrets and Posterity: The Theory of the Transgenerational Phantom" (*SK* 37).

44. Ibid., 166.

45. John Paul Riquelme, "For Whom the Snow Taps: Style and Repetition in 'The Dead,'" in Schwartz, *James Joyce: The Dead*, 224.

46. In the case of *The Uninvited*, visual manifestations of the ghost, through special effects, were required for American audiences, Paramount studios overruling the director's (Lewis Allen's) decision to omit the apparition in the British version. Even when the Irish servant, Lizzie Flynn (Barbara Everest), and the audience see the ethereal ghost in the American version, Rick, one of the leading characters, is still not convinced, and acts as if the servant is adept at special effects: "Lizzie has just conjured up a ghost."

47. Svehla, *"The Uninvited,"* 302–3.

48. Such an approach is central to Abraham and Torok's psychoanalytic concept of "the phantom." Abraham and Torok, "Notes on the Phantom: A Complement to Freud's Metapsychology" (*SK* 165–206).

49. Svehla, *"The Uninvited,"* 202.

50. Janet Egleson Dunleavy, "The Ectoplasmic Truthtellers of 'The Dead,'" *JJQ* 21, no. 4 (Summer 1984): 308.

51. Ibid., 309.

52. Franz K. Stanzel, "Consonant and Dissonant Closure in *Death in Venice* and *The Dead*," 121, cited in Jakob Lothe, *Narrative in Fiction and Film: An Introduction* (Oxford: Oxford University Press, 2000), 155.

53. As Jakob Lothe points out, responding to Stanzel's criticism, Gabriel's subjectively experienced thoughts are placed in a larger narrative frame through the use of images: if this is overlooked by Stanzel, "it is because (by concentrating on the voice) he places too little weight on the distancing effects of Huston's camera." Ibid., 155.

54. Hart, *Joyce, Huston and the Making of "The Dead,"* 13.

55. See Joyce's letters to Stanislaus, 1 February and 11 February 1907, where he recounts details of the Abbey riots, relishing the affront to Yeats and Lady Gregory's self-importance, though his response to Synge is more favorable. Joyce mentions how it put him off working on "The Dead" (*JJL* II, 207–9, 211–13).

56. James Joyce, "The City of the Tribes: Italian Memories of an Irish Port" [1912] (*OCPW* 197).

57. Gordon Bowker, *James Joyce: A Biography* (London: Weidenfield and Nicolson, 2001), 202. In *Finnegans Wake* we encounter "the loftly marconimasts from Clifden sough open tireless secrets (mauveport! mauveport!) to Nova Scotia's listing sisterwands. Tubetube!" (*FW* 407.20–22)—the "Tubetube!" of radio itself reenacting Hamlet's "To be, or not to be."

58. James Joyce, "The Mirage of the Fisherman of Aran: England's Safety Valve in Time of War" [1912] (*OCPW* 205).

59. Allen Tate, "The Dead," in James Joyce, *Dubliners: Text and Criticism*, ed. Robert Scholes and A. Walton Litz (New York: Penguin, 1996), 391.

60. Ibid., 393.

61. For allegory and topographies of memory in "The Dead," see Luke Gibbons, "Identity without a Centre: Allegory, History and Irish Nationalism," *Cultural Studies* 6, no. 3 (October 1992): 358–75, reprinted in *Transformations in Irish Culture* (Cork: Cork University Press, 1996), 134–49; Vincent Cheng, "Empire and Patriarchy in 'The Dead,'" in *Joyce, Race and Empire* (Cambridge: Cambridge University Press, 1996), 128–50; Luke Gibbons, "Where Wolfe Tone's Statue was Not: Ireland, Monuments and Memory," in *History, Memory and Ireland*, ed. Ian McBride (Cambridge: Cambridge University Press, 2001), 127–48; Kevin Whelan, "The Memories of 'The Dead,'" in "The Theatre of Irish Cinema," ed. Dudley Andrew and Luke Gibbons, special issue, *Yale Journal of Criticism* 15, no. 1 (Spring 2002): 59–97; and Cóilín Owens, "'The Charity of Its Silence,'" *Dublin James Joyce Journal* 1 (2008): 30–46.

62. Bruce Robbins, "'The Newspapers Were Right': Cosmopolitanism, Forgetting, and 'The Dead,'" *Interventions* 5, no. 1 (2003): 106–7.

63. As Kevin Barry observes, Joyce drew his arguments for the revitalization of Galway from a pamphlet, *Galway as a Transatlantic Port* [1912], which saw in the coming war an opportunity to open alternative transatlantic shipping routes to those of British ports (*OCPW* 342–33). In the "Cyclops" chapter of *Ulysses*, Galway's former glory as an Atlantic port is part of the nationalist case for the economic regeneration of Ireland.

64. W. B. Yeats, "Swedenborg, Mediums, and the Desolate Places" [1914], in *Explorations* (New York: Collier, 1962), 49, 51–53.

65. Derrida, *Archive Fever*, 86.

Chapter 5

1. L. Paul-Dubois, *Contemporary Ireland*, trans. with introduction by Thomas Kettle (Dublin: Maunsel, 1908), 160.

2. See Sir Horace Plunkett, *Ireland in the New Century* (London: John Murray, 1904); Rev. M. O'Riordan, *Catholicity and Progress in Ireland* (London: Kegan Paul, Trench, Trubner, 1906).

3. Patricia Waugh, *Feminine Fictions: Revisiting the Postmodern* (London: Routledge, 1989), 3.

4. John Wilson Foster, *Fictions of the Irish Literary Revival: A Changeling Art* (Dublin: Gill and Macmillan, 1987), 14. Subsequent references will take the form of *FLR*, followed by page number, in the text. For the classic argument that epic structures militate against interiority, see Erich Auerbach, "Odysseus' Scar," in *Mimesis: The Representation of Reality in Western Literature* (Princeton: Princeton University Press, 2003), 3–13.

5. Wilson Foster is citing Harrison Butterworth, "Motif-Index and Analysis of the Early Irish Hero Tales" (PhD dissertation, Yale University, 1956), 122.

6. Joel Pfister, "On Conceptualizing the Cultural History of Emotional and Psychological Life in America," in *Inventing the Psychological: Toward a Cultural History of Emotional Life in America*, ed. Joel Pfister and Nancy Schnog (New Haven: Yale University Press, 1997), 22.

7. Ibid., 23. Pfister is referring to Joel Kovel, *The Radical Spirit: Essays on Psychoanalysis and Society* (London: Free Association Books, 1988).

8. Gayatri Chakravorty Spivak, *A Critique of Postcolonial Reason: Toward a History of the Vanishing Present* (Cambridge: Harvard University Press, 1999), 258.

9. Pfister, "On Conceptualizing," 27–28, summarizing Michelle Rosaldo, "Toward an Anthropology of Self and Feeling," in *Culture Theory: Essays on Mind, Self, and Emotion*, ed. Richard A. Shweder and Robert A. LeVine (Cambridge: Cambridge University Press, 1994), 13–57.

10. Elleke Boehmer, *Empire, the National, and the Postcolonial, 1890–1920: Resistance in Interaction* (Oxford: Oxford University Press, 2002), 7.

11. Dominick LaCapra, "Revisiting the Historian's Debate: Mourning and Genocide," in *History and Memory after Auschwitz* (Ithaca: Cornell University Press, 1998), 45.

12. Dominick LaCapra, "Conclusion: Acting-out and Working-through," in *Representing the Holocaust: History, Theory, Trauma* (Ithaca: Cornell University Press, 1994), 213–14.

13. Jacques Lacan, "Desire and the Interpretation of Desire in *Hamlet*," in *Literature and Psychoanalysis: The Question of Reading: Otherwise* (Baltimore: Johns Hopkins University Press, 1982), 38. Subsequent references will take the form of *DH*, followed by page number, in the text. According to Stephen Greenblatt, the collapse of ritual was such as to force Shakespeare on the death of his son, Hamnet, in 1595 to create a new way of coping with grief: the staging of interiority itself as the focus of dramatic action in *Hamlet*. Stephen Greenblatt, "The Death of Hamnet and the Making of Hamlet," *New York Review of Books*, 21 October 2004.

14. Jan Goldstein, "The Hysteria Diagnosis and the Politics of Anticlericalism in Late Nineteenth-Century France," *Journal of Modern History* 54 (June 1982): 225.

15. Paul Hirst and Penny Woolley, "Witchcraft and Rationality," in *Social Relations and Human Attributes* (London: Tavistock, 1982), 216.

16. Jacques Derrida, "The Time Is out of Joint," trans. Peggy Kamuf, in *Deconstruction Is/in America: A New Sense of the Political*, ed. Anselm Haverkamp (New York: New York

University Press, 1995), cited in Royle, *The Uncanny*, 281. The classic examples are Father Surin, the exorcist of the Devils of Loudon in 1634, and the hysteria that gripped prosecutors and an entire community in the Salem Witch Trials of 1692–93.

17. Sacks, *Hallucinations*, 234.

18. According to Sacks: "Something has to happen in the mind/brain for imagination to overleap its boundaries and be replaced by hallucinations. Some dissociation or disconnection must occur, some breakdown of the mechanisms." But then he adds: "It is not clear that such a dissociation can explain everything." Ibid., 242.

19. It is worth noting that even the skeptical David Hume extends the kind of uncertainty Todorov associates with the "fantastic" to many critical issues that concern human beings: "Any question of philosophy, on the other hand, which is so *obscure* and *uncertain*, that human reason can reach no fixed determination with regard to it; if it should be treated at all, seems to lead us naturally into the style of dialogue and conversation. Reasonable men may be allowed to differ, where no one can reasonably be positive." David Hume, *Dialogues concerning Natural Religion and Other Writings*, ed. Dorothy Coleman (Cambridge: Cambridge University Press, 2007), 3. It is perhaps in this light that Joyce's recourse to *dialogical* narratives is best viewed, using these open-ended forms to negotiate the acute crises that give rise to the spectral.

20. For the psychological disintegration caused by social death, see Jonathan Lear, *Radical Hope: Ethics in the Face of Cultural Devastation* (Cambridge: Harvard University Press, 2006). On social death, see Orlando Patterson, *Slavery and Social Death: A Comparative Study* (Cambridge: Harvard University Press, 1985).

21. Nicolas Abraham and Maria Torok, "Mourning *or* Melancholia: Introjection *versus* Incorporation" (*SK* 129).

22. This refers to a process whereby "a memory is repressed which has only become a trauma by *deferred action* [*nachträglich*]." Sigmund Freud, "Project for a Scientific Psychology [1895]," in *Standard Edition of the Complete Psychological Works of Sigmund Freud*, vol. 1 (London: Hogarth Press, 1975), 365. Though Freud prevaricates on the actuality of the original scene, the later "recall" does not rule out its happening, only the impossibility of accessing it without "revision" in the present. See also notes 25 and 37 below.

23. Synaesthesia in Joyce also links touch to a kind of "haptic" vision, as in the blind stripling episode in *Ulysses*. See Katherine Mullin, "Joyce, Early Cinema and the Erotics of Everyday Life," in *Roll Away the Reel World: James Joyce and Cinema*, ed. John McCourt (Cork: Cork University Press, 2010), 43–56.

24. Jean-François Lyotard, *Heidegger and "the Jews,"* trans. Andreas Michel and Mark S. Roberts (Minneapolis: University of Minnesota Press, 1990), 13.

25. As Ned Lukacher suggests, "while the earlier event is still to some extent the cause of the later event, the earlier event is nevertheless also the effect of the later event." Ned Lukacher, *Primal Scenes: Literature, Philosophy, Psychoanalysis* (Ithaca: Cornell University Press, 1986), 35, cited in Nicholls, "The Belated Postmodern," 71. The earlier event can only be acknowledged, if at all, belatedly, but to displace it in the service of the present, Jean Laplanche points out, "simply means the fact of creating a past to meet current needs": "Freud insists upon the tensions between the old scene and the recent scenario" but does not cast into doubt, particularly after the acknowledgment of shell shock in World War I, that there *was* an "old scene." Jean Laplanche, *New Foundations for Psychoanalysis*, trans. David Macey (Oxford: Blackwell, 1989), 118, cited in Nicholls, "The Belated Postmodern," 54.

26. Ruth Leys, *Trauma: A Genealogy* (Chicago: University of Chicago Press, 2000), 21.

27. Eleanor Hull, *The Poem Book of the Gael*, xxiv, cited in Bryant, *The Genius of the Gael*, 249.

28. W. R. Wilde, *Irish Popular Superstitions* (Dublin: James McGlashan, 1852), vi.

29. Kimberly J. Devlin, "Visible Shades and Shades of Visibility: The En-Gendering of Death in 'Hades,'" in *"Ulysses"—En-Gendered Perspectives: New Essays on the Episodes*, ed. Kimberly J. Devlin and Marilyn Reizbaum (Columbia: University of South Carolina Press, 1999), 74.

30. Sir James George Frazer, *The Golden Bough: A Study in Magic and Religion* [1890–1915], ed. Robert Fraser (Oxford: Oxford University Press, 1994), 52. Subsequent references will take the form of *GB*, followed by page number, in the text.

31. Angela Bourke, *The Burning of Bridget Cleary: A True Story* (London: Pimlico, 1999), 130.

32. Mary Douglas, *Purity and Danger: An Analysis of the Concepts of Pollution and Taboo* (Harmondsworth: Penguin, 1970), 26.

33. Though Wittgenstein's initial comments on Frazer were written in the early 1930s, he returned to Frazer in 1948, specifically addressing his discussion of Fire Festivals. See Brian R. Clack, *Wittgenstein, Frazer and Religion* (London: Macmillan, 1999), 135.

34. Ludwig Wittgenstein, "Remarks on Frazer's *Golden Bough*," trans. John Beversluis, in *Philosophical Occasions, 1912–1951*, ed. James C. Klagge and Alfred Nordmann (Indianapolis: Hackett, 1993), 149.

35. Ibid., 151.

36. Clack, *Wittgenstein, Frazer and Religion*, 153.

37. Frazer's and related cases of pathological survivals are telling examples of restructuring the past to serve the needs of the present highlighted in note 25 above: "From this point of view, only the occurrence of the second scene [the modern] can endow the first one [the past] with pathogenic force." Jean Laplanche and J. B. Pontalis, *The Language of Psychoanalysis*, trans. Donald Nicholson-Smith (London: Hogarth Press, 1973), 113. Freud further maintains that the primal scene "might have been manufactured" (113), but in this case, there is no need to romanticize ancient societies or to pretend there was no violence; the point is that such primordial violence is not required to explain away the "resurgence" of savagery in the present.

38. Bourke, *Burning of Bridge Cleary*, 125. For Joyce's response to the Maamtrasna murders, see chapter 3 above.

39. Keith Thomas, *Religion and the Decline of Magic* (Harmondsworth: Penguin, 1973), 713–17.

40. W. B. Yeats, "Two Essays and Notes," in Lady Gregory, *Visions and Beliefs in the West of Ireland* [1920] (Gerrards Cross: Colin Smythe, 1976), 360.

41. Clack, *Wittgenstein, Frazer and Religion*, 138.

42. Wittgenstein, "Remarks on Frazer's *Golden Bough*," 131.

43. Though the European "witch craze" was prominent where the Reformation took hold, historians point to a multiplicity of factors in accounting for the persecutions: the liminal spaces of borders and contact zones between country and city, and clashes between elite and popular culture. Secular courts took the lead in Protestant districts, while Catholic Spain and Italy retained ecclesiastical courts. Areas associated with "backwardness," e.g., Ireland and the Scottish Highlands, were mostly exempt, while the Scottish lowlands featured prominently. Pieter Spierenburg, *The Broken Spell: A Cultural and Anthropological History of Preindustrial Europe* (London: Palgrave, 1991), 101–4.

44. Rev. Michael P. Mahon, *Ireland's Fairy Lore* (Boston: Thomas J. Flynn, 1919), 178–79.

45. Thomas, *Religion and the Decline of Magic*, 729.

46. Carole G. Silver, *Strange and Secret Peoples: Fairies and Victorian Consciousness* (New York: Oxford University Press, 1999), 193. As Silver elaborates, Puritan hostility is an abiding trope in Victorian fiction dealing with the disappearance of the fairies from England.

47. Thomas, *Religion and the Decline of Magic*, 745–800.

48. Patricia Lysaght, *The Banshee: The Irish Death Messenger* (Dublin: O'Brien Press, 1986), 234. This tolerance was at the level of practice. In terms of doctrine, the Ultramontane hierarchy was determined to complete the work of the Famine in destroying vernacular religion. Yet though innumerable decrees were issued against "indecorous and indecent behaviour" at wakes and funerals, Lysaght notes that "it is remarkable no mention is made of the banshee," the most feared of all supernatural beings in Irish folklore.

49. See the introduction, 15.

50. Stanislaus Joyce to James Joyce, 10 October 1905 (*JJL* II, 118).

51. See Kevin Rockett and Emer Rockett, *Magic Lantern, Panorama and Moving Picture Shows in Ireland, 1786–1909* (Dublin: Four Courts Press, 2011), 72–78, 279–87.

52. *The Perfect Medium: Photography and the Occult*, ed. Clément Chéroux et al. (New Haven: Yale University Press, 2004); Lynda Nead, *The Haunted Gallery; Painting, Photography, Film, c. 1900* (New Haven: Yale University Press, 2001); Warner, *Phantasmagoria*.

53. Pierre Apraxine and Sophie Schmit, "Photography and the Occult," in Cheroux, *The Perfect Medium*, 15.

54. Cited in Arthur Conan Doyle, *The Coming of the Fairies* (London: George Doran, 1922), 172–73, quoted in R. Brandon Kershner, "Framing Rudy and Photography," *Journal of Modern Literature* 22, no. 2 (Spring 1999): 275. Gardner took his own theories to heart and authenticated the sensational "Cottingley fairies" episode after World War 1. Gardner's main worry about one of the girls, Elsie, was that her sexual maturity might dull her senses to the "subtlety" of the otherworld.

55. Andreas Fischer, "'La Lune au front': Remarks on the History of the Photography of Thought," in Cheroux, *The Perfect Medium*, 139. Hence one explanation of the ghostly emanation of Abraham Lincoln in the famous photograph of his widow, Mary Todd Lincoln, taken by William Mumler, the pioneer of spirit photography, was that she was thinking of her dead husband at the time (143).

56. Abraham and Torok, 'Mourning *or* Melancholia.' (*SK* 130–31).

57. Kershner, "Framing Rudy and Photography," 281.

58. Samuel Beckett, *How It Is* (New York: Grove Press, 1964), 7.

59. The lines of Stephen's poem "On swift sail flaming / From storm and south / He comes, pale vampire / Mouth to my mouth" (*U* 7.522–25), are based on Douglas Hyde's "My Grief on the Sea," translated from Irish in *Love Songs of Connacht* [1893]: Gifford and Seidman (*UA* 62).

60. Kershner, "Framing Rudy and Photography," 286. Kershner adds: "Certainly Yeats's vision of the purity of flight and exile strikes a responsive chord in Stephen. Unfortunately, Stephen's closest approximation to Fairyland is alcohol, and instead of finding himself under the hill in the morning, he is likely to be under the weather" (286).

61. Andreas Fischer, " 'The Most Disreputable Camera in the World': Spirit Photography in the United Kingdom in the Early Twentieth Century," in Cheroux, *The Perfect Medium*, 76–77.

62. Howard Eiland, "Superimposition in Walter Benjamin's *Arcades Project*," *Telos* 138 (Spring 2007): 121–22. The internal quotation is from Walter Benjamin, *The Arcades Project*, trans. Howard Eiland and Kevin McLaughlin (Cambridge: Harvard University Press, 1999), 419.

63. Benjamin, "The Work of Art in the Age of Its Technical Reproducibility," in Walter Benjamin, *Selected Writings*, vol. 4, *1938–1940*, trans. Edmund Jephcott and others, ed. Howard Eiland and Michael W. Jennings (Cambridge: Harvard University Press, 2006), 263.

64. Benjamin, *The Arcades Project*, 471.

65. Walter Benjamin, "On the Concept of History," *Selected Writings* 4:390.

66. As Kimberly Devlin notes: "Like Agamemnon, Bloom has been deprived of the happiness of looking upon his son—he can only fantasize wishful imagos, as he does here." Devlin, "Visible Shades and Shades of Visibility," 75.

67. For the transformative potential of the "Rudy principle," in which loss may preserve relational ties that give birth to a new "son" (Stephen) in "a fetal position," see Vicki Mahaffey, "Joyce and Gender," in *Palgrave Advances in James Joyce Studies*, ed. Jean-Michel Rabaté (London: Palgrave Macmillan, 2004), 121–43.

Chapter 6

1. Mahaffy's imperious dismissal of Joyce has passed into literary folklore: "James Joyce is a living argument in favour of my contention that it was a mistake to establish a separate university for the aborigines of this island—the corner boys who spit into the Liffey" (*JJ* 59).

2. Stephen J. Kern, *The Culture of Time and Space, 1880–1918* (Cambridge: Harvard University Press, 1983), esp. 60–64.

3. Michel Foucault, "Of Other Spaces," *Diacritics* 16 (1986): 22, cited in Edward Soja, *Postmodern Geographies: The Reassertion of Space in Contemporary Social Theory* (London: Verso, 1989), 10.

4. Joseph Frank, "Spatial Form in Modern Literature," [1945], in *The Idea of Spatial Form* (New Brunswick: Rutgers University Press, 1991), 5–66.

5. See Kiberd, "*Ulysses*, Newspapers and Modernism," 463–81.

6. Arnold Hauser, *The Social History of Art*, 4 vols. (London: Routledge and Kegan Paul, 1972), 4:255. The comparison of the novel to a city that could be entered in any direction is derived from Edmund Wilson's pioneering discussion of Joyce's modernism in *Axel's Castle* (New York: Charles Scribner's Sons, 1931), 210.

7. Adams, *Surface and Symbol*, 199.

8. Kern, *Culture of Time and Space*, 77.

9. Gilbert, *James Joyce's "Ulysses*," 200.

10. For Joyce's use of ellipses and cinematic techniques to expose the gaps in both space and time in "Wandering Rocks," see Christopher Butler, "Joyce, Modernism and Postmodernism," in Attridge, *The Cambridge Companion to James Joyce*, 270.

11. For the incongruities of space in "Wandering Rocks," see Ruth Frehner, "Why a Thinsocked Clergyman Walks through Other People's Kitchen: Simultaneity in 'Wandering Rocks,'" in Fritz Senn et al., *James Joyce: "Thought through My Eyes"* (Basel: Schwabe, 2000), 176–89.

12. Very Rev. J. S. Conmee, SJ, *Old Times in the Barony* [1895] (Dublin: Carraig Books, 1976).

13. The leisurely pace of the turfbarge the *Bugaboo* was the butt of the satirical ballad

NOTES TO CHAPTER 6

"On Board the *Bugaboo*," which imagines it as an oceangoing vessel, braving the high seas: "We soon weigh'd anchor and set sail to plow the raging surf / We were bound for the Bog of Allen to get a full load of turf." Colm O'Lochlainn, *More Irish Street Ballads* (Dublin: Sign of the Three Candles, 1965), 25–26. In the *United Ireland* cartoon, it becomes a vehicle for the rudderless Home Rule party after the fall of Parnell, David Sheehy, MP (whose wife Father Conmee meets), being one of those who defected to the anti-Parnellite side.

14. Shari Benstock and Bernard Benstock, *Who's He When He's at Home: A James Joyce Directory* (Urbana: University of Illinois Press, 1980), 170.

15. The "brown straw hat" clearly echoes the "hat of dirty straw" that Father Conmee sees, indicating they are one and the same turfbarge. This feature is taken from "On Board the *Bugaboo*": "The Skipper he wore a wide straw hat and a body coat of blue / He'd made a lovely figure head to adorn the *Bugaboo*."

16. The Latin, screening out impropriety in Father Conmee's mind, is translated by Gifford and Seidman as "ejaculation of semen within the natural female organ" (*UA* 264).

17. Among the few studies to address Joyce's relation to the Irish midlands are Eoin O'Mahony, "Father Conmee and His Associates," *JJQ* 4, no. 4 (Summer 1967): 263–70; Jane Ford, "Why Is Milly in Mullingar?" *JJQ* 14, no. 4 (Summer 1977): 436–49; Tilly Eggers, "Darling Milly Bloom," *JJQ* 12, no. 4 (Summer 1975), 386–96; and Leo Daly's *James Joyce and The Mullingar Connection* (Dublin: Dolmen Press, 1975).

18. James Joyce to Stanislaus Joyce, 13 November 1906 (*JJL* II, 13–14). John T. Gilbert's monumental history was the bible of antiquarian lore about Dublin, and Joyce's interest in it and related histories is hardly consistent with Robert M. Adams's charge that he lacked an antiquarian eye for old Dublin: Adams, *Surface and Symbol*, 199. William Dara owned a house near Belvedere College.

19. O'Mahony, "Father Conmee and His Associates," 270.

20. Benstock and Benstock, *Who's He When He's at Home?*, 182. Kathleen McCormick argues in favor of a "similarity between the countess of Belvedere and the elderly female that goes beyond being involved in court cases . . . three women become associated by the lines that are repeated about them and . . . continue to act out the past events in the repetition and reenactment of phrases and stories as if they were present." McCormick, *"Ulysses," "Wandering Rocks," and the Reader: Multiple Pleasures in Reading* (Lewiston: Edwin Mellen Press, 1991), 10–21. McCormick's argument here draws on Leo Knuth, "A Bathymetric Reading of Joyce's *Ulysses*, Chapter X," *JJQ*, 9, no. 4 (Summer 1972), 412.

21. The elderly female, still "smil[ing] incredulously," reappears at the end of the chapter in the crowd that watches the viceregal cavalcade (*U* 10.1193–94).

22. Fritz Senn, "Charting Elsewhereness: Erratic Interlocations," in *Joyce's "Wandering Rocks," European Joyce Studies 12*, ed. Andrew Gibson and Steven Morrison (Amsterdam: Rodopi, 2002), 176. As Senn points out, the "lawyers of the past" passage was inserted in the margins of the early Rosenbach manuscript, and the "elderly female, no more young" added in later revisions.

23. In reply to Joyce's inquiry whether Lady Rochfort ever lived at Belvedere House, Father Charles Doyle mentions that after her "divorce court proceedings," she was confined in Gaulstown, County Westmeath (*JJL* III, 49–50).

24. Translation of Latin: "Princes have persecuted me without a cause: but my heart standeth in awe of thy word." Gifford and Seidman (*UA* 265).

25. Another suggestion is that it has been "temporarily renamed the Royal in honour

of the Viceroy," though given the racist associations of the Royal with Eugene Stratton, "his blub lips agrin" (*U* 10.1274–75), this hardly seems likely. Ian Gunn and Clive Hart, *James Joyce's Dublin: A Topographical Guide to the Dublin of "Ulysses"* (London: Thames and Hudson, 2004), 60.

26. Kenner, *Ulysses*, 73–45, 127, 151.

27. Whether Bloom was correct in his supposition remains open to dispute. Deborah Warner contends that there is no evidence for Bloom's and Hugh Kenner's (*Ulysses*, 4–75) assertion that "the Ballast Office presents two different times simultaneously: 'Greenwich Time' by the ball for mariners, 'Dunsink Time' by the dial for pedestrians." Deborah Warner, "The Ballast-Office Time Ball and the Subjectivity of Time and Space," *JJQ* 35, no. 4, and 36, no. 1 (1998), 863. As we shall see, the political issue was the perception that Irish national time was being subsumed into English imperial time.

28. Fr. R. S. Devane, SJ, "Summer Time: An Imposition and an Anomaly," *Irish Ecclesiastical Record* 53 (Feb. 1939): 127–28.

29. Rev. C. Mangan, "Greenwich Time in Ireland," *Catholic Bulletin* 8, no. 8 (August 1918): 395.

30. J. F. MacCabe, "Irish Time," *Dublin Magazine* 2, no. 1 (January–March 1927), 35.

31. Ibid., 37. MacCabe goes on to stake a claim for an early Irish contribution to the theory of relativity, citing the discovery by the great Trinity College scientist G. F. Fitzgerald that "a measuring scale in motion would be affected by its own motion" (38).

32. Fredric Jameson, *A Singular Modernity: Essay on the Ontology of the Present* (London: Verso, 2002), 218.

33. See Luke Gibbons, "Coming out of Hibernation: The Myth of Modernization in Irish Culture," in *Transformations in Irish Culture*, 82–94.

34. For the argument that the post–September 11 era, and more generally the post–Cold War era, has intensified *located* rather than abstract forms of globalization, dominated by a renewed American pursuit of global market hegemony, see Perry Anderson, "Force and Consent," *New Left Review* 17 (September/October 2002): 5–30.

35. Dipesh Chakrabarty, "The Two Histories of Capital," in *Provincializing Europe: Postcolonial Thought and Historical Difference* (New Delhi: Oxford University Press, 2001), 69.

36. Max Horkheimer, *Critique of Instrumental Reason* (New York: Continuum, 1994), 22, cited in Chakrabarty, *Provincializing Europe*, 66.

37. Dipesh Chakrabarty, "A Small History of Subaltern Studies," in *Habitations of Modernity: Essays in the Wake of Subaltern Studies* (Delhi: Permanent Black/University of Chicago Press, 2002), 12.

38. See Pier Paolo Pasolini, "Observations on the Long Take," *October* 13 (1980): 3–6.

39. Hansen, "The Mass Production of the Senses: Classical Cinema as Vernacular Modernism"; Mary Ann Doane, *The Emergence of Cinematic Time: Modernity, Contingency, the Archive* (Cambridge: Harvard University Press, 2002), esp. 103–7.

40. Leys, *Trauma: A Genealogy*, 241.

41. Maureen Turim, *Flashbacks in Film: Memory and History* (New York: Routledge, 1989), 27.

42. Turim points out that in Hugo Münsterberg's pioneering critical work *The Psychology of the Photoplay* (1916), the use of dissolves or fades signals subjectively motivated flashbacks, as in memory; by contrast, "flashbacks that are not subjective do not use dissolves or fades, but are simple cuts" (Turim, *Flashbacks in Film*, 31). It is the latter that makes the spectral possible in the "Wandering Rocks."

43. Jo Anna Isaak, *The Ruin of Representation in Modernist Art and Texts* (Ann Arbor, MI: UMI Research Press, 1986), 36.

Chapter 7

1. For discussions of Soyer's soup kitchen at the Phoenix Park and the recurrent anxiety over famine in *Ulysses*, see Mary Lowe-Evans, *Crimes against Fecundity: Joyce and Population Control* (Syracuse: Syracuse University, 1989), esp. 16–29. Evans also links wider questions of "souperism" to the mention of the Rev. Thomas Connellan in "Lestrygonians," as discussed below. See also Nolan, *James Joyce and Nationalism*, 79–119; Julie Ann Ulin, "'Famished Ghosts': Famine Memory in James Joyce's *Ulysses*," *Joyce Studies Annual 2011*, 20–63; and Bonnie Roos, "The Joyce of Eating: Feast, Famine and the Humble Potato in *Ulysses*," in *Hungry Words: Images of Famine in the Irish Canon*, ed. George Cusack and Sarah Goss (Dublin: Irish Academic Press, 2006), 159–96.

2. Patrick Maume, *The Long Gestation: Irish Nationalist Life, 1891–1918* (Dublin: Gill and Macmillan, 1999), 93.

3. Ibid.

4. Eileen Reilly, "Women and Voluntary War Work," in *Ireland and the Great War: "A War to Unite Us All"?* ed. Adrian Gregory and Senia Paseta (Manchester: Manchester University Press, 2002), 51.

5. The threat of famine was particularly acute in Mayo (which Gonne visited) and Kerry, where Connolly spent two weeks investigating conditions at firsthand. The pamphlet, *The Rights of Life and the Rights of Property*, used the teaching of the church fathers to assert the primacy of life over property. See the chapter "Famine" in Maud Gonne McBride, *A Servant of the Queen* [1938] (Gerrards Cross: Colin Smythe, 1994), and Donal Nevin, *James Connolly: "A Full Life"* (Dublin: Gill and Macmillan, 2005), 95–97.

6. Maume, *Long Gestation*, 93.

7. Ibid., 22.

8. *The Unknown Power behind the Irish Nationalist Party: Its present Work and Criminal History*, ed. Lord Ashtown (London: Office of "Grievances from Ireland," 1908).

9. Maume, *Long Gestation*, 22.

10. Rev. Thomas Connellan, *Hear the Other Side*, 12th ed., revised and enlarged (Dublin: Office of "The Catholic," 1908). Subsequent references will take the form of *HTOS*, followed by page number, in the text.

11. See, e.g., James Joyce, *Ulysses*, Modern Library ed. (New York: Random House, 1961), 178. One notable exception is Leo Daly, *James Joyce at the Cross-Keys—Mullingar* (Mullingar: Westmeath Examiner, 1991). Daly's research is exemplary of the kind of local history, drawing both on the archive and cultural memory, often required for interpreting key aspects of Joyce. The same eye for detail is also evident in Daly's better-known work, *James Joyce and the Mullingar Connection*. Apart from Mary Lowe-Evans's reference above (note 1), Connellan's role as the possible real-life source of the runaway priest in George Moore's *The Lake* is discussed in John Cronin, "George Moore's *The Lake*: A Possible Source," in *The Way Back: George Moore's "The Untilled Field" and "The Lake,"* ed. Robert Welsh (Dublin: Wolfhound Press, 1982), 132.

12. Adams, *Surface and Symbol*, 206.

13. As Adams notes: "There was in fact a literal Bird's Nest Institution at 19 and 20 York Street, Kingstown, run by a Protestant Missionary Society" (ibid.).

14. Gifford and Seidman (*UA* 186).

15. Joyce's interest in procuring a copy of Moore's novel, and his caustic response on reading it, feature in his letters to his brother Stanislaus in 1906 (*JJL* II, 129, 152–58, 162–63). In the revised, second edition of *The Lake*, Moore introduced a character, Father Connellan, who, ironically, gets involved in an argument with a number of other priests over whether Irish priests lose their Irishness when they go on missionary work to London. This was dropped in the third edition, 1921.

16. Rev. Thomas Connellan, "Carolan," *Irish Ecclesiastical Record* 4 (September 1885). Turlough O'Carolan, the "Last of the Irish Bards," is buried in Kilronan Abbey, and Connellan describes how "Lady Tennyson [*sic*]," wife of the local landlord, placed a plaque commemorating the harper in the abbey "on the picturesque shore of Lough Meelagh." George Moore's "Kilronan" is set in an indeterminate location but adjoins "Joycetown." George Moore, *The Lake* [1906] (Gerrards Cross: Colin Smythe, 1980).

17. Rev. Thomas Connellan, "Mary Stuart and Elizabeth Tudor," *Irish Ecclesiastical Record* 4 (June 1885): 391.

18. Rev. Joseph Keating, SJ, *"Souperism"* (Dublin: Catholic Truth Society, 1914), 23.

19. Daly, *James Joyce at the Cross-Keys*, 7.

20. Ibid., 28–29.

21. Ibid., 27–28.

22. *The Catholic*, December 1891, cited in ibid., 37.

23. Eleanor Frances Kelly, *Rescued!* (Dublin: Catholic Truth Society, n.d.), 12. Kelly's ardent contributions to the genre also included *Miss Patience Hope Discovers the Soupers* (Dublin: Catholic Truth Society, n.d.).

24. Attridge, *Joyce Effects*, 121.

25. This accords with Terence Killeen's suggestion above that contrary to Joyce's image as system builder and controller of all meaning in *Ulysses*, many resonances and allusions may lie outside his ingenuity and deliberation. See chapter 1, note 74.

26. The Tichborne case is related, in chapter 8 below, to the possibility that Charles Stewart Parnell may have come back from the grave.

27. The O'Brien Institute is in Donnycarney and, like the more famous school at Artane one mile farther north, was run by the Christian Brothers. Both the O'Brien Institute and the Bird's Nest Home, Dun Laoghaire, were listed under the Residential Institutions Redress Board established by the Irish government in 2002 to render compensation for sexual and physical abuse in schools.

28. There is no evidence Joyce was directly familiar with the *Celtic Times*, though he was certainly well schooled in Cusack's journalism, as "Cyclops" shows. In "Eumaeus," one of Cusack's hobby horses in the *Celtic Times* with regard to native industries, the possibility of growing tobacco in Ireland, surfaces in the mouth of "Skin-the-Goat" (*U* 16.995–96).

29. Though Cusack was a founder of the Gaelic Athletic Association in 1884, bitter internal conflicts led to his being forced out of the organization by 1886.

30. "Harmonic Rays," *Celtic Times*, 18 June 1887, 6, reprinted in *"The Celtic Times": Michael Cusack's Gaelic Games Newspaper*, introduction by Marcus de Burca (Ennis: Clasp Press, 2003), italics added.

31. "The Reason Why," *Celtic Times*, 28 May 1887, 4.

32. "Letters to the Editor," *Celtic Times*, 18 June 1887, 3.

33. *Reply to the Catholic Association and its Allies: "The Leader" and "The Irish Rosary"* (Dublin: Society for the Protection of Protestant Interests, 1903), 2, 13. The Catholic Association did not, of course, publicize its principles; these statements were "outed" in

the Protestant press. For a discussion of the Catholic Association and its main adversary, the Protestant Defence Association, in relation to Joyce's Dublin, see Gibson, *Joyce's Revenge*, 46–47.

34. Maume, *Long Gestation*, 94; Rev. Thomas Connellan, *The Catholic Association of Ireland: Its History—Its Aims—Its Results* (Dublin: Office of "The Catholic," 1906), 14.

35. Connellan, *The Catholic Association of Ireland*, 6.

36. Ibid., 3.

37. Michael J. F. McCarthy, "The Irish 'Catholic Association,'" in *Rome in Ireland* (London: Hodder and Stoughton, 1904), 317. McCarthy, a trenchant critic of Catholic power in Ireland, as noted in chapter 2 above, added: "What an alarming discovery it must have been to find that the despised Protestants, of whose intelligence the hierarchy must have been forming such a low estimate, had struck back by closing their purses against the priests and nuns! I strongly advise the Protestants to be in no hurry to open their purses to the priests" (317). Advanced nationalists such as D. P. Moran would have agreed with this, seeing Catholic dependence on aristocratic charity as infection by the "Viceregal microbe" (see note 2 above).

38. Gifford and Seidman (*UA* 345).

39. When "Baby Boardman" (a possible pun on the sandwichboard-men, as well as Edy Boardman's little brother in "Nausicaa") later trips up a fat policeman in "Circe" proclaiming "U. p: up. U. p: up"(*U* 15.1608–9), Cusack is greatly moved: "THE CITIZEN (*choked with emotion, brushes aside a tear in his emerald muffler*) May the good God bless him!" (*U* 15.1616–8).

Chapter 8

1. Bloom's thoughts echo P. J. P. Tynan's sentiments on Trinity College rowdiness on a different occasion: "The Trinity College students' . . . conduct savours more of the rowdy than that of the gentleman—and yet from the ranks of these rowdies will come some of Ireland's magistrates and police officers, to dispense and manipulate alien rule in the country." Patrick J. P. Tynan ["Number One"], *The Irish National Invincibles and Their Times* (London: Chatham and Co., 1896), 258. Subsequent references will take the form of *INI*, followed by page number, in the text. As noted below, Joyce was familiar with Tynan's book.

2. Max Scheler, "Negative Feelings and the Destruction of Values: *Ressentiment*," in *On Feeling, Knowing, and Valuing*, ed. Harold J. Bershady (Chicago: University of Chicago Press, 1992), 123.

3. In some cases, random obstacles prevent recognition (or misrecognition), as when Tom Kernan is not sure who it is he spots across the street: "Is that Ned Lambert's brother over the way, Sam? What? Yes. He's as like as damn it. No. The windscreen of the motorcar in the sun there. Just a flash like that. Damn like him" (*U* 10.757–59).

4. Scheler, "Negative Feelings," 123.

5. Walter Benjamin, "Short History of Photography," in *One Way Street*, trans. Edmund Jephcott and Kingsley Shorter (London: New Left Books, 1979), 249.

6. Maurice Merleau-Ponty, *Sense and Non-Sense*, trans. H. L. Dreyfus and P. A. Dreyfus (Evanston: Northwestern University Press, 1964), 52.

7. As Scheler notes: "We might perhaps go further and say that [for the premodern mind] everything whatsoever is given . . . as 'expression,' and that what we call development through learning, is not a subsequent addition of a mental element to an already

given inanimate world of material objects, but a continuous process of disenchantment, in that only a proportion of sensory appearances retain their function as vehicles of expression, while others do not." Scheler, *The Nature of Sympathy*, 239. Though disenchantment is akin to subtraction, it is at another level a subjective *accretion*, a detached intellectual construct "imposed" on our senses, often with great effort, akin to the elaborate "context" required to understand scientific constructs, as noted by W. V. O. Quine above, chapter 2, note 14.

8. Henry Glassie, "Eighteenth-Century Cultural Process in Delaware Valley Folk Building," *Winterthur Portfolio* 7 (1972): 43, cited in Locke, *Eavesdropping*, 97.

9. Benjamin, "Short History of Photography," 243.

10. Ibid., 245, 243.

11. Ezra Pound, "*Dubliners* and Mr. James Joyce," *JJCH* I, 66.

12. See chapter 2 above.

13. Barbara Johnson, *Persons and Things* (Cambridge, MA: Harvard University Press, 2008), 6–10, 23–28; Melvin J. Friedman, "Lestrygonians," in *James Joyce's "Ulysses": Critical Essays*, 16–37.

14. Kelly, *Our Joyce*, 16; Pound, "*Dubliners* and Mr. James Joyce," 67.

15. Peter Costello, *James Joyce: The Years of Growth, 1882–1915: A Biography* (London: Kyle Cathie, 1992), 136.

16. "*Ulysses* Notesheets: 'Cyclops 1,'" in *Joyce's "Ulysses" Notesheets in the British Museum*, ed. Phillip Herring (Charlottesville: University of Virginia Press, 1972), 83. According to Hugh Staples, Joyce copied this coded dialogue of agrarian secret societies such as Whiteboys or Ribbonmen from A. M. Sullivan's *New Ireland: Political Sketches* (Glasgow, 1877), 40. Hugh Staples, "'Ribbonmen,' Signs and Passwords in *Ulysses*," *Notes and Queries* 13, no. 3 (March 1966): 95–96.

17. John Wyse Jackson and Peter Costello, *John Stanislaus Joyce* (London: Fourth Estate, 1997), chapter 20. In Peter Costello's estimation, John Kelly's "great moral stature" was such that he was, "outside of the Jesuits, perhaps the finest man that Joyce knew at this time." Costello, *James Joyce: The Years of Growth*, 136.

18. In "The Boarding House" it is noted: "Dublin is such a small city. Everyone knows everyone else's business" (*D* 61).

19. See Michael Seidel's spectral definition: "Gnomon means the shape of a smaller parallelogram taken away from a larger one, a missing piece or ghost of a form not quite there." Seidel, *James Joyce: A Short Introduction*, 45. Joyce's exploitation of familiarity in modes of address is discussed in Gerald Bruns, "Eumaeus," in Hart and Hayman, *James Joyce's "Ulysses": Critical Essays*, 367–68.

20. Wim Van Mierlo, "The Subject Notebook: A Nexus in the Composition History of *Ulysses*—A Preliminary Analysis," http://www.geneticjoycestudies.org/GJS7 /GJS7mierlo.html, accessed 17 January 2012. Van Mierlo notes that there is no conclusive proof Joyce read these books, but passages in "Eumaeus" would suggest some familiarity.

21. Tynan's designation of himself as "Number One" appears to be picked up in "Eumaeus": "And then, number one, you came up against the man in possession" (*U* 16.1341–42).

22. Malcolm Brown, *The Politics of Irish Literature: From Thomas Davis to W. B. Yeats* (Seattle: University of Washington Press, 1973), 281. James Fairhall notes of Tynan that "we learn more than he wants to tell us," but it is precisely this excess that destroys narrative cohesion. Fairhall, *James Joyce and the Question of History* (Cambridge: Cambridge University Press, 1993), 28.

23. Colleen Lamos, "The Double Life of 'Eumaeus,'" in Devlin and Reizbaum, *Ulysses—En-Gendered Perspectives*, 242–53.

24. Iain McCalman, "Popular Constitutionalism and Revolution in England and Ireland," in *Revolution and the Meanings of Freedom in the Nineteenth Century*, ed. Isser Wolloch (Stanford: Stanford University Press, 1996), 167.

25. As noted in chapter 7, it may also allude to the return from a watery grave of the Rev. Thomas Connellan.

26. Joyce's term, from the Linati scheme for *Ulysses*: Richard Ellmann, *"Ulysses" on the Liffey* (Oxford: Oxford University Press, 1972), 186.

27. Patrick Pearse, "Ghosts," [Christmas 1915], in *Collected Works of Padraic H. Pearse: Political Writings and Speeches* (Dublin: Phoenix, 1924), 268–69.

28. Carlos Fuentes, *Terra Nostra*, trans. Margaret Sayers Peden (Harmondsworth: Penguin Books, 1976), 646.

29. It is also the ghostly call of the Irish past—extending to the Fenian leader James Stephens, but stopping short of Parnell—that is redirected through Africa (in a spatial as well as a temporal realignment) to summon the young man Dan to join the Boers in South Africa in George Moore's story "The Voice of the Mountain," discussed in chapter 3 above.

INDEX

Abbey Theatre, 135, 237n26, 256n55
Aberdeen, Lady, "Lady Microbe," 190
Abraham, Nicolas, and Maria Torok: encryptment, 130, 145, 160–61; hope in, 146; "Imago" in, 146, 164; melancholia, 14, 130–31, 146, 160; phantom, 131, 255n48; suspension of literal and figural, 146–47; transgenerational memory, 146. *See also* incorporation; introjection
Adams, Robert Martin, 17, 168, 191–92, 197–98, 232n42, 262n18; Joyce lacking antiquarian's eye, 262n18; surface and symbol in Joyce, 40–41; on totalizing designs of *Ulysses*, 241n74
Adorno, Theodor W., 59, 68
advertising, 17, 55, 140, 150
"After the Race" (*Dubliners*), 211; first publication, 251n43; free indirect discourse, absence of, 251n53; Joyce not satisfied with, 96–97; resentment in, 65
Agamemnon, 261n66
Alighieri, Dante, 47
Ancient Order of Hibernians, 190
Anderson, Margaret C., 232n36
Anderson, Perry, 263n34
Anna Karenina (Tolstoy), 64
Aquinas, Saint Thomas ("Tommaso Mastino"), 47
"Araby" (*Dubliners*), 20
Aran Islands, 92–93, 135–36
Aristotle, 40, 241n69

Atget, Eugène, 211
Attridge, Derek: bodily dimension of speech, 43, 44; on modernist universalism, 40; self-sufficiency of modernist works, 41; on unforeseen connection in Joyce's work, 41–42, 198
Auden, W. H., xiv
Auerbach, Erich, 252n70, 257n4
Austen, Jane, 85, 91, 97
Australia, 57, 98; Wagga Wagga, 221

Baedeker's Guide, 4
Bakhtin, Mikhail, 74, 77, 231n30, 250n47; chronotopes, 186; language not private property, 101; on *skaz*, 99
Bakhtin, Nicholas, 250n47
Ball, Sir Robert, 179; *The Story of the Heavens*, 180
Banim, John, and Michael Banim, 85; *The Bit o'Writin*, 89; *The Boyne Water*, 86; "Crohoore of the Billhook," 86
Barnes, Djuna, 229n7
Barry, Kevin, 253n12, 256n63
Barthes, Roland, 12; on "reality effect," 35, 239n53
Battaillard, Pascal, 253n12
Battle, Mary, 154–55
Bazargan, Susan, 72
Beauregard, Raphaëlle Costa de, 112
Beckett, Samuel, 161, 239n55; *Happy Days*, 242n89
Belloc, Hilaire, 181

Benjamin, Walter, 42; on photography, 211–12; physiognomy, 211–13; superimposition and the past, 163–64

Benstock, Bernard, 28, 172, 176

Benstock, Shari, 172, 176

Bird's Nest home, 19, 191, 196–97, 199, 264n13, 265n27

Bishop, John, 239n55

"Boarding House, A" (Dubliners), 18, 267n18

Bodin, Jean, 143

Boehmer, Elleke, 140–41

Boer War, 220, 221, 222, 224; calling character in "A Voice of the Mountain" (Moore), 98–99, 268n29; Irish demonstrations in support of Boers, 20, 207–9; Parnell and, 220–25

Bog of Allen, 262n13

Borch-Jacobsen, Mikkel, 13; Freud's metaphysics of the subject, 233n56

Borges, Jorge Luis, 51

Boucicault, Dion: Arrah-na-Pogue, 80; "Harvey Duff" (The Shaughran), 72, 73, 215, 246n54

Boyd, Ernest, 87; on Joyce and cosmopolitanism, 84; on Joyce and the Revival, 83, 87, 248n16; on Moore, 95

Brodsky, Joseph, xv

Brown, Malcolm, 216

Bruns, Gerald, 91, 267n19

Bryant, Sophie, 65–66, 259n27; Celtic psychology, 65–66; subconscious becoming the conscious in others, 78

Budgen, Frank, 2, 36, 67, 100, 165, 247n4

"Bugabu, The," 172, 177, 261n13, 262n15

Buller, Captain, 38, 240n64

Burke, Colonel Richard, 215–16

Burke, Edmund, 57

Burke, Thomas, 46, 217

Butler, Christopher, 261n10; on Riffaterre, 36; on Wordsworth, 36

Butler, Judith: critique of Freud on mourning and melancholia, 20, 224; on interiority, 4; performance and identity formation, 68, 246nn41–42; performativity of identity, 68; on relational ties, xv, 224

Byron, Lord, 38, 240n65

Cage, John, 37, 40, 41, 241n72

Cahalan, James, 87

Caird, James A., 204

capitalism, 19–20, 138, 140: cultural logic of development, 181–83; Fordism, 182; individualist ethic, xv, 138; time discipline, 182–83; world-system, 182–83, 263n34

Carleton, William, 85; Rody the Rover', or, The Ribbonman, 87, 203; "Wild Goose Lodge," 87

Carlyle, James, 203

Carlyle, Thomas, 86

Casey, Joseph, 49, 215–16

Castle, Terry, 230n9

Castle Rackrent (Edgeworth), 88

Catholicism, Roman, 2 , 14, 47, 59, 62, 63, 83, 119, 152, 175, 193, 198, 203–4, 206, 236n13, 237n23, 250n47, 266n37; "Castle Catholics," 190, 205; Catholic Association, 204–5, 265n33; Catholic Truth Society, 197; coexisting with folk belief, 14, 155–57, 254n26; as cultural presence, 83, 138, 152; devotional revolution, 15, 198; orphanages, 169, 199; witch craze, 259n43

—tracts: Miss Patience Hope Discovers the Soupers, 265n23; Rescued!, 197; Souperism, 196

cattle trade, Irish, 99, 182, 183–84

Cavell, Marcia, on psychoanalysis presupposing interiority, 233n58, 234n59

Chakrabarty, Dipesh, 181–82

Chamberlain, Joseph, M.P., 20, 207–9

Chandler, Raymond, 129, 255n39

Charcot, Jean-Martin, 143

Chatman, Seymour, 109–11

Chesterton, G. K., 181

Chevalier, Ann, on Joyce's cosmopolitanism, 84

Chiniquy, Rev. Charles, 192

Cholodenko, Alan, 118

cinema: camera as ghost, xv, 117–19; and free indirect discourse, 116–17; Joyce and, 103, 110–35; structuring inner life, 184–86; and subjective narration, 109–10, 132–33; as technology, xv

—techniques: cross-cutting, 167, 169, 171;

flashbacks, 184–86, 261n10, 263n42; montage, xv, 110, 116, 163, 168, 183, 184; parallel action, 110, 167

city, 10, 12, 35, 95–96; cultural and political underworld, 47, 50–51, 59, 214–19; inner speech and inner life, 3–4, 41, 44, 51, 53–55, 59–66, 163–64; and language, xv, 22, 34, 36, 62; material textures of, xv, 17, 31, 38–39, 60, 64, 125–26; physiognomy of, 212–15; spectrality, 8, 51, 128–29, 176–79, 207–11, 222–25; time and space in, 165–69, 178–83; transformation of, 32, 167

Civil War: American, 157; English, 156

Clack, Brian, 154

Clarke, Austin, 24

"Clay" (Dubliners), 119, 239n56, 251n55; Maria's forgotten verse, 18

Cleary, Bridget, 15, 153, 154–55, 161, 234n65

Cleary, Michael, 153

Clerkenwell explosion, 48–49, 215

Cohn, Dorrit, on free indirect discourse, 4

Colum, Mary, 21; Joyce's appreciation of reviews of Ulysses, 245n23; on Joyce's relationship to Dublin, 21–22, 28, 62–63

Comte, Auguste, 150

Conmee, Rev. John, S.J., 19, 64, 168, 169–78, 184, 199, 262n13; Old Times in the Barony, 174

Connellan, Rev. Thomas, 19, 20, 264n1, 265n16; bookstore, 191–93; brothers James and Patrick, 197; critic of Catholic church, 191, 193–96, 205–6; featuring in The Lake (Moore), 193, 264n11, 264n15; founds The Catholic mission, 194–98; Hear the Other Side, 191, 193–96; priest in Catholic church, 193–94; stages drowning, 191–92, 268n25

Connolly, James: collectivism and syndicalism, 138–39; on threats of contemporary famine in Ireland, 190, 264n5

Connolly, S. J.: absence of internal psychological constraints, 15; on popular supernaturalism, 15–16

Connor, Steven, 7–8

Coogan, Amanda, Molly Blooms, 68–69

Costello, Peter, 215, 229n3, 267n17

"Counterparts" (Dubliners), resentment in, 65

Culler, Jonathan, on deictic language in literature, 237n28

Curran, Constantine, 23

Cusack, Michael, 102, 200–204, 265nn28–29, 266n39; Celtic Times, 200–204, 265n28

Daly, Leo, 197, 262n17, 264n11

Dara, William, 174, 262n18

Darwinism, social, 153

Davis, Deborah R., on famine specters, 234n64

Davitt, Michael, 107–8, 131, 190

"Dead, The" (Dubliners), 6, 8, 17, 39–40, 67–68, 96, 103–37, 141, 151, 251n51; association of ghost with "air," 126–27, 136, 148; Duke of Wellington, 136; "gas" and ghost, 114, 126; gaslight, 8, 123, 126–27; gasworks, 8, 123; and King Conaire, 128, 253n17; King William, 136; noises in, 129; political underworld in, 135–36, 256n61; power-cuts on night of, 125–26, 255n32; O'Connell, 136; ritual in, 141; street lighting in, 8, 125–29; "Taps" in, 125–26, 129–30, 136; weather in, 136. See also "Lass of Aughrim" (song)

—characters. Gabriel Conroy: disturbances in his speech, 8; encounter with Lily, 115; ghostly interception of voice, 116; imagining ghost of Michael Furey, 6, 117–18; rehearsing speech, 68; viewing himself in the mirror, 251n51; and west of Ireland, 115, 151. Gretta Conroy, 67; relation to Lily, 123; and west of Ireland, 115, 125, 151. Lily, 6; accent, 253n17; and back answers, 115; plight of, 113–15; relation to Gretta, 123; use of language, 113, 253n13; voice framing story, 112–17. Michael Furey, 8, 124, 136; ghost of, 117–18; job in gasworks, 123, 126, 151; and west of Ireland, 125, 134. Molly Ivors, 67, 135–36

Dead, The (Huston), xv, 38–39, 103–37; "Broken Vows" ("Donall Óg"), 113–14, 116, 119–22, 134; and Dublin middle-

Dead, The (Huston) (continued)
class society, 125; historical ruins in,
134–35; John Huston and the Dubliners
(Sievernich), 124; servant's story in,
112–17, 122–24; tripartite structures in,
122; voice-over in, 133–34, 256n53. See
also "Lass of Aughrim" (song)
—cast: Helena Carroll (Aunt Kate), 115;
Cathleen Delany (Aunt Julia), 119;
Rachael Dowling (Lily), 104, 112, 122,
123; Anjelica Huston (Gretta Conroy), 104, 119, 121, 123; Donal McCann
(Gabriel Conroy), 104, 115, 121; Sean
McClory (Mr. Grace), 119, 122
—characters. Gabriel: east of Ireland,
121–23; encounter with Lily, 115; west
of Ireland, 115, 120. Mr. Grace, 113, 119–
22. Gretta: association with west of Ireland, 116; experiences trance, 119–21;
relation to Lily, 122–23. Lily: accent,
253n17; and "Broken Vows," 120–22;
as framing presence, 112–17, 122–24;
plight of, 113–15; relation to Gretta,
122–23; use of language, 113, 253n13.
Michael Furey, 8, 124; ghost off-screen,
117–18, 255n40; job in gasworks, 123,
126; and west of Ireland, 125, 134
Deane, Emma, 163
Deane, Seamus, 19; on cosmopolitan style
in Joyce, 26
Debord, Guy, 105
Deleuze, Gilles, 92, 117, 233n57, 254n24
Derrida, Jacques, 53, 71; on exorcism, 143;
on Freud, 5, 230n22, 232n49; idioms
of haunting, 137; on Molly Bloom's
soliloquy, 53, 68–70; on non-contem-
poraneity of the ghost, 19; other versus
mother tongue, 86, 101
Dettmar, Kevin, 232n39, 232n41
Devane, Fr. R. S., S.J., 180
Devlin, Kimberly, 71, 72, 150, 214, 261n66
De Wet, Christiaan, 20, 220, 222–25
DiBattista, Maria, on ghosts in Ulysses, 16
Dickens, Charles, 106; Oliver Twist, 48
disenchantment: modernity as, 212, 266–
67n7; of night, 14; Scheler on, 212,
266–67n7
Don Quixote (Cervantes), 64
Douglas, Mary, 153

Dowie, Dr Alexander, 189
Dowland, John, 11
Doyle, Arthur Conan, 50, 260n54
Doyle, Father Charles, 175, 262n23
Doyle, J. C., 16–17
Dracula (Stoker), 232n34
Dublin: Bible wars in, 19, 204–5; city
breaking into text, 28; descriptive
writing, lack of in Ulysses, 38; and
Empire, 51, 59, 119; "hungry for illusion," 20; irrelevance to Ulysses, 27;
Joyce's attachment to, 21–24; knowledge of required for reading Ulysses,
3, 28, 31, 46–47; negative topography,
58–59, 243n6; and Paris, 16; as physiognomy, 211; Pound on, 214; precision
in sense of place, 214, 239n56; relation
to Europe, 22, 24; statues, 56–58, 136,
243n3
—places: Annesley Bridge, 178; Antient
Concert Rooms, 16; Artane, 199; Ballast Office, 179; Bank of Ireland, 57;
Barney Kiernan's, 60, 61, 205; Belvedere College, 169, 174–75, 199, 262n23;
Bird's Nest home, 191; Byron Lodge,
Sutton, 38; Chapelizod, 147; Charleville Mall, 171; City Hall, 54–55; Clarence Hotel, 56; Commons-lane, 94;
The Coombe, 92; Crossguns Bridge,
172; Davey Byrne's, 189, 191; DBC restaurant, 225; Dignam's Court, 170; Dillon's auction rooms, 189; Dollymount,
25, 170; Donnycarney, 169, 265n27;
Dublin Castle, 59, 68, 69, 212, 216;
Dunsink, 179; Finn's Hotel, 55; Four
Courts, 128; Glasnevin, 7, 14, 150, 172,
183, 210; Graham Lemon's, 189; Grand
Canal, 178, 262n25; Gray's confectioner, 191; Gresham Hotel, 8, 125–26,
254n30, 255n32; Guinness's brewery, 51;
Hely's, 206; Hill of Howth, 97; Kingsbridge, 4, 78, 213; King William monument, 136; Liffey, 51, 55, 235n3; Loopline Bridge, 46; Mountjoy Square, 169;
Mud Island, 171; National Library, 2,
11, 16, 64; Newcomen Bridge, 170, 171,
176; O'Brien Institute, 169, 265n27;
O'Connell Bridge, 179, 189; O'Connell monument, 136; O'Neill's funeral

establishment, 172; Ormond Quay, 55–56, 71; Pembroke, 178; Phibsborough, 172; Philip Crampton's fountain, 189; Phoenix Park, 46, 49, 119, 148–49, 189, 217, 239n56, 264n1; Red Bank restaurant, 16–17; Ringsend, 158; Rotunda hospital, 158; Royal Canal, 172–73, 198, 262n25; Rutland Square, 158; Queen's Theatre, 16; Sandycove (Martello tower), 9, 162; Sandymount, 45, 98, 161, 198; Scotch House, 203; Sisters of Charity home, 189; St Agatha's church, 171; St Francis Xavier's church, 170; Thomas Cook's travel agency, 56, 58; Ushers Island, 117; Walter Sexton's, 207; Wellington monument, 136; Wellington Quay, 56
—streets: Bachelors Walk, 56, 189; Capel Street, 24; College Green, 57; Dawson Street, 19, 191, 194; D'Olier Street, 16; Duke Lane, 191; Eccles Street, 46, 171; Fitzgibbon Street, 170; Fleet Street, 125; Gardiner Street, 170, 189; Grafton Street, 204, 207, 225; Great Brunswick Street, 16; Lower Mount Street, 178; Malahide Road, 173–74, 177: Nassau Street, 55; North Strand Road, 170; North William Street, 171; Sackville Street (O'Connell Street), 170, 189, 255n32; Thomas Street, 24, 59; Upper Gardiner Street, 170; Westland Row, 76; Westmoreland Street, 179, 199, 213
Dubliners: aimed at Irish and international readership, 26, 214; formal innovations already present in, 85; Joyce's difficulties in publishing, 26; substitutability of place names in, 35. See also titles of separate stories
Dublin Magazine, 178, 181
Dubois, L. Paul, 138, 257n1
Dudley, Lady, 49, 59
Dudley, Lord, 59
Duffy, Enda: local knowledge in Ulysses, 39; on surveillance in Ulysses, 47, 214–15; on unsaid in Ulysses, 17
Dujardin, Édouard, 105, 119; Joyce's relation to, 251n55; Moore's relation to, 249n22
Dun Laoghaire, 196

Eco, Umberto, 51, 62; on "open" work, 27
Ecstasy (Machatý), 103
Edgeworth, Maria, 87, 88
Egleson Dunleavy, Janet, 133
Eglinton, John (W. G. Magee), 1, 2, 269n22
Ehrlich, Howard, 42
Eichenbaum, Boris, 91
Eiland, Howard, 163
Eisenstein, Sergei, 119
Eliot, George, 194
Eliot, T. S., xiv, 239n49
Ellmann, Maud, 2, 20
Ellmann, Richard, 17, 252n68
Elphin, Diocese of, 193
Emmet, Robert, 37, 98, 243n8
Empire, British, xiv, 22, 28, 59, 62, 119, 222, 224
"Encounter, An" (Dubliners), 18
Engels, Friedrich, 231
"Eveline"(Dubliners): "Derevaun Seraun," 18; failure of eye contact in, 45; first publication, 251n43; narrative style of, 81–82
Everest, Barbara, 255n46
everyday life: aesthetic representation of, 29–33; defamiliarization of, 31, 33; direct access to, 34; Lefebvre on, 29; Perec on the "infra-ordinary," 29; Woolf on, 34

Fairhall, James, 257n22
famine, 161, 199; contemporary threats of famine, 190, 264n5;Great Famine, xiv; impact on popular supernaturalism, 15, 260n48; and "The Lass of Aughrim," 114–15, 124; potato in Ulysses, 199; "Souperism," 19, 189–90, 196, 198, 264n1; Soyer's soup kitchen, 189, 264n1; and specters, 15, 19, 189, 199, 234n64; starvation in Dublin, 189, 199
Ferenczi, Sándor, 14, 253n59
Ferrer, Daniel, 229n4
Finnegans Wake, 6, 7, 22, 33, 36, 80, 85, 128, 130, 225, 229n4; address to Dublin, 24; cinema in, 130, 252n1; Clifden and Marconi, 135, 256n57; dissolution of time and place in, 239n55; Maamtrasna trial, 247n2; thunder in, 1

Fire Festival (Bealtaine), 153–54

Fitzgerald, G. F., 263n31

Flanagan, Thomas, 85

Flaubert, Gustave, 6, 81, 91, 95, 97, 101, 231n29, 252n70

Fleischmann, Martha, reminder of bird-girl, 25

Foley, John Henry, 57

folk beliefs: banshee, 15, 128, 157, 260n48; changeling, 153, 155, 159, 161, 162, 164; fairies, 1, 15, 128, 154, 155, 156, 157, 162, 229n1, 254n26, 260n46, 260n54, 260n60; vampire, 162, 199, 260n59. See also superstition

form: density of aesthetic, 238n38; disrupted by real-life intrusions, 41–42, 51; forging sympathetic ties, 4; formal innovations already present in Dubliners, 85; modernist innovations and Irish culture, xiv, 3, 28, 59, 83–85; rendering the everyday intelligible, 32; search for in Irish culture, 85; and structuralism, 35–39; transformative power of, 32, 238n38; Ulysses contesting self-sufficiency of, 240n62

Foster, John Wilson: arrested growth of realist fiction, 139; eclipse of self in Ireland, 139; retarding influence of ritual, 141

Foucault, Michel, 39, 167

Francini Bruni, Alessandro, 96, 234n66

Frank, Joseph, 167

Frazer, Sir James: The Golden Bough, 152–53, 155, 259n37; Wittgenstein, comments on, 153–54, 259n35

free indirect discourse: against authority, 87; Bally first to identify, 250n47; as condescension, 87, 101, 252n70; contesting inner and outer worlds, 131–32; definitions of, 4, 77, 81; dual vantage point, 112; and film, 116–17, 132; and free association, 74–75; hallucinations, 27; and idiolect, 81, 100, 216, 247n7; and idiomatic language, xiv, 4, 81–83, 92; intersubjective, 91; intonation in, 82–83, 101, 247n4; Irish literature, use in, 26–27, 88–95; "liberating the modern subject," 77; primarily literary device, 27; operating at psychological

level, 81, 91; questioning individualism, 77; and relational ties, 26; as response to hearing voices, 5; in Old Testament, 7; and skaz, 91–92; and telepathy, 11; no textual markers to identify, 92, 102, 247n3, 250n47; "Uncle Charles Principle," 81, 100, 102; and the unconscious, 13

Freud, Sigmund, xiv, 2, 150, 237n24; accidents and parapraxes in, 75–77; Borch-Jacobsen on, 13–14, 233n56; Cavell on, 233n58; Derrida on, 5, 230n23; on ego formation, 233–34n59; ghost as projection of inner life, xiv, 5, 12–13; on "Gradiva"(Jensen), 5; Joyce's attitude to "Viennese school," xiv, 2, 229n4, 229n7, 232n49; on Judge Schreber, 14; Laplance and Leclaire on, 13, 24; on melancholia, xv, 20, 37, 131, 142, 146–47; on memory as relational structure rather than event, 24; on mourning, xv, 2, 20, 37, 142, 224; nachträgichkeit (belatedness), 147–48, 236n11, 258n22, 258n25, 259n37; presupposing anterior subjectivity, 13–15, 146, 149, 233n57, 233n59; psychological basis of superstition, 12–13; on superstition, 12–13, 150–51; talking cure, 74; on trauma, 149, 233n37, 236n11, 258n25; "Wolf Man," case of, 236n11

Friedman, Melvin J., 64

Fuentes, Carlos, 222–23

Gabler, Hans Walter, 38, 192

Gaelic Athletic Association, 201, 265n29

Galway (county), 238n34; Aughrim, 114, 136; Clifden, 135; Connemara, 79, 89, 135; and Danish fisherman, 135; Derrygimlagh bog, 135; Galway city, 8, 89, 93, 114, 123, 125, 126, 129; Galway harbour scheme, 137, 183, 186, 256n63; outpost of modernity, 135–37, 151; Tuam, 89. See also Maamtrasna trial

Gardner, Edward L., 158; and Cottingley fairies, 260n54

Garnett, Richard, 250n49

Gauntier, Gene, 184

ghost, 207–9, 220–22, 224; as absence, 16; accents, speaking with, 137; "air," asso-

ciations with, 126–27, 148; and "apophatic" language, xv, 17; appearing at moments of crisis in Joyce's fiction, 7, 258n19; banished by electric light, 14, 128; belief in, xiii, 125; as breakdown in social system, 144; as camera, xv, 117–19; and change in manners, 16; and commodity culture, 20, 163–64; contesting inner and outer life, xiii, 2–3, 5, 12–14, 64, 127, 131–32, 208; of Paddy Dignam, 20, 210–11; as failed internalization, 132; and the future, 19, 20, 160, 234nn71–72; "ghostly light," 126; as "gnomen," 267n19; gothic genre, xiii, 2, 217; as hallucination, 5, 6, 12, 27, 144, 230n22, 231n29, 258n18; in Hamlet, 16, 18; and incorporation, 145–46; madness, as symptom of, xiii, 11–13, 142–43, 150; and modernity, xiii, 7; Native Americans, 144, 163; noncontemporaneity of, 18; off-screen forces, 117–18, 132–33, 255n46; projection and witch craze, 259n43; as projection of inner life, xiv, 5, 8, 12–13, 14, 161; projections as against voices of others, 230; Samuel, ghost of, appearing to Saul, 7; "social death," 144, 258n20; and textual phantoms, 18. See also haunting; superstition
Gibson, Andrew, 49
Gifford, Don, 192
Gilbert, John T., 174, 262n18
Gilbert, Stuart, 2, 168
Gilhooly, Bishop Laurence, 193–94
Gilligan, David, 86
Glassie, Henry, 212, 214
Gogol, Nikolai, 91
Gogarty, Fr. Oliver (The Lake), 193
Gonne, Maud, on threats of contemporary famine in Ireland, 190, 264n5
Gottfried, Roy, on Joyce's cosmopolitanism at the expense of his Irishness, 235n13
"Grace" (Dubliners), Mrs. Kernan, 14, 156, 252n66
"Gradiva"(Jensen), 5, 230n21, 232n49
Grattan, Henry, 57; Grattan's Parliament, 58
Greenblatt, Stephen, 257n13

Gregory, Lady, 113–14, 116, 134, 253n14, 256n55
Gregory, Lord, 114–15, 253n16
Grice, H. P., on implicature, 235n79
Griffin, Gerald, 85, 86
Griffith, Arthur, 23, 49, 207, 235n4, 241n71; on anti-TB measures, 190; aversion to cosmopolitanism of Ryan, 235n5; on Irish afforestation, 190; lack of leadership abilities, 207
Griffith, D. W., 178
Grimshaw, Atkinson, 128

Halbwachs, Maurice, 2
Halloween (John Carpenter), 132
Hansen, Miriam Bratu, 70
Harrington, John, 117
Hart, Clive, 28, 38, 113, 135, 239n56, 240n62, 253n13
haunting: as cultural, 125, 144; disenchantment and, xiii, 14, 157, 266n7; and habitation, 137; in Heaney's Station Island, xiii; in Ibsen's Ghosts, 22; and Irish history, 37;rational responses to, 2, 151–53, 157; in Ulysses, 37, 207–9, 220–22, 224; spiritualism, 124, 128, 134, 143, 157, 159, 162, 255n38; spirituality, 152, 156, 189. See also ghost; superstition
Hauptmann, Gerhart, 149
Hauser, Arnold, 167–68
Hayman, David, on "arranger" in Joyce's fiction, 239n49
Heaney, Seamus, Station Island, xiii, xv
Heflin, Van, 44
Hegarty, Frances: For Dublin (Hegarty and Stones), 53–59; and women's movement in Ireland, 73–74
Hegel, G. W. F., 70
Heidegger, Martin, on "enworlding," 32
Herr, Cheryl, 32, 71, 238n41, 245n41
Herring, Philip: tension between factual accuracy and indeterminacy in Joyce, 242n101; uncertainty principle, 237n25
Hertz waves, 128, 157
Hiltpold, Rudolf, 25
Hirst, Paul, 143
history, Irish: Act of Union (1800), 58; Battle of Aughrim, 136; Battle of the

history, Irish (continued)
  Boyne, 86; Danes, 98, 161; Druids,
  98; Dynamite War, 49, 215–16; Easter
  Rising of 1916, 26, 180; Fenian move-
  ment, 216–17; Flight of the Wild Geese,
  98; Land War, 49, 89, 190; Molly
  Maguires, 190; Norman invasion, 98;
  Poor Law Act (1847), 114; Ribbonism,
  190, 215, 267n16; Siege of Limerick,
  98; Whiteboy movement, 101, 190, 215,
  252n68, 267n16. See also Invincibles
Hobsbawm, Eric J., 63
Hogan, Patrick Colm, 248n7
Holocaust, 153
Holy Ghost, 15, 126, 255n34
Holyhead, 26
hope, xiii, xv, 20, 31, 49, 77, 146, 162, 164,
  222–24; and phantom limb, 25
Horkheimer, Max, 163, 183
Horne, Donald, 57
Hull, Eleanor, 149
Hume, David, 258n19
Husserl, Edmund, 168
Huston, John, xv, 103. See also Dead, The
  (Huston)
Hutchins, Patricia, on Joyce's memories
  of Dublin, 236n10
Hyde, Douglas, 162, 260n59
hysteria, 6, 12, 143–44, 258n16

implicature, 18, 235n79
incorporation, 14, 145–46, 160; eating and
  drinking, 14, 145–47, 233n59; relation to
  ritual, 145. See also Abraham, Nicolas,
  and Maria Torok
India, 182
individualism: absence of in non-Western
  societies, 140; conformity of American individualism, 140; historical
  emergence of, 14, 183; lack of in Irish
  society, xiv–xv, 62, 138–39; materialist
  critique of egoism, 109, 231n26; negative self-control, 15, 65; performativity
  of personal identity, 68; questioning of
  personal identity, 3, 62–63
Industrial Development Authority (Ireland), 182
Industrial Revolution, 182; absence of in
  Ireland, 15

inner speech, 3, 41; as abbreviated speech,
  64; complexity of, 64–65; as dialogue,
  247n65; egocentric speech, 244n12,
  247n65; and the image, 111; and official
  speech, 68; social as well as internal, 3,
  4, 59–60, 62–64, 68, 70–71, 244n12. See
  also Vygotsky, Lev
interiority, 160; and Cartesian theory, 32,
  60; Cavell, 233n58; consciousness of
  others, 65; divided against itself, 66;
  emergence of, 32, 183; lack of historically in Irish culture, xv, 14–15, 33, 37,
  65, 139–41; lacking unity, 14, 65–66, 149,
  231;limits of, 2, 3, 4, 31, 140; linked to
  external world, 4, 31, 59, 63–64, 70–71,
  186–87, 233n57; mass production of
  the senses, 70, 184; and performativity, 246n42; porousness of, 62, 70–71,
  165–66, 232n43; removal of ghost to,
  160, 208; Rosaldo on myth of universal "inner space," 140; self as specter, 6,
  149, 231; self illusion, compared to God
  illusion, 5; social affirmation of, 64–66,
  68, 140; social structuring of, 3, 59–61,
  107–8, 139–40, 211, 230n19; staging of
  in Hamlet, 257n13; synaesthesia, 130,
  258n23; and time, 165, 168. See also subjectivity
internalization: failure as psychological
  mechanism in Ireland, xiv, 14, 15, 65–
  66, 149; ghost as resistance to, 132; relation to mourning, 14, 142; Vygotsky
  on, 60–61, 107
intimacy, cultural, xiv, 45, 64; and cultural
  underworld, 47, 73; Dublin, in relation to, 3, 267n18; and everyday life,
  29; Herzfeld on, 62; and inner speech,
  64, 247n65
intimacy, of returned gaze, 25, 44–45
introjection, 14, 145–46, 160; failure
  of, 144–46, 161; term introduced by
  Ferenczi, 233n59. See also Abraham,
  Nicolas, and Maria Torok
Invincibles: assassination of Lord
  Fredrick Cavendish and Thomas
  Burke, 46, 49–50, 216–19; informers,
  215; Joyce on Parnell forging links
  with, 52; Tynan on, 216–19. See also
  history, Irish

involuntary memory. *See* memory, involuntary

Isaak, JoAnna, 186

Jakobson, Roman, 42; on metaphor and metonomy, 240n57, 242n80

James, Henry, 91

James, William, 254n29

Jameson, Fredric, 3, 100, 182, 230n12, 231n29; on "autonomization," 241n72

Jaurretche, Colleen, on "apophatic" writing and negative theology, 234n70

Jay, Martin, 27, 253n4

Jesuits, 62

Jesus Christ, 157, 210

Johnson, Barbara, 213

Johnson, Jeri, 13, 100, 253n6

Johnson, Rev. Jimmy, 205

Joly, John, 179

Joyce, James: on Abbey riots, 256n55; "arranger" in fiction, 239n49; aversion to instant familiarity, 21; Berlitz teacher, 22, 234n66; chance, attitude to, 11; and cinema, xv, 103–37, 167–68, 171, 184, 186, 211, 231n33, 261n10; cosmopolitanism of, xiv, 4, 21, 26, 84; and Cusack, 265n28; Dublin, relation to, 21–23, 28, 62, 236n10; eyesight, poor, 231n33; factual accuracy in, 243n101; favorite photograph by Giedion-Welcker, 22, 235n2; and Fenianism, 49, 215; formal innovations and Irish culture, 3, 28, 59; free indirect discourse, emergence of, 96–97; Freud, possession of works by, 229n4; ghost of, xiii, xv, 1; interest in plans for the revitalization of Galway port, 256n63; interest in the conscious as well as the unconscious, 2, 229n7; Ireland, anxieties about, 237n16; on Ireland as specter, 16; interest in Irish history, 83–84, 174; *Irish Homestead*, stories in, 96–97; on the Irish language, 79–80; and Irish midlands, 262n17; Irishness and cosmopolitanism, 83–85, 237n23; and Irish Revival, 1, 23, 79, 83–85, 135, 229n1, 248n16; law, attitude towards, 80; and madness, 12; on James Clarence Mangan, 124–25; on "Mildred Lawson," 96–97; and Moore, 96–100,

265n15; on Mozart, 17; and Mullingar, 197–98; on "nightmare of history," xiv; paranormal, interest in, 229n3; police, attitude to, 80; present at apparition of mother's ghost, 1, 231n33; responses to psychoanalysis, 2, 229; on sight and sound, 252n2; singing in Antient Concert Rooms, 17; skepticism towards rationalism, 2; skepticism towards religion, xiv, 1, 2; subjection to English society (Moretti), 27; and superstition, 1; theosophy, attitude to, 2, 124, 254n28; and vision, 103–5; works as "letters of desire"(Lawrence), 30; on the "world of faery," 229n1

—mainland European residences: Paris, 21, 24, 26, 49, 84, 168, 211, 215, 251n55; Pola, 24, 236n10; Trieste, 16, 22, 24, 26, 84, 229n4, 232n49, 234n66, 235n3, 236n10, 245n24; Zurich, 24, 25, 26, 84, 192, 197, 235n2, 236n10

—works: "Ireland at the Bar," 79–80; "The Mirage of the Fisherman on Aran," 136–37; "The Shade of Parnell," 51. *See also separate titles*

Joyce, Josephine, 235n76

Joyce, Margaret ("Poppie"), 1

Joyce, May, 1

Joyce, Myles, execution of, 79–80

Joyce, Nora Barnacle, 17, 55, 97; Joyce's objections to Stanislaus's criticisms of, 251n56; loneliness of, 251n56; unimpressed by "Mildred Lawson," 97

Joyce, Stanislaus, 34, 80, 96–97, 156, 174, 230n16, 245n24, 254n28, 256n55, 265n15; on characters in Joyce's stories, 238n31, 251n56

Kalem Film Company, 184–85

Kavanagh, Patrick, 63

Kelleher, John V., 128, 253n17

Kelleher, Margaret, 250n49

Kelly, Eleanor Frances, 265n23

Kelly, John, 215, 267n17

Kelly, Joseph, 26, 214

Kenealy, Edward: Chartist "Angel Street" conspiracy, 221; and Tichborne Claimant, 221

Kenner, Hugh, 102, 178, 252n74, 263n27;

Kenner, Hugh (*continued*) on "arranger" in Joyce's fiction, 239n49; parallax, 178–79; relation of Joyce's modernism to Ireland, 85; on textual indeterminacy, 241n70, 252n66, 252n74; "Uncle Charles Principle," 81

Kern, Stephen, 165–69, 170, 175

Kerry (county), 190, 264n5; Killarney, 105

Kershner, R. Brandon, 116, 158–59, 161, 162, 260n60

Kickham, Charles, *Knocknagow*, 89–91

Kidd, John, 37–38, 240n64

Kierkegaard, Soren, 68

Kildare (county): Clongowes College, 106–7, 108, 109, 110, 177; Maynooth, 193; Rathcoffey, 17

Killeen, Terence: on author as collective voice, 41; on autonomy of narrative details, 241n74, 245n31, 265n25

Klitgaard, Ida, on free indirect discourse, 81

Knuth, Leo, 28, 38, 239n56, 240n62, 262n20

Kovel, Joel, 140

Kristensen, Tom, 229n3

Kuhns, Richard, on what is shown and what is said, 242n84

Lacan, Jacques: on breakdown of ritual, 142–43; on *Hamlet*, 143; on madness, 144; on mirror-stage, 233n53; unconscious as discourse of the other, 13, 232–33n52; unconscious not instinctual, 233n52; unconscious structured like a language, 233n52; unified self as "Imaginary," 231n24

LaCapra, Dominick, 151; on mourning and melancholia, 142; ritual and "working through," 142

Ladd, Alan, 44

Lad from Old Ireland, The (Olcott), 184–86

Laffan, May: "The Game Hen," 94–95; neglect of in Irish criticism, 250n49

Lamarr, Hedy, 103

Lamos, Colleen, 219

language: "apophatic," 17, 234n70, 237n26; Attridge on, 41–42; contingency, 29, 39–40, 198; decidable and undecidable

meaning, 28, 80, 240n58, 241n74; deictic, 29, 237n28; ellipses, 18, 28, 39, 64, 115, 237n25, 262n10; fictive contrasted with language of real life, xv, 19, 39–40, 240n61, 241nn70–71; foreground and background in, 3, 28–30, 34, 42, 242n83; Hiberno-English, 80, 88; idiolect, 81, 100, 216, 247n7; indirect language, 18, 44; inflated diction, 216–19; internalization of, 60; linguistic commons, 101; literal and figurative uses, 6, 112, 127, 132, 146–47; meanings "off the page," 17, 28, 37, 115, 170, 197–98, 214, 234n70, 240n62, 242n80, 249n28; landscape, 36; Standard English, xiv, 85–86, 88, 89, 94, 100–101; and the unsaid, 30, 43, 58–59; what is shown and what is said, 243n84. *See also* text

Laplanche, Jean, 13; on interiority in Freud, 233n55; on memory of relational structures rather than events, 24; *nachträgichkeit* (belatedness), 236n11, 258n25

Larbaud, Valery, on Joyce's Irishness contributing to his modernism, 83–84

"Lass of Aughrim" (song), 18, 112, 114–16, 120, 122, 126, 127, 130, 136, 253n15; missing lines of, 18, 114–15; "old Irish tonality" in, xv. *See also* "Dead, The" (*Dubliners*); *Dead, The* (Huston)

Latour, Bruno, critique of psychological explanations of supernatural, 4

Lawless, Emily, *Grania*, 92–94

Lawrence, Karen, 30, 245n41; on centrality of free indirect discourse in *Ulysses*, 248n12

Leclaire, Serge. *See* Laplanche, Jean

Lefebvre, Henri, 29, 248n21

Léon, Paul, 103

Leonardo da Vinci, 47

Leskov, Nikolai, 91

Leslie, Shane: review of *Ulysses*, 23, 235n4, 241n71; on *Ulysses* as literary explosion, 48

Levin, Harry, 4

Levi-Strauss, Claude, 151

Lincoln, Mary Todd, 260n55

"Little Cloud, A" (*Dubliners*), resentment in, 65

Little Review, 192

Liverpool, 49, 183

Lloyd, David: on "differential space,"
248n21; oral culture and Irish modernity, 244n21

local knowledge, 28–29, 39, 41, 46–47, 165,
197, 214, 242n63; in *Portrait*, 237n26;
precision of, 239n56; resisting surveillance, 47–48; as "subjugated knowledge" (Foucault), 39

Lock, Charles, 77

Locke, John L., 230n22

Lodge, David, 253n6

London, 16, 26, 27, 134, 180, 194

Lothe, Jakob, 256n53

Lowe-Evans, Mary, 264n1

Lukacher, Ned, 258n25

Luther, Martin, 143

Lyotard, Jean Francois, 148

Lysaght, Patricia, 128, 156, 260n48

Maamtrasna trial, 79–80, 82, 92, 101, 154;
in *Finnegans Wake*, 247n2

Macardle, Dorothy, 254n20

Macintosh, H. M., 203

Maddox, James, 101

Madrid, 213

Maginni, Denis J., 170

Mahaffey, Vicki, 252n55, 261n67

Mahaffy, J. P., 165; on Joyce, 261n1

Mahon, Rev. Michael P., 155–56

Malcolm, Janet, 233n57

Mallarmé, Stéphane, 68

Mander, Miles, 117

Mangan, James Clarence, 124

Mangan, Rev. C., 181

Marconi, Guigielmo, 135

Martyn, Edwards, 205

Marx, Karl, 140, 231

Masson, Jeffrey, 233n57

Maume, Patrick, 190–91

Maupassant, Guy de, 109

Mayo (county), 190, 264n5; Knock, 157;
Westport, 99

McCabe, Colin, 37

McCabe, J. F., 178, 181–82

McCalman, Iain, 221

McCarthy, Michael J. F., 266n37; on absence of individualism in Ireland, 62;

Joyce's and Stanislaus Joyce's familiarity with his books, 245n24

McCarthy, Tom, 4

McCormack, John, 16–17

McCorristine, Shane, 6, 231

McHale, Brian, 87, 92, 250n47

memory: "akasic," 124; alternative pasts,
76; collective, 11, 120–21, 131, 134, 146;
completed by the future, xv, 26, 76;
contrasted with romantic regression,
xv; modernism, xv, 165; and monuments, 57–58; private, xiii, xv; public,
xiii, xv, 2; of relational structure rather
than event, 24; spectral, 20, 119, 175–77;
standardization of time, 165. *See also*
past, the

memory, involuntary: in Freud, 76; and
negative topography, 58–59, 243n6; and
phantom limb, 24; in Proust, 75; public
nature of in Joyce, 75–76; and topography, 38–39, 243n8, 256n61; transgenerational, 146; transpersonal, 254n29;
trauma, 187

Mercanton, Jacques, 12, 33

Merleau-Ponty, Maurice: dethroning
vision, 105; on facial expressions, 212;
on phantom limb, 23–24, 25–26, 236n7;
on structures of experience, 44

Metz, Christian, 104

microbes, 190

Mies van der Rohe, Ludwig, 41

Mill, John Stuart, 213

Miller, D. A., 48, 87

Miller, Nicholas, 243n6

Milton, John, "Lycidas," 198

Mitry, Jean, 117

Moby Dick (Melville), 28

modernism: collage, 17; and contingency,
26, 212; Irish, xiv, 27–28; self-sufficiency of modernist works, 41, 240n62;
and simultaneity, 165–69, 172, 178; and
space, 165–68; synchronicity, 165, 180;
universalism, 41

modernism, vernacular: and form, xiv,
95–97; free indirect discourse, xiv,
91–92; and idiomatic language, xiv

modernity: colonial, xiii–xiv, xv, 138–40,
181–82, 212; ghosts of, xiii, 7; and inner
life, 70; as metropolitan, xiv; and oral

modernity (*continued*)
culture, 244n21; progress, 150; singular modernity, 182; and social distributivism, 181; and western periphery, xiv, 135–36
Mondrian, Piet, 41
monologue, interior (stream of consciousness): Bryant on, 66; as confining, 67; as dialogue, 59, 64, 67, 71–72, 105, 247n65; in Dujardin, 85; as "exterior consciousness," 4–5; flowing through the city, 64; and free indirect discourse, 72, 77, 83–84; and Irish culture, 85; as Joyce's signature style, 83; Moore's experiments in, 85; and parallax, 77; social structuring of, 230n19; and subjectivity, xiv, 4
Moore, George, 84; experiments with free indirect discourse, 96–100, 251n58; and interior monologue, 85, 95–96; relationship to Dujardin, 85, 95–96, 249n22
—works: "A Faithful Heart," 97; *The Lake*, 193, 197, 265n15; "Mildred Lawson," 96–97, 251n51; *The Untilled Field* ("The Exile," "Fugitives," "Home Sickness," and "The Wedding Feast"), 99–100; "A Voice of the Mountain," 97–99, 268n29
Moran, D. P., 190, 266n37
Moretti, Franco, 27, 50, 83
Morley, Christopher, 66
Morrison-Miller, A., 201–2
"Mother, A" (*Dubliners*): colloquial idioms in, 82; ressentiment and Mrs. Kearney, 65
Mozart, Wolfgang Amadeus, 17
Münsterberg, Hugo, 263n41
Myers, Frederick W. H, 229n3
"My Love She Was Born in the North Countree" (song), 17

narration: and allegory, 256n61; "arranger" (Hayman and Kenner) in Joyce's fiction, 239n49; asserting and naming in, 109, 111; communal, 41, 90; and compassion, 34, 63; and contingency, 40–41, 74–75, 77, 197–98, 212, 241n69; details, use of, 18, 39, 116,

241n74, 267n22; dual vantage point, 112; factual reportage, 39–40; first-person, absence of, 13; first-person narration, 110–12 (*see also* monologue, interior); foreground and background in, 42, 242n83; of history versus fiction (Aristotle), 40, 241nn69–70; idiomatic, 88; impersonal, 33; indeterminacy, 76; and loose ends, 63, 74; and panoptical gaze, 47–48, 50–51; real-life, 41, 51, 240n61, 241n64; third-person, 4, 6, 9, 13, 39–40, 47, 61, 63, 68, 73, 77, 81–82, 90, 100, 133; undecidable, 177; and voice, 110–12; and voice-over, 132–33. *See also* free indirect discourse; monologue, interior
New Christy Minstrels, 123
newspapers, 29–30, 147–48, 150, 167, 218; *Daily Express*, 119; *Dublin Evening Mail*, 147, 154; *Evening Telegraph*, 40; *Freeman's Journal*, 32, 203, 210, 211; inaccuracy of, 40; *Irish Times*, 126, 203–4, 255n32
New Zealand, 98
Nicholls, Peter, 258n25; on phantoms in psychoanalysis, 236n11
Nietzsche, Friedrich, 61, 65, 149; on ressentiment, 245n32
Noël, Lucie, 104
Nolan, Emer, 90, 102, 249n3
Norris, Margot: on implicature, 18, 235n79; on Lily in "The Dead," 115

O'Carolan, Turlough, 265n16
O'Connell, Daniel, 136
O'Conor Don, the, 205
O'Donovan Rossa, Jeremiah, 49
O'Higgins, Brian, 190
Olivier, Laurence, 117
O'Mahony, Eoin, 175
O'Neill, Eithne, 117
O'Riordan, Monsignor Michael, 138
Owens, Cóilín, 7, 243n8
Owenson, Sydney (Lady Morgan): *Patriotic Sketches*, 88; *The O'Briens and the O'Flahertys*, 88–89

"Painful Case, A" (*Dubliners*), 4, 213
—characters. Mr. *Duffy*, 4; creature of

habit, 76–77, 141–42; distant from his own body, 77; face, 211; ear of intimacy, 76, 147; incorporation and ingestion, 147–48; *nachträgichkeit* (belatedness), 147–48; of thought, 78. *Mrs. Sinico*, 4, 18, 147–48, 150; cause of death unclear, 76

parallax: and free direct discourse, 27; and time, 27, 77, 178, 179, 180

paralysis, xv, 31, 59, 212, 238n41

Paris Commune, 157

Parnell, Charles Stewart, 17, 20, 190, 268n29; and De Wet, 20, 220–22; fall and death of, xiv, 20, 37, 51, 106–9, 111, 201, 207, 219–23, 262n13; ghost, 17, 20, 207–9, 220–22, 224; "hillside men" and insurrection, 52; Invincibles, forging links with, 52; leadership abilities, 207–8; O'Shea, 219–20; in *Portrait*, 106–12; return of his hat, 240n61

Parnell, John Howard, 207–9, 225

Parsons, Deborah, on free indirect discourse, 77

Pascal, Fania, 250n43

Pascal, Roy, 250n43

Pasolini, Pier Paolo, 92, 183, 254n19, 254n24; blurring of past and present, 184; on free indirect image, 116

past, the, xiii, 10, 12, 14, 24–25, 32, 35, 78, 83, 84, 120; anachronism, 125, 167, 176, 182, 183; cultural pasts, 124–25, 131, 134, 135, 136, 151; superimposition of past and present, 163–64, 184–87; "survivals," 183; unrequited pasts, xv, 12, 15, 16, 17, 20, 24–26, 65, 74–77, 132, 142, 145, 148–51, 186–87, 222–23. *See also* memory

Pearse, P. H., "Ghosts," 222

Pepper's Ghost, 19

Perec, Georges, 29–30, 241n71

Pfister, Joel, 139–40

phantom limb: and death, 25; as "gestalt," 236n8; hinging on difference, 25; and involuntary memory, 24; and memory, 11, 22–23, 24; in Merleau-Ponty, 23–25; normal experience of loss, 11, 232n44; phantom histories, 24; vestige of hope, 25

Phillips, Adam: critique of coherent nar-

ratives of the self, 74–76; on free association, 74

Piaget, Jean, 60–61

Pierce, David, 3

place, sense of: comparative absence of in Wordsworth, 35–36; in Joyce's work, 35–41

Plunkett, Sir Horace: on co-operative ideals, 138–39; on lack of individualism in Ireland, 138; persistence of superstition in Ireland, 144

Pollexfen, George, 155

Pope, Alexander, 31

Portrait of the Artist as a Young Man, A: bird-girl episode in, 25, 44–45; first-person narrative not dominant in, 13; impersonal narration in, 33; intonations of speech in the title, 247n4; local knowledge in, 237n26; review of, in *Freeman's Journal*, 32

—characters. *Dante*, 107–8. *Stephen Dedalus*: colors green and red, relation to, 106–12; mother, sundering of relationship to, 25; politics of perception in, 106–12; returned gaze of bird-girl, 44–45; and vision, 104–5

Portrait of the Artist as a Young Man, A (Strick), treatment of political coloring of vision, 110–11

—cast: Rosaleen Linehan (May Dedalus), 110; T. P. McKenna (Simon Dedalus), 110; Desmond Perry (Mr. Casey), 110; Maureen Potter (Dante), 111

Pound, Ezra, xiv; on *Portrait* and Irish Troubles, 48; review of *Dubliners*, 35, 213–14

Protestantism: ascendancy, 138, 190, 191, 204; *The Catholic*, 19, 191, 194, 196, 197; evangelicalism, 19, 169, 189, 190; orphanages, 19, 196; Protestant Defence Association, 266n33; Protestant work ethic, 138–39, 182–83; Reformation, lack of in Ireland, xiii, 15, 155–56; reformatories, 199; ritual, 156; Society for Promoting Christianity among the Jews, 206; "United Presbyterians," 201–3

—tracts: *Learning to Float; or, Saved by*

Protestantism (*continued*)
  Faith, 205; *Learning to Walk in the
    Paths of Righteousness*, 205; *The Lily in
    the Pool; or, A Pure Life in a Polluted
    World*, 205; *Walled Up Nuns*, 192; *Why
    I Left the Church of Rome*, 191–92, 197
Proust, Marcel, 24, 75, 167
psychoanalysis. *See* Abraham, Nicolas,
  and Maria Torok; Freud, Sigmund;
  Lacan, Jacques
public sphere, 47; contested, 51, 76, 186–
  87, 216; counterpublic sphere, 218;
  opacity of in colonial societies, 37, 216–
  20; patriarchal, 67, 73, 93; and private
  sphere, 37, 50, 55–66, 67, 73, 107, 111, 168,
  183, 186, 219

Quine, W. V. O., 244n14

Radcliffe, Ann, 2
Raleigh, Sir Walter, 199
Rand, Nicholas T., 121
Rauschenberg, Robert, 36–37, 40, 237n21
Redmond, John, 190
Rée, Jonathan, 101
Rees, W. D., 144
relational ties: and affective states, 25–26;
  and free indirect discourse, 26; in
  Judith Butler, xv, 20, 224; relational
  aesthetic in Joyce, 24; relational forms
  in Scheler, 214, 222, 224, 225
Renoir, Jean, 109
ressentiment (resentment), 59, 61, 65,
  244n19
Rickard, John S., 8, 232n37; on proleptic
  memory in Joyce, 234n71; on transper-
  sonal memory, 254n29
Riffaterre, Michael, 35–36, 239n53, 239n55,
  240n58
Rigney, Ann, on real-life individuals in
  realist fiction, 42
Riquelme, John Paul, 92, 131–32, 133
ritual, 14, 15, 139, 141–44, 149, 152, 153, 155,
  156, 161, 237n25; and incorporation, 145
Robbins, Bruce, 136
Robson, Flora, 117
Romains, Jules, 84
Romanyshyn, Robert, 24
Ronen, Ruth, 42

Rosaldo, Michelle, 120
Roscommon (county): Kilronan Abbey,
  193, 265n16; *Roscommon Messenger*,
  194; Strokestown, 193
Royle, Nicholas, 18
Ruskin, John, 250n49
Russell, George (AE), 84, 204
Russell, Rev. Matthew, S.J., 250n49

Sacks, Oliver: on apparitions, 144; hallucinations, 258n18; hearing voices, 11;
  imaginary friends, 12; phantom limb,
  11, 232n44
Schatzman, Morton, 14
Scheler, Max: on disenchantment, 211–12,
  266n7; on relational forms, 210, 214,
  222, 224, 225; representing the everyday, 32; on stream of consciousness,
  31–32; transformative power of aesthetic form, 32; uncanny in facial resemblance, 208–10, 211–12
Schivelbusch, Wolfgang, 234n61
Scholes, Robert: on "double context,"
  43, 242nn82; on text and context, 43,
  242n83
Schreber, Judge Daniel: Deleuze and
  Guattari on, 233n57; Freud on, 14,
  233n57; Schatzman on, 14; Moritz
  Schreber (father), 14
science, 2, 34, 63, 127, 129, 143–44, 152, 156,
  157, 161, 163–64, 229n3, 244n14, 255n38,
  263n31
Scotland, 201–2, 204, 259n43; Caledonian
  Games, 201, 204
secrets, 9, 19, 37, 41, 43, 44, 53, 94, 97, 143;
  161; open secrets, 53, 94, 219–20; public
  secrets, 62, 63, 204, 205, 215–19
Seidel, Michael, 267n19
Senn, Fritz, 176, 262n22; relation of
  Joyce's modernism to Ireland, 85
Shakespeare, William: death of son Hamnet, 11; *Hamlet*, 11, 16, 18, 29, 64, 142,
  154, 160, 198, 220, 234n68, 257n13; *Ham-
  let*, playing ghost in, 234n68; *Macbeth*,
  xiii, 154, 241n70; *The Tempest*, 198
Shane (Stevens), 44
Shannon, River, 19, 193, 194
Sheehy, David, M.P., 169, 208, 262n13
Sheehy, Mrs. David, 169

Sheehy-Skeffington, Hannah, 23
Sherlock Holmes, 50
Shields, Hugh, 253n15
Schloss, Carol, on Molly's soliloquy, 240n68
Seidman, Robert J., 192
Sigerson, George, 1, 75, 234n72, 246n63
Silver, Carol G., 260n46
Simmel, Georg, 83
Sinn Féin, 73
Sipière, Dominique, 253n12
"Sisters, The" (*Dubliners*), 7; first publication, 251n43; gnomon in, 18, 237n26, 267n19; incorporation in, 145–46
—characters: narrator, 8; Fr. Flynn, 8, 18
skaz, 91–92, 100, 250n41; linked to folklore (Eichenbaum), 91; and storytelling (Bakhtin), 99; Titunik on, 91, 230n45; Vinogradov on, 250n46
"Skin-the-Goat"(Fitzharris), 46, 51, 218–19
Sligo (county): Bishop's Palace, Sligo, 193; Geevagh, 193
Smyley, Mrs., 19, 196–97
South Africa, 10, 98–99, 220, 222, 268n29
space, 48, 105, 120, 136, 151, 163, 165, 167, 168, 182; differential, 85, 184, 261n10; dislocations, 170, 177–78; haunted, 163; private and public space, 37, 53, 55, 63, 68, 70, 165, 183, 261n6; spatial form, 167–68, 171–72
Spain, 259n43
Spencer, Herbert, 150
Spivak, Gayatri Chakravorty, on critique of bourgeois subject, 140
Stalin, Joseph, 61
Stam, Robert, 110–11
Stanzel, Franz, 133, 256n53
Staples, Hugh, 267n16
Steinberg, Leo, 28
Stephen Hero, 2, 61
Stephens, James (Fenian leader), 73, 98, 268n29
Stephens, James (writer), 248n17
Stirner, Max, 231
Stoker, Bram, 232n34
Stoker, Dr Thornley, 250n49
Stones, Andrew. *See* Hegarty, Frances
Stratton, Eugene, 178, 263n25

stream of consciousness. *See* monologue, interior
Strick, Joseph, 110–11
subjectivity: in crisis, 11; incomplete formation of in Ireland, xiv–xv; and interior monologue, xiv; intersubjectivity and solidarity, 140; polyphony challenging subjectivity, 77; in postcolonial societies, 139, 140–41; trans-subjectivity, 8, 10–11, 124–25. *See also* interiority
Sullivan, A. M., 267n16
superstition, 150–53, 161; Bloom on, 1; dispelling of, 128; Freud on, 12; Joyce's susceptibility to, 1; magic, 152; persistence in Irish society, 144, 154–57; resisting the Reformation, xii, 156. *See also* folk beliefs
surveillance: church, 2, 72; and local knowledge, 47–48; police, 37, 47, 50, 59, 61, 73, 214–20
Svehla, Gary J., 132–33
Sword, Helen, 128
Synge, J. M., 83, 84, 248n17; *Playboy of the Western World*, 135, 256n55

Tara, 26
Tate, Allen, 125–26
technology: cinema, xv, 186; electric light, 14, 125, 128, 129; electric power, 126–27, 136; magic lantern, 8, 129, 157, 159, 161; phonograph (gramophone), 7, 157, 232n34; photography, xv, 29, 36, 119, 151, 157–58, 159, 161, 162, 211–13, 260n55; power-cuts on night of "The Dead," 125–26, 255n32; radio, 128, 135; relation to spectrality, xiv, 7, 14, 128, 150, 157–58, 162, 163–64, 255n38; street-lighting, xv, 7, 125–26, 266n32; telephone, 7, 8, 157; television, 128; and time, 165; transport, 70, 126, 165, 167, 183; x-rays, 157, 158
telepathy, 8–9; between Stephen and Bloom, 9–10, 232n42
Tennison, Lady Louisa, 265n16
text: context, 27, 37, 42–43, 60, 64, 240n58, 242n80, 242nn82–83; "double-context," 43, 242n82; extra-textual matter, 28, 42, 239n49, 242n80; internal

text (*continued*)
context, 240n58; language of science as context-dependent, 244n14; negative topography, 58–59, 243n6; textual omissions, 235n77; and topography, 38–39, 240n62, 243n8. *See also* language
Theosophy, 2, 124, 137, 254n28
Thomas, Keith, 156
Thompson, E. P., 182
Thom's Directory, xv, 36
Thornton, Weldon, 112
"Those Lovely Seaside Girls"(song), 173
Tichborne Claimant (Thomas Castro), 198, 220–21; Lady Tichborne, 220; Roger Charles, 220–21
time, 165; chronotopes, 186; Daylight Saving Time, 180; different temporalities, 167; Dunsink time, 180–81, 263n27; Greenwich Mean Time, 167, 179, 180; International Meridian Conference, 167, 180; overlapping, 186; and parallax, 179; "Summer Time," 182; "Time (Ireland) Act," (1916), 180; Timeball, Ballast Office, 179; triumph over space, 167
Tipperary (county), 153, 154, 155; Clonmel, 153
Titunik, I. R., 92
Todorov, Tzvetan, on the fantastic, 2–3, 258n19
Tone, Theobald Wolfe, 98
Torok, Maria. *See* Abraham, Nicolas, and Maria Torok
trauma, 9, 10, 37, 51, 158; external source, 146, 149; and flashbacks, 184–86; and hope, 224; and interiority, 149; melancholia, 146, 160; and memorials, 243; public, xiv, 51, 189; ritual and, 144–45, 151; working through, 142; World War I, 184, 258n25
Trench, Frederick (Third Baron Ashtown), 190–91
Trinity College, Dublin, 38, 165, 263n31; awarding degree to Chamberlain, 20, 208; pro-Boer demonstrations in front of, 20, 208–9; Provost's House, 207; statues, 57
Turim, Maureen, 184, 263n42
Twigg, Lizzie, 204

Tynan, P. J. ("Number One'), 266n1, 267nn21–22; inflated diction in "Eumaeus," 216–19; *The Irish National Invincibles and Their Times*, 216–19

Ullmann, Stephen, 6
Ulysses: affording cultural intimacy to Dublin, 3, 4, 21–22, 28, 63; "Agenbite of inwit," 14, 162, 199; Byronic theme in, 38; conscience as physical, 14; contesting self-sufficiency of form, 63, 240n62; deictic language in, 237n28; descriptive writing, lack of, 38, 100; drowning in, 198; as encyclopedia, 33, 37; excess of detail in, 18, 39, 241n74, 267n22; facial resemblances in, 210; as ghost story, 1, 225; haunting of May Dedalus, 1, 9, 254n26; irrelevance of Dublin to, 37; "a kind of retrospective arrangement," 148–49; Leslie's review of, 23; Linati scheme, 268n26; as literary explosion, 47–48; maternal associations in, 9; "matutinal cloud" in, 9–10; "metempsychosis," 198, 222; as open book (Eco), 27; personal identity, questioning of, 3, 62–63; phantasmagoria of "Circe," 9; reproducing reality, 32; Rosenbach manuscript, 192; "shout in the street," 64; "striking of the match," 50; and telepathy, 9–11; textual phantoms in, 18; totalizing designs of, 241n74; uncertainty principle in, 243n101; U.p: up, 63, 189, 199–206; U.p: up, possible meanings of, 201
—characters. *Bargeman*, 171–73, 176, 262n15. *Blazes Boylan*, 173; great organizer, 63; sexual performance, 70; as singer, 16, 234n69. *Buck Mulligan*, 9, 126, 198. *The Citizen* (*see* Cusack, Michael). *Denis Breen*, 188, 190, 199, 205. *Gerty McDowell*, and returned gaze, 45. *Mrs. Josie (Powell) Breen*, 188, 199, 205. *Kevin Egan*: real-life counterpart, 49. *Leopold Bloom*: adopting Catholicism, 206; carrying potato, 199; criticisms of police, 50; exchanging glances with Stephen, 46, 50; on death, 16; haunting by dead son, Rudy, 37, 158–64; media technologies

and the next world, 7; returned gaze with Gerty McDowell, 45; "Sherlock-holmesing," 50; speculating on signs of death, 7; suffering from premonitions, 234n71; suicide of father, Rudolf Virag, 37; telepathy with Stephen, 10–11; voice mimicked by Molly, 72; Zionism, 10. *Man in brown mackintosh*, 40, 63, 178, 200. *Mary Rochfort* (Lady Belvedere), 174–78, 262n23; "elderly female," 176, 262nn20–22; "no more young," 176, 262n22. *May Dedalus*, 1, 9–10, 37, 162, 199. *Milly Bloom*, 71, 173. *Molly Bloom*, 10, 102, 171; British army background, 67; contesting private and public life, 67–68, 73; links between internal and external words, 70–71, 246n46; lunar cycles of Molly's "period piece," 71; masquerading the voice, 68, 245n41; mimicry of other voices, 71; natural imagery in soliloquy, 71, 246n48; photograph, 212–13; polyphony in, 72, 250n46; and Rudy, 158; secret life of, 53; as singer, 234n69; soliloquy as exemplar of inner life, 67; stream of consciousness, 55, 67–74; as "subjugated knowledge," 240n68; trains of thought, 70–71, 78. *Paddy Dignam*: funeral, 7, 40, 172–73, 183, 201; ghost, 20, 210–11; home, 255n77; son, 19, 169, 199. *Rudy*: apparition of, 150, 158–61, 162, 164; Bloom in his eyes, 158; "Rudy Principle" (Mahaffey), 261n67. *Stephen Dedalus*: exchanging glances with Bloom, 46, 50; on *Hamlet*, 16; haunted by mother's death, 9–10, 37, 162; on pier as disappointed bridge, 17, 20; speculations on ghost in *Hamlet*, 16; telepathy, 9; telepathy with Bloom, 10–11. *Throwaway*, 63, 76. *Tom Kernan*, 59, 148–49, 266n3
uncertainty principle in Joyce, 3
undead, the: in Joyce, xiii; and return from drowning, 19; vampire, 162, 199, 260n59
Uninvited, The (Allen), 132, 254n20, 255n46; Ray Milland as Roderick Fitzgerald, 254n20; "Stella by Starlight"(song), 254n20

unionism, Irish Unionist Association, 190
USSR, 61

Valente, Joseph, on polyphony in Joyce, 77
Van Mierlo, Wim, 267n20
Victoria, Queen, 51, 59
Vinogradov, V., 250n43, 250n46
vision: addressivity of the eye, 45, 105, 242n87; Eisenstein on polyphonic image, 119; free indirect image, 131; and inner speech, 111; and light, 130; ocularcentrism in western culture, 253n4; and optics, 129; politics of, 105–12; resisting voyeurism, 43, 104–5; returned gaze, 44–45, 149, 158, 160, 218–19, 242n89; spectacle, 42, 59, 105, 123; visual tonality, 13; vocalizing of, xv, 242n87, 252n2
voice, 82–83, 91, 92–95, 100, 127, 247n4, 256n53; eavesdropping, 214; Eisenstein on polyphonic image, 119; Pasolini on, 116; visualizing the voice, xv, 103–12, 130–31; voice-over, 133–34
voices, hearing, 11, 116, 231n28; Joyce and, 23; as ventriloquism, 4–5; "The Voice of the Mountain" (Moore), 97–99
Volosinov, V. N., 88, 102; intonation and free indirect discourse, 82–83
Vygotsky, Lev: on egocentric speech, 244n12; on inner speech, 3, 55, 59–61, 64, 68–71, 244n12. *See also* inner speech

Wakefield, Edward, 229n5
wakes (for the dead), 14, 260n48
Wales, 156, 201
Wales, Katie, 59; public nature of Molly's soliloquy, 246n44; unconscious as dialogical, 74
Walsh, Archbishop William, 205
Warner, Deborah, 263n27
Warner, Marina, 129–30, 255n34
Waugh, Patricia, 139
Weber, Max, 138
Wertsch, James, 61, 64; on conformity without internalization, 61, 244n14; on inner speech as dialogue, 247n65
Westmeath (county), 171–72, 173;

Westmeath (county) (*continued*)
Athlone, 19, 173, 193, 196, 199; Gaulstown, 262n23; Lough Ennell, 174–76; Lough Owel, 173; Lough Ree, 192; Mullingar, 173, 174, 177, 198, 199, 264n11; *Westmeath Independent*, 194; *Westmeath Nationalist*, 196, 197, 198
Whitley, Catherine, 67, 68
Wilde, Sir William, 150; on famine specters, 15
Willemen, Paul, 111, 253n10
Williams, Raymond, 31
Winch, Peter, 44
witchcraft, 7; in Ireland, 153, 155; witch craze in Europe, 143–44, 257–58n16, 259n43; Witch of Endor, 7
Wittgenstein, Ludwig, 50; on aesthetics of the everyday, 29–31, 241n71; comments on Frazer's *Golden Bough*, 153–54; on forms of life, 34, 42–43; philosophy leaving the world as it is, 33–34; private language, 230; relationship to Nicholas Bakhtin, 250n47; what is shown and what is said, 242n84
Wooley, Penny, 143
Woolf, Virginia, 34
Woolsey, Judge, 66
world literature, address to national as well as international readership, 26, 43–44, 47–48
Wuthering Heights (Bronte), 86
Wuthering Heights (Wyler), camera as ghost in, 117

Yeats, W. B., xiv, 83, 104, 222, 256n55; burning of Bridget Cleary, 155; "Countess Cathleen," 237n26; over-familiarity of audiences with characters in plays, 238n34; spirits with accents, 137
"Yew Trees"(Wordsworth), 35–36

Zach, Wolfgang, 85
Ziarek, Ewa, 70–71
Zionism, 159